The Essential Homer

Selections from
the *Iliad* and the *Odyssey*

The Essential Homer

Selections from

the *Iliad* and the *Odyssey*

Translated and Edited by
STANLEY LOMBARDO

Introduction by
SHEILA MURNAGHAN

Hackett Publishing Company, Inc.
Indianapolis/Cambridge

Copyright © 2000 by Hackett Publishing Company, Inc.

For further information, please address

Hackett Publishing Company, Inc.
P. O. Box 44937
Indianapolis, Indiana 46244–0937

www.hackettpublishing.com

Cover art: Hiroshige, *Angry Seas at Naruto, Awa Province*.
Reproduced by permission of Japan Gallery, New York

Cover design by Abigail Coyle and Brian Rak

Interior design by Meera Dash

Library of Congress Cataloging-in-Publication Data

Homer.
   [Iliad. English. Selections]
   The essential Homer : selections from the Iliad and Odyssey /
translated and edited by Stanley Lombardo ; introduction by
Sheila Murnaghan.
       p. cm.
   Abridgment of the translator's version of Iliad, published in 1997;
and the Odyssey, published in 2000.
   Includes bibliographical references.
   ISBN 0-87220-541-X (cloth : alk. paper)—
   ISBN 0-87220-540-1 (paper : alk. paper)
   1. Homer—Translations into English   2. Epic poetry, Greek—
Translations into English.   3. Odysseus (Greek mythology)—
Poetry.   4. Achilles (Greek mythology)—Poetry.   5. Trojan War—
Poetry.   I. Homer. Odyssey. English. Selections.   II. Lombardo,
Stanley, 1943–   III. Title.

PA4025.A15 L66   2000
883'.01—dc21   00-040934

Contents

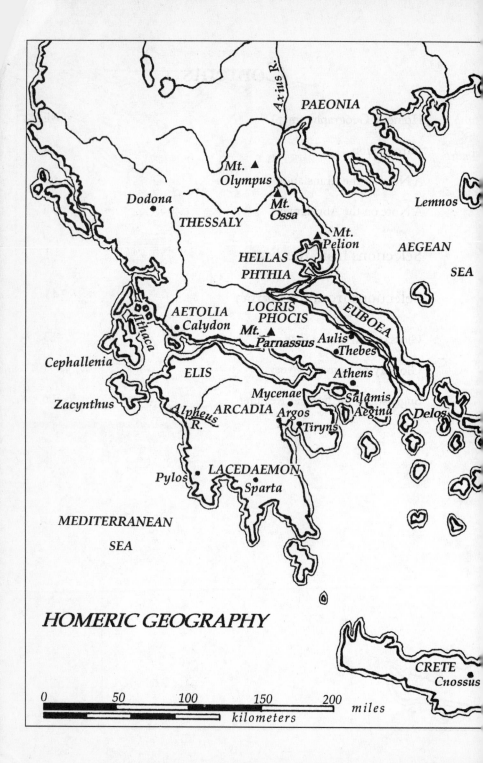

PAEONIA

Axius R.

Mt. ▲
Olympus

Mt. ▲
Ossa

Dodona

THESSALY

Lemnos

Mt. ▲
Pelion

HELLAS
PHTHIA

AEGEAN

SEA

AETOLIA
Calydon

LOCRIS
PHOCIS

EUBOEA

Ithaca

Mt. ▲
Parnassus

Aulis

Cephallenia

ELIS

Thebes

Athens

Zacynthus

Mycenae

Salamis

Delos

*Alpheus
R.*

ARCADIA

Argos

Aegina

Tiryns

Pylos

LACEDAEMON

Sparta

MEDITERRANEAN

SEA

HOMERIC GEOGRAPHY

CRETE
Cnossus

0   50   100   150   200   *miles*

kilometers

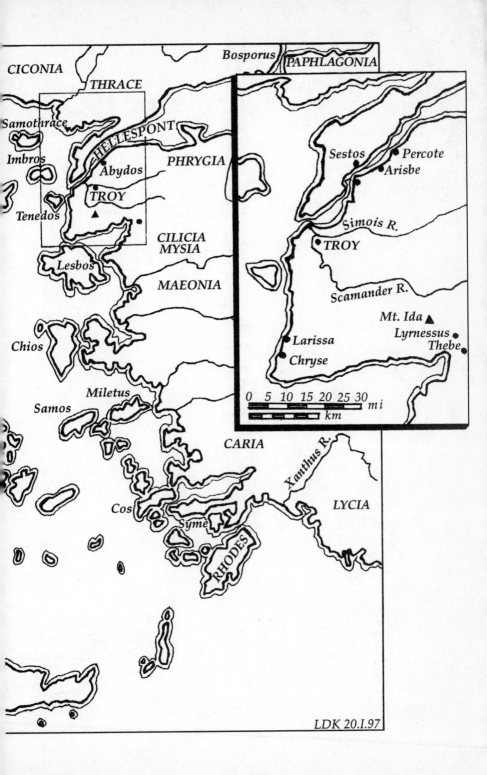

CICONIA

THRACE

Bosporus

PAPHLAGONIA

Samothrace

HELLESPONT

Imbros

PHRYGIA

Abydos

TROY

Tenedos

CILICIA
MYSIA

Lesbos

MAEONIA

Chios

Miletus

Samos

CARIA

Cos

Syme

Xanthus R.

LYCIA

RHODES

Sestos

Percote

Arisbe

Simois R.

TROY

Scamander R.

Mt. Ida

Lyrnessus

Thebe

Larissa

Chryse

0 5 10 15 20 25 30   mi
km

LDK 20.I.97

Introduction

The earliest works of ancient Greek literature are two epic poems, the *Iliad* and the *Odyssey*, both attributed to a single poet, Homer. Although very different in their themes, settings, and outlooks, both of these poems display the expansive scope of epic, which typically recounts events with far-reaching historical consequences, sums up the values and achievements of an entire culture, and documents the fullness and variety of the world. And both poems deal with the same event in Greek mythology, the war against Troy.

In the myth of the Trojan War, the Greeks band together and sail to Troy, on the coast of Asia Minor (present-day Turkey). Their purpose is to recover Helen, the beautiful wife of a Greek chieftain, Menelaus, who has been stolen by the Trojan prince Paris, and to punish Troy for Helen's abduction. The Greeks spend ten hard years fighting around Troy until they finally succeed in taking the city and can return at last to their homes. Each of the Homeric epics relates a major portion of this legend, but each does so by concentrating on the events of a very short period and on the experiences of a particular hero.

The *Iliad* focuses on the greatest fighter of the Greeks, Achilles, and describes a crucial period late in the war, in which Achilles quarrels with the Greek commander Agamemnon and refuses to fight any longer, then changes course and returns to battle to kill the Trojan champion Hector. Not only is this episode decisive (since Hector's loss assures Troy's fall), but it is also told in a way that evokes the entire war. The poem looks back to the war's origins and ahead both to the defeat of Troy and to Achilles' own death in battle, portraying all the major heroes and surveying the glorious successes and painful losses of both sides.

The *Odyssey* concerns the war's aftermath, the difficult journey home from Troy, and focuses on Odysseus, the wily hero whose return is both the most challenging and the most successful. Concentrating on the last leg of Odysseus' ten-year journey and his recovery of a home that has been taken over by enemies, the *Odyssey* nonetheless incorporates accounts of what happened to the other major Greek heroes after the war, fills in Odysseus' adventures from the time he left Troy, and describes the long period of anxious waiting endured by his wife and son in his absence.

This sophisticated technique of using a single episode to evoke a larger body of legendary material is one indication that these poems are not the earliest tellings of these stories. Although they represent for us the beginning of Western literature, the *Iliad* and the *Odyssey* are also themselves the products of a long poetic tradition, now lost to us, that developed over several periods of early Greek history.

The Trojan legend, which includes tales of disaster and destruction for both the defeated Trojans and the victorious Greeks, is a mythic account of the end of the first stage of ancient Greek history, which is known as the Bronze Age, after the widespread use of bronze (rather than iron, which was not yet in common use), or the Mycenaean period, after the city of Mycenae, one of the main power centers of that era. Mycenaean civilization developed in the centuries after 2000 B.C.E., which is approximately when Greek-speaking people first arrived in the area at the southern end of the Balkan peninsula that we now know as Greece. Those Greek-speakers gradually established there a rich civilization dominated by a few powerful cities built around large, highly organized palaces. These palaces were at once fortified military strongholds and centers for international trade, in particular trade with the many islands located in the Aegean Sea, to the east of the Greek mainland. On the largest of those islands, the island of Crete, there was already flourishing, by the time the Mycenaeans arrived in Greece, a rich and sophisticated civilization, known as Minoan civilization, by which the Mycenaeans were heavily influenced and which they came ultimately to dominate.

From the Minoans the Mycenaeans gained, along with many other crafts and institutions, a system of writing: a syllabary, in which each symbol stands for a particular syllable, as opposed to an alphabet, in which each symbol stands for a particular sound. The Mycenaeans adapted to the writing of Greek the syllabary that the Minoans used to write their own language, a language that, although we have examples of their writing, still has not been identified. This earliest Greek writing system is known to present-day scholars as

Linear B, and archaeologists excavating on Crete and at various mainland centers including Mycenae and Pylos have recovered examples of it incised on clay tablets. These tablets contain not—as was hoped when they were found—political treaties, mythological poems, or accounts of religious rituals—but detailed accounts of a highly bureaucratic palace economy: inventories of grain or livestock, lists of palace functionaries assigned to perform such specialized roles as "unguent boiler," "chair-maker," or "bath-pourer."

Mycenaean civilization reached its height at about 1600 B.C.E. and was essentially destroyed in a series of natural disasters and political disruptions about 400 years later, around 1200 B.C.E. We do not really know what happened, but all of the main archaeological sites show some evidence of destruction, burning, or hasty abandonment at about that time, and a sharp decline thereafter in the ambition and complexity of their material culture. Among these is the site of Troy itself, which was discovered in the late nineteenth century by Heinrich Schliemann, who followed the topographical details given in the *Iliad;* through this discovery, Schliemann both vindicated the historical validity of Homer and helped to found the field of archaeology.

Related in some way to the disruptions that ended the Bronze Age was the emergence of a new group of Greek-speakers as the dominant people on the mainland. The classical Greeks referred to these people as the Dorians and believed that they had invaded Greece from the north. Modern historians are uncertain whether they were new migrants or people already present in Greece who newly came to power in the upheavals of this period. In any case, many people left the mainland as a consequence and moved east, settling on various islands of the Aegean and along the coast of Asia Minor, in the area that is now western Turkey but that then became, in its coastal region, as much a part of the Greek world as was the mainland itself.

Both the Greeks who remained on the mainland and those who migrated to Asia Minor lived in conditions that involved less material prosperity and less highly organized concentrations of political and military power than were characteristic of the Mycenaean period. Their period is traditionally known as the "Dark Age" because their physical remains suggest a less magnificent level of civilization and because we know relatively little about it, although recent work in archaeology is increasing our knowledge and revealing more evidence of prosperity and artistic achievement than had previously been available.

In the transition to the Dark Age, writing, which was probably practiced in the Mycenaean period only by a small class of professional scribes, fell out of use, and the Greeks became once again a culture without writing. On the other hand, they had always relied, and they continued to rely, on oral communication as their central means of recalling, preserving, and transmitting the historical memories, religious beliefs, and shared stories that in our culture would be committed to writing—or now to various forms of electronic media. In particular, the Greeks of Asia Minor, known as the Ionians, developed a tradition of heroic poetry, through which they recalled their own history, looking back and recounting the experiences of that earlier lost era. This poetry centered on certain legendary figures and events, among them the events surrounding the Trojan War, which, as mentioned before, appear to reflect the final moments of Mycenaean civilization.

The so-called Dark Age came to an end during a period roughly corresponding to the eighth century—the 700s—B.C.E. The cultural shift that we label the end of the Dark Age and the beginning of the Archaic period involved, not a series of upheavals, as with the end of the Bronze Age, but the emergence of new activity in a variety of fields. A growth in population led to a wave of colonization, with established Greek centers sending out colonies to such places as the Black Sea, Sicily, southern Italy, and southern France. There was also greater contact among the various Greek communities, which were politically distinct and remained so for centuries. This contact led to the development of institutions designed to unite those communities culturally and to reinforce a shared Greek, or Panhellenic, heritage, such as the oracle of Apollo at Delphi and the Olympic games (founded in 776 B.C.E.). Around this time, the Greeks began to build large-scale stone temples and to make large-scale statues and a new kind of pottery decorated with elaborate geometric patterns. Many of the features of Greek culture that we associate with the Classical Period—the period that loosely corresponds to the fifth and fourth centuries B.C.E.—had their origins in the eighth century.

In addition to colonization, this was also a time of increased trade and thus of greater contact with other Mediterranean cultures.

One consequence of this trade was the renewal of contacts, which had been intensive in the Mycenaean period, with cultures of the Near East. Through their dealings with the Phoenicians, a Semitic people living in present-day Lebanon, the Greeks learned a new system of writing—not a syllabary like Linear B, but an alphabet, the alphabet that is still used to write Greek and that was adapted to become the Roman alphabet, now widely used for many languages, including English. This new way of writing Greek quickly became much more widespread than Linear B had been, and it was put to a greater variety of uses. Among these was the writing down of poetry, and it is generally believed among scholars (although by no means universally agreed) that the *Iliad* and the *Odyssey* came into being in the written form in which we know them at that time.

Although we know these poems in written form, we can see in their style and in their narrative techniques traces of their oral origins, even if there is considerable disagreement among scholars over how close to those origins these particular works may be. Specifically, these poems manifest a use of repeated elements—phrases, lines, groups of lines, and types of episodes—that are an essential feature of an oral poet's style. Because a poet who performs orally does not memorize and recite an unchanging artifact but composes his song as he goes at the same rate at which he delivers it, he relies on a supply of stock elements; acquiring that supply is a vital part of his training. Analysts of Homeric style have discovered that the repeated features that are immediately noticeable to readers form an elaborate system both of ready-made whole lines and of short phrases that allowed the poet easily to generate new lines that conformed to the requirements of the meter in which he composed, a meter known as the dactylic hexameter. Among the most striking of these are the phrases used to identify the characters, which link their names with their attributes or their ancestry, and which exist in different forms to be used as needed at different places in the line and in different grammatical cases. But the use of repeated patterns extends to much larger units as well, including obvious repetition of whole blocks of lines, as when, for example, a character reports on an event in the same words in which it was originally narrated, or the more subtle use of repeated sequences of actions to describe such recurrent circumstances as a host welcoming a guest or one character visiting another in search of important information.

Because repeated elements such as epithets have such a clear usefulness as aids to oral composition, it is hard to be sure how much further significance they are meant to bear in any particular context, although they certainly are meaningful as general expressions of a character's nature. For example, the central heroes of both poems have epithets that sum up their distinctive forms of excellence. The semidivine warrior Achilles is known as *dios* (godlike) and *podas ôkus* (swift-footed), whereas the wily survivor Odysseus is known as *polumêtis* (extremely clever) and *polutlas* (enduring much), but that usage does not mean that Achilles is displaying his speed when he is called *podas ôkus* (which is sometimes applied to him when he is sitting down) or that Odysseus is being especially clever at the points at which he is called *polumêtis*. The question of how integral these repeated elements are to the meaning of Homeric poetry is especially pressing for the translator, who has to decide whether to carry this stylistic feature over to a new language and a poetic form that does not have the same strict metrical rules as Homer's hexameters. The modern translator is also involved in a different relationship between the poem and the audience—not a live performance at which all parties were present at once and at which the conventions of Homeric style were familiar and unremarkable, but a less direct form of communication over large stretches of time and space, mediated through the printed page.

Stanley Lombardo has played down the repetitive dimension of the Greek original more than some other translators do, for the sake of a swift narrative pace and of making the characters speak in English as real people do. He has also taken advantage of some of Homer's repetitions for a creative solution to one of the most difficult problems of translation, the way in which there is almost never a single word or phrase that captures what is in the original. The fact that the same expressions occur over and over again gives him a chance to try a range of different versions that cumulatively add up to what is in the Greek. For example, one of the most famous lines in Homeric poetry is one that appears twenty times in the *Odyssey* and twice in the *Iliad*, which is used to describe the coming of dawn. This time-marker is, in part, a routine building block of Homeric poetry, a convenient, efficient way of marking a new phase in the action that corresponds to the start of a new day. But the announcement of dawn's appearance is made to fill an entire line through the addition of two epithets, which mean "early-born" and "rosy-fingered." By offering us several different versions of this line, Lombardo is able to bring out much more fully the many meanings of these wonderfully suggestive adjectives, as shown in these examples from the *Odyssey*: "Dawn's pale rose fingers brushed across the sky" (2.1); "Dawn came early, touching the sky with rose" (5.228); "Dawn spread her rose-light over the sky" (8.1); "Dawn came early, with palmettoes of rose" (9.146); "Light blossomed like roses in the eastern sky" (12.8); "At the first blush of Dawn. . . . " (half of 12.324).

The relationship between oral poetry and Homeric style was not fully understood until earlier in this century. A crucial step in this understanding was the comparative work of an American scholar, Milman Parry, who during the 1920s and 1930s studied oral poets who were then still practicing their art in the Balkan region. Parry saw that many of their techniques corresponded to the conventions of Homeric style. For well over a century before Parry's discoveries, scholars had been worrying over the ways in which Homeric poetry is different from later poetry produced through the medium of writing, speculating about how these poems were produced, or what came to be known as "the Homeric question." Much attention was given to inconsistencies between different sections of the narrative or to places in which sections of the narrative seem to be awkwardly joined. For example, the *Iliad* relates the death of the same minor warrior in two different places and includes passages in which some of the characters seem unaware of the stubborn way in which Achilles goes on refusing to fight even after Agamemnon has tried to make peace with him. In the *Odyssey*, Odysseus is told by the seductive sorceress Circe that he must visit the land of the dead, but when he gets there, things do not go at all the way that she has said they will. Or, at the end of the poem, some of Odysseus' defeated enemies give an account of how he regained his house that does not match the actual narrative.

These inconsistencies were seen by scholars who were known as "analysts" as supporting a theory according to which the *Iliad* and the *Odyssey* were each created through the joining together by editors of several shorter traditional poems composed by illiterate bards. According to this theory, the *Iliad* might have been put together from a poem about Achilles and from several other battle narratives about the Trojan War; and the *Odyssey* might have been put together from one poem about Odysseus' exotic journey from Troy, from another about his homecoming, and from yet another about the adventures of his son Telemachus. The analysts were countered by "unitarians," scholars who found in each poem an overall unity of theme and conception that outweighs those inconsistencies and points to a single intelligence shaping the entire work. Parry's discoveries have tended to uphold the unitarian position because they reveal that the kinds of small inconsistencies that concerned the analysts are both common and unimportant in the context of oral performance.

Although the answers to the Homeric question proposed during the 18th and 19th centuries are not generally accepted today, the scholars who wrestled with it helped to show how different these works are from modern poetry, and they recognized early on that an important clue to their origins might be provided by the singers actually portrayed in the *Odyssey*, Phemius and Demodocus, who perform songs as entertainment for groups of people gathered in aristocratic households. Phemius and Demodocus are like the modern bards studied by Parry in that they perform songs that are at once new and traditional, original retellings of legendary material that is the common property of the singer and the audience. Also like modern oral poets, they display a high degree of responsiveness to their audiences as they give shape to each particular version of a story.

The fact that one of these poets, Demodocus, is blind marks the poet as a figure who relies on inner resources. In Homeric terms, that reliance means that the poet is divinely inspired, instilled by the Muses with knowledge of past events that he has not himself witnessed. For divine inspiration, we might substitute the inherited skills and familiarity with poetic tradition of an oral poet, but in either case, those inner resources can be contrasted to the external aid of writing, which is never alluded to in the *Odyssey*, and alluded to only once in the *Iliad*. It is interesting that ancient legends about Homer, the poet to whom both the *Odyssey* and the *Iliad*—along with other poems—were attributed, claim that he was blind, so that he too was seen as both a visionary figure—in myth, prophets are also often blind—and one who did not write. It should be noted, though, that ancient stories about Homer, like most of the biographical information we have about early Greek poets, are largely fictitious, based mainly on the events of the *Odyssey*, so that Homer is portrayed as an itinerant beggar, which happens to be a role adopted by Odysseus as a disguise for much of the *Odyssey*.

We have no reliable information about Homer that would allow us to decide whether, for example, he really was responsible for both the *Iliad* and the *Odyssey* or to determine just what role he played in the process by which the poems that we have came into being. A key step in that process was the point at which the traditions of oral performance intersected with the new practice of writing and the epics took on the written form in which we now know them. One of the main challenges now facing Homeric scholars is that of figuring out to what extent the distinctive qualities of the *Iliad* and the *Odyssey* are due to the use of writing. On the one hand, the poems bear all the marks of oral style, which tend to disappear quickly once a poet learns to write. On the other hand, they are far too long to have ever been performed on a single occasion like the ones depicted in the *Odyssey*, and there is considerable debate about whether the large-scale design and complex structure exhibited by both the *Iliad* and the *Odyssey* could have been produced without the aid of writing. And, even though most scholars believe that the poems were written down in the eighth century B.C.E. when writing first became available, others argue that the first written texts were produced later, possibly in Athens in the sixth century B.C.E., where we know an effort was made to produce official versions of both epics.

Whenever they were actually written down and however much they may have been shaped by writing, the Homeric epics were still primarily oral works, in the sense that they were regularly performed and were known to their audiences through performance, well into the classical period. The process of transmission by which the *Iliad* and the *Odyssey* became what they are today—that is, poems experienced almost exclusively through reading, whether in Greek or in translation—is a long and complicated one. It starts with that first, still mysterious moment when the epics were first written down and encompasses many stages of editing and copying: by ancient scholars, especially those working in Alexandria in the third century B.C.E., who were responsible, for example, for the division of both poems into twenty-four books; by medieval scribes, who copied out the manuscripts on which our modern editions are based; and by modern scholars who have produced the texts from which translations like the ones in this volume are made.

Amid such uncertainty, the idea that the singers in the *Odyssey*, Phemius and Demodocus, might represent poets of the kind who helped to shape the *Iliad* and the *Odyssey* is not at all implausible. Many of the customs and institutions represented in the poems reflect the times in which the poems and their traditions took shape rather than the earlier period during which the events depicted supposedly occurred. Historians and archaeologists who have compared the culture described in the Homeric epics with what we know of Greek history have discovered that the epics describe a world that does not correlate to any one period but that combines elements of the Bronze Age with elements of the Dark Age: memories of the earlier time in which the Trojan legend is set have been woven together with circumstances borrowed from the period during which the Trojan legend evolved. The many depictions of daily life in peacetime communities found in the *Odyssey* tend to reflect that later period. The kingdoms depicted there are much smaller and much less highly organized than those of the Mycenaean period, and many details of their material culture and social organization accord more closely to what we know of Dark Age life—a way of life that, we then assume, must have seemed quite familiar to the poem's original audience.

From the way that each of the Homeric epics begins, we can sense that they are building on a long, preexisting tradition. The *Iliad* plunges into the quarrel between Achilles and Agamemnon with confidence that its audience will already be familiar with these characters and the legends to which they belong. That the *Odyssey* is not the first telling of Odysseus' story seems clear from the opening lines, in which the subject is simply identified as "the cunning hero, the wanderer, who was blown off course"; his name is not mentioned until many lines later—a fitting introduction for a hero who will turn out to specialize in concealing his identity and waiting for the strategic moment. Throughout both poems, various characters, especially the oldest and wisest, make comparisons with similar situations outside the poem, apparently drawing on an inherited fund of similar legends. For the most part, however, we can only speculate about the ways in which the epics that we have reshape earlier versions of their stories, creating through shifts of focus or the addition of new details a kind of commentary on previous traditions that would have added to the interest and pleasure of these poems for their original audiences.

We can get some sense of the interplay of different narratives within a tradition from the relationship between the *Iliad* and the *Odyssey* themselves. The nature of this relationship has been discussed ever since antiquity, when there was already a debate about whether both poems were by the same author. An English scholar of the late 19th century, David Munro, compared the two poems and discovered an interesting phenomenon (now known as "Munro's law"), which is that there is no overlap in their contents: neither poem recounts any events that are told in the other. This discovery lends itself to several conclusions, such as that the two poems were composed in complete ignorance of each other, but the most likely conclusion is that they were designed to complement one another. The *Odyssey* seems, in fact, to go out of its way to fill in the rest of the story of the *Iliad*, including events that are implicit but still untold at the end of the *Iliad*, such as the death and burial of Achilles and the taking of Troy. As a pair, the two poems seem designed to give, through a complex combination of their own main events and the wider experiences they include through reminiscences and other kinds of allusions, a comprehensive account of the Trojan War.

The *Iliad* and the *Odyssey* complement each other, not only in their contents but also in their visions of human life and their definitions of heroism. The *Iliad* is entirely focused on war, and one of the main themes of the poem is the inescapability of war even when people are fully aware of its evils. The story of Achilles turns on his attempt to leave the war and his discovery that he cannot, and his story is necessarily limited to the battlefield; he knows from a prophecy that if he stays and fights at Troy, he will never go home. Achilles' qualities are preeminently those of a warrior: physical courage and strength, skill in battle, and the single-minded pursuit of honor even at the cost of his life. The *Odyssey* tells another story of hardship and struggle, but it is also one of survival and eventual success, as Odysseus finally achieves the satisfying homecoming that is lost for Achilles and for most of the other Greeks. The *Odyssey* includes a wide range of settings, some fantastic, some quite ordinary and domestic, and has a broader sense of human possibilities. Correspondingly, Odysseus is a different kind of hero: versatile, adaptable, and as dependent on his wits as on his physical powers.

In some of the *Odyssey*'s allusions to the *Iliad*, we can even detect an element of rivalry between the two poems. At one point,

Odysseus encounters the bard Demodocus, who is singing a song that, like the Homeric epics, concerns the Trojan War. Demodocus' song is a curious one because it seems to be a kind of alternate version of the *Iliad*. Whereas the *Iliad* focuses on a quarrel between the two major Achaean heroes Achilles and Agamemnon, this song focuses on a quarrel between Achilles and Odysseus. From other sources, we know what this quarrel must have been about, for the two heroes were evidently supposed to have disputed whether Troy would ultimately be taken by *biê*, "force," the quality at which Achilles' excelled, or *mêtis*, "cleverness," the quality at which Odysseus excelled. When Odysseus then asks Demodocus for another song and specifies that its subject should be the story of the Trojan Horse, he is implicitly pointing to the resolution of this dispute. Although, as the *Iliad* recounts, Achilles' might is essential to the Trojan defeat, especially through his killing of Hector, the city is taken in the end only through a clever trick contrived by Odysseus with the help of the goddess Athena, the infiltration of the city by a band of men hidden within a huge statue of a horse. In having Demodocus sing, at Odysseus' request, a kind of alternative *Iliad* concerned with the opposition between Achilles and Odysseus, the *Odyssey* sets up a competition with both the *Iliad* and its hero that Odysseus wins. If Achilles has to choose between staying at Troy and winning glory there or going home again, Odysseus, the *Odyssey* tells us, is the hero who does not have to make that choice, who manages to have it all.

Taken together, these two poems offer us a full-scale introduction to the Trojan War, a mythic event that encapsulated for the Greeks their own early history and that has played a central role in the subsequent traditions of Western art and literature. Through this myth, they portray an entire world, within which their very different heroes struggle to define themselves, and offer us two powerful, compelling perspectives on war itself. As seen in the *Iliad* through the figure of Achilles, war is an overwhelming experience that dominates human life and the arena of preeminent human achievement; as seen in the *Odyssey* through the figure of Odysseus, war is one of many challenges to be mastered with cunning intelligence, survived, and crowned with a glorious and adventurous homecoming.

Sheila Murnaghan
University of Pennsylvania

A Note on the Translation

The poetics of this translation of Homer's *Iliad* and *Odyssey* are easily and briefly stated: rhythms and language drawn from natural speech, in the tradition of American poetry; emphasis on the physicality, rapidity, and suppleness of the verse; varied treatment of epithets and formulae, often heightening their effect as poetic events; treatment of similes as partially independent poetic moments, indicated by italics and indentation; close attention to presentation of the text on the page; commitment to the poetic line. Above all, this translation reflects the oral performance nature of the original poems. It began as scripts for performance, and it has been shaped by the complementary pressures of poetic composition and oral performance. Throughout the period of composing the translation as poetry on the page, I continued reciting it to audiences, voicing the text as I crafted it and crafting it to capture the voice that I heard.

Stanley Lombardo

A Note on the Abridgment

Homer's *Iliad* and *Odyssey* are presented here in versions approximately one-half as long as the original epics. The passages that have been retained appear exactly as in the original Lombardo translation and have not been condensed or digested in any way. Omitted passages are indicated by book and line number and are summarized very briefly. The selections have been made with an eye toward keeping the major characters in play and highlighting the interventions of the gods in human affairs.

ILIAD 1

Rage:
> Sing, Goddess, Achilles' rage,
Black and murderous, that cost the Greeks
Incalculable pain, pitched countless souls
Of heroes into Hades' dark,
And left their bodies to rot as feasts   5
For dogs and birds, as Zeus' will was done.
> Begin with the clash between Agamemnon—
The Greek warlord—and godlike Achilles.

Which of the immortals set these two
At each other's throats?   10
> Apollo,
Zeus' son and Leto's, offended
By the warlord. Agamemnon had dishonored
Chryses, Apollo's priest, so the god
Struck the Greek camp with plague,   15
And the soldiers were dying of it.
> Chryses
Had come to the Greek beachhead camp
Hauling a fortune for his daughter's ransom.
Displaying Apollo's sacral ribbons   20
On a golden staff, he made a formal plea
To the entire Greek army, but especially
The commanders, Atreus' two sons:

"Sons of Atreus and Greek heroes all:
May the gods on Olympus grant you plunder   25
Of Priam's city and a safe return home.
But give me my daughter back and accept
This ransom out of respect for Zeus' son,

Lord Apollo, who deals death from afar."

A murmur rippled through the ranks: 30
"Respect the priest and take the ransom."
But Agamemnon was not pleased
And dismissed Chryses with a rough speech:

"Don't let me ever catch you, old man, by these ships again,
Skulking around now or sneaking back later.   35
The god's staff and ribbons won't save you next time.
The girl is mine, and she'll be an old woman in Argos
Before I let her go, working the loom in my house
And coming to my bed, far from her homeland.
Now clear out of here before you make me angry!"   40

The old man was afraid and did as he was told.
He walked in silence along the whispering surf line,
And when he had gone some distance the priest
Prayed to Lord Apollo, son of silken-haired Leto:

"Hear me, Silverbow, Protector of Chryse,   45
Lord of Holy Cilla, Master of Tenedos,
And Sminthian God of Plague!
If ever I've built a temple that pleased you
Or burnt fat thighbones of bulls and goats—
    Grant me this prayer: 50
Let the Danaans pay for my tears with your arrows!"

Apollo heard his prayer and descended Olympus' crags
Pulsing with fury, bow slung over one shoulder,
The arrows rattling in their case on his back
As the angry god moved like night down the mountain.   55

He settled near the ships and let loose an arrow.
Reverberation from his silver bow hung in the air.
He picked off the pack animals first, and the lean hounds,
But then aimed his needle-tipped arrows at the men
And shot until the death-fires crowded the beach.   60

Nine days the god's arrows rained death on the camp.
On the tenth day Achilles called an assembly.
Hera, the white-armed goddess, planted the thought in him
Because she cared for the Greeks and it pained her
To see them dying. When the troops had all mustered,   65
Up stood the great runner Achilles, and said:

"Well, Agamemnon, it looks as if we'd better give up
And sail home—assuming any of us are left alive—
If we have to fight both the war and this plague.
But why not consult some prophet or priest   70
Or a dream interpreter, since dreams too come from Zeus,
Who could tell us why Apollo is so angry,
If it's for a vow or a sacrifice he holds us at fault.
Maybe he'd be willing to lift this plague from us
If he savored the smoke from lambs and prime goats."   75

Achilles had his say and sat down. Then up rose
Calchas, son of Thestor, bird-reader supreme,
Who knew what is, what will be, and what has been.
He had guided the Greek ships to Troy
Through the prophetic power Apollo   80
Had given him, and he spoke out now:

"Achilles, beloved of Zeus, you want me to tell you
About the rage of Lord Apollo, the Arch-Destroyer.
And I will tell you. But you have to promise me and swear
You will support me and protect me in word and deed.   85
I have a feeling I might offend a person of some authority
Among the Greeks, and you know how it is when a king
Is angry with an underling. He might swallow his temper
For a day, but he holds it in his heart until later
And it all comes out. Will you guarantee my security?"   90

Achilles, the great runner, responded:

"Don't worry. Prophesy to the best of your knowledge.
I swear by Apollo, to whom you pray when you reveal
The gods' secrets to the Greeks, Calchas, that while I live

And look upon this earth, no one will lay a hand   *95*
On you here beside these hollow ships, no, not even
Agamemnon, who boasts he is the best of the Achaeans."

And Calchas, the perfect prophet, taking courage:

"The god finds no fault with vow or sacrifice.
It is for his priest, whom Agamemnon dishonored   *100*
And would not allow to ransom his daughter,
That Apollo deals and will deal death from afar.
He will not lift this foul plague from the Greeks
Until we return the dancing-eyed girl to her father
Unransomed, unbought, and make formal sacrifice   *105*
On Chryse. Only then might we appease the god."

He finished speaking and sat down. Then up rose
Atreus' son, the warlord Agamemnon,
Furious, anger like twin black thunderheads seething
In his lungs, and his eyes flickered with fire   *110*
As he looked Calchas up and down, and said:

                                    "You damn soothsayer!
You've never given me a good omen yet.
You take some kind of perverse pleasure in prophesying
Doom, don't you? Not a single favorable omen ever!   *115*
Nothing good ever happens! And now you stand here
Uttering oracles before the Greeks, telling us
That your great ballistic god is giving us all this trouble
Because I was unwilling to accept the ransom
For Chryses' daughter but preferred instead to keep her   *120*
In my tent! And why shouldn't I? I like her better than
My wife Clytemnestra. She's no worse than her
When it comes to looks, body, mind, or ability.
Still, I'll give her back, if that's what's best.
I don't want to see the army destroyed like this.   *125*
But I want another prize ready for me right away.
I'm not going to be the only Greek without a prize,
It wouldn't be right. And you all see where mine is going."

And Achilles, strong, swift, and godlike:

"And where do you think, son of Atreus, 130
You greedy glory-hound, the magnanimous Greeks
Are going to get another prize for you?
Do you think we have some kind of stockpile in reserve?
Every town in the area has been sacked and the stuff all divided.
You want the men to count it all back and redistribute it? 135
All right, you give the girl back to the god. The army
Will repay you three and four times over—when and if
Zeus allows us to rip Troy down to its foundations."

The warlord Agamemnon responded:

"You may be a good man in a fight, Achilles, 140
And look like a god, but don't try to put one over on me—
It won't work. So while you have your prize,
You want me to sit tight and do without?
Give the girl back, just like that? Now maybe
If the army, in a generous spirit, voted me 145
Some suitable prize of their own choice, something fair—
But if it doesn't, I'll just go take something myself,
Your prize perhaps, or Ajax's, or Odysseus',
And whoever she belongs to, it'll stick in his throat.

But we can think about that later. 150
                              Right now we launch
A black ship on the bright salt water, get a crew aboard,
Load on a hundred bulls, and have Chryseis board her too,
My girl with her lovely cheeks. And we'll want a good man
For captain, Ajax or Idomeneus or godlike Odysseus— 155
Or maybe you, son of Peleus, our most formidable hero—
To offer sacrifice and appease the Arch-Destroyer for us."

Achilles looked him up and down and said:

"You shameless, profiteering excuse for a commander!
How are you going to get any Greek warrior 160
To follow you into battle again? You know,

I don't have any quarrel with the Trojans,
They didn't do anything to *me* to make me
Come over here and fight, didn't run off *my* cattle or horses
Or ruin *my* farmland back home in Phthia, not with all   165
The shadowy mountains and moaning seas between.
It's for *you*, dogface, for your precious pleasure—
And Menelaus' honor—that we came here,
A fact you don't have the decency even to mention!
And now you're threatening to take away the prize   170
That I sweated for and the Greeks gave me.
I never get a prize equal to yours when the army
Captures one of the Trojan strongholds.
No, I do all the dirty work with my own hands,
And when the battle's over and we divide the loot   175
You get the lion's share and I go back to the ships
With some pitiful little thing, so worn out from fighting
I don't have the strength left even to complain.
Well, I'm going back to Phthia now. Far better
To head home with my curved ships than stay here,   180
Unhonored myself and piling up a fortune for you."

The warlord Agamemnon responded:

"Go ahead and desert, if that's what you want!
I'm not going to beg you to stay. There are plenty of others
Who will honor me, not least of all Zeus the Counselor.   185
To me, you're the most hateful king under heaven,
A born troublemaker. You actually *like* fighting and war.
If you're all that strong, it's just a gift from some god.
So why don't you go home with your ships and lord it over
Your precious Myrmidons. I couldn't care less about you   190
Or your famous temper. But I'll tell you this:
Since Phoebus Apollo is taking away my Chryseis,
Whom I'm sending back aboard ship with my friends,
I'm coming to your hut and taking Briseis,
Your own beautiful prize, so that you will see just how much   195
Stronger I am than you, and the next person will wince
At the thought of opposing me as an equal."

Achilles' chest was a rough knot of pain
Twisting around his heart: should he
Draw the sharp sword that hung by his thigh, 200
Scatter the ranks and gut Agamemnon,
Or control his temper, repress his rage?
He was mulling it over, inching the great sword
From its sheath, when out of the blue
Athena came, sent by the white-armed goddess 205
Hera, who loved and watched over both men.
She stood behind Achilles and grabbed his sandy hair,
Visible only to him: not another soul saw her.
Awestruck, Achilles turned around, recognizing
Pallas Athena at once—it was her eyes— 210
And words flew from his mouth like winging birds:

"Daughter of Zeus! Why have you come here?
To see Agamemnon's arrogance, no doubt.
I'll tell you where I place my bets, Goddess:
Sudden death for this outrageous behavior." 215

Athena's eyes glared through the sea's salt haze.

"I came to see if I could check this temper of yours,
Sent from heaven by the white-armed goddess
Hera, who loves and watches over both of you men.
Now come on, drop this quarrel, don't draw your sword. 220
Tell him off instead. And I'll tell you,
Achilles, how things will be: You're going to get
Three times as many magnificent gifts
Because of his arrogance. Just listen to us and be patient."

Achilles, the great runner, responded: 225

"When you two speak, Goddess, a man has to listen
No matter how angry. It's better that way.
Obey the gods and they hear you when you pray."

With that he ground his heavy hand
Onto the silver hilt and pushed the great sword 230

Back into its sheath. Athena's speech
Had been well-timed. She was on her way
To Olympus by now, to the halls of Zeus
And the other immortals, while Achilles
Tore into Agamemnon again: 235

                          "You bloated drunk,
With a dog's eyes and a rabbit's heart!
You've never had the guts to buckle on armor in battle
Or come out with the best fighting Greeks
On any campaign! Afraid to look Death in the eye,   240
Agamemnon? It's far more profitable
To hang back in the army's rear—isn't it?—
Confiscating prizes from any Greek who talks back
And bleeding your people dry. There's not a real man
Under your command, or this latest atrocity   245
Would be your last, son of Atreus.
Now get this straight. I swear a formal oath:
  By this scepter, which will never sprout leaf
Or branch again since it was cut from its stock
In the mountains, which will bloom no more   250
Now that bronze has pared off leaf and bark,
And which now the sons of the Greeks hold in their hands
At council, upholding Zeus' laws—
                          By this scepter I swear:
When every last Greek desperately misses Achilles,   255
Your remorse won't do any good then,
When Hector the man-killer swats you down like flies.
And you will eat your heart out
Because you failed to honor the best Greek of all."

Those were his words, and he slammed the scepter,   260
Studded with gold, to the ground and sat down.

Opposite him, Agamemnon fumed.
                          Then Nestor
Stood up, sweet-worded Nestor, the orator from Pylos
With a voice high-toned and liquid as honey.   265
He had seen two generations of men pass away

In sandy Pylos and was now king in the third.
He was full of good will in the speech he made:

"It's a sad day for Greece, a sad day.
Priam and Priam's sons would be happy indeed, 270
And the rest of the Trojans too, glad in their hearts,
If they learned all this about you two fighting,
Our two best men in council and in battle.
Now you listen to me, both of you. You are both
Younger than I am, and I've associated with men 275
Better than you, and they didn't treat me lightly.
I've never seen men like those, and never will,
The likes of Peirithous and Dryas, a shepherd to his people,
Caineus and Exadius and godlike Polyphemus,
And Aegeus' son, Theseus, who could have passed for a god, 280
The strongest men who ever lived on earth, the strongest,
And they fought with the strongest, with wild things
From the mountains, and beat the daylights out of them.
I was their companion, although I came from Pylos,
From the ends of the earth—they sent for me themselves. 285
And I held my own fighting with them. You couldn't find
A mortal on earth who could fight with them now.
And when I talked in council, they took my advice.
So should you two now: taking advice is a good thing.
    Agamemnon, for all your nobility, don't take his girl. 290
Leave her be: the army originally gave her to him as a prize.
Nor should you, son of Peleus, want to lock horns with a king.
A scepter-holding king has honor beyond the rest of men,
Power and glory given by Zeus himself.
You are stronger, and it is a goddess who bore you. 295
But he is more powerful, since he rules over more.
Son of Atreus, cease your anger. And I appeal
Personally to Achilles to control his temper, since he is,
For all Greeks, a mighty bulwark in this evil war."

And Agamemnon, the warlord: 300

"Yes, old man, everything you've said is absolutely right.
But this man wants to be ahead of everyone else,

He wants to rule everyone, give orders to everyone,
Lord it over everyone, and he's not going to get away with it.
If the gods eternal made him a spearman, does that mean   *305*
They gave him permission to be insolent as well?"

And Achilles, breaking in on him:

"Ha, and think of the names people would call me
If I bowed and scraped every time you opened your mouth.
Try that on somebody else, but not on me.   *310*
I'll tell you this, and you can stick it in your gut:
I'm not going to put up a fight on account of the girl.
You, all of you, gave her and you can all take her back.
But anything else of mine in my black sailing ship
You keep your goddamn hands off, you hear?   *315*
Try it. Let everybody here see how fast
Your black blood boils up around my spear."

So it was a stand-off, their battle of words,
And the assembly beside the Greek ships dissolved.
Achilles went back to the huts by his ships   *320*
With Patroclus and his men. Agamemnon had a fast ship
Hauled down to the sea, picked twenty oarsmen,
Loaded on a hundred bulls due to the god, and had
         Chryses' daughter,
His fair-cheeked girl, go aboard also. Odysseus captained,
And when they were all on board, the ship headed out to sea.   *325*

Onshore, Agamemnon ordered a purification.
The troops scrubbed down and poured the filth
Into the sea. Then they sacrificed to Apollo
Oxen and goats by the hundreds on the barren shore.
The smoky savor swirled up to the sky.   *330*

That was the order of the day. But Agamemnon
Did not forget his spiteful threat against Achilles.
He summoned Talthybius and Eurybates,
Faithful retainers who served as his heralds:

"Go to the hut of Achilles, son of Peleus;   335
Bring back the girl, fair-cheeked Briseis.
If he won't give her up, I'll come myself
With my men and take her—and freeze his heart cold."

It was not the sort of mission a herald would relish.
The pair trailed along the barren seashore   340
Until they came to the Myrmidons' ships and encampment.
They found Achilles sitting outside his hut
Beside his black ship. He was not glad to see them.
They stood respectfully silent, in awe of this king,
And it was Achilles who was moved to address them first: 345

"Welcome, heralds, the gods' messengers and men's.
Come closer. You're not to blame, Agamemnon is,
Who sent you here for the girl, Briseis.
                              Patroclus,
Bring the girl out and give her to these gentlemen.   350
You two are witnesses before the blessed gods,
Before mortal men and that hard-hearted king,
If ever I'm needed to protect the others
From being hacked to bits. His mind is murky with anger,
And he doesn't have the sense to look ahead and behind   355
To see how the Greeks might defend their ships."

Thus Achilles.
                    Patroclus obeyed his beloved friend
And brought Briseis, cheeks flushed, out of the tent
And gave her to the heralds, who led her away.   360
She went unwillingly.
                      Then Achilles, in tears,
Withdrew from his friends and sat down far away
On the foaming white seashore, staring out
At the endless sea. Stretching out his hands,   365
He prayed over and over to his beloved mother:

"Mother, since you bore me for a short life only,
Olympian Zeus was supposed to grant me honor.
Well, he hasn't given me any at all. Agamemnon

Has taken away my prize and dishonored me."   370

His voice, choked with tears, was heard by his mother
As she sat in the sea-depths beside her old father.
She rose up from the white-capped sea like a mist,
And settling herself beside her weeping child
She stroked him with her hand and talked to him: 375

"Why are you crying, son? What's wrong?
Don't keep it inside. Tell me so we'll both know."

And Achilles, with a deep groan:

"You already know. Why do I have to tell you?
We went after Thebes, Eëtion's sacred town,   380
Sacked it and brought the plunder back here.
The army divided everything up and chose
For Agamemnon fair-cheeked Chryseis.
Then her father, Chryses, a priest of Apollo,
Came to our army's ships on the beachhead,   385
Hauling a fortune for his daughter's ransom.
He displayed Apollo's sacral ribbons
On a golden staff and made a formal plea
To the entire Greek army, but especially
The commanders, Atreus' two sons.   390
You could hear the troops murmuring,
'Respect the priest and take the ransom.'
But Agamemnon wouldn't hear of it
And dismissed Chryses with a rough speech.
The old man went back angry, and Apollo   395
Heard his beloved priest's prayer.
He hit the Greeks hard, and the troops
Were falling over dead, the god's arrows
Raining down all through the Greek camp.
A prophet told us the Arch-Destroyer's will,   400
And I demanded the god be appeased.
Agamemnon got angry, stood up
And threatened me, and made good his threat.
The high command sent the girl on a fast ship

Back to Chryse with gifts for Apollo, 405
And heralds led away my girl, Briseis,
Whom the army had given to me.
Now you have to help me, if you can.

   Go to Olympus
And call in the debt that Zeus owes you. 410
I remember often hearing you tell
In my father's house how you alone managed,
Of all the immortals, to save Zeus' neck
When the other Olympians wanted to bind him—
Hera and Poseidon and Pallas Athena. 415
You came and loosened him from his chains,
And you lured to Olympus' summit the giant
With a hundred hands whom the gods call
Briareus but men call Aegaeon, stronger
Even than his own father Uranus, and he 420
Sat hulking in front of cloud-black Zeus,
Proud of his prowess, and scared all the gods
Who were trying to put the son of Cronus in chains.

   Remind Zeus of this, sit holding his knees,
See if he is willing to help the Trojans 425
Hem the Greeks in between the fleet and the sea.
Once they start being killed, the Greeks may
Appreciate Agamemnon for what he is,
And the wide-ruling son of Atreus will see
What a fool he's been because he did not honor 430
The best of all the fighting Achaeans."

And Thetis, now weeping herself:

"O my poor child. I bore you for sorrow,
Nursed you for grief. Why? You should be
Spending your time here by your ships 435
Happily and untroubled by tears,
Since life is short for you, all too brief.
Now you're destined for both an early death
And misery beyond compare. It was for this
I gave birth to you in your father's palace 440
Under an evil star.

                I'll go to snow-bound Olympus
And tell all this to the Lord of Lightning.
I hope he listens. You stay here, though,
Beside your ships and let the Greeks feel   *445*
Your spite; withdraw completely from the war.
Zeus left yesterday for the River Ocean
On his way to a feast with the Ethiopians.
All the gods went with him. He'll return
To Olympus twelve days from now,   *450*
And I'll go then to his bronze threshold
And plead with him. I think I'll persuade him."

And she left him there, angry and heartsick
At being forced to give up the silken-waisted girl.

  Meanwhile, Odysseus was putting in   *455*
At Chryse with his sacred cargo on board.
When they were well within the deepwater harbor
They furled the sail and stowed it in the ship's hold,
Slackened the forestays and lowered the mast,
Working quickly, then rowed her to a mooring, where   *460*
They dropped anchor and made the stern cables fast.
The crew disembarked on the seabeach
And unloaded the bulls for Apollo the Archer.
Then Chryses' daughter stepped off the seagoing vessel,
And Odysseus led her to an altar   *465*
And placed her in her father's hands, saying:

"Chryses, King Agamemnon has sent me here
To return your child and offer to Phoebus
Formal sacrifice on behalf of the Greeks.
So may we appease Lord Apollo, and may he   *470*
Lift the afflictions he has sent upon us."

Chryses received his daughter tenderly.

Moving quickly, they lined the hundred oxen
Round the massive altar, a glorious offering,
Washed their hands and sprinkled on the victims   *475*

Sacrificial barley. On behalf of the Greeks
Chryses lifted his hands and prayed aloud:

"Hear me, Silverbow, Protector of Chryse,
Lord of Holy Cilla, Master of Tenedos,
As once before you heard my prayer, 480
Did me honor, and smote the Greeks mightily,
So now also grant me this prayer:
                                        Lift the plague
From the Greeks and save them from death."

Thus the old priest, and Apollo heard him. 485

After the prayers and the strewing of barley
They slaughtered and flayed the oxen,
Jointed the thighbones and wrapped them
In a layer of fat with cuts of meat on top.
The old man roasted them over charcoal 490
And doused them with wine. Younger men
Stood by with five-tined forks in their hands.
When the thigh pieces were charred and they had
Tasted the tripe, they cut the rest into strips,
Skewered it on spits and roasted it skillfully. 495
When they were done and the feast was ready,
Feast they did, and no one lacked an equal share.
When they had all had enough to eat and drink,
The young men topped off mixing bowls with wine
And served it in goblets to all the guests. 500
All day long these young Greeks propitiated
The god with dancing, singing to Apollo
A paean as they danced, and the god was pleased.
When the sun went down and darkness came on,
They went to sleep by the ship's stern-cables. 505

Dawn came early, a palmetto of rose,
Time to make sail for the wide beachhead camp.
They set up mast and spread the white canvas,
And the following wind, sent by Apollo,
Boomed in the mainsail. An indigo wave 510

Hissed off the bow as the ship surged on,
Leaving a wake as she held on course through the billows.

When they reached the beachhead they hauled the black ship
High on the sand and jammed in the long chocks;
Then the crew scattered to their own huts and ships.			*515*

All this time Achilles, the son of Peleus in the line of Zeus,
Nursed his anger, the great runner idle by his fleet's fast hulls.
He was not to be seen in council, that arena for glory,
Nor in combat. He sat tight in camp consumed with grief,
His great heart yearning for the battle cry and war.			*520*

Twelve days went by. Dawn.
The gods returned to Olympus,
Zeus at their head.
				Thetis did not forget
Her son's requests. She rose from the sea			*525*
And up through the air to the great sky
And found Cronus' wide-seeing son
Sitting in isolation on the highest peak
Of the rugged Olympic massif.
She settled beside him, and touched his knees			*530*
With her left hand, his beard with her right,
And made her plea to the Lord of Sky:

"Father Zeus, if I have ever helped you
In word or deed among the immortals,
	Grant me this prayer:			*535*
Honor my son, doomed to die young
And yet dishonored by King Agamemnon,
Who stole his prize, a personal affront.
Do justice by him, Lord of Olympus.
Give the Trojans the upper hand until the Greeks			*540*
Grant my son the honor he deserves."

Zeus made no reply but sat a long time
In silence, clouds scudding around him.
Thetis held fast to his knees and asked again:

"Give me a clear yes or no. Either nod in assent 545
Or refuse me. Why should you care if I know
How negligible a goddess I am in your eyes."

This provoked a troubled, gloomy response:

"This is disastrous. You're going to force me
Into conflict with Hera. I can just hear her now, 550
Cursing me and bawling me out. As it is,
She already accuses me of favoring the Trojans.
Please go back the way you came. Maybe
Hera won't notice. I'll take care of this.
And so you can have some peace of mind, 555
I'll say yes to you by nodding my head,
The ultimate pledge. Unambiguous,
Irreversible, and absolutely fulfilled,
Whatever I say yes to with a nod of my head."

And the Son of Cronus nodded. Black brows 560
Lowered, a glory of hair cascaded down from the Lord's
Immortal head, and the holy mountain trembled.

    Their conference over, the two parted. The goddess
Dove into the deep sea from Olympus' snow-glare
And Zeus went to his home. The gods all 565
Rose from their seats at their father's entrance. Not one
Dared watch him enter without standing to greet him.
And so the god entered and took his high seat.
                            But Hera
Had noticed his private conversation with Thetis, 570
The silver-footed daughter of the Old Man of the Sea,
And flew at him with cutting words:

"Who was that you were scheming with just now?
You just love devising secret plots behind my back,
Don't you? You can't bear to tell me what you're thinking, 575
Or you don't dare. Never have and never will."

The Father of Gods and Men answered:

"Hera, don't hope to know all my secret thoughts.
It would strain your mind even though you are my wife.
What it is proper to hear, no one, human or divine,   580
Will hear before you. But what I wish to conceive
Apart from the other gods, don't pry into that."

And Lady Hera, with her oxen eyes wide:

"Oh my. The awesome son of Cronus has spoken.
Pry? You know that I never pry. And you always   585
Cheerfully volunteer—whatever information you please.
It's just that I have this feeling that somehow
The silver-footed daughter of the Old Man of the Sea
May have won you over. She *was* sitting beside you
Up there in the mists, and she did touch your knees.   590
And I'm pretty sure that you agreed to honor Achilles
And destroy Greeks by the thousands beside their ships."

And Zeus, the master of cloud and storm:

"You witch! Your intuitions are always right.
But what does it get you? Nothing, except that   595
I like you less than ever. And so you're worse off.
If it's as you think it is, it's my business, not yours.
So sit down and shut up and do as I say.
You see these hands? All the gods on Olympus
Won't be able to help you if I ever lay them on you."   600

Hera lost her nerve when she heard this.
She sat down in silence, fear cramping her heart,
And gloom settled over the gods in Zeus' hall.
Hephaestus, the master artisan, broke the silence,
Out of concern for his ivory-armed mother: 605

"This is terrible; it's going to ruin us all.
If you two quarrel like this over mortals
It's bound to affect us gods. There'll be no more
Pleasure in our feasts if we let things turn ugly.
Mother, please, I don't have to tell you,   610

You have to be pleasant to our father Zeus
So he won't be angry and ruin our feast.
If the Lord of Lightning wants to blast us from our seats,
He can—that's how much stronger he is.
So apologize to him with silken-soft words,   615
And the Olympian in turn will be gracious to us."

He whisked up a two-handled cup, offered it
To his dear mother, and said to her:

"I know it's hard, Mother, but you have to endure it.
I don't want to see you getting beat up, and me   620
Unable to help you. The Olympian can be rough.
Once before when I tried to rescue you
He flipped me by my foot off our balcony.
I fell all day and came down when the sun did
On the island of Lemnos, scarcely alive.   625
The Sintians had to nurse me back to health."

By the time he finished, the ivory-armed goddess
Was smiling at her son. She accepted the cup from him.
Then the lame god turned serving boy, siphoning nectar
From the mixing bowl and pouring the sweet liquor   630
For all of the gods, who couldn't stop laughing
At the sight of Hephaestus hustling through the halls.

And so all day long until the sun went down
They feasted to their hearts' content,
Apollo playing beautiful melodies on the lyre,   635
The Muses singing responsively in lovely voices.
And when the last gleams of sunset had faded,
They turned in for the night, each to a house
Built by Hephaestus, the renowned master craftsman,
The burly blacksmith with the soul of an artist.   640

And the Lord of Lightning, Olympian Zeus, went to his bed,
The bed he always slept in when sweet sleep overcame him.
He climbed in and slept, next to golden-throned Hera.

ILIAD 2

The gods slept soundly that night,
And the men, by their warhorses.

But Zeus lay awake in the dark,
Thinking of how to honor Achilles
And destroy Greeks by the shipload.   5
His thoughts parted like stormclouds,
And in the clear space between them
He saw what seemed to be the best plan:
To send to Agamemnon, son of Atreus,
A wooly menace, a Dream,   10
And to it he spoke these feathery words:

"Go, deadly Dream, along the Greek ships
Until you come to the hut of Agamemnon,
And deliver this message to him exactly:
Order him to arm his long-haired Greeks.   15
Now is his time to capture Troy.
The Olympian gods are no longer divided;
Hera has bent them all to her will
And targeted the Trojans for pain."

The Dream listened and went. Shadows flew   20
Around the Greek ships. It found Agamemnon
Wrapped in deep, starlit slumber.

The Dream stood above his head. It looked
Like Nestor, the old man that Agamemnon
Respected the most, looked just like Nestor,   25
And this dream that was a god addressed the king:

"Asleep, son of Atreus, horsebreaker,
Wise man? You can't sleep all night.
All those decisions to make, so many people

Depending on you. I'll be brief.   *30*
I am a messenger from Zeus, who is
Far away, but loves you and pities you.
He orders you to arm your long-haired Greeks.
Now is your time to capture Troy.
The Olympian gods are no longer divided;   *35*
Hera has bent them all to her will
And targeted Troy for sorrow from Zeus.
Think it over. Keep your wits about you,
And don't forget this when sleep slips away."

And the voice trailed off, leaving him there   *40*
Dreaming of things that were never to be.
He thought he would take Priam's city that day,
The fool. He didn't know what Zeus had in mind,
The pain and groans for both Trojans and Greeks
In the unendurable crush of battle.   *45*
He woke from sleep, the god's voice
Eddying around him. He sat upright,
Pulled on a silky shirt, threw on a cloak,
Laced a pair of sandals on his shining feet,
And hung from his shoulder a silver-worked sword.   *50*
And he held his imperishable, ancestral staff
As he walked through the ships of the bronze-kilted Greeks.

Dawn had just reached the peak of Olympus,
Speaking light to Zeus and the other immortals.

[Lines 55–225 are omitted. Agamemnon tests the troops' morale by suggesting that they lift the siege and sail for home. They are barely restrained from doing so by Odysseus, who brings them back to assembly.]

And so Odysseus mastered the army. The men all
Streamed back from their ships and huts and assembled
With a roar.

> *A wave from the restless, churning sea*
> *Crashes on a beach, and the water seethes and thunders.*   *230*

They had all dropped to the sand and were sitting there,
Except for one man, Thersites, a blathering fool
And a rabble rouser. This man had a repertory
Of choice insults he used at random to revile the nobles,
Saying anything he thought the soldiers would laugh at.   235
He was also the ugliest soldier at the siege of Troy,
Bowlegged, walked with a limp, his shoulders
Slumped over his caved-in chest, and up top
Scraggly fuzz sprouted on his pointy head.
Achilles especially hated him, as did Odysseus,   240
Because he was always provoking them. Now
He was screaming abuse at Agamemnon.
The Achaeans were angry with him and indignant,
But that didn't stop him from razzing the warlord:

"What's wrong, son of Atreus, something you need?   245
Your huts are filled with bronze, and with women
We Achaeans pick out and give to you first of all
Whenever we take some town. Are you short of gold?
Maybe some Trojan horse breeder will bring you some
Out of Ilion as ransom for his son   250
Whom I or some other Achaean has captured.
Maybe it's a young girl for you to make love to
And keep off somewhere for yourself. It's not right
For a leader to march our troops into trouble.
You Achaeans are a disgrace, Achaean women, not men!   255
Let's sail home in our ships and leave him here
To stew over his prizes so he'll have a chance to see
Whether he needs our help or not. Furthermore,
He dishonored Achilles, who's a much better man.
Achilles doesn't have an angry bone in his body,   260
Or this latest atrocity would be your last, son of Atreus!"

That was the abuse Agamemnon took
From the mouth of Thersites. Odysseus
Was on him in a flash, staring him down
With a scowl, and laid into him: 265

"Mind your tongue, Thersites. Better think twice

About being the only man here to quarrel with his betters.
I don't care how bell-toned an orator you are,
You're nothing but trash. There's no one lower
In all the army that followed Agamemnon to Troy. 270
You have no right even to mention kings in public,
Much less badmouth them so you can get to go home.
We have no idea how things are going to turn out,
What kind of homecoming we Achaeans will have.
Yet you have the nerve to revile Agamemnon, 275
Son of Atreus, the shepherd of his people,
Because the Danaan heroes are generous to him?
You think you can stand up in public and insult him?
Well, let me tell you something. I guarantee
That if I ever catch you running on at the mouth again 280
As you were just now, my name isn't Odysseus
And may I never again be called Telemachus' father
If I don't lay hold of you, strip your ass naked,
And run you out of the assembly and through the ships,
Crying at all the ugly licks I land on you." 285

And with that he whaled the staff down
On Thersites' back. The man crumpled in pain
And tears flooded his eyes. A huge bloody welt
Rose on his back under the gold stave's force,
And he sat there astounded, drooling with pain 290
And wiping away his tears. The troops, forgetting
Their disappointment, had a good laugh
At his expense, looking at each other and saying:

"Oh man! You can't count how many good things
Odysseus has done for the Greeks, a real leader 295
In council and in battle, but this tops them all,
The way he took that loudmouth out of commission.
I don't think he'll ever be man enough again
To rile the commanders with all his insults."

That's what they were saying in the ranks. 300

[Lines 301–471 are omitted. Odysseus and Nestor advance powerful argu-
ments for continuing the war.]

   The warlord Agamemnon
Ordered the heralds to muster the troops
In battle formation. They gave their skirling cry,
And all the commanders around Atreus' son   *475*
Hurried to have their men fall in.
And in their midst Athena, eyes like slate,
Carried the aegis, priceless and out of all time,
Pure gold tassels flying in the wind, each
Woven strand worth a hundred oxen.   *480*
And the goddess herself, glowing like moonlight,
Rushed over the sand, sweeping them on
And stiffening their hearts, so that for each of them
To die in battle was sweeter than going home.

> *A fire raging through endless forests*   *485*
> *In a mountain range can be seen far away*
> *As a distant glow.*

               Likewise the glare
From the advancing army's unimaginable bronze,
An eerie light that reached the stratosphere.   *490*

> *Migratory birds—cranes, geese, or long-necked swans—*
> *Are gathering in a meadow in Asia*
> *Where the river Caystrius branches out in streams.*
> *For a while they fly in random patterns*
> *For the pure joy of using their wings,*   *495*
> *But then with a single cry they start to land,*
> *One line of birds settling in front of another*
> *Until the whole meadow is a carpet of sound.*

Likewise from the ships and huts, tribe after tribe
Poured out onto the Scamander's floodplain,   *500*
And the ground groaned and reverberated
Under their feet and the hooves of their horses.

And they stood in the flowering meadow there,
Countless as leaves, or as flowers in their season.

> *Innumerable throngs of buzzing flies*   505
> *Will swarm all over a herdsman's yard*
> *In springtime, when milk wets the pails—*

Likewise the throngs of long-haired Greeks
Who stood on the plain facing the Trojans,
Intent on hammering them to pieces.   510

> *And as goatherds easily separate out*
> *Wide flocks of goats mingled in pasture,*

So the commanders drew up their troops
To enter battle, and Lord Agamemnon
Moved among them like Zeus himself,   515
The look in his eyes, the carriage of his head,
With a torso like Ares', or like Poseidon's.

> *Picture a bull that stands out from the herd*
> *Head and horns above the milling cattle—*

Zeus on that day made the son of Atreus   520
A man who stood out from the crowd of heroes.

[Lines 522–872 are omitted. In a passage known as the Catalogue of the Ships, the poet lists the contingents of the Greek army and their leaders.]

> But tell me now, Muse, who were the best
> Of men and of horses in the Atreides' army?

The best horses were the mares of Eumelus,   875
Swift as birds, of the same age, with matching coats,
And their backs were as even as a levelling line.
Apollo Silverbow had bred them in Pereia,
A team of mares who bore Panic in battle.

The best warrior was Telamonian Ajax—   880
While Achilles was in his rage. For Achilles
Was second to no one, as were the horses
That bore Peleus' flawless son. But now he lay idle
Among his beaked, seagoing hulls, furious
With Agamemnon, the shepherd of the people,   885
The son of Atreus. Achilles' men
Amused themselves on the shore, throwing
The discus and javelin and shooting their bows.
The horses stood beside their chariots
Champing lotus and marsh parsley.   890
The chariots lay covered in their owners' huts.
The men missed their leader. They tramped
Through the camp and had no part in fighting.

The army marched, and it was as though the land
Were swept with fire. Earth groaned beneath them,   895

As beneath Zeus when in his wrath he thunders
And lashes the country of the Arimi with lightning
Where men say Typhoeus lies in the ground.

So the earth groaned under their feet
As they pressed on quickly over the plain.   900

Zeus notified the Trojans of all this
By sending Iris streaking down to Ilion.
She found the citizens assembled in one body,
Young and old alike, near Priam's gate, talking.
Iris positioned herself nearby   905
And made her voice sound like Polites'—
A son of Priam who, trusting his speed,
Often sat as lookout on top of the barrow
Of old Aesytes, watching for any movement
Of Greek troops from their ships.   910
Using his voice, the goddess said to Priam:

"Sir, you are as fond of endless speeches now
As you were in peacetime. But this is war.

I have been in a battle or two, but never
Have I seen an army like this,   *915*
Covering the plain like leaves, or like sand,
As it advances to attack the city.
Hector, you're in charge of this operation.
But because there are so many allies here
With different languages from points abroad,   *920*
Each captain should give the word to his own men
And lead them out marshalled by cities."

Hector knew this was a goddess' speech
And dismissed the assembly. They rushed to arms.
All the gates were opened, and the troops   *925*
Poured through them, on foot and in war cars.
In front of the city there is a steep hill
Out in the plain, level terrain all around it.
Men call this hill Batieia. Immortals call it
The barrow of Myrine the Dancer.   *930*
It was here that the Trojans and their allies
Drew up their troops in companies.

*[The rest of Book 2 (lines 933–97) is omitted. The poet lists the contingents
of the Trojan army.]*

ILIAD 3

Two armies,
The troops in divisions
Under their commanders,

The Trojans advancing across the plain

> *Like cranes beating their metallic wings*   5
> *In the stormy sky at winter's onset,*
> *Unspeakable rain at their backs, their necks stretched*
> *Toward Oceanic streams and down*
> *To strafe the brown Pygmy race,*
> *Bringing strife and bloodshed from the sky at dawn,*   10

While the Greeks moved forward in silence,
Their breath curling in long angry plumes
That acknowledged their pledges to die for each other.

> *Banks of mist settle on mountain peaks*
> *And seep into the valleys. Shepherds dislike it*   15
> *But for a thief it is better than night,*
> *And a man can see only as far as he can throw a stone.*

No more could the soldiers see through the cloud of dust
The armies tramped up as they moved through the plain.

And when they had almost closed—   20
Was it a god?—no, not a god
But Paris who stepped out from the Trojan ranks,
Leopard skin on his shoulders, curved bow, sword,
And shaking two bronze-tipped spears at the Greeks
He invited their best to fight him to the death.   25

When Menelaus, who was Ares' darling, saw him
Strutting out from the ranks, he felt

As a lion must feel when he finds the carcass
Of a stag or wild goat, and, half-starving,
Consumes it greedily even though hounds and hunters   30
Are swarming down on him.

It was Paris all right,
Who could have passed for a god,
And Menelaus grinned as he hefted his gear
And stepped down from his chariot. He would   35
Have his revenge at last. Paris' blood
Turned milky when he saw him coming on,
And he faded back into the Trojan troops
With cheeks as pale as if he had seen—
Had almost stepped on—a poisonous snake   40
In a mountain pass. He could barely stand
As disdainful Trojans made room for him in the ranks,
And Hector, seeing his brother tremble at Atreus' son,
Started in on him with these abusive epithets:

"Paris, you desperate, womanizing pretty boy!   45
I wish you had never been born, or had died unmarried.
Better that than this disgrace before the troops.
Can't you just hear it, the long-haired Greeks
Chuckling and saying that our champion wins
For good looks but comes up short on offense and defense?   50
Is this how you were when you got up a crew
And sailed overseas, hobnobbed with the warrior caste
In a foreign country and sailed off with
A beautiful woman with marriage ties to half of them?
You're nothing but trouble for your father and your city,   55
A joke to your enemies and an embarrassment to yourself.
No, don't stand up to Menelaus: you might find out
What kind of a man it is whose wife you're sleeping with.
You think your lyre will help you, or Aphrodite's gifts,
Your hair, your pretty face, when you sprawl in the dust?   60
It's the Trojans who are cowards, or you'd have long since
Been dressed out in stones for all the harm you've done."

And Paris, handsome as a god, answered him:

"That's only just, Hector. You've got a mind
Like an axe, you know, always sharp,   65
Making the skilled cut through a ship's beam,
Multiplying force—nothing ever turns your edge.
But don't throw golden Aphrodite's gifts in my face.
We don't get to choose what the gods give us, you know,
And we can't just toss their gifts aside.   70
So all right, if you want me to fight, fine.
Have the Trojans and the Greeks sit down,
And Menelaus and I will square off in the middle
To fight for Helen and all her possessions.
Winner take all.   75
And everyone else will swear oaths of friendship,
You all to live here in the fertile Troad,
And they to go back to bluegrass Argos
And Achaea with its beautiful women."

Hector liked what he heard.   80
He went out in front along the Trojan ranks
Holding a spear broadside and made them all sit down.
Greek archers and slingers were taking aim at him
And already starting to shoot arrows and stones
When Agamemnon boomed out a command   85
For them to hold their fire. Hector was signalling
That he had something to say, and his helmet
Caught the morning sun as he addressed both armies:

"Listen to me, Trojans, and you warriors from Greece.
Paris, on account of whom this war began, says this: 90
He wants all the Trojan and Greek combatants
To lay their weapons down on the ground.
He and Menelaus will square off in the middle
And fight for Helen and all her possessions.
Winner take all.   95
And everyone else swears oaths of friendship."

Utter silence,
Until Menelaus, who was good at the war shout, said:

"Now listen to me, since my pain is paramount
In all this. It may be that the Greeks and Trojans   *100*
Can at last call it quits. We've had enough suffering
From this quarrel of mine that Paris began.
Whichever of us is due to die, let him die.
Then the rest of you can be done with each other.
Bring a pair of lambs, a white one and a black,   *105*
For Earth and Sun. Our side will bring another for Zeus.
And have Priam come, so he can swear oaths himself,
In person, since his sons are arrogant perjurers
Who would just as soon trample on Zeus' solemn word.
Younger men always have their heads in the clouds.   *110*
An old man looks ahead and behind, and the result
Is far better for both parties involved."

You could see their mood brighten,
Greeks and Trojans both, with the hope
That this wretched war would soon be over.   *115*
They pulled their chariots up in rows,
Dismounted, and piled up their weapons.

There was not much space between the two armies.

Hector dispatched two heralds to the city
To fetch the lambs and summon Priam.   *120*
Agamemnon sent Talthybius back to the ships
With orders to bring back a lamb.

While these human heralds were off on their missions,
Iris, the gods' herald (who is also the rainbow),
Came to white-armed Helen disguised as Laodice,   *125*
Her sister-in-law and Priam's most beautiful daughter.
She found Helen in the main hall, weaving a folding mantle
On a great loom and designing into the blood-red fabric
The trials that the Trojans and Greeks had suffered
For her beauty under Ares' murderous hands.   *130*
Iris stood near Helen and said:

"Come and see, dear lady, the amazing thing

The Greek and Trojan warriors have done.
They've fought all these years out on the plain,
Lusting for each other's blood, but now   *135*
They've sat down in silence—halted the war—
They're leaning back on their shields
And their long spears are stuck in the sand.
But Paris and Menelaus are going to fight
A duel with lances, and the winner   *140*
Will lay claim to you as his beloved wife."

The goddess' words turned Helen's mind
Into a sweet mist of desire
For her former husband, her parents, and her city.
She dressed herself in fine silvery linens   *145*
And came out of her bedroom crying softly.
Two maids trailed behind, Aethrê,
Pittheus' daughter, and cow-eyed Clyménê.
They came to the Western Gate,
Where a knot of old men sat—   *150*

Priam, Panthous, Thymoetes,
Lampus, Clytius, Hicetaon
(Who was in Ares' bloodline),
Ucalegon and Antenor,
Who lived and breathed wisdom—   *155*

These veterans sat on the wall by the Western Gate,
Too old to fight now, but excellent counsellors.

   Think of cicadas perched on a branch,
   Their delicate voices shrill in the woods.

Such were the voices of these Trojan elders   *160*
Sitting on the tower by the Western Gate.
When they saw Helen coming
Their rasping whispers flew along the wall:

"Who could blame either the Trojans or Greeks
For suffering so long for a woman like this."   *165*

"Her eyes are not human."

"Whatever she is, let her go back with the ships
And spare us and our children a generation of pain."

But Priam called out to her:

"Come here, dear child, sit next to me   *170*
So you can see your former husband
And dear kinsmen. You are not to blame
For this war with the Greeks. The gods are.
Now tell me, who is that enormous man
Towering over the Greek troops, handsome,   *175*
Well-built? I've never laid eyes on such
A fine figure of a man. He looks like a king."

And Helen,
The sky's brightness reflected in her mortal face:

"Reverend you are to me dear father-in-law,   *180*
A man to hold in awe. I'm so ashamed.
Death should have been a sweeter evil to me
Than following your son here, leaving my home,
My marriage, my friends, my precious daughter,
That lovely time in my life. None of it was to be,   *185*
And lamenting it has been my slow death.
But you asked me something, and I'll answer.
That man is Agamemnon, son of Atreus,
A great king and a strong warrior both.
He was also my brother-in-law—shameless bitch   *190*
That I am—if that life was ever real."

The old man was lost in reverie and wonder:

"The son of Atreus. Born to power and wealth.
Blessed by the gods. Now I see
How many Greek lads you command.   *195*
I thought I saw it all when I went
To Phrygia once and saw thousands

Of soldiers and gleaming horses
Under the command of Otreus and Mygdon
Massed by the banks of the Sangarios,   200
An army in which I myself served
On that fateful day when the Amazons
Swept down to fight against men.
They were nothing compared to these wild-eyed Greeks."

Then he saw Odysseus and asked: 205

"Now tell me about this one, dear child,
Shorter than Agamemnon by a head
But broader in the shoulders and chest.
His armor is lying on the ground
And he's roaming the ranks like a ram,   210
That's it, just like a thick-fleeced ram
Striding through a flock of silvery sheep."

And Helen, Zeus' child:

                    "That is Laertes' son,
The master strategist Odysseus, born and bred   215
In the rocky hills of Ithaca. He knows
Every trick there is, and his mind runs deep."

Antenor turned to her and observed astutely:

"Your words are not off the mark there, madam.
Odysseus came here once before, on an embassy   220
For your sake along with Menelaus.
I entertained them courteously in the great hall
And learned each man's character and depth of mind.
Standing in a crowd of Trojans, Menelaus,
With his wide shoulders, was more prominent,   225
But when both were seated Odysseus was lordlier.
When it came time for each to speak in public
And weave a spell of wisdom with their words,
Menelaus spoke fluently enough, to the point
And very clearly, but briefly, since he is not   230

A man of many words. Being older, he spoke first.
Then Odysseus, the master strategist, rose quickly,
But just stood there, his eyes fixed on the ground.
He did not move his staff forward or backward
But held it steady. You would have thought him   235
A dull, surly lout without any wit. But when he
Opened his mouth and projected his voice
The words fell down like snowflakes in a blizzard.
No mortal could have vied with Odysseus then,
And we no longer held his looks against him."   240

The third hero old Priam saw was Ajax.

"And who is that giant of a Greek over there,
Head and shoulders above the other Achaeans?"

And Helen, shining in her long trailing robes:

"That is big Ajax, the army's mountain.   245
Standing beyond him is Idomeneus,
Like a god, with his Cretan commanders.
He used to come often from Crete
And Menelaus would entertain him
In our house. And now I can make out   250
All the other Greeks, those I know
And whose names I could tell you.
But there are two commanders I do not see,
Castor the horsebreaker and the boxer
Polydeuces, my brothers, born of one mother.   255
Either they didn't come here from lovely Lacedaemon,
Or else they did come in their seagoing ships
But avoid the company of the fighting men
In horror of the shame and disgrace that are mine."

But they had long been held by the life-giving earth   260
There in Lacedaemon, their ancestral land.

And now the heralds came up to the town
With the sacrificial victims, the two rams,

And as fruit of the fields, hearty wine
In a goatskin bag. The herald Idaeus   265
Held a gleaming bowl and a golden chalice
And roused the old man with this speech:

"Rise, son of Laomedon.
The best men of Troy and Achaea summon you
Down to the plain to swear solemn oaths.   270
Paris and Menelaus will fight
A duel for the woman, and she will
Follow the winner with all her possessions.
Everyone else will swear oaths of friendship,
We to live here in the fertile Troad,   275
And they to go back to bluegrass Argos
And Achaea with its beautiful women."

The old man stiffened.
He ordered his companions to yoke his horses,
Then mounted himself and took the reins.   280
Antenor rode with him in the beautiful chariot
And they drove out through the Western Gate
And onto the plain. They pulled up in the space
Between the two armies and stepped down to the earth.

Agamemnon rose,   285
And Odysseus, deep in thought.

Heralds brought the animals for the oaths
And mixed wine in the great bowl.
They poured water over the kings' hands,
Then Agamemnon drew the knife   290
That hung by his sword scabbard
And cut hairs from the rams' heads.
The heralds gave these to the leaders on both sides,
And Agamemnon lifted his palms to the sky:

"Zeus, Father, Lord of Ida,   295
Greatest and most glorious;
Helios, who sees all and hears all;

Rivers and Earth, and Powers below
Who punish perjurers after death,
Witness and protect these sacred Oaths: *300*
If Paris Alexander kills Menelaus,
Helen and all her goods are his,
And we will sail away in our ships.
But if Menelaus kills Paris,
The Trojans will surrender Helen   *305*
With all her goods and pay the Argives
A fit penalty for generations to come.
If Priam and Priam's sons refuse,
Upon Paris' death, this penalty to me,
I swear to wage this war to its end."   *310*

He spoke, then slashed the rams' throats
And put the gasping animals on the ground,
Their proud temper undone by whetted bronze.

Then they all filled their cups
With wine from the bowl and poured libations   *315*
To the gods eternal and prayed,
Greek and Trojan alike, in words like these:

"Zeus almighty and most glorious
And all you other immortal gods,
Whoever breaks this oath and truce,   *320*
May their brains spill to the ground
Like this wine, theirs and their children's,
And may other men master their wives."

But Zeus would not fulfill their prayers.

Then Priam spoke his mind: *325*

"Hear me, Trojans and Achaean soldiers:
I am going back now to windswept Ilion
Since I cannot bear to see with my own eyes
My dear son fighting with Menelaus,
Who is dear to Ares. Zeus and the other immortals   *330*

Doubtless know whose death is destined."

And this man who was a god's equal
Loaded the rams onto his chariot
For interment in Trojan soil, mounted,
And took the reins. Antenor stood behind him   335
And together they drove back to Ilion.

Priam's son Hector and brilliant Odysseus
First measured off an arena and then
Shook lots in a bronze helmet to decide
Which of the two would cast his spear first.   340
You could see hands lifted to heaven
On both sides and hear whispered prayers:

"Death, Lord Zeus,
For whichever of the two
Started this business,   345
But grant us your peace."

Great Hector shook the helmet, sunlight
Glancing off his own as he looked away,
And out jumped Paris' lot.

                    The armies   350
Sat down, rank after rank, tooled weapons
And high-stepping horses idle by each man.

The heroes armed.

Paris, silken-haired Helen's present husband,
Bound greaves on his shins with silver clasps,   355
Put on his brother Lycaon's breastplate,
Which fit him well, slung around his shoulders
A bronze sword inlaid with silver
And a large, heavy shield. On his head he placed
A crested helmet, and the horsehair plume   360
Nodded menacingly.

Likewise Menelaus' gear.
They put their armor on in the ranks
And then stepped out into no-man's-land,
A cold light in their eyes.   *365*

Veterans on both sides, horse-breaking Trojans
And bronze-kneed Greeks, just sat and stared.
They stood close, closer, in the measured arena,
Shaking their spears, half-mad with jealousy.
And then Paris threw. A long shadow trailed his spear   *370*
As it moved through the air, and it hit the circle
Of Menelaus' shield, but the spearpoint crumpled
Against its tough metal skin. It was Menelaus' turn now,
And as he rose in his bronze he prayed to Zeus:

"Lord Zeus, make Paris pay for the evil he's done to me,   *375*
Smite him down with my hands so that men for all time
Will fear to transgress against a host's offered friendship."

With this prayer behind it Menelaus' spear
Carried through Paris' polished shield
And bored into the intricate breastplate,   *380*
The point shearing his shirt and nicking his ribs
As Paris twisted aside from black fatality.
Menelaus drew his silver-hammered sword
And came down with it hard on the crest
Of Paris' helmet, but the blade shattered   *385*
Into three or four pieces and fell from his hands.
Menelaus groaned and looked up to the sky:

"Father Zeus, no god curses us more than you.
I thought Paris was going to pay for his crimes,
And now my sword has broken in my hands,   *390*
And my spear's thrown away. I missed the bastard!"

As Menelaus spoke he lunged forward
And twisted his fingers into the thick horsehair
On Paris' helmet, pivoted on his heel,
And started dragging him back to the Greeks.   *395*

The tooled-leather chinstrap of Paris' helmet
Was cutting into his neck's tender skin,
And Menelaus would have dragged him
All the way back and won no end of glory.
But Aphrodite, Zeus' daughter, had all this   400
In sharp focus and snapped the oxhide chinstrap,
Leaving Menelaus clenching an empty helmet,
Which the hero, spinning like a discus thrower,
Heaved into the hands of the Greek spectators.
Then he went back for the kill.   405
                                    But Aphrodite
Whisked Paris away with the sleight of a goddess,
Enveloping him in mist, and lofted him into
The incensed air of his vaulted bedroom.
Then she went for Helen, and found her   410
In a crowd of Trojan women high on the tower.

A withered hand tugged at Helen's fragrant robe.

The goddess was now the phantom of an old woman
Who had spun wool for Helen back in Lacedaemon,
Beautiful wool, and Helen loved her dearly.   415
In this crone's guise Aphrodite spoke to Helen:

"Over here. Paris wants you to come home.
He's propped up on pillows in your bedroom,
So silky and beautiful you'd never think
He'd just come from combat, but was going to a dance,   420
Or coming from a dance and had just now sat down."

This wrung Helen's heart. She knew
It was the goddess—the beautiful neck,
The irresistible line of her breasts,
The iridescent eyes. She was in awe   425
For a moment, and then spoke to her:

"You eerie thing, why do you love
Lying to me like this? Where are you taking me now?
Phrygia? Beautiful Maeonia? Another city

Where you have some other boyfriend for me?   *430*
Or is it because Menelaus, having just beaten Paris,
Wants to take his hateful wife back to his house
That you stand here now with treachery in your heart?
Go sit by Paris yourself! Descend from the gods' high road,
Allow your precious feet not to tread on Olympus,   *435*
Go fret over him constantly, protect him.
Maybe someday he'll make you his wife—or even his slave.
I'm not going back there. It would be treason
To share his bed. The Trojan women
Would hold me at fault. I have enough pain as it is."   *440*

And Aphrodite, angry with her, said:

"Don't vex me, bitch, or I may let go of you
And hate you as extravagantly as I love you now.
I can make you repulsive to both sides, you know,
Trojans and Greeks, and then where will you be?"   *445*

Helen was afraid, and this child of Zeus
Pulled her silvery-white linens around her
And walked silently through the Trojan women,
Eluding them completely. The goddess went ahead
And led her to Paris' beautiful house. The servants   *450*
Suddenly all found something to do.
Helen moved like daylight to the vaulted bedroom,
Where Aphrodite, smiling, placed a chair for her
Opposite Paris. Helen, daughter of Zeus,
Sat down and, averting her eyes, said reproachfully: *455*

"Back from the war? You should have died out there,
Beaten by a real hero, my former husband.
You used to boast you were better than Menelaus,
When it came to spear work and hand-to-hand combat.
Why don't you go challenge him to fight again,   *460*
Right now? I wouldn't recommend it, though,
A fair fight between you and Ares' redhead darling.
You'd go down in no time under his spear."

Paris answered her:

"Don't insult me, Helen.   465
Menelaus beat me this time—with Athena's help.
Next time I'll beat him. We have gods on our side too.
Enough of this.
                    Let's go to bed now and make love.
I've never wanted you so much,   470
Not even when I first took you away
From Lacedaemon in my sailing ship
And made love to you on the island of Cranae.
I want you even more now than I wanted you then."

He walked to the bed, and Helen followed.   475

While the two of them slept in their bed,
Menelaus prowled the ranks looking for Paris.
The Trojan troops, as much as they would have liked to,
Could not produce him. To a man,
They hated Paris as they hated death itself.   480
So Agamemenon, as commander-in-chief, proclaimed:

"Hear me, Trojans, allied troops, and Dardanians:
The victory clearly belongs to Menelaus.
Surrender therefore Argive Helen
And all the possessions that come with her.   485
We will further assess a suitable penalty,
A tribute to be paid for generations to come."

Thus Agamemnon. And the Greeks cheered.

ILIAD 4

The gods were seated with Zeus
On his golden terrace, and Hebe
Was pouring them nectar. They toasted
Each other with golden cups
As they looked out at Troy.   5

               Zeus all at once
Started to provoke Hera with taunts:

"Well, Menelaus has a pair of goddesses
To help him, Hera of Argos
And Athena the Defender,   10
But they prefer to sit on the sidelines
Enjoying themselves. Aphrodite, now,
Smiling as always, stays with her hero
And manages to stave off his doom.
Did you see how she saved him just now   15
When it looked like he was about to die!
Still, Menelaus, Ares' favorite, clearly won.
But we should decide all this now.
Should we let war rage again
Or establish peace between the two sides?   20
If somehow we all could agree to do this
Priam's city might still be a place to live,
And Menelaus could take Argive Helen home."

He had no sooner finished
Than Athena and Hera were whispering   25
To each other with their heads together,
Plotting trouble for the Trojans.
                  Athena
Didn't say a word, although she was furious
With her father.   30
          Hera, however,

Couldn't contain her anger, and said:

"Awesome son of Cronus! What a thing to say!
How dare you undo all my hard work.
The sweat I sweated driving my poor team   35
To raise an army against Priam and his sons!
Do it. But don't expect us all to approve."

Zeus brooded like a thunderhead, and answered:

"I don't understand you, woman. What have
Priam and his children done to you   40
That you are so fixed on demolishing
Ilion's stronghold down to its last well-laid brick?
Do you think if you were to enter its gates,
Get inside its long walls, and chew up Priam
And Priam's children raw, and the rest of the Trojans,   45
You might find some relief from this livid hate?
Do as you please. I don't want this quarrel
To become a source of strife between us.
But I'll tell you this, and you take it to heart.
The next time I have a passion to smash a city   50
And I choose one with men dear to you in it,
Don't try to curb my anger. Just let me do it.
I've given in to you, though unwilling at heart.
For of all the cities under the sun and stars,
Of all the cities on earth that men inhabit,   55
Sacred Ilion is the dearest to my soul,
And Priam and the people of ashen-spear Priam.
My altar there has never lacked libations
Or the steamy savor that is our due worship."

And Hera, the queen, her eyes big as an ox's: 60

"There are three cities especially dear to me:
Argos, Sparta, and broad Mycenae.
Waste these if they ever annoy you.
I won't stand in the way or take it too hard.
Even if I begrudged you their destruction,   65

What could I do against your superior strength?
Still, it's not right to cancel all my hard work.
I too am a god, from the same stock as you,
The eldest daughter of devious Cronus,
And honored both by position of birth   70
And as the wife of the lord of all the immortals.
Let's call this a draw and yield to each other,
I to you, and you to me, and the other gods
Will all fall in line. Quickly now,
Dispatch Athena into the war zone   75
To maneuver the Trojans to break the truce
And do some damage to the exultant Greeks."

Zeus had no wish to argue this,
And he winged these words to Pallas Athena:

"Go down instantly to the battlefield.   80
Get the Trojans to break the truce
And do some damage to the exultant Greeks."

Athena had been longing for action.
She flashed down from the peaks of Olympus

> *Like a star that the son of devious Cronus*   85
> *Sends as a portent to sailors, or to an army*
> *Camped on a wide plain, a brilliant meteor*
> *That sheds sparks all along its shining furrow.*

This was Pallas Athena rocketing down
Into no-man's-land. They were frozen with awe,   90
Horse-breaking Trojans and bronze-kneed Greeks,
Soldiers glancing at each other, saying things like:

"We'll be fighting again soon."

                         "This could mean peace."

"It means war, if Zeus wants to bring it."   95

While they exchanged words to this effect,
Athena blended into the crowd, disguised
As a Trojan, Antenor's son Laodocus,
A good man with a spear, and went in search
Of Pandarus and found that son of Lycaon,   *100*
Strong and not a blemish on him, standing
With rank on rank of tough, shield-bearing troops
Around him, his men from the banks of Aesepus.
Athena stood next to him and her words flew fast:

"If you listened to me, wise son of Lycaon,   *105*
You would take a shot at Menelaus
And win glory and gratitude from the Trojans,
Especially from prince Alexander.
He would give you splendid gifts
If he saw Menelaus, Atreus' warrior son,   *110*
Felled by your arrow and laid on the pyre.
Come on, one swift arrow aimed at Menelaus,
And vow to Apollo, the Wolf-born Archer,
That you will offer a hundred firstling lambs
When you come home to your city, sacred Zeleia."   *115*

Athena spoke and convinced the fool.
He took out his polished bow, made of the horns
Of a wild ibex that he himself had killed
As it came from behind a rock. Waiting for it,
He shot it in the chest, and it fell back in a cleft.   *120*
The horns measured sixteen palms from the head,
And the worker in horn fitted them together,
Smoothed it all and tipped it with gold.
This was the bow he bent, bracing it
Carefully on the ground while his men concealed him   *125*
With shields, so the Greeks couldn't react
Before Menelaus was hit. He took the lid
From the quiver and drew out a feathered arrow,
Barbed with black pain, that had never been shot.
He fit the bitter arrow quickly to the string   *130*
And vowed to Apollo, the Wolf-born Archer,
He would offer a hundred firstling lambs

When he came home to his city, sacred Zeleia.
He drew back the notched arrow until the string
Reached his nipple and the iron arrowhead the bow,   135
Which bent until it arched into a circle,
Then snapped back twanging, and the string hummed
As the arrow needled over the crowded plain.

But the gods were watching you, Menelaus,
Yes, and especially Athena, who stretched out   140
Her immortal hand and whisked the arrow away
From your bare flesh as lightly as a mother
Sweeps a fly from her sleeping child.
The goddess redirected the arrow
To the golden clasps of your belt   145
Where the corselet had an extra fold.
The bitter arrow hit the buckled belt
And drove right through its rich design
And pierced the filigreed corselet
And penetrated even the kilt-piece beneath   150
That he wore as proof against javelins.
The arrow's tip just grazed the human skin,
And dark blood started to flow from the wound.

> *In Maeonia and Caria women stain ivory*
> *With scarlet, to be cheek pieces for horses.*   155
> *Such a piece will lie in a treasure chamber,*
> *And though many horsemen pray to use it*
> *As an ornament for the horse and glory*
> *For the driver, it lies there as a king's prize.*

That, Menelaus, was how your thighs were stained   160
With blood, and your fine shins and ankles beneath.

The warlord Agamemnon went numb
When he saw black blood flowing from the wound,
As did Menelaus himself, whom Ares loved.
But when he saw that the ferrule and barbs   165
Had not gone in, he breathed easier and revived.
Agamemnon, though, was still groaning deeply,

Holding Menelaus' hand, and his comrades
Added their groans. Agamemnon spoke for them all:

"Dear brother, my oath was your death,   *170*
Setting you up to fight the Trojans for us,
And now they've trampled their oath and hit you.
But oaths are not empty: we pledged lambs' blood,
Poured strong wine, and clasped our right hands.
If the Olympian does not act on this immediately   *175*
He will in good time, and they will pay heavily
With their heads, their wives, and their children.
Deep down inside I know this for sure:
There will come a day when holy Troy will perish,
And Priam and the people under Priam's ashen spear.   *180*
Zeus himself, throned in heaven on high,
Will shake his dark aegis over them all
In his wrath for this treachery. This shall be done.
But dreadful grief will be mine if you die,
Menelaus, and meet your destiny now.   *185*
I will return to Argos in utter disgrace,
For the Greeks will turn their minds homeward now,
And we will leave Priam and the Trojans to boast
They have Argive Helen. And your bones will rot
As you lie in Trojan soil, your work unfinished.   *190*
And some arrogant Trojan will say as he leaps
Onto the barrow of glorious Menelaus:
'So much for the wrath of Agamemnon,
Who led the Greek army here for nothing
And has now gone home to his native land   *195*
With empty ships, and without good Menelaus.'
On that day may the earth gape open for me."

And Menelaus, cheering him up:

"It's all right. Don't frighten the others.
The arrow didn't hit a fatal spot. My belt   *200*
Stopped it before it got in very far, that
And the banded kilt-piece the bronzesmiths made."

And lord Agamemnon's response:

"May it be so, dear Menelaus.
But our physician will palpate the wound   *205*
And apply medications to stop the pain."

And he said to Talthybius, the godlike herald:

"Talthybius, call Machaon here on the double,
Asclepius' son, our faultless physician,
To see Menelaus. Someone has shot him,   *210*
Someone really good with a bow, a Trojan
Or Lycian, to his glory and our grief."

Following his orders, the herald
Went through the welter of Greek bronze,
Looking for Machaon, and spotted him   *215*
Standing in the midst of his men, tough
Shield-bearing troops from Tricca's pastures.
He came up to him and spoke winged words:

"Son of Asclepius, lord Agamemnon calls you
To see Menelaus. Someone has shot him,   *220*
Someone really good with a bow, a Trojan
Or Lycian, to his glory and our grief."

Machaon's heart was pounding as he made his way
Across the crowded sand and through the troops
Until he came to where Menelaus lay wounded,   *225*
All the army's best gathered around him
In a circle, into which he stepped like a god
And quickly drew the arrow from the clasped belt.
As it came out the barbs were broken backward.
Then he undid the metallic belt and, beneath it,   *230*
The band with the beaten bronze kilt-piece.
When he saw the wound the arrow had made
He sucked out the blood and smeared on
Soothing ointments Chiron had given his father.

While they were attending to Menelaus,   *235*
The Trojans came on under their shields,
As the Greeks strapped on their gear,
And reminded themselves of the joys of war.

[Lines 239–448 are omitted. Agamemnon reviews the troops.]

> *A swollen wave pushed by the West Wind*
> *Moves closer and closer to a thundering beach.*   *450*
> *It crests in deep water and then breaks*
> *Onto the shore with a huge roar and curls over*
> *And around the jutting rocks in a spray of brine.*

So too wave after wave of Greek battalions
Moving into combat.   *455*
                        The captains
Issued commands; the rest marched on
In such an eerie silence you would have said
That not a soldier in the army had a voice,
But in fact the silence was terror   *460*
Of their commanders, and only the mute glow
From their detailed weaponry signalled their advance.

Not so with the Trojan army.

> *More ewes than anyone could ever count*
> *Are penned in the court of a man of means,*   *465*
> *Waiting, waiting to give their white milk*
> *And bleating incessantly when they hear the lambs.*

Thus the clamor from the immense Trojan muster,
Not one voice, one language,
But a cacophony of tongues from different lands.   *470*

Behind them, Ares, as behind the Greeks
The goddess Athena with sea-grey eyes,
And on both sides Terror and Panic
And Ares' murderous sister, Eris,

Small when her crest first appears 475
But so ravenous and relentless in her ways
That she soon thrusts her head into the sky
Even while she keeps her feet on the earth.
This horror now infused equal parts of strife
Into both armies as she patrolled their ranks, 480
Swelling the volume of human suffering.

When the two sides closed with each other
They slammed together shields and spears,
Rawhide ovals pressed close, bronze thoraxes
Grinding against each other amid the groans 485
And exultations of men being slain
And of those slaying, as the earth ran with blood.

> *Swollen winter torrents flow together*
> *Where two valleys meet. The heavy water*
> *From both streams joins in a gorge,* 490
> *And far off in the mountains*
> *A shepherd hears a single, distant roar.*

Equally indistinguishable the shrieking
Of these warriors laboring in union.

[Lines 495–584 are omitted. The battle rages.]

No one could trust his immunity any longer, 585
Not even those who had danced their way through
Unscathed until now, led by the hand by Pallas Athena
Through the hail of whetted bronze instruments.
This was a day many Greeks and Trojans
Paired off with each other to lie in the dust. 590

ILIAD 5

Pallas Athena now gave to Diomedes,
Tydeus' son, the strength and courage
That would make him shine
Among the Greeks and win him glory.
Starlight flowed from his helmet and shield,   5
As if Sirius had just risen from the sea
Before dawn in autumn, and that brightest of stars
Was blazing from his torso and face
Instead of from the sky.
                            Athena aimed him   10
To where the battle was thickest.

[Lines 12–107 are omitted. The Greeks, led by Diomedes, begin to rout the Trojans.]

When Pandarus saw him storming across the plain
And driving entire battalions before him,
He bent his curved bow and, taking aim at Diomedes,   110
Hit him on the fly in his right shoulder,
The arrow piercing the corselet plate
And spattering it with blood as it punched through.
And Pandarus whooped:

"Got him! Take heart, Trojan horsemen,   115
The best of the Achaeans is hit! I don't think
He will hold up long under that stiff shaft
If Apollo in truth sent me forth from Lycia."

Half prayer, half boast. But the arrow didn't kill him.
Diomedes took cover next to his horses and car   120
And, still standing, said to Sthenelus, his driver:

"Son of Capaneus, get down from the car
And pull this arrow out of my shoulder."

Sthenelus vaulted down to the ground,
Steadied himself, and drew the arrow   *125*
Clean through his shoulder and out the other side.
Blood spurted through the linked tunic,
And Diomedes, good at the war shout, prayed:

"Hear me, daughter of Zeus! If ever
You stood by my father's side, a friend   *130*
In the heat of battle, stand by me now,
Goddess Athena. Deliver unto me
And place within the range of my spear
The man who hit me before I saw him
And boasted I would not see for long   *135*
The brilliant light of Helios the Sun."

Pallas Athena heard Diomedes' prayer.
She made his body lithe and light,
Then feathered these words into his ear:

"Go after the Trojans for all you're worth,   *140*
Diomedes. I have put into your heart
Your father's heroic temper, the fearless
Fighting spirit of Tydeus the horseman,
Tydeus the Shield. And I have removed
The mist that has clouded your eyes   *145*
So that now you can tell god from man.
Do not fight with any immortal
Who might come and challenge you,
Except Aphrodite, daughter of Zeus.
If she comes you may wound her with bronze."   *150*

With these words the grey-eyed one was gone,
And Diomedes returned to the front.
He had been eager before to fight the Trojans
But now his fury was tripled.

[Lines 155–86 are omitted. Diomedes continues his killing rampage.]

Aeneas saw him wrecking the Trojan ranks
And made his way through the busy spears
Searching for Pandarus. When he found him,
Looking like the match for a god that he was,   *190*
He went up to him and had this to say:

"Pandarus, where are your arrows and bow,
And your fame? No one here or in all Lycia
Can compete with you or claim to be better.
Say a prayer to Zeus and take a shot at this man—   *195*
Whoever he is—who is beating the daylights
Out of the Trojans, some of our best too.
It could be he's a god, angry with the Trojans
Over some sacrifice. That would be tough."

Lycaon's splendid son came back with this: *200*

"Aeneas, he looks like Diomedes to me,
His shield, his grooved helmet, his horses.
I'm not at all sure that he's not a god,
But if he is who I think he is, Tydeus' son,
He's not fighting like this without some god   *205*
Standing at his side and cloaked in mist.
I swear one of the immortals turned aside
An arrow I already shot at him
Just as it struck. It wound up hitting him
In the right shoulder, clean through his breastplate.   *210*
I thought I had sent him down to Hades,
But I didn't get him. *Some* god is sure angry.
Anyway, I don't have a chariot now,
Or horses to pull it—not that there aren't eleven
Beautiful new chariots back in Lycaon's palace,   *215*
Covered with cloths, and a yoke of horses
Beside each one eating white barley and spelt.
Yes, and Lycaon, the old spearman,
Told me as I left to go to war mounted,
Advice I should have taken but didn't,   *220*
Sparing the horses because I was afraid
That in an army this big they would lack feed,

And they had been used to eating all they wanted.
So I left them, and came to Ilion on foot,
Trusting my bow, for all the good it has done. *225*
I've taken shots at two of their best,
Diomedes and Menelaus, and hit them both,
Drew blood for sure, and only made them madder.
Curse the day I took my bow from its peg
And led my Trojan troops to lovely Ilion *230*
As a favor to Hector. If I ever return
And see my land, my wife, and my high-roofed home,
May my throat be cut by a thief in the night
If I fail to smash my bow in pieces
And throw it in the fire. It's been a piece of junk." *235*

And Aeneas, the Trojan commander, replied:

"Don't talk like that. Things won't get any better
Until you and I take a chariot
And face him in combat. Come on, get in mine,
And you'll see what the horses of Tros can do. *240*
They know how to eat up the plain, and how to
Cut and turn, in pursuit or flight,
And they will get us back to the city in safety
If Zeus gives Diomedes the glory again.
Get in and take the lash and the reins, *245*
And I'll dismount to fight; or you
Take him on, and leave the horses to me."

Lycaon's splendid son came back with this:

"Keep the reins, Aeneas, and drive your own horses.
They will pull better for a driver they know *250*
In case we have to run from the son of Tydeus.
I wouldn't want them to be spooked, and shy
From pulling us out because they miss your voice—
Not with Diomedes all over us. He'd kill us both
And make off with your horses. No, you drive them, *255*
And I'll meet his charge with my spear."

So they mounted the chariot and drove off
Full speed ahead toward the son of Tydeus.

Sthenelus saw them coming and said to Diomedes:

"Here comes a duo now with muscle to spare   260
And hot to fight you. One is good with a bow,
Pandarus, who boasts he is Lycaon's son.
The other is Aeneas, who says his mother
Is Aphrodite, and Anchises his father.
Let's retreat in the chariot. Calm down   265
And get out of action or you'll get yourself killed."

Diomedes looked him up and down and said:

"Don't talk to me about retreating, Sthenelus.
It's not in me to dodge a fight. Besides,
I still have my strength. I'm not even going   270
To get in the chariot, much less retreat in it.
I'll take them on just like this. Pallas Athena
Won't *let* me back down. As for these two,
Their horses won't be carrying them both away,
Even if one of them manages to escape.   275
And one thing more. Athena has many plans,
But if she does give me the glory here
And I kill them both, hold our horses
On this spot, tying the reins to the chariot rail,
And rush Aeneas' horses. Drive them back   280
Away from the Trojans and to the Greek lines.
These horses come from the stock that Zeus
Gave to Tros as payment for his son Ganymede.
The finest horses under the sun. Anchises
Stole some of the breed from Laomedon   285
By secretly putting his mares to them,
And so got six colts born in his own palace.
Four he kept for himself and reared at the stall,
And two he gave to Aeneas, superb warhorses.
If we could take these, it'd be a real coup."   290

Thus Diomedes and his driver.
                              Their two opponents
Drove their thoroughbreds hard
And quickly closed the gap, and Pandarus,
Lycaon's splendid son, called out: 295

"You're tough, Diomedes, a real pedigreed hero.
So I only stung you with that arrow?
Well, let's see what I can do with a spear."

The shaft cast a long shadow as it left his hand
And hit Diomedes' shield. The bronze apex   300
Sheared through and stopped
Just short of his breastplate.
Pandarus, thinking he had hit him, whooped again:

"Got you right through the belly, didn't I?
You're done for, and you've handed me the glory."   305

Diomedes answered him levelly:

"You didn't even come close, but I swear
One of you two goes down now
And gluts Ares with his blood."

His javelin followed his voice, and Athena   310
Guided it to where the nose joins the eye-socket.
The bronze crunched through the pearly teeth
And sheared the tongue at its root, exiting
At the base of the chin.
                         Pandarus fell from the car,   315
His armor scattering the hard light
As it clattered on his fallen body.
His horses shied—
                   Quick movement of hooves—
As his soul seeped out into the sand.   320

Aeneas vaulted down with his shield and spear,
Afraid that the Greeks might drag the body away.

He straddled it like a lion sure of its strength,
Spear straight out, crouched behind his shield's disk,
Only too glad to kill whoever stood up to him,   *325*
His mouth open in a battle-howl.
                                    But Tydeus' son
Levered up in one hand a slab of stone
Much too large for two men to lift—
As men are now—lifted it and smashed it   *330*
Into Aeneas' hip, where the thighbone turns
In the socket that medics call the cup.
The rough stone shattered this joint and severed
Both tendons, ripping open the skin. The hero
Sank to his knees, clenching the dirt with one hand,   *335*
While midnight settled upon both his eyes.

That would have been the end of Aeneas,
But his mother Aphrodite, Zeus' daughter
(Who bore Aeneas to Anchises the oxherd),
Had all this in sharp focus. Her milk-white arms   *340*
Circled around him and she enfolded him
In her radiant robe to prevent the Greeks
From killing him with a spear to the chest.

As she was carrying him out of the battle,
Sthenelus remembered the instructions   *345*
Diomedes had given him. He held his own horses
Away from the boiling dust, tying the reins
To the chariot rail, and, on foot, stampeded
Aeneas' beautiful horses toward the Greek lines,
Giving them to Deipylus, the boyhood friend   *350*
He valued most and whose mind was like his,
To drive back to the ships. Then he mounted
His own chariot, took the glossy reins in hand,
And drove his heavy-hooved horses off to find
Tydeus' son, who was himself in armed pursuit   *355*
Of Aphrodite. Diomedes knew
This was a weakling goddess, not one of those
Who control human warfare—no Athena,
No Enyo here, who demolishes cities—

And when he caught up to her in the mêlée 360
He pounced at her with his spear and, thrusting,
Nicked her on her delicate wrist, the blade
Piercing her skin through the ambrosial robe
That the Graces themselves had made for her.
The cut was just above the palm, and the goddess' 365
Immortal blood oozed out, or rather
The ichor that flows in the blessed gods' veins,
Who, eating no bread and drinking no wine,
Are bloodless and therefore deathless as well.
The goddess shrieked and let her son fall, 370
And Phoebus Apollo gathered him up
In an indigo cloud to keep the Greeks
From killing him with a spear to the chest.
And Diomedes, yelling above the battle noise:

"Get out of the war, daughter of Zeus! 375
Don't you have enough to do distracting
Weak women? Keep meddling in war and
You'll learn to shiver when it's even mentioned."

The goddess, in extreme distress now,
Went off in a daze. Wind-footed Iris 380
Took her and led her through the throng,
Throbbing with pain, her pale skin bruised.
After a while she found Ares, sitting
On the left of the battle, his spear propped
Against a bank of mist, his horses standing by. 385
Aphrodite fell to her knees and begged
Her brother for his gold-frontleted horses:

"Brother dear, lend me your horses
And help me get to Olympus. I'm hurt,
Wounded by a mortal, Diomedes, 390
Who would fight even Father Zeus."

Ares gave her the gold-frontleted horses.
She mounted the chariot gingerly,
And Iris stepped in and took the reins.

She cracked the whip and the team flew off   *395*
And came in no time to steep Olympus,
The gods' homestead.
                                    Iris, a blur of windy light,
Halted the team, unyoked them,
And cast before them their ambrosial fodder.   *400*

Aphrodite went in to her mother,
Dione, and fell in her lap.
                                    And Dione,
Cradling her daughter in her arms,
And stroking her with her hand, said: *405*

"Oh my poor baby, who did this to you?
To treat you like this! What did you do?"
And Aphrodite, the goddess who loved to smile:

"Tydeus' son wounded me, that bully
Diomedes, because I was carrying my son   *410*
Out of range, Aeneas, who is my dearest.
The war has gone far beyond Trojans and Greeks.
The Greeks are fighting the immortal gods."

Dione answered in her lustrous voice:

"You must bear it, my child. I know it hurts.   *415*
Many of us Olympians have suffered harm
From men, giving tit for tat to each other.
Ares did, when Otus and Ephialtes,
Those bullies, sons of Aloeus, kept him tied him up
In a bronze jar for thirteen months.   *420*
They would have destroyed the God of War
If their stepmother, beautiful Eëriboea,
Hadn't told Hermes. He got Ares out,
But the painful bonds had about done him in.
Hera suffered too, when Heracles shot her   *425*
Right in the breast with a triple-pronged arrow,
And there was no helping the pain she had then.
Hades too, formidable as he is, had to endure

An arrow the same man shot him with
Among the dead in Pylos, making him suffer.   *430*
He went to the house of Zeus on Olympus
In agony, pierced with pain. The arrow
Had driven right through his shoulder.
Paieon rubbed on an anodyne
And healed him, Hades being no mortal.   *435*
Heracles was simply outrageous and reckless
To provoke the Olympian gods with arrows.
And now Athena has set this man upon you,
This fool Diomedes, who doesn't understand
That a man who fights with gods doesn't last long,   *440*
His children don't sit on his lap calling him 'Papa'
To welcome him home from the horrors of war.
So as strong as he is, he had better watch out
Or someone braver than you might fight him,
And Aegialeia, Adrastus' heroic daughter,   *445*
The wife of Diomedes, tamer of horses,
Will wake her family from sleep with lamenting
Her wedded husband, the best of the Achaeans."

And with both her hands she wiped off the ichor.
The wrist was healed, and the pain subsided.   *450*

Athena and Hera were looking on
And making snide remarks to provoke Zeus.
The grey-eyed goddess opened with this:

"You won't get angry if I say something,
Will you, Father Zeus? The truth is this: *455*
Aphrodite has been urging some Greek lady
To traipse after her beloved Trojans,
And while she was stroking this gowned beauty
She scratched her frail little hand on a golden brooch."

The Father of Gods and Men smiled   *460*
And calling Aphrodite said to her:

"Dear child, war isn't your specialty, you know.

You just take care of the pleasures of love
And leave the fighting to Ares and Athena."

While these gods were talking to each other,   465
Diomedes leapt upon Aeneas, even though
He knew Apollo's hands were there above him.
Great as Apollo was, Diomedes meant
To kill the Trojan and strip off his armor.
Three times he leapt in homicidal frenzy,   470
Three times Apollo flicked his lacquered shield,
But when he charged a fourth, last time,
He heard a voice that seemed to come
From everywhere at once, and knew it was
Apollo's voice, saying to him: 475

"Think it over, son of Tydeus, and get back.
Don't set your sights on the gods. Gods are
To humans what humans are to crawling bugs."

Even at this, Diomedes only backed up a little,
Just out of range of the wrathful god.   480

And Apollo took Aeneas from the swarm
Up to his temple on sacred Pergamum.
There Leto and arrowy Artemis healed him
In the great sanctuary, and made him glorious.
And silver-bowed Apollo made a phantom   485
To look like Aeneas, armor and all,
And over this wraith the Greeks and Trojans
Battered each other with their rawhide shields
Until the edges were tattered into leather fringe.
Apollo then called out to the God of War: 490

"Ares, you bloodthirsty marauder,
Would you be so kind as to take this Diomedes
Out of action, before he goes up against Zeus?
He's already wounded Cypris on the wrist,
And came after me like a raging demon."   495

Apollo then sat down on Pergamum's height,
While Ares went to spur on the Trojans.

[Lines 498–763 are omitted. The Trojans attack.]

The havoc continued, and when Hera noticed
That the Greeks were being crushed in battle,   765
Her words flew fast to Pallas Athena:

"This is a disaster, daughter of Zeus.
Our word to Menelaus that he would go home
With Troy demolished will come to nothing
If we allow Ares to rage on like this.   770
Come. It's time we remembered how to fight."

Athena, the grey-eyed goddess, agreed.
And Hera, queen of heaven, daughter of Cronus,
Got busy harnessing the horses, gold-frontleted,
While Hebe slid the bronze, eight-spoked wheels   775
Onto the car's iron axle, wheels with pure gold rims
Fitted with bronze tires, a stunning sight,
And the hubs spinning on both sides were silver.
The car's body was made of gold and silver straps
Stretched tight, and had a double railing.   780
From it projected a silver pole, and at its end
Hebe bound the golden yoke, and on that she hung
The golden harness. Hera led the quick-hooved horses
Beneath the yoke, her heart pounding for war.

Athena, meanwhile, Zeus' favorite daughter,   785
Let her supple robe slip down to her father's floor,
This embroidered garment her own handiwork.
She put on one of cloudy Zeus' tunics
And strapped on her armor. Around her shoulders
She flung the tasselled aegis, bordered with Rout   790
And inset with the blood-chilling horrors of War,
In the center of which was a Gorgon's head,
The dread insignia of Zeus Aegis-Holder.

On her head she put a gold helmet, knobbed and horned,
And embossed with a hundred cities' soldiery.   *795*
She stepped into the blazing chariot cradling a spear
Long and thick enough for heaven's daughter
To level battalions of heroes in her wrath.

Hera quickly flicked the horses with the lash,
And the automatic gates of heaven   *800*
Groaned open, as willed by the Hours,
Who control access to Olympus and heaven,
Opening and shutting the dense cloudbanks.
Through this gate they drove the patient horses
And found Zeus sitting apart from the other gods   *805*
On the highest peak of ridged Olympus.
White-armed Hera reined in the horses there
And put her questions to the Most High:

"Father Zeus, doesn't Ares infuriate you
With his reckless destruction of so many Greeks,   *810*
Much to my sorrow, while Cypris and Apollo,
Smug at their success, are lounging around
With this mindless bully who knows no law?
Father Zeus, will you be angry with me
If I knock Ares silly and out of the battle?"   *815*

And Zeus, clouds scudding around him:

"Better to put Athena onto him;
She's always been the best at giving him grief."

White-armed Hera did not disobey.
She lashed the horses and they flew with a will   *820*
Between the starry heavens and earth.
One bound of the gods' horses
Takes them as far into the misty distance
As a lookout can see over the wine-blue Aegean.

When they came to Troy and to the confluence   *825*
Of the Scamander and Simois rivers,

The white-armed goddess reined in the horses,
Unyoked them, and shed a thick mist around them.
Simois made ambrosia sprout up for them.

The two goddesses, though passionate to come   830
To the aid of the Greeks, stepped forward
As quietly as doves. They were soon in the thick of things
Where the army's elite, drawn to Diomedes' strength,
Clustered around him like huge animals, lions
Or razorback hogs that can rip a man apart.   835
Hera took her stance there and transformed herself
To look like Stentor, whose bronze voice sounds as loud
As fifty voices combined. And she yelled:

"For shame, Greeks! You're all show and no fight.
When godlike Achilles used to enter battle   840
The Trojans wouldn't so much as leave their gates
Out of fear for what his spear could do.
Now they have us backed up against our ships."

This got their fighting spirit up. Meanwhile,
Grey-eyed Athena flashed to Diomedes' side.   845
She found that prince beside his horses and car,
Cooling the wound from Pandarus' arrow.
The sweat where his broad shield strap rubbed
Was bothering him, and his arm was sore.
He was lifting the strap and wiping off   850
The dark, clotted blood when the goddess,
Casually grasping the horses' yoke, said to him:

"You're not very much like your father, you know.
Tydeus had a small build, but he was a fighter—
Even when I wouldn't allow him to fight   855
Or show his stuff. Like the time he came to Thebes
As a solo envoy to all those Cadmeians.
I ordered him to keep his peace at the banquet,
But he had a lot of heart, as he always had,
And challenged the Cadmeian youths and beat them all,   860
Effortlessly. Of course I was there beside him.

But you, I stand by you, I protect you,
I tell you not to worry, to fight the Trojans,
And here you are, either bone-tired
Or paralyzed with fear. No, you're no son   865
Of Tydeus or grandson of sharp old Oeneus."

And Diomedes, as tough as they come, answered:

"I know it's you, goddess, daughter of Zeus,
And so I will answer you frankly. No, I'm not
Paralyzed by fear, and I'm not slacking off.   870
But I am following the orders you gave me
When you told me not to fight face to face
With any of the gods except Aphrodite.
If she came, you said I could wound her with bronze.
That's why I've withdrawn and given orders   875
For all of the troops to fall back to this spot.
I know that Ares is controlling the battle."

And Athena, whose eyes were as grey as owls:

"Diomedes, son of Tydeus, I do love you.
You don't have to fear Ares or any other   880
Of the immortals. Look who is here beside you.
Drive your horses directly at Ares
And when you're in range, strike.
Don't be in awe of Ares. He's nothing but
A shifty lout. He promised Hera and me   885
He would fight against Troy and help the Greeks.
Now he's turned Trojan and abandoned us."

With that, she pulled Sthenelus back and pushed him
Off the chariot. Sthenelus went flying,
And Athena got in next to Diomedes,   890
Who seemed to glow beside the eager goddess,
And the solid-oak axle groaned under the load
Of an awesome deity and a hero at his best.
Pallas Athena handled the reins and whip
And drove the horses directly at Ares,   895

Who at that moment was stripping the armor
From a warrior named Periphas, a huge man,
Aetolia's finest and his father's glory.
Ares was busy removing the dead man's armor
And getting smeared with blood. Athena   900
Put on Hades' helmet so Ares couldn't see her.
But Ares did see Diomedes, and when he did,
He dropped Periphas to lie in his own gore
And headed straight for the hero.
As soon as they were in range of each other   905
Ares leaned out over his horses' backs
And thrust, frantic for a kill. Athena's hand
Deflected the spear in mid-air and sent it
Sailing harmlessly over Diomedes' chariot,
And when Diomedes thrust next,   910
She drove his spear home to the pit
Of Ares' belly, where the kilt-piece covered it.
The spearhead sliced right through to the flesh,
And when Diomedes pulled it out,
Ares yelled, so loud you would have thought   915
Ten thousand warriors had shouted at once,
And the sound reverberated in the guts of Greeks and Trojans,
As if Diomedes had struck not a god in armor
But a bronze gong nine miles high.

After a period of heat, when the low clouds   920
Are massed like wool, you will sometimes see
A darker clot of air whirling off
On its way to becoming a tornado—

That is how Ares appeared to Diomedes,
Moving off through the clouds and up the big sky.   925

He quickly scaled the heights of Olympus,
Sat down sulking beside Cronion Zeus,
Showed him the immortal blood oozing
From his wound, and whined these winged words:

"Father Zeus, doesn't it infuriate you   930

To see this violence? We gods
Get the worst of it from each other
Whenever we try to help out men.
Why did you have to give birth to that madwoman,
Your marauding daughter who is always   *935*
Breaking the rules? All the rest of us gods,
Every one on Olympus, listen to you.
But she can say or do whatever she wants.
You even urge her on, your grey-eyed girl.
Just now she's been egging on Diomedes   *940*
To rampage against the immortal gods.
He wounded Cypris first, got her on the wrist,
Then charged at me like an avenging spirit.
My fast footwork saved me, or I would be
Lying in a heap of gruesome corpses,   *945*
Or barely alive from taking hits from his spear."

And Zeus, from under thunderhead brows:

"Shifty lout. Don't sit here by me and whine.
You're the most loathsome god on Olympus.
You actually like fighting and war.   *950*
You take after your hardheaded mother,
Hera. I can barely control her either.
One way or another, she got you into this.
Be that as it may, I cannot tolerate your being in pain.
Your mother did, after all, bear you to me.   *955*
But if you were born to any other god,
You'd be long buried in hell below the Titans."

And he called Paieon to doctor his wound.
Paieon rubbed on an anodyne to kill the pain.
And then,   *960*

> *As quickly as white milk*
> *Thickened with fig juice*
> *Curdles when stirred,*

Paieon healed impetuous Ares.

And Hebe bathed him and dressed him handsomely,   *965*
And he sat beside Zeus exulting in glory.
Then back to the palace of great Zeus
Came Argive Hera and Athena the Protector,
Having stopped brutal Ares from butchering men.

ILIAD 6

The battle was left to rage on the level expanse
Between Troy's two rivers. Bronze spearheads
Drove past each other as the Greek and Trojan armies
Spread like a hemorrhage across the plain.

*[Lines 5–102 are omitted. The Greeks counterattack. The Trojan seer Hele-
nus, Hector's brother, persuades him to return to Troy and ask the women
to pray to Athena.]*

Hector took his brother's advice.
He jumped down from his chariot with his gear
And toured the ranks, a spear in each hand.   *105*
He urged them on, and with a trembling roar
The Trojans turned to face the Achaeans.
The Greeks pulled back. It looked to them
As if some god had come from the starry sky
To help the Trojans. It had been a sudden rally.   *110*
Hector shouted and called to the Trojans:

"Soldiers of Troy, and illustrious allies,
Remember to fight like the men that you are,
While I go to the city and ask the elders
Who sit in council, and our wives, to pray   *115*
To the gods and promise bulls by the hundred."

And Hector left, helmet collecting light
Above the black-hide shield whose rim tapped
His ankles and neck with each step he took.

Then Glaucus, son of Hippolochus,   120
Met Diomedes in no-man's-land.
Both were eager to fight, but first Tydeus' son
Made his voice heard above the battle noise:

"And which mortal hero are you? I've never seen you
Out here before on the fields of glory,   125
And now here you are ahead of everyone,
Ready to face my spear. Pretty bold.
I feel sorry for your parents. Of course,
You may be an immortal, down from heaven.
Far be it from me to fight an immortal god.   130
Not even mighty Lycurgus lived long
After he tangled with the immortals,
Driving the nurses of Dionysus
Down over the Mountain of Nysa
And making them drop their wands   135
As he beat them with an ox-goad. Dionysus
Was terrified and plunged into the sea,
Where Thetis received him into her bosom,
Trembling with fear at the human's threats.
Then the gods, who live easy, grew angry   140
With Lycurgus, and the Son of Cronus
Made him go blind, and he did not live long,
Hated as he was by the immortal gods.
No, I wouldn't want to fight an immortal.
But if you are human, and shed blood,   145
Step right up for a quick end to your life."

And Glaucus, Hippolochus' son:

"Great son of Tydeus, why ask about my lineage?
Human generations are like leaves in their seasons.
The wind blows them to the ground, but the tree   150
Sprouts new ones when spring comes again.

Men too. Their generations come and go.
But if you really do want to hear my story,
You're welcome to listen. Many men know it.
Ephyra, in the heart of Argive horse country,   *155*
Was home to Sisyphus, the shrewdest man alive,
Sisyphus son of Aeolus. He had a son, Glaucus,
Who was the father of faultless Bellerophon,
A man of grace and courage by gift of the gods.
But Proetus, whom Zeus had made king of Argos,   *160*
Came to hate Bellerophon
And drove him out. It happened this way.
Proetus' wife, the beautiful Anteia,
Was madly in love with Bellerophon
And wanted to have him in her bed.   *165*
But she couldn't persuade him, not at all,
Because he was so virtuous and wise.
So she made up lies and spoke to the king:
'Either die yourself, Proetus, or kill Bellerophon.
He wanted to sleep with me against my will.'   *170*
The king was furious when he heard her say this.
He did not kill him—he had scruples about that—
But he sent him to Lycia with a folding tablet
On which he had scratched many evil signs,
And told him to give it to Anteia's father,   *175*
To get him killed. So off he went to Lycia,
With an immortal escort, and when he reached
The river Xanthus, the king there welcomed him
And honored him with entertainment
For nine solid days, killing an ox each day.   *180*
But when the tenth dawn spread her rosy light,
He questioned him and asked to see the tokens
He brought from Proetus, his daughter's husband.
And when he saw the evil tokens from Proetus,
He ordered him, first, to kill the Chimaera,   *185*
A raging monster, divine, inhuman—
A lion in the front, a serpent in the rear,
In the middle a goat—and breathing fire.
Bellerophon killed her, trusting signs from the gods.
Next he had to fight the glorious Solymi,   *190*

The hardest battle, he said, he ever fought,
And, third, the Amazons, women the peers of men.
As he journeyed back the king wove another wile.
He chose the best men in all wide Lycia
And laid an ambush. Not one returned home;   195
Blameless Bellerophon killed them all.
When the king realized his guest had divine blood,
He kept him there and gave him his daughter
And half of all his royal honor. Moreover,
The Lycians cut out for him a superb   200
Tract of land, plow-land and orchard.
His wife, the princess, bore him three children,
Isander, Hippolochus, and Laodameia.
Zeus in his wisdom slept with Laodameia,
And she bore him the godlike warrior Sarpedon.   205
But even Bellerophon lost the gods' favor
And went wandering alone over the Aleian plain.
His son Isander was slain by Ares
As he fought against the glorious Solymi,
And his daughter was killed by Artemis   210
Of the golden reins. But Hippolochus
Bore me, and I am proud he is my father.
He sent me to Troy with strict instructions
To be the best ever, better than all the rest,
And not to bring shame on the race of my fathers,   215
The noblest men in Ephyra and Lycia.
This, I am proud to say, is my lineage."

Diomedes grinned when he heard all this.
He planted his spear in the bounteous earth
And spoke gently to the Lycian prince: 220

"We have old ties of hospitality!
My grandfather Oeneus long ago
Entertained Bellerophon in his halls
For twenty days, and they gave each other
Gifts of friendship. Oeneus gave   225
A belt bright with scarlet, and Bellerophon
A golden cup, which I left at home.

I don't remember my father Tydeus,
Since I was very small when he left for Thebes
In the war that killed so many Achaeans.   230
But that makes me your friend and you my guest
If ever you come to Argos, as you are my friend
And I your guest whenever I travel to Lycia.
So we can't cross spears with each other
Even in the thick of battle. There are enough   235
Trojans and allies for me to kill, whomever
A god gives me and I can run down myself.
And enough Greeks for you to kill as you can.
And let's exchange armor, so everyone will know
That we are friends from our fathers' days."   240

With this said, they vaulted from their chariots,
Clasped hands, and pledged their friendship.
But Zeus took away Glaucus' good sense,
For he exchanged his golden armor for bronze,
The worth of one hundred oxen for nine.   245

W hen Hector reached the oak tree by the Western Gate,
Trojan wives and daughters ran up to him,
Asking about their children, their brothers,
Their kinsmen, their husbands. He told them all,
Each woman in turn, to pray to the gods.   250
Sorrow clung to their heads like mist.
Then he came to Priam's palace, a beautiful
Building made of polished stone with a central courtyard
Flanked by porticoes, upon which opened fifty
Adjoining rooms, where Priam's sons   255
Slept with their wives. Across the court
A suite of twelve more bedrooms housed
His modest daughters and their husbands.
It was here that Hector's mother met him,
A gracious woman, with Laodice,   260
Her most beautiful daughter, in tow.
Hecuba took his hand in hers and said:

"Hector, my son, why have you left the war

And come here? Are those abominable Greeks
Wearing you down in the fighting outside, 265
And does your heart lead you to our acropolis
To stretch your hands upward to Zeus?
But stay here while I get you
Some honey-sweet wine, so you can pour a libation
To Father Zeus first and the other immortals, 270
Then enjoy some yourself, if you will drink.
Wine greatly bolsters a weary man's spirits,
And you are weary from defending your kinsmen."

Sunlight shimmered on great Hector's helmet.

"Mother, don't offer me any wine. 275
It would drain the power out of my limbs.
I have too much reverence to pour a libation
With unwashed hands to Zeus almighty,
Or to pray to Cronion in the black cloudbanks
Spattered with blood and the filth of battle. 280
But you must go to the War Goddess' temple
To make sacrifice with a band of old women.
Choose the largest and loveliest robe in the house,
The one that is dearest of all to you,
And place it on the knees of braided Athena. 285
And promise twelve heifers to her in her temple,
Unblemished yearlings, if she will pity
The town of Troy, its wives, and its children,
And if she will keep from holy Ilion
Wild Diomedes, who's raging with his spear. 290
Go then to the temple of Athena the War Goddess,
And I will go over to summon Paris,
If he will listen to what I have to say.
I wish the earth would gape open beneath him.
Olympian Zeus has bred him as a curse 295
To Troy, to Priam, and all Priam's children.
If I could see him dead and gone to Hades,
I think my heart might be eased of its sorrow."

Thus Hector. Hecuba went to the great hall

And called to her handmaidens, and they 300
Gathered together the city's old women.
She went herself to a fragrant storeroom
Which held her robes, the exquisite work
Of Sidonian women whom godlike Paris
Brought from Phoenicia when he sailed the sea 305
On the voyage he made for high-born Helen.
Hecuba chose the robe that lay at the bottom,
The most beautiful of all, woven of starlight,
And bore it away as a gift for Athena.
A stream of old women followed behind. 310

They came to the temple of Pallas Athena
On the city's high rock, and the doors were opened
By fair-cheeked Theano, daughter of Cisseus
And wife of Antenor, breaker of horses.

The Trojans had made her Athena's priestess. 315
With ritual cries they all lifted their hands
To Pallas Athena. Theano took the robe
And laid it on the knees of the rich-haired goddess,
Then prayed in supplication to Zeus' daughter:

"Lady Athena who defends our city, 320
Brightest of goddesses, hear our prayer.
Break now the spear of Diomedes
And grant that he fall before the Western Gate,
That we may now offer twelve heifers in this temple,
Unblemished yearlings. Only do thou pity 325
The town of Troy, its wives and its children."

But Pallas Athena denied her prayer.

While they prayed to great Zeus' daughter,
Hector came to Paris' beautiful house,
Which he had built himself with the aid 330
Of the best craftsmen in all wide Troy:
Sleeping quarters, a hall, and a central courtyard
Near to Priam's and Hector's on the city's high rock.

Hector entered, Zeus' light upon him,
A spear sixteen feet long cradled in his hand,   335
The bronze point gleaming, and the ferrule gold.
He found Paris in the bedroom, busy with his weapons,
Fondling his curved bow, his fine shield, and breastplate.
Helen of Argos sat with her household women
Directing their exquisite handicraft.   340

Hector meant to shame Paris and provoke him:

"This is a fine time to be nursing your anger,
You idiot! We're dying out there defending the walls.
It's because of you the city is in this hellish war.
If you saw someone else holding back from combat   345
You'd pick a fight with him yourself. Now get up
Before the whole city goes up in flames!"

And Paris, handsome as a god:

"That's no more than just, Hector,
But listen now to what I have to say.   350
It's not out of anger or spite toward the Trojans
I've been here in my room. I only wanted
To recover from my pain. My wife was just now
Encouraging me to get up and fight,
And that seems the better thing to do.   355
Victory takes turns with men. Wait for me
While I put on my armor, or go on ahead—
I'm pretty sure I'll catch up with you."

To which Hector said nothing.

But Helen said to him softly: 360

                              "Brother-in-law
Of a scheming, cold-blooded bitch,
I wish that on the day my mother bore me
A windstorm had swept me away to a mountain
Or into the waves of the restless sea,   365

Swept me away before all this could happen.
But since the gods have ordained these evils,
Why couldn't I be the wife of a better man,
One sensitive at least to repeated reproaches?
Paris has never had an ounce of good sense   *370*
And never will. He'll pay for it someday.
But come inside and sit down on this chair,
Dear brother-in-law. You bear such a burden
For my wanton ways and Paris' witlessness.
Zeus has placed this evil fate on us so that   *375*
In time to come poets will sing of us."

And Hector, in his burnished helmet:

"Don't ask me to sit, Helen, even though
You love me. You will never persuade me.
My heart is out there with our fighting men.   *380*
They already feel my absence from battle.
Just get Paris moving, and have him hurry
So he can catch up with me while I'm still
Inside the city. I'm going to my house now
To see my family, my wife and my boy. I don't know   *385*
Whether I'll ever be back to see them again, or if
The gods will destroy me at the hands of the Greeks."

And Hector turned and left. He came to his house
But did not find white-armed Andromache there.
She had taken the child and a robed attendant   *390*
And stood on the tower, lamenting and weeping–
His blameless wife. When Hector didn't find her inside,
He paused on his way out and called to the servants:

"Can any of you women tell me exactly
Where Andromache went when she left the house?   *395*
To one of my sisters or one of my brothers' wives?
Or to the temple of Athena along with the other
Trojan women to beseech the dread goddess?"

The spry old housekeeper answered him:

"Hector, if you want the exact truth, she didn't go   *400*
To any of your sisters, or any of your brothers' wives,
Or to the temple of Athena along with the other
Trojan women to beseech the dread goddess.
She went to Ilion's great tower, because she heard
The Trojans were pressed and the Greeks were strong.   *405*
She ran off to the wall like a madwoman,
And the nurse went with her, carrying the child."

Thus the housekeeper, but Hector was gone,
Retracing his steps through the stone and tile streets
Of the great city, until he came to the Western Gate.   *410*
He was passing through it out onto the plain
When his wife came running up to meet him,
His beautiful wife, Andromache,
A gracious woman, daughter of great Eëtion,
Eëtion, who lived in the forests of Plakos   *415*
And ruled the Cilicians from Thebes-under-Plakos—
His daughter was wed to bronze-helmeted Hector.
She came up to him now, and the nurse with her
Held to her bosom their baby boy,
Hector's beloved son, beautiful as starlight,   *420*
Whom Hector had named Scamandrius
But everyone else called Astyanax, Lord of the City,
For Hector alone could save Ilion now.
He looked at his son and smiled in silence.
Andromache stood close to him, shedding tears,   *425*
Clinging to his arm as she spoke these words:

"Possessed is what you are, Hector. Your courage
Is going to kill you, and you have no feeling left
For your little boy or for me, the luckless woman
Who will soon be your widow. It won't be long   *430*
Before the whole Greek army swarms and kills you.
And when they do, it will be better for me
To sink into the earth. When I lose you, Hector,
There will be nothing left, no one to turn to,
Only pain. My father and mother are dead.   *435*
Achilles killed my father when he destroyed

Our city, Thebes with its high gates,
But had too much respect to despoil his body.
He burned it instead with all his armor
And heaped up a barrow. And the spirit women   440
Came down from the mountain, daughters
Of the storm god, and planted elm trees around it.
I had seven brothers once in that great house.
All seven went down to Hades on a single day,
Cut down by Achilles in one blinding sprint   445
Through their shambling cattle and silver sheep.
Mother, who was queen in the forests of Plakos,
He took back as prisoner, with all her possessions,
Then released her for a fortune in ransom.
She died in our house, shot by Artemis' arrows.   450
Hector, you are my father, you are my mother,
You are my brother and my blossoming husband.
But show some pity and stay here by the tower,
Don't make your child an orphan, your wife a widow.
Station your men here by the fig tree, where the city 455
Is weakest because the wall can be scaled.
Three times their elite have tried an attack here
Rallying around Ajax or glorious Idomeneus
Or Atreus' sons or mighty Diomedes,
Whether someone in on the prophecy told them   460
Or they are driven here by something in their heart."

And great Hector, helmet shining, answered her:

"Yes, Andromache, I worry about all this myself,
But my shame before the Trojans and their wives,
With their long robes trailing, would be too terrible 465
If I hung back from battle like a coward.
And my heart won't let me. I have learned to be
One of the best, to fight in Troy's first ranks,
Defending my father's honor and my own.
Deep in my heart I know too well   470
There will come a day when holy Ilion will perish,
And Priam and the people under Priam's ash spear.
But the pain I will feel for the Trojans then,

For Hecuba herself and for Priam king,
For my many fine brothers who will have by then   475
Fallen in the dust behind enemy lines—
All that pain is nothing to what I will feel
For you, when some bronze-armored Greek
Leads you away in tears, on your first day of slavery.
And you will work some other woman's loom   480
In Argos or carry water from a Spartan spring,
All against your will, under great duress.
And someone, seeing you crying, will say,
'That is the wife of Hector, the best of all
The Trojans when they fought around Ilion.'   485
Someday someone will say that, renewing your pain
At having lost such a man to fight off the day
Of your enslavement. But may I be dead
And the earth heaped up above me
Before I hear your cry as you are dragged away."   490

With these words, resplendent Hector
Reached for his child, who shrank back screaming
Into his nurse's bosom, terrified of his father's
Bronze-encased face and the horsehair plume
He saw nodding down from the helmet's crest.   495
This forced a laugh from his father and mother,
And Hector removed the helmet from his head
And set it on the ground all shimmering with light.
Then he kissed his dear son and swung him up gently
And said a prayer to Zeus and the other immortals: 500

"Zeus and all gods: grant that this my son
Become, as I am, foremost among Trojans,
Brave and strong, and ruling Ilion with might.
And may men say he is far better than his father
When he returns from war, bearing bloody spoils,   505
Having killed his man. And may his mother rejoice."

And he put his son in the arms of his wife,
And she enfolded him in her fragrant bosom
Laughing through her tears. Hector pitied her

And stroked her with his hand and said to her: *510*

"You worry too much about me, Andromache.
No one is going to send me to Hades before my time,
And no man has ever escaped his fate, rich or poor,
Coward or hero, once born into this world.
Go back to the house now and take care of your work,   *515*
The loom and the shuttle, and tell the servants
To get on with their jobs. War is the work of men,
Of all the Trojan men, and mine especially."

With these words, Hector picked up
His plumed helmet, and his wife went back home,   *520*
Turning around often, her cheeks flowered with tears.
When she came to the house of man-slaying Hector,
She found a throng of servants inside,
And raised among these women the ritual lament.
And so they mourned for Hector in his house   *525*
Although he was still alive, for they did not think
He would ever again come back from the war,
Or escape the murderous hands of the Greeks.

                                        P aris meanwhile
Did not dally long in his high halls.   *530*
He put on his magnificent bronze-inlaid gear
And sprinted with assurance out through the city.

   Picture a horse that has fed on barley in his stall
   Breaking his halter and galloping across the plain,
   Making for his accustomed swim in the river,   *535*
   A glorious animal, head held high, mane streaming
   Like wind on his shoulders. Sure of his splendor
   He prances by the horse-runs and the mares in pasture.

That was how Paris, son of Priam, came down
From the high rock of Pergamum,   *540*
Gleaming like amber and laughing in his armor,
And his feet were fast.
                        He caught up quickly

With Hector just as he turned from the spot
Where he'd talked with his wife, and called out: 545

"Well, dear brother, have I delayed you too much?
Am I not here in time, just as you asked?"

Hector turned, his helmet flashing light:

"I don't understand you, Paris.
No one could slight your work in battle.   550
You're a strong fighter, but you slack off—
You don't have the will. It breaks my heart
To hear what the Trojans say about you.
It's on your account they have all this trouble.
Come on, let's go. We can settle this later,   555
If Zeus ever allows us to offer in our halls
The wine bowl of freedom to the gods above,
After we drive these bronze-kneed Greeks from Troy."

[Book 7 is omitted. Hector and Paris return to battle. Hector offers to fight a duel with any Greek. Ajax responds to the challenge and the two fight to a draw. The Greeks and Trojans agree to a truce so that they can bury the dead. The Greeks build a wall and a trench around their camp.]

ILIAD 8

Dawn.
Saffron light over all the earth.

Zeus, who plays in thunder, had the gods
Assembled on the utmost peak
Of the rugged Olympic massif,   5
And now enjoyed their undivided attention:

"Listen to me, divine ones,
So I can tell you what I want.
What I don't want is any god—male or female—
Attempting to brook my word. You are all   10
To assent, so we can get this over with.
If I catch any one of you with a private plan
To assist either the Greeks or Trojans,
He—or she—will return to Olympus
A crippled wreck—unless of course I hurl   15
Him—or her—into moldy Tartarus,
Down into the deepest underground abyss,
Iron-gated and bronze-stooped,
As far beneath Hades as the sky is above earth.
Then you will know who is supreme around here.   20
Or would you like to find out now?
Come on. Hang a gold cable down from the sky.
All you gods and goddesses holding the end
Couldn't drag down from sky to earth
Zeus the Master, no matter how hard you tried.   25
But if I wanted to I could haul up all of you,
With the earth itself and the very sea,
Then loop the cable around a spur of Olympus,
And the totality would hang suspended in space.
That's how superior I am to gods and men."   30

They were stunned to silence, aghast

At his words. It had been a masterful speech.
Finally, grey-eyed Athena spoke up:

"Well, our Father who art the highest,
We know very well your might is unyielding.   *35*
Still, we have pity for the Danaan spearmen
Who are now destined to die an ugly death.
We will withdraw from the war if you
Command it. But we will still advise the Greeks,
So they won't all be casualties of your wrath."   *40*

And Zeus, smiling at her, answered:

"There, there, daughter. My heart really
Isn't in it. I want to be gentle to you, child."

With that, he harnessed his horses,
Bronze-hooved, gold-maned, and swift,   *45*
And clothed himself in gold, and gripped
His golden whip, and stepped onto his chariot,
And with a touch of his lash they were off,
Flying between earth and the starry universe.
He came to Ida, with its springs and wild beasts,   *50*
A mountain mother, and to Gargaros there,
Where his precinct and smoking altar stood.
There Zeus reined in his horses, unhitched them
From the car, and shed upon them a heavy mist.
Then he sat among the peaks exulting in glory   *55*
With the city of Troy and the Greek ships in view.

The Greeks were taking a hurried meal
In their huts, and then armed themselves quickly.
Likewise the Trojans throughout the city,
A smaller army but much more desperate   *60*
To engage the enemy: they were fighting
For their children and for their wives.
All the gates were opened, and the troops
Poured through them, on foot and in war cars.
When the two sides closed with each other   *65*

They slammed together shields and spears—
Rawhide ovals pressed close, bronze thoraxes
Grinding against each other, and the groans
Of men being slain and the cries of those slaying
Hung in the air as the earth ran with blood.   70

As long as the holy light climbed toward noon
Soldiers on both sides were hit and fell.
But when the sun straddled heaven's meridian,
The Father stretched out his golden scales.
On them he placed two dooms of agonizing death,   75
One for the Trojans, one for the Greeks.
He held the scales in the middle, and down sank
The Greek day of doom, down to the fertile earth,
While the Trojans' soared up to the sky's expanse.
Then Zeus thundered from Ida, and sent a blazing flash   80
Into the Greek army. The soldiers gaped
In wonder, and their blood turned milky with fear.

*[Lines 83–356 are omitted. The battle sways, but the Trojans, with Zeus'
support, gain the upper hand.]*

Watching all this, Hera was moved to pity
And said to Athena in a flurry of words:

"Don't the two of us care any more that the Greeks
Are being beaten? This may be the end.   360
One single man, Priam's son Hector,
Is pushing them all to the brink of doom.
His rampage is no longer bearable.
Just look at how much harm he has done!"

And the grey-eyed goddess said to her: 365

"I would love to have this man snuffed out,
Killed by the Argives in his own native land.
But my father is on a rampage himself now,
And constantly thwarts all my best efforts.

He has conveniently forgotten how many times   370
I rescued his son Heracles when he was struggling
With Eurystheus' labors. He would cry to heaven
And Zeus would dispatch me to save his neck.
Had I been sharp enough to know all this
When he was sent to Hades to fetch the hellhound,   375
He never would have made it back up from Styx.
At any rate, Zeus hates me now and has executed
The plan Thetis sold him on when she kissed his knees
And grabbed his beard, begging him to honor
Her son Achilles, sacker of cities.   380
Well, one day he'll call me his grey-eyed girl again.
But for now, you get our horses ready
While I go to the house of Zeus Aegis-Holder
And put on my war gear. I want to see
The expression on Hector's helmeted face   385
When we two appear in the lanes of battle.
Many a Trojan will glut the dogs and birds
With their soft flesh after they fall by the ships."

Hera, the white-armed goddess, agreed,
And the queen of heaven, daughter of Cronus,   390
Hastened to harness the gold-frontleted horses.
Athena, meanwhile, Zeus' favorite daughter,
Let her supple robe slip down to her father's floor,
This embroidered garment her own handiwork.
She put on one of cloudy Zeus' tunics,   395
Strapped on her battle gear, and then stepped
Into the blazing chariot cradling a spear
Long and thick enough for heaven's daughter
To level battalions of men in her wrath.

Hera quickly flicked the horses with the lash,   400
And the automatic gates of heaven
Groaned open, as willed by the Hours,
Who control access to Olympus and heaven,
Opening and shutting the dense cloudbanks.
Through this gate they drove the patient horses.   405

Zeus saw them from Ida and seethed with anger.
He sent golden-winged Iris to bear this message:

"Go, swift Iris. Turn them back,
And don't let them come face to face with me.
It would not be pretty if we had to fight.   410
This is my solemn word on the subject:
I will maim their horses, throw them
From the chariot, and smash it to bits.
Not in ten circling years will they be healed
Of the wounds the thunderbolt will inflict.   415
The grey-eyed one must learn what it means
To fight with her father. As for Hera,
I am not so angry with her, since she
Always opposes whatever I say."

He spoke, and Iris stormed from Ida's peaks   420
To the Olympic range, and caught them
Just at the gates and repeated Zeus' words:

"Where are you two off to in such a hurry?
Zeus will not allow you to help the Greeks.
This is his solemn word on the subject: 425
He will maim your horses, throw you
From the chariot, and smash it to bits.
Not in ten circling years will you be healed
Of the wounds the thunderbolt will inflict.
That's so you, grey eyes, will see   430
What it means to fight with your father.
Hera he's not so upset with, since she
Always opposes whatever he says.
But you are awesome indeed, and a fearless bitch,
If you dare lift your spear against Zeus."   435

Iris spoke and was gone in a blur of wind.
Hera turned to Athena and said:

"Daughter of the Aegis-Holder, I can no longer
Countenance our fighting with Zeus

For the sake of mere mortals. Let one fall   440
And another live, as chance may have it.
And let Zeus judge by his own lights
Between Trojans and Greeks, as is only proper."

With that she turned her hooved horses around.
The Hours unyoked them for the goddesses,   445
And tethered them at their ambrosial stalls,
And leaned the chariot on the shining gateway.
They went inside and sat on golden thrones
With the other immortals, and nursed their grief.

Zeus wheeled his chariot from Ida   450
To Olympus, where the gods sat assembled.
No one less than Poseidon unyoked his team,
Set the car on its stand, and draped it with a cloth
While Zeus rumbled onto his golden throne
And mighty Olympus trembled under his feet.   455
Only Hera and Athena sat apart from Zeus
And failed to address him or ask him a question.
He knew what was wrong and said:

"Why are you two so upset, Athena and Hera?
It's not battle fatigue. You two never get tired   460
Of pulverizing Trojans, your mortal enemies.
It all comes down to this: these two hands are more powerful
Than all the gods on Olympus combined.
As for you two, your shining limbs trembled
Before you got close enough to see the front lines.   465
And it's just as well, because one thing is certain:
Once you had been struck by my thunderbolt
You would never have made it back to Olympus."

The two goddesses murmured to each other,
Huddling close and still scheming against Troy.   470
Athena kept silent and said nothing out loud,
Although she was furious at her father Zeus.
Hera, however, could not contain her anger:

"The awesome son of Cronus has spoken again!
We're all too familiar with your irresistible strength,   475
But we still feel pity for the Danaan spearmen
Who are now destined to die an ugly death.
Fine! We will withdraw from the war,
If you command it. But we will still advise the Greeks,
So they won't all be casualties of your wrath."   480

And Zeus, clouds gathering around him:

"At dawn you will see Cronus' almighty son,
If you wish, my ox-eyed lady Hera,
Making casualties of much of the Greek army.
Hector will not be absent from the war   485
Until Achilles has risen up from beside his ship
On the day when the fighting for Patroclus' dead body
Reaches its fever pitch by the ships' sterns.
That is divinely decreed.
                              Your wrath is nothing to me,   490
Not even if you go to the deepest foundations
Of Earth and Sea, where Cronus and Iapetus
Dwell out of the light of Hyperion the Sun,
Cooled by no winds, in the trench of Tartarus—
Not even then will I care that you are angry,   495
Because there is nothing more shameless than you."

He spoke, and white-armed Hera said nothing.

The sunlight fell into the Ocean, drawing
Black night over earth's fields, a sunset
The Trojans resented, but to the Greeks   500
Welcome, thrice-prayed-for ebony night.

Hector made camp, leading the Trojans
Along the river some distance from the ships
To an open space that was clear of the dead.
They stepped to the ground from their chariots   505
To hear Hector speak. In his hand was a spear
Sixteen feet long, bronze point gleaming, the ferrule gold.

Leaning on this spear, he addressed the troops:

"Hear me, Trojans, Dardanians, and allies.
I had thought to destroy the Greeks and their ships   *510*
And be back by now to windy Ilion.
But darkness intervened. This more than anything
Has saved them and their fleet parked on our beach.
So for now, let us yield to black night
And prepare our supper. Unyoke your horses   *515*
And feed them. Bring cattle and sheep from the city,
And get bread and mellow wine from your houses.
And gather tons of firewood, so that all night long
Until early dawn we can burn fires enough
To light up the sky, in case the long-haired Greeks   *520*
Have any idea of sailing off by night.
We'll not let them board their ships at ease
Or without a fight. Let them each have a wound
From an arrow or spear to brood over at home,
A going-away present as they jump on their ships,   *525*
And a lesson to others not to make war on Troy.
Heralds should proclaim throughout the city
That boys and greybeards bivouac tonight
All around the city on our god-built walls.
As for the women, each of them should light   *530*
A fire in her house. The city needs to guard
Against a sneak attack while the army is away.
Enough for now. This is sound strategy.
In the morning I will address the troops again.
I hope and pray to Zeus and all gods   *535*
To drive off this visitation of foreign dogs
The fates have brought us in the black ships.
For tonight, we will take care of ourselves.
At the crack of dawn we arm ourselves
And hit the Greeks hard in their beachhead camp.   *540*
I will find out whether the great Diomedes
Will drive me back from the ships to our wall,
Or whether I will walk off with his bloody gear.
And tomorrow he will know what he is made of,
And whether he can stand up to my spear.   *545*

My hunch is that he will find himself lying wounded
In the front lines, with his friends all around him,
At sunup tomorrow. I wish I were as sure
Of immortality and eternal youth
And honor like Apollo's and Pallas Athena's   550
As I am that this is a black day for the Greeks."

Thus Hector, and the Trojans cheered.
They unyoked their sweating horses
And tethered them with thongs to their chariots.
They brought cattle and sheep from the city,   555
Got bread and mellow wine from their houses,
And gathered firewood. They offered
Bulls by the hundred to the immortal gods,
And onshore winds carried the smoky savor
Up to the sky. But the blessed ones disdained   560
To partake. They abhorred holy Ilion,
And Priam, and the people under Priam's ash spear.

But the Trojans had great notions that night,
Sitting on the bridge of war by their watchfires.

>   *Stars: crowds of them in the sky, sharp*   565
>   *In the moonglow when the wind falls*
>   *And all the cliffs and hills and peaks*
>   *Stand out and the air shears down*
>   *From heaven, and all the stars are visible*
>   *And the watching shepherd smiles.*   570

So the bonfires between the Greek ships
And the banks of the Xanthus, burning
On the plain before Ilion.
                              And fifty men
Warmed their hands by the flames of each fire.   575

And the horses champed white barley,
Standing by their chariots, waiting for Dawn
To take her seat on brocaded cushions.

ILIAD 9

*[Lines 1–185 are omitted. Agamemnon sends Odysseus, Phoenix, and Ajax
to apologize to Achilles on his behalf and to ask him to return to battle.]*

They went in tandem along the seething shore,
Praying over and over to the god in the surf
For an easy time in convincing Achilles.
They came to the Myrmidons' ships and huts
And found him plucking clear notes on a lyre—   190
A beautiful instrument with a silver bridge
He had taken when he ransacked Eëtion's town—
Accompanying himself as he sang the glories
Of heroes in war. He was alone with Patroclus,
Who sat in silence waiting for him to finish.   195
His visitors came forward, Odysseus first,
And stood before him. Surprised, Achilles
Rose from his chair still holding his lyre.
Patroclus, when he saw them, also rose,
And Achilles, swift and sure, received them: 200

"Welcome. Things must be bad to bring you here,
The Greeks I love best, even in my rage."

With these words Achilles led them in
And had them sit on couches and rugs
Dyed purple, and he called to Patroclus: 205

"A larger bowl, son of Menoetius,
And stronger wine, and cups all around.
My dearest friends are beneath my roof."

Patroclus obliged his beloved companion.
Then he cast a carving block down in the firelight   210
And set on it a sheep's back and a goat's,
And a hog chine too, marbled with fat.

Automedon held the meat while Achilles
Carved it carefully and spitted the pieces.
Patroclus, godlike in the fire's glare,   215
Fed the blaze. When the flames died down
He laid the spits over the scattered embers,
Resting them on stones, and sprinkled the morsels
With holy salt. When the meat was roasted
He laid it on platters and set out bread   220
In exquisite baskets. Achilles served the meat,
Then sat down by the wall opposite Odysseus
And asked Patroclus to offer sacrifice.
After he threw the offerings in the fire,
They helped themselves to the meal before them,   225
And when they had enough of food and drink,
Ajax nodded to Phoenix. Odysseus saw this,
And filling a cup he lifted it to Achilles:

"To your health, Achilles, for a generous feast.
There is no shortage in Agamemnon's hut,   230
Or now here in yours, of satisfying food.
But the pleasures of the table are not on our minds.
We fear the worst. It is doubtful
That we can save the ships without your strength.
The Trojans and their allies are encamped   235
Close to the wall that surrounds our black ships
And are betting that we can't keep them
From breaking through. They may be right.
Zeus has been encouraging them with signs,
Lightning on the right. Hector trusts this—   240
And his own strength—and has been raging
Recklessly, like a man possessed.
He is praying for dawn to come early
So he can fulfill his threat to lop the horns
From the ships' sterns, burn the hulls to ash,   245
And slaughter the Achaeans dazed in the smoke.
This is my great fear, that the gods make good
Hector's threats, dooming us to die in Troy
Far from the fields of home. Up with you, then,
If you intend at all, even at this late hour,   250

To save our army from these howling Trojans.
Think of yourself, of the regret you will feel
For harm that will prove irreparable.
This is the last chance to save your countrymen.
Is it not true, my friend, that your father Peleus   255
Told you as he sent you off with Agamemnon:
'My son, as for strength, Hera and Athena
Will bless you if they wish, but it is up to you
To control your proud spirit. A friendly heart
Is far better. Steer clear of scheming strife,   260
So that Greeks young and old will honor you.'
You have forgotten what the old man said,
But you can still let go of your anger, right now.
Agamemnon is offering you worthy gifts
If you will give up your grudge. Hear me   265
While I list the gifts he proposed in his hut:
Seven unfired tripods, ten gold bars,
Twenty burnished cauldrons, a dozen horses—
Solid, prizewinning racehorses
Who have won him a small fortune—   270
And seven women who do impeccable work,
Surpassingly beautiful women from Lesbos
He chose for himself when you captured the town.
And with them will be the woman he took from you,
Briseus' daughter, and he will solemnly swear   275
He never went to her bed and lay with her
Or did what is natural between women and men.
All this you may have at once. And if it happens
That the gods allow us to sack Priam's city,
You may when the Greeks are dividing the spoils   280
Load a ship to the brim with gold and bronze,
And choose for yourself the twenty Trojan women
Who are next in beauty to Argive Helen.
And if we return to the rich land of Argos,
You would marry his daughter, and he would honor you   285
As he does Orestes, who is being reared in luxury.
He has three daughters in his fortress palace,
Chrysothemis, Laodice, and Iphianassa.
You may lead whichever you like as your bride

Back to Peleus' house, without paying anything, 290
And he would give her a dowry richer than any
A father has ever given his daughter.
And he will give you seven populous cities,
Cardamyle, Enope, grassy Hire,
Sacred Pherae, Antheia with its meadowlands, 295
Beautiful Aepeia, and Pedasus, wine country.
They are all near the sea, on sandy Pylos' frontier,
And cattlemen live there, rich in herds and flocks,
Who will pay you tribute as if you were a god
And fulfill the shining decrees of your scepter. 300
All this he will do if you give up your grudge.
But if Agamemnon is too hateful to you,
Himself and his gifts, think of all the others
Suffering up and down the line, and of the glory
You will win from them. They will honor you 305
Like a god.
          And don't forget Hector.
You just might get him now. He's coming in close,
Deluded into thinking that he has no match
In the Greek army that has landed on his beach." 310

And Achilles, strong, swift, and godlike:

"Son of Laertes in the line of Zeus,
Odysseus the strategist—I can see
That I have no choice but to speak my mind
And tell you exactly how things are going to be. 315
Either that or sit through endless sessions
Of people whining at me. I hate like hell
The man who says one thing and thinks another.
So this is how I see it.
I cannot imagine Agamemnon, 320
Or any other Greek, persuading me,
Not after the thanks I got for fighting this war,
Going up against the enemy day after day.
It doesn't matter if you stay in camp or fight—
In the end, everybody comes out the same. 325
Coward and hero get the same reward:

You die whether you slack off or work.
And what do I have for all my suffering,
Constantly putting my life on the line?
Like a bird who feeds her chicks   330
Whatever she finds, and goes without herself,
That's what I've been like, lying awake
Through sleepless nights, in battle for days
Soaked in blood, fighting men for their wives.
I've raided twelve cities with our ships   335
And eleven on foot in the fertile Troad,
Looted them all, brought back heirlooms
By the ton, and handed it all over
To Atreus' son, who hung back in camp
Raking it in and distributing damn little.   340
What the others did get they at least got to keep.
They all have their prizes, everyone but me—
I'm the only Greek from whom he took something back.
He should be happy with the woman he has.
Why do the Greeks have to fight the Trojans?   345
Why did Agamemnon lead the army to Troy
If not for the sake of fair-haired Helen?
Do you have to be descended from Atreus
To love your mate? Every decent, sane man
Loves his woman and cares for her, as I did,   350
Loved her from my heart. It doesn't matter
That I won her with my spear. He took her,
Took her right out of my hands, cheated me,
And now he thinks he's going to win me back?
He can forget it. I know how things stand.   355
It's up to you, Odysseus, and the other kings
To find a way to keep the fire from the ships.
He's been pretty busy without me, hasn't he,
Building a wall, digging a moat around it,
Pounding in stakes for a palisade.   360
None of that stuff will hold Hector back.
When I used to fight for the Greeks,
Hector wouldn't come out farther from his wall
Than the oak tree by the Western Gate.
He waited for me there once, and barely escaped.   365

Now that I don't want to fight him anymore,
I will sacrifice to Zeus and all gods tomorrow,
Load my ships, and launch them on the sea.
Take a look if you want, if you give a damn,
And you'll see my fleet on the Hellespont 370
In the early light, my men rowing hard.
With good weather from the sea god,
I'll reach Phthia after a three-day sail.
I left a lot behind when I hauled myself here,
And I'll bring back more, gold and bronze, 375
Silken-waisted women, grey iron—
Everything except the prize of honor
The warlord Agamemnon gave me
And in his insulting arrogance took back.
So report back to him everything I say, 380
And report it publicly—get the Greeks angry,
In case the shameless bastard still thinks
He can steal us blind. He doesn't dare
Show his dogface here. Fine. I don't want
To have anything to do with him either. 385
He cheated me, wronged me. Never again.
He's had it. He can go to hell in peace,
The half-wit that Zeus has made him.
His gifts? His gifts mean nothing to me.
Not even if he offered me ten or twenty times 390
His present gross worth and added to it
All the trade Orchomenus does in a year,
All the wealth laid up in Egyptian Thebes,
The wealthiest city in all the world,
Where they drive two hundred teams of horses 395
Out through each of its hundred gates.
Not even if Agamemnon gave me gifts
As numberless as grains of sand or dust,
Would he persuade me or touch my heart—
Not until he's paid in full for all my grief. 400
His daughter? I would not marry
The daughter of Agamemnon son of Atreus
If she were as lovely as golden Aphrodite
Or could weave like owl-eyed Athena.

Let him choose some other Achaean   *405*
More to his lordly taste. If the gods
Preserve me and I get home safe
Peleus will find me a wife himself.
There are many Greek girls in Hellas and Phthia,
Daughters of chieftains who rule the cities.   *410*
I can have my pick of any of them.
I've always wanted to take a wife there,
A woman to have and to hold, someone with whom
I can enjoy all the goods old Peleus has won.
Nothing is worth my life, not all the riches   *415*
They say Troy held before the Greeks came,
Not all the wealth in Phoebus Apollo's
Marble shrine up in craggy Pytho.
Cattle and flocks are there for the taking;
You can always get tripods and chestnut horses.   *420*
But a man's life cannot be won back
Once his breath has passed beyond his clenched teeth.
My mother Thetis, a moving silver grace,
Tells me two fates sweep me on to my death.
If I stay here and fight, I'll never return home,   *425*
But my glory will be undying forever.
If I return home to my dear fatherland
My glory is lost but my life will be long,
And death that ends all will not catch me soon.
As for the rest of you, I would advise you too   *430*
To sail back home, since there's no chance now
Of storming Ilion's height. Zeus has stretched
His hand above her, making her people bold.
What's left for you now is to go back to the council
And announce my message. It's up to them   *435*
To come up with another plan to save the ships
And the army with them, since this one,
Based on appeasing my anger, won't work.
Phoenix can spend the night here. Tomorrow
He sails with me on our voyage home,   *440*
If he wants to, that is. I won't force him to come."

He spoke, and they were hushed in silence,

Shocked by his speech and his stark refusal.
Finally the old horseman Phoenix spoke,
Bursting into tears. He felt the ships were lost. 445

"If you have set your mind on going home,
Achilles, and will do nothing to save the ships
From being burnt, if your heart is that angry,
How could I stay here without you, my boy,
All by myself? Peleus sent me with you 450
On that day you left Phthia to go to Agamemnon,
A child still, knowing nothing of warfare
Or assemblies where men distinguish themselves.
He sent me to you to teach you this—
To be a speaker of words and a doer of deeds. 455
I could not bear to be left behind now
Apart from you, child, not even if a god
Promised to smooth my wrinkles and make me
As young and strong as I was when I first left
The land of Hellas and its beautiful women. 460
I was running away from a quarrel with Amyntor,
My father, who was angry with me
Over his concubine, a fair-haired woman
Whom he loved as much as he scorned his wife,
My mother. She implored me constantly 465
To make love to his concubine so that this woman
Would learn to hate the old man. I did as she asked.
My father found out and cursed me roundly,
Calling on the Furies to ensure that never
Would a child of mine sit on his knees. 470
The gods answered his prayers, Underworld Zeus
And dread Persephone. I decided to kill him
With a sharp sword, but some god calmed me down—
Putting in my mind what people would say,
The names they would call me—so that in fact 475
I would not be known as a parricide.
From then on I could not bear to linger
In my father's house, although my friends
And my family tried to get me to stay,
Entreating me, slaughtering sheep and cattle, 480

Roasting whole pigs on spits, and drinking
Jar after jar of the old man's wine.
For nine solid days they kept watch on me,
Working in shifts, staying up all night.
The fires stayed lit, one under the portico   *485*
Of the main courtyard, one on the porch
In front of my bedroom door. On the tenth night,
When it got dark, I broke through the latches
And vaulted over the courtyard fence,
Eluding the watchmen and servant women.   *490*
I was on the run through wide Hellas
And made it to Phthia's black soil, her flocks,
And to Lord Peleus. He welcomed me kindly
And loved me as a father loves his only son,
A grown son who will inherit great wealth.   *495*
He made me rich and settled me on the border,
Where I lived as king of the Dolopians.
I made you what you are, my godlike Achilles,
And loved you from my heart. You wouldn't eat,
Whether it was at a feast or a meal in the house,   *500*
Unless I set you on my lap and cut your food up
And fed it to you and held the wine to your lips.
Many a time you wet the tunic on my chest,
Burping up wine when you were colicky.
I went through a lot for you, because I knew   *505*
The gods would never let me have a child
Of my own. No, I tried to make you my child,
Achilles, so you would save me from ruin.
But you have to master your proud spirit.
It's not right for you to have a pitiless heart.   *510*
Even the gods can bend. Superior as they are
In honor, power, and every excellence,
They can be turned aside from wrath
When humans who have transgressed
Supplicate them with incense and prayers,   *515*
With libations and savor of sacrifice.
Yes, for Prayers are daughters of great Zeus.
Lame and wrinkled and with eyes averted,
They are careful to follow in Folly's footsteps,

But Folly is strong and fleet, and outruns them all,   *520*
Beating them everywhere and plaguing humans,
Who are cured by the Prayers when they come behind.
Revere the daughters of Zeus when they come,
And they will bless you and hear your cry.
Reject them and refuse them stubbornly,   *525*
And they will ask Zeus, Cronus' son, to have
Folly plague you, so you will pay in pain.
No, Achilles, grant these daughters of Zeus
The respect that bends all upright men's minds.
If the son of Atreus were not offering gifts   *530*
And promising more, if he were still raging mad,
I would not ask you to shrug off your grudge
And help the Greeks, no matter how sore their need.
But he is offering gifts and promising more,
And he has sent to you a delegation   *535*
Of the best men in the army, your dearest friends.
Don't scorn their words or their mission here.
     No one could blame you for being angry before.
We all know stories about heroes of old,
How they were furiously angry, but later on   *540*
Were won over with gifts or appeased with words.
I remember a very old story like this, and since
We are all friends here, I will tell it to you now.
     The Curetes were fighting the Aetolians
In a bloody war around Calydon town.   *545*
The Aetolians were defending their city
And the Curetes meant to burn it down.
This was all because gold-throned Artemis
Had cursed the Curetes, angry that Oeneus
Had not offered her his orchard's first fruits.   *550*
The other gods feasted on bulls by the hundred,
But Oeneus forgot somehow or other
Only the sacrifice to great Zeus' daughter.
So the Archer Goddess, angry at heart,
Roused a savage boar, with gleaming white tusks,   *555*
And sent him to destroy Oeneus' orchard.
The boar did a good job, uprooting trees
And littering the ground with apples and blossoms.

But Oeneus' son, Meleager, killed it
After getting up a party of hunters and hounds   560
From many towns: it took more than a few men
To kill this huge boar, and not before
It set many a hunter on the funeral pyre.
But the goddess caused a bitter argument
About the boar's head and shaggy hide   565
Between the Curetes and Aetolians.
They went to war. While Meleager still fought
The Curetes had the worst of it
And could not remain outside Calydon's wall.
But when wrath swelled Meleager's heart,   570
As it swells even the hearts of the wise,
And his anger rose against Althaea his mother,
He lay in bed with his wife, Cleopatra,
Child of Marpessa and the warrior Idas.
Idas once took up his bow against Apollo   575
To win lissome Marpessa. Her parents
Called the girl Halcyone back then
Because her mother wept like a halcyon,
The bird of sorrows, because the Archer God,
Phoebus Apollo, had stolen her daughter.   580
Meleager nursed his anger at Cleopatra's side,
Furious because his mother had cursed him,
Cursed him to the gods for murdering his uncle,
Her brother, that is, and she beat the earth,
The nurturing earth, with her hands, and called   585
Upon Hades and Persephone the dread,
As she knelt and wet her bosom with tears,
To bring death to her son. And the Fury
Who walks in darkness heard her
From the pit of Erebus, and her heart was iron.   590
Soon the enemy was heard at the walls again,
Battering the gates. The Aetolian elders
Sent the city's high priests to pray to Meleager
To come out and defend them, offering him
Fifty acres of Calydon's richest land   595
Wherever he chose, half in vineyard,
Half in clear plow-land, to be cut from the plain.

And the old horseman Oeneus shook his doors,
Standing on the threshold of his gabled room,
And recited a litany of prayers to his son,   600
As did his sisters and his queenly mother.
He refused them all, and refused his friends,
His very best friends and boon companions.
No one could move his heart or persuade him
Until the Curetes, having scaled the walls   605
Were burning the city and beating down
His bedroom door. Then his wife wailed
And listed for him all the woes that befall
A captured people—the men killed,
The town itself burnt, the women and children   610
Led into slavery. This roused his spirit.
He clapped on armor and went out to fight.
And so he saved the Aetolians from doom
Of his own accord, and they paid him none
Of those lovely gifts, savior or not.   615
   Don't be like that. Don't think that way,
And don't let your spirit turn that way.
The ships will be harder to save when they're burning.
Come while there are gifts, while the Achaeans
Will still honor you as if you were a god.   620
But if you go into battle without any gifts,
Your honor will be less, save us or not."

And strong, swift-footed Achilles answered:

"I don't need that kind of honor, Phoenix.
My honor comes from Zeus, and I will have it   625
Among these beaked ships as long as my breath
Still remains and my knees still move.
Now listen to this. You're listening? Good.
Don't try to confuse me with your pleading
On Agamemnon's behalf. If you're his friend   630
You're no longer mine, although I love you.
Hate him because I hate him. It's as simple as that.
You're like a second father to me. Stay here,
Be king with me and share half the honor.

These others can take my message. Lie down   *635*
And spend the night on a soft couch. At daybreak
We will decide whether to set sail or stay."

And he made a silent nod to Patroclus
To spread a thick bed for Phoenix. It was time
For the others to think about leaving. Big Ajax,   *640*
Telamon's godlike son, said as much:

"Son of Laertes in the line of Zeus,
Resourceful Odysseus—it's time we go.
I do not think we will accomplish
What we were sent here to do. Our job now   *645*
Is to report this news quickly, bad as it is.
They will be waiting to hear. Achilles
Has made his great heart savage.
He is a cruel man, and has no regard
For the love that his friends honored him with,   *650*
Beyond anyone else who camps with the ships.
Pitiless. A man accepts compensation
For a murdered brother, a dead son.
The killer goes on living in the same town
After paying blood money, and the bereaved   *655*
Restrains his proud spirit and broken heart
Because he has received payment. But you,
The gods have replaced your heart
With flint and malice, because of one girl,
One single girl, while we are offering you   *660*
Seven of the finest women to be found
And many other gifts. Show some generosity
And some respect. We have come under your roof,
We few out of the entire army, trying hard
To be the friends you care for most of all."   *665*

And Achilles, the great runner, answered him:

"Ajax, son of Telamon in the line of Zeus,
Everything you say is after my own heart.
But I swell with rage when I think of how
The son of Atreus treated me like dirt   *670*

In public, as if I were some worthless tramp.
Now go, and take back this message:
I won't lift a finger in this bloody war
Until Priam's illustrious son Hector
Comes to the Myrmidons' ships and huts 675
Killing Greeks as he goes and torching the fleet.
But when he comes to my hut and my black ship
I think Hector will stop, for all his battle lust."

He spoke. They poured their libations
And headed for the ships, Odysseus leading. 680
Patroclus ordered a bed made ready
For Phoenix, and the old man lay down
On fleeces and rugs covered with linen
And waited for bright dawn. Achilles slept
In an inner alcove, and by his side 685
Lay a woman he had brought from Lesbos
With high, lovely cheekbones, Diomede her name,
Phorbas' daughter. Patroclus lay down
In the opposite corner, and with him lay Iphis,
A silken girl Achilles had given him 690
When he took steep Scyrus, Enyeus' city.

By now Odysseus and Ajax
Were in Agamemnon's quarters,
Surrounded by officers drinking their health
From gold cups and shouting questions. 695
Agamemnon, the warlord, had priority:

"Odysseus, pride of the Achaeans, tell me,
Is he willing to repel the enemy fire
And save the ships, or does he refuse,
His great heart still in the grip of wrath?" 700

Odysseus, who endured all, answered:

"Son of Atreus, most glorious Agamemnon,
Far from quenching his wrath, Achilles
Is filled with even more. He spurns you
And your gifts, and suggests that you 705

Think of a way to save the ships and the army.
He himself threatens, at dawn's first light,
To get his own ships onto the water,
And he said he would advise the others as well
To sail for home, since there is no chance now　　　710
You will storm Ilion's height. Zeus has stretched
His hand above her, making her people bold.
This is what he said, as these men here
Who came with me will tell you, Ajax
And the two heralds, prudent men both.　　　715
Phoenix will spend the night there. Tomorrow
He sails with Achilles on his voyage home,
If he wants to. He will not be forced to go."

They were stunned by the force of his words
And fell silent for a long time, hushed in grief,　　　720
Until at last Diomedes said in his booming voice:

"Son of Atreus, glorious Agamemnon,
You should never have pleaded with him
Or offered all those gifts. Achilles
Was arrogant enough without your help.　　　725
Let him do what he wants, stay here
Or get the hell out. He'll fight later, all right,
When he is ready or a god tells him to.
Now I want everyone to do as I say.
Enjoy some food and wine to keep up　　　730
Your strength, and then get some sleep.
When the rosy light first streaks the sky
Get your troops and horses into formation
Before the ships. Fight in the front yourselves."

The warlords assented, taken aback　　　735
By the authority of Diomedes' speech.
Each man poured libation and went to his hut,
Where he lay down and took the gift of sleep.

[Book 10 is omitted. Odysseus and Diomedes raid the Trojan camp by night.]

ILIAD 11

Dawn left her splendid Tithonus in bed
And rose to bring light to immortals and men,
As Zeus launched Eris, the goddess Strife,
Down to the Greek ships, a talisman of War
Clutched in her hands. She took her stand 5
Near the great black hull of Odysseus' ship,
Which lay in the middle, so a shout could reach
Ajax's huts on one end of camp and Achilles'
On the other. These two had beached their ships
On the flanks, confident in their manhood. 10
Standing there, she emitted a yell that rose
In volume and pitch until it seemed to each Greek
That fighting to the death was far preferable
To sailing home in their hollow ships.

Agamemnon boomed out a command 15
For his men to arm, and did so himself,
Strapping on sunlit bronze, his greaves first,
Works of art, trimmed with silver at the ankles.
Then he covered his chest with a corselet,
A gift from the Cypriot king, Cinyras. 20
News had reached Cyprus that the Greeks
Were launching a fleet for Troy, and Cinyras
Sent this corselet as homage to the warlord.
It had ten bands of dark blue enamel,
Twelve of gold, and twenty of tin. 25
On either side were three enameled dragons
With arching necks—iridescent as rainbows
That Zeus anchors in cloud as portents for men.
And he slung a sword around his shoulders,
Golden bolts shining in the hilt. The sheath 30
Was silver, fitted with golden straps.
Then he took up his shield, a crafted glory
Of metalwork, ringed with bronze, bossed

With white tin, and inlaid with dark cyan,
A Gorgon flanked by Terror and Rout   35
Glaring out of the midnight blue center.
The shield was hung with a baldric of silver
Upon which writhed an enameled dragon
With three heads twisting from a single neck.
He set upon his head a two-horned helmet   40
With four bosses and a horsehair plume
That nodded menacingly on its crest.
The spears that he took tapered to bronze points
Honed with light. The sky caught their glare,
And Hera and Athena thundered in response,   45
Honoring the lord of gold-crusted Mycenae.

The drivers had orders to keep their horses
In a steady line up and down the trench
While the heroes moved forward on foot
In full battle gear. The shout the troops gave   50
When they finally charged filled the dawn sky.
The charioteers let them have a long lead
And then closed the gap from behind. Thunder
Rolled up from the plain like black dust, and Zeus,
Soon to be pitching strong souls into Hades,   55
Rained drops of blood from the crystal air.

Opposite them the Trojans, on rising ground,
Gathered around their heroes, great Hector,
Polydamas, Aeneas, and Antenor's three sons,
Polybus, Agenor, and young Acamas—   60
All of whom could have passed as immortal gods.
Hector, behind the perfect circle of his shield,
Shone like a death star in a bank of clouds,
Sometimes passing behind them as he moved
From the front lines to the rear, issuing commands,   65
And his bronze flashed like Zeus' lightning.

    Reapers are working toward each other
    In a rich man's field, cutting huge swaths
    Of barley or wheat, and the grain falls in piles.

The Greeks and Trojans kept coming on.   70
Turning their backs would have meant
A disastrous rout. They fought on equal terms,
Head to head, going after each other
Like rabid wolves. Eris looked on rejoicing,
The only god who took the field that day.   75
All of the others kept their peace,
Idle in their homes on Olympus' ridges,
Sulking because the Dark Cloud, Zeus,
Meant to cover the Trojans with glory.
The Patriarch paid them no mind. He sat   80
Apart from the others in glorious solitude,
Looking down at Troy and the Achaean ships,
The flash of bronze, men killing and being killed.

As long as the holy light climbed toward noon,
Men were hit and fell on both sides of battle.   85

> *Toward evening, the woodsman turns home,*
> *His hands sore from swinging his axe*
> *And his heart weary from felling tall trees,*
> *And all his desire is for the sweetness of food.*

About that time in the long afternoon   90
The Danaans broke through, their captains calling,
Calling each other through the ranks of men,
Until their valor split the enemy lines.
Agamemnon led the way, taking out Bienor,
A Trojan commander, and his driver, Oïleus.   95
Oïleus at least had the chance to jump down
And face Agamemnon, but as he charged
The warlord's spear drove into his forehead.
Oïleus' heavy bronze helm had little effect
On the spear's sharp point, which penetrated   100
Not only the helmet's rim but the skull's bone,
Scrambling the grey stuff inside. So much
For these two. The warlord left them there,
Their naked chests gleaming in the level light,
And went on to kill Isus and Antiphus,   105

Two sons of Priam, bastard and legitimate,
Riding in one car. The bastard held the reins
And Antiphus stood by. Achilles once
Had bound these two with willow branches,
Surprising them as they watched their sheep   *110*
On Ida's hills, and later released them for ransom.
Now Agamemnon, Atreus' wide-ruling son,
Hit Isus with his spear above the nipple
And Antiphus with his sword beside his ear,
Knocking both from the car. As he was busy   *115*
Stripping their armor he recognized their faces
From the time when Achilles had brought them
Down from Ida and to the beachhead camp.

> *Imagine how easily a lion crushes*
> *A pair of fawns in his powerful jaws.*   *120*
> *He has come to where they lie huddled together*
> *On the forest floor, and has ripped out their hearts.*
> *And though their mother is near she can do*
> *Nothing to save them. Trembling herself,*
> *She bolts through the thick woods, and sweat*   *125*
> *Glazes her skin as she flees the great cat.*

The Trojans were chased off, none of them able
To help Agamemnon's two victims.

Peisander and Hippolochus were next,
Battle-hardened sons of Antimachus,   *130*
Who in the shrewdness of his heart
And in consideration of Paris' substantial gifts
Had argued against surrendering Helen
To blond Menelaus. Agamemnon now took
His two sons instead. Together in one car   *135*
They were trying to get their rearing horses
Under control—the reins had slipped from their hands—
When Agamemnon charged them like a lion.
They fell to their knees in their chariot's basket:

"Take us alive, son of Atreus, for ransom.   *140*

Antimachus' palace is piled high with treasure,
Gold and bronze and wrought iron our father
Would give you past counting once he found out
We were alive and well among the Greek ships."

Sweet words, and they salted them with tears.   *145*
But the voice they heard was anything but sweet:

"Your father Antimachus—if you really are
His sons—once urged the Trojan assembly
To kill Menelaus on the spot
When he came with Odysseus on an embassy.   *150*
Now you will pay for his heinous offense."

He spoke, and knocked Peisander backward
Out of his chariot with a spear through his chest
And sent him sprawling on the ground.
Hippolochus leapt down. Agamemnon   *155*
Used his sword to slice off both arms
And lop off his head, sending his torso
Rolling like a stone column through the crowd.
He didn't bother them further, but pressed on
To where the fighting was thickest, Greeks   *160*
In their leg-armor crowding in behind him,
Killing Trojans on foot, from chariots,
Dust rolling up from the plain like thunder
Under the horses' hooves, and all the while
In the blood-red bronze, Agamemnon killing,   *165*
Calling to his Greeks, the great warlord

> *Like fire consuming dry manzanita*
> *When the winds rise up*
> *And the scrub forest is burned to its roots,*

The Trojans falling as they fled,   *170*
And the horses, arching their necks,
Rattled empty cars along the lanes of war,
Feeling the absence of their faultless masters
Who lay sprawled on the ground

Dearer now to vultures than to their wives.   *175*

Zeus drew Hector out of the boiling dust,
Out of the blood, out of the noise and the slaughter,
While Agamemnon pressed on,
Howling to his Greeks to follow him.
Past the ancient tomb of Ilus,   *180*
Over the middle of the plain,
Beyond the windy fig tree
They rushed toward the city,
Yearned for it, the son of Atreus calling them,
Calling, his hard hands spattered with gore.   *185*
But when they came to the Western Gate
And the oak tree there, the two armies halted,
Waiting. There were still some Trojan stragglers
Being driven across the plain like cattle.

> *In the dead of night a lion rushes a herd,*   *190*
> *Scattering them all, though only one heifer will die.*
> *He crushes her neck first in his teeth,*
> *Then greedily laps up all her soft insides.*

Agamemnon picked off the hindmost Trojans
One by one, toppling them from their chariots,   *195*
And was coming up to Ilion's steep wall
When the Father of Gods and Men
Came down from heaven and onto Ida's peaks
In one step, a thunderbolt in his hands,
And sent gold-winged Iris off with a message: *200*

"Go, swift Iris, and take word to Hector
That as long as he sees Lord Agamemnon
Storming through the ranks and laying them low
He should hold back and order other troops
To engage the enemy. But when at last   *205*
Agamemnon is wounded by an arrow or spear
And mounts his chariot, then will I
Loan Hector strength to kill and keep killing
Until he comes to the thwarted ships

And the sun sets and sacred darkness falls." 210

Thus Zeus, and Iris moved like rain
Down from Ida's hills and to holy Ilion
Seeking Hector, splendor of Priam's house,
And found him standing in his chariot.
Iris hovered nearby on windy feet: 215

"Hector, son of Priam, Father Zeus
Has sent me here with a message for you.
As long as you see Lord Agamemnon
Storming through the ranks and laying them low
You should hold back and order other troops 220
To engage the enemy. But when at last
Agamemnon is wounded by an arrow or spear
And mounts his chariot, then will Zeus
Loan you the strength to kill and keep killing
Until you come to the thwarted ships 225
And the sun sets and sacred darkness falls."

Iris spoke and was gone, and Hector
Vaulted from his chariot with all his gear.
Brandishing a pair of spears he toured the troops
And worked them into a frenzy for battle. 230
A ripple moved through their lines as they turned
And faced the Greeks. Over against them
The Achaean forces stiffened their lines.
The two armies were poised for battle, but one man,
Agamemnon, charged forward first, 235
Determined to fight far in advance of all.

And now, Muses, who reside on Olympus,
Tell me who came, of all the Trojans
And their famed allies, to face Agamemnon.
It was Iphidamas, one of Antenor's sons, 240
A good man, tall, bred on Thracian farmland.
His mother was Theano, and her father,
Cisseus, raised the boy from infancy.
When he came of age, Cisseus gave him

His own daughter in marriage to keep him there.   *245*
But Iphidamas left her in the bridal chamber
And went chasing after glory when he heard
The Achaeans were coming. He sailed
With twelve trim ships, left them at Percote,
And came overland to Troy. Now he faced   *250*
Agamemnon, son of Atreus. When they closed
To within range of each other, Agamemnon
Cast and missed. Iphidamas stepped in
And stabbed him just beneath the corselet,
Putting his weight behind the thrust   *255*
And trusting his strong wrist to drive the spear home
Through the glittering belt, but the point
Bent like lead as soon as it hit the silver.
The great warlord seized the spear's haft
And with a lion's ferocity pulled it toward him   *260*
And out of Iphidamas' hands. A sword stroke
To the neck made his body go slack,
And Iphidamas fell in a sleep of bronze,
The town hero, far from his wedded wife,
Who gave him no joy, though he gave much for her,   *265*
A hundred head of cattle, a thousand sheep and goats
On promise from his countless herds.
Agamemnon stripped his costly armor
And paraded it through the Achaean troops.

When Antenor's eldest son, Coön,   *270*
Saw his brother fall, his eyes stung with grief.
Working his way to Agamemnon's blind side
He lunged with his spear and hit him
Below his left elbow, the point piercing
The forearm's sinew. The great warlord   *275*
Shuddered, but without missing a step
Jumped at Coön, who was now hauling
His brother Iphidamas away by his foot.
The son of Atreus' wind-hardened spear
Caught him under his shield, and as his limbs   *280*
Went slack, Agamemnon reached over
His brother's body to sever his head.

So Antenor's two sons fulfilled their destiny
Under the warlord's hands and sank into the gloom.

Agamemnon continued his killing rampage   285
With spear, sword, and chunks of rock
As long as blood flowed warm from the wound.
But when the wound dried and the blood caked,
The pain set in, needling and sharp,

    As if he were a woman in labor   290
    Struggling with the stabbing pain
    Hera's daughters dispense
    When they preside at a childbirth.

Agamemnon, in agony, leapt onto his chariot
And told the driver to make for the ships,   295
Then boomed out a final order to his men:

"Commanders of Greece, the battle is yours!
Keep the war from our ships. Zeus almighty
Has not seen fit to let me fight the whole day."

And the charioteer lashed the horses on   300
To the beached ships. Manes streaming,
Chests flecked with foam, bellies dust-stained,
They bore the wounded warlord from battle.

When Hector saw Agamemnon leaving,
He called to the Trojans and Lycians: 305

"Trojans and Lycians, Dardanian warriors,
Be men, my friends, and remember your valor.
Their best man is gone, and Zeus has granted me
A great victory. Drive your horses
Directly at them and win the power and glory."   310

And he set them on the Greeks
The way a hunter sets his grinning dogs
On a boar or a lion, leading the way himself,

Hector, son of Priam, peer of Ares, bane of mortals,
Falling on the conflict the way a windstorm   *315*
Falls on the sea and churns the violet water.

*[Lines 317–631 are omitted. Hector leads the Trojans against the Greeks
and turns them back. Odysseus and Diomedes are wounded.]*

So the fight went on, like wildfire burning.

  Meanwhile, the sweat-glazed mares of Neleus
Had pulled Nestor, and Machaon with him,
Out of the battle and into the Greek camp,   *635*
And Achilles saw them as they went by.
Achilles was standing on the stern of his ship
Gazing out at the blood, sweat, and tears
Of the Greeks in rout. And the great runner
Called to his comrade Patroclus from the ship,   *640*
And Patroclus heard him and came out of the hut
Like the god Ares. This was the beginning of evil
For Menoetius' strong son, who now asked:

"Why have you called me, Achilles? What do you want?"

And Achilles, the great runner, answered: *645*

"Son of Menoetius, my heart's companion,
If I have it right, the Greeks will soon be
Grovelling before me. They've reached their limit.
But I want you to go now and ask Nestor
Whom he is bringing wounded from battle.   *650*
From behind, it looked just like Machaon,
Son of Asclepius, but I didn't see his face.
The horses went by at a pretty good clip."

Patroclus did as his beloved friend asked
And sprinted through the camp.   *655*

Nestor had just reached his hut

And was stepping down from the chariot
With Machaon. His squire Eurymedon
Unhitched the old man's horses,
And the two dried the sweat from their tunics   660
By standing in the onshore breeze for a while.
Then they went into the hut and sat on chairs
While Hecamede prepared a drink for them.
This woman, who had long, beautiful hair,
Nestor had taken out of Tenedos   665
When Achilles sacked it. She was the daughter
Of a great man, Arsinous, and the Greeks
Had chosen her for Nestor, their best in council.
She now drew up for them a polished table
With blue enamelled feet, and set on it   670
A bronze basket, and next to it an onion
Grated for their drink, and pale green honey,
And sacred barley meal. Then she set down
A magnificent cup the old man had brought from home,
Studded with gold rivets. It had four handles,   675
With a pair of golden doves pecking at each,
And a double base beneath. Anyone else
Would have strained to lift the cup from the table
When full, but old Nestor raised it easily.
Into this cup Hecamede, beautiful as a goddess,   680
Poured Pramnian wine, grated goat cheese into it
With a brazed grater, and sprinkled white barley on top.
She motioned for them to drink. They did so,
And when they had slaked their parching thirst,
They began to swap tales and were enjoying themselves   685
When Patroclus stood in the door, more like a god
Than a man. Seeing him, the old man jumped up
From his gleaming chair, took him by the hand,
Led him inside, and asked him to sit down.
Patroclus refused, in no uncertain terms: 690

"No thank you, venerable sir, no seat for me.
I have too much respect for Achilles, who sent me
To ask you whom you have brought back wounded.
But I see for myself it is Machaon,

And I will bring this news back to Achilles now.   695
You know, sir, what a hard man he is,
Quick to blame even the blameless."

And Nestor, the horseman from Gerenia:

"And why does Achilles feel any sorrow
For wounded Greeks? He has no idea   700
Of the grief that has spread through the army.
Our best men have been hit and are lying
Wounded in camp. Diomedes is out,
And Odysseus, a good man with a spear,
Even Agamemnon has taken a hit.   705
Eurypylus, too, an arrow in his thigh.
Machaon here I have just brought back
With an arrow wound. But Achilles
For all his valor has no feeling for us.
Is he waiting until our ships go up in flames   710
On the shore of the sea, in spite of our efforts,
And we are all killed in a row? For my strength
Is not as it once was in my knotted limbs.
Oh to be young again, with my strength firm,
As I was in the cattle wars with the Eleans   715
When I killed Itymoneus, the valiant son
Of Hypeirochus, a man of Elis,
During the drive back. Leading the charge
In the fight for his cattle, he was hit by my spear
And fell, and the country folk all fled in terror.   720
The spoils we corralled from out of the plain!
Fifty herds of cattle and as many flocks of sheep,
As many droves of pigs, as many herds of goats.
And one hundred and fifty chestnut horses,
All mares, many with foals underneath.   725
We drove them all into Pylos by night,
Up to the citadel. And Neleus was glad
I had done so well, going to war as a boy.

[Lines 729–805 are omitted. Nestor tells a story about his youthful exploits.]

That is the sort of man I was. But Achilles?
His valor is for himself alone. And yet I think
He will sorely lament the army's destruction.
Ah yes, my young friend—Menoetius,
On the day he sent you forth from Phthia   *810*
To join Agamemnon, laid a charge on you.
Mustering the army throughout Achaea,
We had come to the well-built house of Peleus,
And we found the hero Menoetius inside
With you and Achilles. The old horseman Peleus   *815*
Was burning a bull's fat thighbones to Zeus
Out in the courtyard. He held a golden cup
And poured flaming wine as the sacrifice blazed.
You two were busy with the flesh of the bull
When we appeared in the doorway. Achilles   *820*
Jumped up in astonishment, took us by the hand,
And led us inside. He had us sit down,
Then set before us all that guests should have.
When we had our fill of food and drink
I began to speak, urging that you come with us.   *825*
You were both right eager, and your fathers
Laid on you both many commands. Old Peleus
Told Achilles to be preeminent always,
But to you Menoetius gave this command:
'My son, Achilles is higher born than you,   *830*
But you are older, though he is much stronger.
Advise him, speak to him wisely, direct him,
And he will be better off for obeying.'
Thus spoke the old man, but you have forgotten.
Still, you should speak to Achilles.   *835*
It is not too late, and he just might listen.
Who knows but that with the help of some god
You might rouse his spirit? You are his friend,
And it is good for friends to persuade each other.
If some oracle, or a secret his mother   *840*
Has learned from Zeus, is holding him back,
Let him send *you* out, let *you* lead a troop
Of Myrmidons and light the way for our army.
If you wear his armor, and the Trojans think

You are he, they will back off and give the Greeks   *845*
Some breathing space, what little there is in war.
Our rested men will turn them with a shout
And push them back from our ships to Troy."

This speech put great notions in Patroclus' head,
And he went sprinting down the line of ships   *850*
To Achilles. But when he reached Odysseus' hulls,
Where the assembly grounds and altars stood,
He ran into Eurypylus limping in from battle
With an arrow in his thigh. Sweat poured down
His neck and shoulders, and black blood pulsed   *855*
From his terrible wound, but his spirit was strong.
When Patroclus saw him he cried out in dismay:

"Ah, you Greek heroes, you were all destined
To die far from home and glut Trojan dogs
With your white fat. Eurypylus, tell me,   *860*
Is there any way to hold back Hector now,
Or will we all go down beneath his spear?"

And the wounded Eurypylus:

"We'll all be piling into our black ships soon.
We have no defense left. All our best   *865*
Have been hit and are laid up in camp,
And the Trojans only get stronger.
Lend me a hand here. Lead me back to my ship
And cut this arrow out of my thigh.
Wash the blood off in warm water   *870*
And put some soothing poultices on it,
The good stuff. They say Achilles taught you
And that he learned from Chiron, the just centaur.
Our medics, Podalirius and Machaon—
One is laid up wounded and needs a doctor himself,   *875*
And the other is out there fighting the Trojans."

Menoetius' valiant son answered:

"What are we going to do, Eurypylus?
I am on my way to Achilles now
With a message from Lord Nestor.   *880*
But you're hurting, and I won't let you down."

He put his arm around Eurypylus' chest
And helped him to his hut. His attendant,
When he saw them, spread hides on the floor.
Patroclus had him lie down, and with a knife   *885*
Cut from his thigh the barbed arrow.
He washed the wound off with warm water
And patted into it a bitter root
That he had rubbed between his hands,
An anodyne that took away the pain.   *890*
The bleeding stopped, and the wound was dry.

ILIAD 12

While Patroclus doctored Eurypylus
The battle raged on. The Greeks
Still had the protection of their trench
And the wide wall above it they had built
As the last line of defense for their ships—   *5*
For the time being. When they built that wall
And drove the trench around it to protect their ships
And all their plunder, they neglected to offer
Formal sacrifice to the immortal gods.
Built against the will of the immortals,   *10*
The wall could not endure for long.
While Hector lived and Achilles raged
And the city of Priam was still unpillaged,
The great wall of the Greeks stood firm.
But when all the best Trojans had died   *15*
And many Greeks had fallen or had left

And after ten years Priam's city had fallen
And the Greeks had sailed back to their native land,
Then Poseidon and Apollo conspired
To sweep away the wall, bringing against it   20
The might of all the rivers that flow down
From Ida's mountains to the sea—
Rhesus and Heptaporus, Caresus and Rhodius,
Granicus and Aesepus, shining Scamander
And Simois, along the banks of which   25
Many bullhide shields and helmets fell in the dust,
And a generation of men who were half-divine.
Phoebus Apollo turned all their mouths together
And for nine days sent their flood against the wall.
Zeus poured down rain continually, the sooner   30
To wash the wall into the sea. The Earthshaker
Led the way, holding a trident in his hands,
And pushed into the waves all the foundations
Of beams and stones the Greeks had laid with toil.
He made all smooth along the mighty Hellespont   35
And again covered the great shore with sand.
The wall was gone. He turned the beautiful rivers
Back to flow in their original channels.

This Poseidon and Apollo were to do
In time to come. But now the battle raged   40
On both sides of the well-built wall. The beams
Rang as they were struck, and the Greeks,
Whipped back by Zeus, were penned in with their ships,
Terrified of Hector, who had engineered the rout
And who still fought like a howling wind.   45

[Lines 46–258 are omitted. Hector leads the Trojans across the trench and
up to the wall around the Greek camp.]

To the noise of their advance Zeus now added
A wind from Ida's mountains that blew dust   260
Straight at the ships and the bewildered Greeks.
The sky god was giving the glory to the Trojans

And to Hector.

    Trusting these portents
And their own strength, the Trojans did their best   *265*
To breach the wall. Pulling down pickets
And battlements, they threw them to the ground
And set to work prying up the huge beams
The Greeks had used to reinforce the wall.
They were dragging these out, hoping to topple   *270*
The entire structure, but even then the Greeks
Refused to give way, patching the battlements
With bullhide and beating off the invaders.

Both Ajaxes were on the wall, patrolling it
And urging on the troops, using harsh words,   *275*
Gentle words, whatever it took
To get the men back into the fight:

"Friends!—and I mean everyone from heroes
To camp followers—no one ever said
Men are equal in war. There is work for us all.   *280*
You know it yourselves. I don't want a single man
To return to the ships now that you have heard
The rallying cry. Keep the pressure on.
Olympian Zeus may still grant us
To drive the enemy back to the city."   *285*

And they roused the Greeks to battle.

> *Snow flurries fall thick on a winter's day*
> *When Zeus in his cunning rouses himself*
> *To show humans the ammunition he has.*
> *He lulls the winds and he snows and snows*   *290*
> *Until he has covered all the mountain tops,*
> *Headlands and meadows and men's plowed fields.*
> *And the snow falls over the harbors*
> *And the shores of the grey sea, and only*
> *The waves keep it off. The rest of the world*   *295*
> *Is enveloped in the winter tempest of Zeus.*

The stones flew thick upon the Trojans
And upon the Greeks, and the wooden wall
Was beaten like a drum along its whole length.

For all this, though, Hector and his Trojans   *300*
Would never have broken the barred gate
Had not Zeus roused his own son, Sarpedon,
Against the Greeks, as a lion against cattle.
Sarpedon held before him a perfect shield,
Its bronze skin hammered smooth by the smith,   *305*
Who had stitched the leather beneath with gold
All around the rim. Holding this shield
And brandishing two spears, Sarpedon advanced.

> *The mountain lion has not fed for days*
> *And is hungry and brave enough to enter*   *310*
> *The stone sheep pen and attack the flocks.*
> *Even if he finds herdsmen on the spot*
> *With dogs and spears to protect the fold,*
> *He will not be driven back without a try,*
> *And either he leaps in and seizes a sheep*   *315*
> *Or is killed by a spear, as human heroes are.*

Godlike Sarpedon felt impelled
To rush the wall and tear it down.

He turned to Glaucus and said:

"Glaucus, you know how you and I   *320*
Have the best of everything in Lycia—
Seats, cuts of meat, full cups, everybody
Looking at us as if we were gods?
Not to mention our estates on the Xanthus,
Fine orchards and riverside wheat fields.   *325*
Well, now we have to take our stand at the front,
Where all the best fight, and face the heat of battle,
So that many an armored Lycian will say,
'So they're not inglorious after all,
Our Lycian lords who eat fat sheep   *330*

And drink the sweetest wine. No,
They're strong, and fight with our best.'
Ah, my friend, if you and I could only
Get out of this war alive and then
Be immortal and ageless all of our days.   *335*
I would never again fight among the foremost
Or send you into battle where men win glory.
But as it is, death is everywhere
In more shapes than we can count,
And since no mortal is immune or can escape,   *340*
Let's go forward, either to give glory
To another man or get glory from him."

Thus Sarpedon. Glaucus nodded, and the two of them
Moved out at the head of a great nation of Lycians.
Menestheus, Peteos' son, saw them and shuddered,   *345*
For they were advancing toward his part of the wall
And bringing ruin with them. Menestheus
Looked along the wall for a Greek captain
Who would be able to avert this disaster.
He saw both Ajaxes, who never seemed to tire,   *350*
And Teucer, who had just come from his hut.
They were near enough, but there was no way
To make a shout reach them, not with all the noise
Filling the air, the crash of shields and helmets
And the pounding on the gates, which were all closed now   *355*
And before each one of which the enemy stood,
Trying their best to break them and enter.
So Menestheus turned to the herald Thoötes:

"Run, Thoötes, and call Ajax, or better yet
Call both of them. All hell is going to break loose here.   *360*
The Lycian leaders are bearing down on us,
And they've been awfully tough in the big battles.
If the fighting is too heavy for them both to come,
At least get Telamonian Ajax here,
And Teucer too, who is good with a bow."   *365*

And the herald was off, running along the wall

Until he came to the two Ajaxes, to whom he said:

"My lords Ajax, captains of the Achaeans,
The son of Peteos, nurtured of Zeus,
Bids you come make a stand, however briefly,   370
In the battle there—both of you would be best—
Since all hell is going to break loose there.
The Lycian leaders are bearing down on us,
And they've been awfully tough in the big battles.
If the fighting is too heavy for both of you to leave,   375
At least let Telamonian Ajax come,
And Teucer too, who is good with a bow."

Telamonian Ajax heard the herald out
And said to his Oïlean counterpart:

"Ajax, stay here with Lycomedes   380
And keep these Danaans in the fight.
I'm going to make a stand over there.
When I've helped them out I'll come back here."

Big Ajax left, and with him Teucer,
His natural brother, and Pandion,   385
Who carried Teucer's curved bow.
Moving along the inside of the wall
They came to Menestheus' sector—
And to men hard-pressed. The Lycians
Were swarming up the battlements   390
Like black wind. The Greeks pushed back
With a shout. In the combat that ensued
It was Telamonian Ajax who first killed his man,
Sarpedon's comrade Epicles, hitting him
With a jagged piece of marble that lay on top   395
Of the heap of stones inside the wall there.
You couldn't find a man alive now
Who could lift that stone with both hands,
But Ajax swung it high and hurled it
With enough force to shatter the four-horned helmet   400
And crush Epicles' skull inside. He fell

As if he were doing a high dive from the wall,
And his spirit left his bones. Then Teucer hit
A fast charging Glaucus with an arrow
Where he saw his arm exposed. This stopped him cold,   *405*
And he leapt back from the wall, hiding his wound
From Greek eyes and his pride from their taunts.
It pained Sarpedon to see Glaucus withdraw
But it didn't take away any of his fight.
He hit Alcmaon, son of Thestor, with his spear,   *410*
Jabbing it in, and as he pulled it out again
Alcmaon came forward with it, falling headfirst
And landing with a clatter of finely tooled bronze.
Sarpedon wrapped his hands around the battlement
And pulled. The whole section gave way, exposing   *415*
The wall above and making an entrance for many.

Ajax and Teucer attacked him together.
Teucer's arrow hit his shield's bright belt
Where it slung across his chest, but Zeus
Beat off the death spirits. He would not allow   *420*
His son to fall by the ships. Big Ajax
Leapt upon him at the same moment,
Thrusting his spear into Sarpedon's shield,
But could not push the point through.
He did make him reel backward, though.   *425*
Sarpedon collected himself a short distance
Back from the wall. He was not giving up.
His heart still hoped to win glory here.
Wheeling around he called to his godlike Lycians:

"Lycians! Why are you slacking off from the fight?   *430*
Do you think I can knock this wall down alone
And clear a path to the ships? Help me out here.
The more men we have the better the work will go."

The Lycians cowered before their warlord's rebuke,
Then tightened the ranks around him even more.   *435*
The Greeks strengthened their positions on the wall
And steeled themselves for a major battle.

For all their strength the Lycians were unable
To break the wall, nor could the Greek spearmen
Push them back once they were close in.   *440*
They fought at close quarters,

> *like two men*
> *Disputing boundary stones in a common field*
> *And defending their turf with the measuring rods*
> *They had brought with them to stake their claims.*   *445*

Likewise the Trojans and Greeks, separated
By the palisade and reaching over it
To hack away at each other's leather shields.
Many were wounded, mostly those who turned
Their unprotected backs to the enemy,   *450*
But many through their shields too, until
The whole wooden wall dripped with the blood
Of soldiers from both sides. But the Trojans
Could do nothing to drive the Greeks back.

> *An honest woman who works with her hands*   *455*
> *To bring home a meager wage for her children*
> *Will balance a weight of wool in her scales*
> *Until both pans are perfectly level.*

So too this battle,
Until Zeus exalted Priam's son Hector,   *460*
First to penetrate the Achaean wall.

His shout split the air:

> "Move, Trojans!
Let's tear down this Greek fence
And make a bonfire out of their ships!"   *465*

They heard him, all right, and swarmed
Right up the wall, climbing to its pickets
With spears in their hands, while Hector
Scooped up a stone that lay by the gates,

A massive boulder tapering to a point.   *470*
It would take two men to heave it onto a cart—
More than two as men are now—but Hector
Handled it easily alone. Zeus
Lightened it for him, so that the stone
Was no more to Hector than the fleece   *475*
Of a ram is to a shepherd who carries it
Easily in his free hand. This was how
Hector carried it up to the gates,
A set of heavy double doors, solidly built
And bolted shut by interlocked inner bars.   *480*
Standing close to these towering doors, Hector
Spread his feet to get his weight behind the throw
And smashed the stone right into the middle.
The hinges broke off, and the stone's momentum
Carried it through, exploding the doors   *485*
And sending splintered wood in every direction.
Hector jumped through, a spear in each hand.

His face was like sudden night,
And a dark gold light played about the armor
That encased his zealous bones. No one   *490*
Could have stopped him, except the gods,
In his immortal leap through the ruined gate,
And his eyes glowed with fire.
                            Wheeling around
In the throng, Hector called to his Trojans,   *495*
Who needed no persuasion, to scale the wall.
Those who couldn't swarmed through the gate.
And the Greeks? In rout to their hollow ships,
With a noise like the damned stampeded into hell.

ILIAD 13

After Zeus had brought Hector and the Trojans
To the Greek ships, he left the combatants
To their misery and turned his luminous eyes
Far away, scanning the horse country of Thrace,
The Mysians, who fight in tight formation,   5
The Hippemolgi, whose diet is mares' milk,
And the Abii, most righteous of humans,
And turned his eyes no more to Troy.
He never dreamed that any of the immortals
Would go to help the Trojans or the Greeks.   10

But Poseidon wasn't blind. He sat high
On the topmost peak of wooded Samothrace,
Marvelling at the war going on beneath him.
He could see all of Ida, and Priam's city,
And the Greek ships, from where he sat.   15
The sea crawled beneath him. He pitied
The Greeks being beaten by the Trojans,
And he was furious with Zeus.

Three enormous strides took him down
The craggy mountain, and each footfall   20
Sent tremors through the wooded massif
As the immortal sea god descended.
A fourth step took him to his goal, Aegae,
Where his fabulous palace was built,
Shimmering gold in the depths of the bay.   25
He harnessed to his chariot a team of horses,
Bronze-hooved, gold-maned, and swift,
And clothed himself in gold, and gripped
His golden whip, and stepped onto his chariot
And went driving over the waves. The sea   30
Parted in joy before him, and all its denizens
Frolicked beneath him, acknowledging their lord.
The chariot flew on—the bronze axle below

Never got wet—and the prancing horses
Took Poseidon to the Achaean ships.   *35*

A wide cave is submerged in the deep water
Midway betweeen Tenedos and rocky Imbros.
The Earthshaker reined in his horses there,
Unhitched them, and threw out ambrosial fodder
For them to eat. And he put hobbles of gold   *40*
On their feet so that they would wait there until
Their master returned. Then he went off to the Greeks.

The Trojans were swarming behind Hector
Like flame or rumbling wind, and their howls
Expressed their belief they would take the ships   *45*
Of the Greeks and kill beside them all their best.
But Poseidon, who circles the earth and shakes it,
Had emerged from the sea to urge on the Argives.
He assumed the form and voice of Calchas
And spoke to the Ajaxes, who were ready to hear: *50*

"You two men will save the Greek army
If you just summon your strength and don't panic.
The Trojans aren't invincible. The Greek line
Will hold everywhere else they've climbed the wall.
It's only here that I have a premonition   *55*
We might be hurt, where a firestorm rages
In the person of Hector, son of Zeus, as he says.
May some god put in your hearts the will
To stand firm yourselves and encourage the others.
You could force Hector back from the ships then,   *60*
Even if the Olympian is behind his charge."

And the Lord of Earthquake struck them both
With his staff and pumped strength into them,
Lightening their limbs and their hands and feet.

And the god himself rose like a hawk   *65*
That lifts itself from a sheer precipice
And soars downwind after another bird.

So Poseidon was gone across the dusty plain.

*[Lines 70–836 are omitted. Poseidon rallies the Greeks. The Greek heroes
Idomeneus and Meriones meet behind the lines, and then Idomeneus dis-
tinguishes himself in battle. The fighting is furious on both sides.]*

> *Aching winds sweep down to the ground*
> *Under rolling thunder from the patriarch Zeus*
> *And then clash with the sea. The water moans*
> *And is whipped into wave after wave of arching,*   840
> *Seething breakers capped with white foam.*

The Trojans kept coming, rank on rank
Flashing with bronze, behind their captains.
Hector, son of Priam, led them all,
And he was like the War God himself   845
Behind his balanced shield, thick with hide
And layered with welded bronze, and on his head
The crest of his helm rippled in shining wind.
He kept testing the Greek lines here and there
To see if they would yield before him   850
As he came on behind his shield, but the Greeks
Didn't flinch. Then big Ajax strode forward:

"Come closer, sweetheart. No need to be coy.
We're not exactly inexperienced in war,
You know. It was Zeus who whipped us before.   855
I'm sure you'd like to rip our ships apart,
But be just as sure we have hands to defend them.
Your city, with all its people, will likely fall
A lot sooner, captured by us and plundered.
As for you, the day will soon be here   860
When you pray to Zeus and all immortals
For your combed horses to outfly falcons
And take you through the dusty plain to Troy."

His words were not out before a bird flew past
On the right, a high-soaring eagle.   865

The Achaeans shouted, taking heart
At the omen. But Hector answered him:

"You bumbling ox, what a stupid thing to say.
I wish it were as certain that I were Zeus' son
And Hera my mother, and that I were honored   *870*
Equally with Apollo and Athena
As it is that this day will bring doom
To every last Greek, and you among them,
Killed by my long spear, if you have the guts
To wait for it to pierce your lily-white skin   *875*
And leave your larded flesh to glut the dogs and birds
Of Troy, after you have fallen amid the ships."

With that he led the charge, followed by
Trojans shrieking at the top of their lungs.
The Greeks answered with cries of their own,   *880*
Digging in their heels as Troy's best came on,
And the noise from both armies blended together
And rose through the air to the brightness of Zeus.

ILIAD 14

[Lines 1–148 are omitted. Nestor meets with the wounded heroes Agamemnon, Odysseus, and Diomedes. Poseidon, now disguised as an old man, is still helping the Greeks.]

Standing on a crag of Olympus
Gold-throned Hera saw her brother,   150
Who was her husband's brother too,
Busy on the fields of human glory,
And her heart sang. Then she saw Zeus
Sitting on the topmost peak of Ida
And was filled with resentment. Cow-eyed Hera   155
Mused for a while on how to trick
The mind of Zeus Aegis-Holder,
And the plan that seemed best to her
Was to make herself up and go to Ida,
Seduce him, and then shed on his eyelids   160
And cunning mind a sleep gentle and warm.
She went to the bedroom her darling son
Hephaestus had built for her, and closed
Behind her the solid, polished doors
He had fitted out with a secret latch   165
And that no other god could open.
First she cleansed her lovely skin
With ambrosia, then rubbed on scented oil
So immortally perfumed that if the jar
Were just shaken in Zeus' bronze-floored house   170
The fragrance would spread to heaven and earth.
She rubbed this into her beautiful skin,
And she combed her hair and plaited
The lustrous, ambrosial locks that fell
Gorgeously from her immortal head.   175
Then she put on a robe that Athena
Had embroidered for her, pinning it
At her breast with brooches of gold.

A sash with a hundred tassels
Circled her waist, and in her pierced ears   *180*
She put earrings with three mulberry drops
Beguilingly bright. And the shining goddess
Veiled over everything with a beautiful veil
That was as white as the sun, and bound
Lovely sandals on her oiled, supple feet.   *185*
When everything was perfect, she stepped
Out of her room and called Aphrodite
And had a word with her in private:

"My dear child, will you do something for me,
I wonder, or will you refuse, angry because   *190*
I favor the Greeks and you the Trojans?"

And Zeus' daughter Aphrodite replied:

"Goddess revered as Cronus' daughter,
Speak your mind. Tell me what you want
And I'll oblige you if I possibly can."   *195*

And Hera, with every intention to deceive:

"Give me now the Sex and Desire
You use to subdue immortals and humans.
I'm off to visit the ends of the earth
And Father Ocean and Mother Tethys   *200*
Who nursed and doted on me in their house
When they got me from Rhea, after Zeus
Had exiled Cronus to the regions below.
I'm going to see them and try to resolve
Their endless quarrel. For eons now   *205*
They've been angry and haven't made love.
If I can talk to them and have them make up—
And get them together in bed again—
They will worship the ground I walk on."

And Aphrodite, who loved to smile: *210*

"How could I, or would I, refuse someone
Who sleeps in the arms of almighty Zeus?"

And with that she unbound from her breast
An ornate sash inlaid with magical charms.
Sex is in it, and Desire, and seductive   215
Sweet Talk, that fools even the wise.
She handed it to Hera and said:

"Here, put this sash in your bosom.
It has everything built in. I predict
You will accomplish what your heart desires."   220

She spoke, and ox-eyed Hera,
Smiling, tucked the sash in her bosom.

Then Zeus' daughter Aphrodite went home,
But Hera streaked down from Olympus' peak,
Used Pieria and Emathia as stepping stones,   225
And sped over the snowcapped mountains
Of Thrace. Her feet never touched earth.

At Athos she stepped on the billowing sea
And so came to Lemnos, Thoas' city,
Where she met Sleep, the brother of Death.   230
She took Sleep's hand, and said to him:

"Sleep, lord of all, mortal and immortal,
If ever you've listened to me before,
Listen now, and I will be grateful forever.
Lull Zeus' bright eyes to sleep for me   235
As soon as I lie beside him in love.
I will give you gifts: a handsome throne
Of imperishable gold that Hephaestus,
My strong-armed son, will build you.
It comes with a stool to rest your feet on   240
As you sit at banquet and sip your wine."

Sweet Sleep answered her:

"Goddess revered as Cronus' daughter,
If this were any other of the gods eternal
I'd lull him to sleep without any trouble,   *245*
Even if it were the River Ocean,
Which was the origin of them all.
But not Zeus. I wouldn't go near
The son of Cronus, much less lull him
To sleep, unless he himself asked me.   *250*
I learned my lesson from your last request,
That day Heracles, Zeus' high-hearted son,
Sailed from Troy, having wasted the city.
Yes, I slipped my sweet self around the mind
Of Zeus Aegis-Holder, while you brewed up   *255*
Storms at sea to drive his son Heracles
Off course to Cos, far from his friends.
And when Zeus woke up was he angry!
Throwing gods all over the house, and looking
For me especially. He would have pitched me   *260*
From aether to sea, no more to be seen,
If Night, the Mistress, had not saved me.
I ran to her, and he relented, reluctant
To do anything to offend swift Night.
And now this, another impossible mission."   *265*

Hera, the ox-eyed Lady, said to him:

"Sleep, what are you worried about?
Do you think that Zeus will help the Trojans
And be as angry now as he was then
For Heracles, his own son? Come on.   *270*
Look, I'll give you one of the young Graces
To have and to hold and be called your wife,
Pasithea, the object of all your desire."

Sleep's mood brightened at this. He said:

"Swear by the inviolable water of Styx,   *275*
One hand on fertile Earth and the other
On glistering Sea, so that all the gods

Below with Cronus will be witnesses,
That you will give me one of the Graces,
Pasithea, the object of all my desire."   280

The white-armed goddess Hera agreed
And swore the oath, naming all the gods
In Tartarus below. Titans they are called.
When she had sworn and finished the oath,
The two of them left Lemnos and Imbros   285
And came like swirling fog to Ida,
A mountain wilderness dotted with springs.
They left the sea at Lecton and headed inland.
The treetops quivered under their feet.
Sleep halted before Zeus could see him,   290
Perching in the highest fir tree on Ida
That rose through mist to pure bright air.
Sleep nestled in its long-needled branches
And looked just like the shrill mountain owl
Gods call Chalcis, and men Cymindis.   295

Hera was fast approaching Gargarus,
Ida's highest peak, when Zeus saw her.
And when he saw her, lust enveloped him,
Just as it had the first time they made love,
Slipping off to bed behind their parents' backs.   300
He stood close to her and said:

"Hera, why have you left Olympus?
And where are your horses and chariot?"

And Hera, with every intention to deceive:

"I'm off to visit the ends of the earth   305
And Father Ocean and Mother Tethys
Who nursed and doted on me in their house.
I'm going to see them and try to resolve
Their endless quarrel. For eons now
They've been angry and haven't made love.   310
My horses stand at the foot of Ida,

Ready to bear me over land and sea.
I came here from Olympus for your sake,
So you wouldn't be upset that I left
To visit Ocean without a word to you."   *315*

And Zeus, clouds scudding about him:

"You can go there later just as well.
Let's get in bed now and make love.
No goddess or woman has ever
Made me feel so overwhelmed with lust,   *320*
Not even when I fell for Ixion's wife,
Who bore Peirithous, wise as a god;
Or Danae, with lovely, slim ankles,
Who bore Perseus, a paragon of men;
Or the daughter of far-famed Phoenix,   *325*
Who bore Minos and godlike Rhadamanthus;
Or Semele; or Alcmene in Thebes,
Who bore Heracles, a stouthearted son;
And Semele bore Dionysus, a joy to humans;
Or Demeter, the fair-haired queen;   *330*
Or glorious Leto; or even you—
I've never loved anyone as I love you now,
Never been in the grip of desire so sweet."

And Hera, with every intention to deceive:

"What a thing to say, my awesome lord.   *335*
The thought of us lying down here on Ida
And making love outdoors in broad daylight!
What if one of the Immortals saw us
Asleep, and went to all the other gods
And told them? I could never get up   *340*
And go back home. It would be shameful.
But if you really do want to do this,
There is the bedroom your dear son Hephaestus
Built for you, with good solid doors. Let's go
There and lie down, since you're in the mood."   *345*

And Zeus, who masses the clouds, replied:

"Hera, don't worry about any god or man
Seeing us. I'll enfold you in a cloud so dense
And golden not even Helios could spy on us,
And his light is the sharpest vision there is."   350

With that he caught his wife in his arms.
Beneath them the shining soil sprouted
Fresh grass, and dewy lotus, and crocus,
And hyacinth, soft and thick, that kept them
Up off the ground. And as they lay there   355
A beautiful, golden cloud enfolded them
And precipitated drops of glimmering dew.

    And so the Father slept soundly on Gargaron's peak,
Mastered by Sleep and Love, and held his wife close.

*[The rest of Book 14 (lines 360–535) is omitted. The Greeks rout the
Trojans. Ajax knocks out Hector with a huge stone.]*

ILIAD 15

The Trojans had retreated through the palisade
And trench, a beaten army, and had halted
Beside their chariots, their faces pale
With terror, when Zeus awoke
On Ida's summit with Hera by his side.   5
He jumped to his feet and saw the Trojans
Being routed by howling Greeks
With Poseidon Lord among them,
And Hector lying on the plain, his friends
Crouched around him while he gasped for breath   10
In a haze of pain, and vomited blood.
It was no flyweight Greek who had hit him.
The Father of Gods and Men felt pity for him
And, scowling at Hera, delivered this speech:

"Hera, you scheming bitch, this trick of yours   15
Has taken Hector out and routed his army.
And you may be the first to profit from your plot—
When I whip the living daylights out of you.
Or don't you remember when I strung you up
With anvils hanging from your feet and gold   20
Unbreakable bands on your wrists? You dangled
In the air among the clouds, and all the gods
On high Olympus protested, but none
Could come to your rescue. If anyone tried
I'd send him sailing off our balcony—   25
There wouldn't be much left when he hit the ground.
Even so, my heart still ached for Heracles.
You and Boreas, whose squalls you suborned,
Had maliciously driven him over the desert sea
And brought him later to the great city of Cos.   30
I got him out of there and led him back
To bluegrass Argos, after many labors.
I remind you of this so you'll quit playing games

And see where this gets you, making love to me
The way you did just now, and tricking me."   35

The ox-eyed lady Hera stiffened at this,
And she feathered her words home carefully:

"All right. I swear by Earth and Heaven above,
And the subterranean water of Styx, the greatest
And the most awesome oath a god can swear,   40
By your sacred head and by our marriage couch,
Upon which I would never perjure myself—
That it is not by my will that Poseidon
Is hurting the Trojans and helping the Greeks.
He's acting of his own free will, out of pity   45
For the beating the Greeks are taking by their ships.
But I would advise even him to toe the line
And follow wherever you lead, Dark Cloud."

Zeus, the Father of Gods and Men,
Smiled at this and issued a swift reply: 50

"Well, my ox-eyed Lady, if your mind
Really were to be the same as mine, Poseidon
Would find it difficult not to follow us.
So if you mean what you say, go back now
To the gods and send Iris here, and Apollo,   55
She to go down to the bronze-coated Greeks
And tell Lord Poseidon to desist from the war;
And Phoebus Apollo to rouse Hector to fight,
Breathe strength into him again, so that he may
Forget the pain that now distresses him and   60
Drive the Achaeans back once more in flight.
So shall they flee in panic and fall dead among
The hollow ships of Peleus' son Achilles,
Who will send forth his comrade Patroclus,
Whom illustrious Hector will kill with his spear   65
Before Ilion, after Patroclus himself has killed
Many a youth, among them Sarpedon, my son.
In wrath for Patroclus Achilles will kill Hector.

From that time on I shall cause the Trojans
To be driven back from the ships, until the Greeks   70
Capture steep Ilion through Athena's counsel.
But until that time comes I will not cease
From my wrath or allow any immortal
To bear aid to the Danaans until the desire
Of the son of Peleus is fulfilled, as I   75
Promised at the first with a nod of my head
On the day when Thetis begged me by my knees
To honor Achilles, sacker of cities."

White-armed Hera was obedient to his word
And went from Ida's mountains to long Olympus.   80

> *The thought of a man who has seen the world*
> *Travels quickly to any spot on the globe*
> *When he wishes he were there—*

So Hera flew with the speed of desire
And came to Olympus.   85

She found the immortal gods assembled
In the house of Zeus. When they saw her
They were quick to toast her arrival.
She ignored them all, but did take a cup
From lovely Themis, who had run up to greet her   90
And who now addressed her with winged words:

"Hera, why have you come? You look so upset. Zeus
Must have really frightened you—your own husband!"

The goddess, ivory-armed Hera, replied:

"Don't get me started, Themis. You know yourself   95
What a bully he is, and how stubborn. No,
Let's get on with the feast, and you will hear
Along with the others what Zeus means to do.
It's not very pretty, and I rather doubt
That anyone, mortal or god, will be pleased—   100

Or if anyone will still have an appetite left."

Hera composed herself and sat down.
The gods' mood darkened. Hera smiled
With her lips, but her dark brows were tense,
And at last she burst out indignantly: *105*

"We're all simpering idiots to be angry with Zeus!
We all want to get to him, to talk him down,
To beat some sense into him, but does he care?
He doesn't even notice! No, he sits apart,
Secure in his supreme, almighty power.   *110*
You'll just have to take whatever grief
He dishes out to you. I'm afraid that now
It's Ares' turn to suffer, seeing that his son,
Whom he loves more than any mortal man,
His dear Ascalaphus, has died in battle."   *115*

When Ares heard this he smacked his muscled thighs
With the flat of his hands and wailed out loud:

"None of you Olympians can blame me now
If I go to the Greek ships and avenge my son,
Not even if I am to be blasted by Zeus   *120*
And lie among corpses in the blood and dust."

And he ordered his sons, Panic and Rout,
To yoke his team while he buckled on armor.
The hostility between the gods and Zeus
Would have reached new heights then,   *125*
Had not Athena, afraid for them all,
Jumped from her throne, sped through the door,
And disarmed Ares. She plucked the helmet
From his head, the shield from his shoulders,
Took the stiff, bronze spear from his hands,   *130*
And gave the furious War God a tongue-lashing:

"Are you out of your mind? Didn't you hear
What Hera just said, or don't you care?

Do you want more trouble than you can handle,
Forced to crawl back to Olympus yourself   *135*
And sowing disaster for the rest of us?
He'll leave the Trojans and Greeks, you know,
And come back here to raise hell with us,
Mauling us all in turn, guilty or not.
So please get over your anger for your son.   *140*
Better men than he have been killed or will be.
Human offspring are hard to save."

Ares gave in, and sat back down on his throne.
Then Hera called Apollo out of the palace,
And Iris, too, the immortals' messenger,   *145*
And said to them in a quick flurry of words:

"Zeus wants you to go to Ida immediately.
When you arrive you will look upon his face
And do whatever he orders you to do."

Having said that, Lady Hera turned away   *150*
And sat down on her throne.
                        The pair darted off
And came to Ida, mountain mother of beasts,
And found Cronus' son on Gargaron Peak,
Sitting in a wreath of fragrant cloud.   *155*
They stood respectfully before the face of Zeus,
And his mood brightened when he saw how promptly
The two of them had obeyed his wife's words.
He addressed Iris first, with words on wings:

"Go, swift Iris, to Lord Poseidon   *160*
And tell him this as true messenger.
Bid him cease from war and battle
And go off to the other gods, or to the bright sea.
If he is inclined to disregard my words
Have him consider in his mind and heart   *165*
That strong as he is he cannot withstand
My onset, since I am mightier by far
And elder born. Yet he has the gall to claim

He is equal to me, whom all the gods dread."

He spoke, and Iris was off in a blur of wind,   *170*
Moving down Ida's mountain to holy Troy

> *Like snow or hail flying from the clouds*
> *Under a cold blast from the brilliant North.*

So Iris flew with the speed of desire
And confronted the glorious Shaker of Earth: *175*

"A message for you, blue-maned Sea God.
I come here from Zeus who bears the aegis
And who bids you cease from war and battle
And go off to the other gods, or to the bright sea.
If you are inclined to disregard his words,   *180*
He threatens to come here himself and wage war
Against you, and he strongly advises you
To avoid his hands, since he is mightier by far
And elder born. Yet you have the gall to claim
You are equal to him, whom all the gods dread."   *185*

The Earthshaker made this angry reply:

"He may be strong, but this is outrageous,
To force me, his peer, to stop against my will.
We three brothers, whom Rhea bore to Cronus,
Zeus, myself, and Hades, lord of the dead,   *190*
Divided up the universe into equal shares.
When we shook the lots, I got the grey sea
As my eternal domain; Hades, the nether gloom;
Zeus, the broad sky with clouds and bright air.
Earth and high Olympus remain common to all.   *195*
I will not follow Zeus' whims. Mighty as he is,
Let him remain content with his third share,
And not try to frighten me as if I were a coward.
Better for him to threaten his own children
With abusive language, the sons and daughters   *200*
He begot himself, who will listen because they must."

And Iris, her feet soft in the offshore wind:

"Is this the message, blue-maned Sea God,
I should take to Zeus, this hard, unyielding speech?
Will you not relent, as noble hearts often do?   205
You know how the Furies always side with the elder."

And Poseidon Earthshaker answered her:

"That is very well spoken, Iris. It is good
When a messenger understands how things are.
But bitter pain comes to my heart and soul   210
Whenever anyone attacks an equal,
A peer of equal status, with angry words.
Although I am offended, I will yield for now.
But I will say this, and make this threat from my heart:
If in spite of me and Pallas Athena,   215
And Hera and Hermes and Hephaestus Lord,
He spares steep Ilion, and is not willing
To lay it waste, nor give power to the Greeks,
He can be sure of eternal strife between us."

And with that Poseidon left the Greek army   220
And dove into the sea. They missed him sorely.

Cumulus clouds piled high on Ida's summit.

Zeus turned and spoke to Apollo:

"Go now, Phoebus, to bronze-clad Hector.
Tremendous Poseidon has gone into the sea   225
That laps the earth, avoiding my precipitous
Wrath. Too bad. The fight would have been legend,
Even among the gods below with Cronus.
But it was better for us both that he yielded
Before me, angry and indignant as he was.   230
It would not have been settled without some sweat.
At any rate, take the tasselled aegis in your hands
And shake it over the Greeks to rout their heroes.

And see to Hector yourself. Fortify him
Until the Greeks have run back to their ships   235
On the Hellespont. I'll take it from there
And see the Achaeans get some breathing space."

Apollo did not disobey his father's words.
He came down from Ida's peaks like a falcon
That bloodies doves in flight, swift on the wing,   240
And found Hector, light of Troy, sitting up—
He no longer lay down—and catching his breath.
He recognized his friends, and his gasping
And sweating had stopped, since Zeus now had
A mind to revive him. Apollo stood close and said: 245

"Hector, son of Priam, why are you sitting here
Apart from the rest, scarcely alive? What is wrong?"

Hector's helmet shone in the light. He said weakly:

"Which god are you, questioning me face to face?
Haven't you heard that while I was killing his friends   250
At the rear of the ships, booming Ajax hit me
In the chest with a stone and took the fight out of me?
I thought I would see the dead in Hades' house
This very day, after I had breathed forth my last."

And Apollo, Lord of bright distances: 255

"Courage. The Son of Cronus has sent me from Ida
To help and stand by you—no one less than me,
Phoebus Apollo, the Gold Sword, who has in the past
Saved both you and your steep citadel.
Come now and rally your many charioteers   260
To drive their horses against the hollow ships.
I will go ahead and smooth all the ground
For the chariots, and I will turn the Greek heroes."

And he breathed strength into the man
Who tended Troy's army as a shepherd his flock.   265

Picture a horse that has eaten barley in its stall
Breaking its halter and galloping across the plain,
Making for his accustomed swim in the river,
A glorious animal, head held high, mane streaming
Like wind on his shoulders. Sure of his splendor   270
He prances by the horse-runs and the mares in pasture.

That was Hector, knees and feet like wind,
As he rallied the chariots. He had heard the god's voice.

And the Greeks?

Hunters and hounds have been hot on the trail   275
Of an antlered stag or a mountain goat,
But a sudden sheer rock or a tangled wood
Saves the animal, which was not theirs to catch,
And their shouting brings a bearded lion
Into their path. Then the eager hunters turn back.   280

Hordes of Greeks had been advancing relentlessly,
Carving their way forward with spears and swords.
But when they saw Hector patrolling the ranks,
They tensed up with fear and stopped in their tracks.

[Lines 285–620 are omitted. The Greeks are driven back to their camp.]

It was then that the Trojans, like lions
Who have tasted raw meat, charged the ships
And completed this part of Zeus' design.
He steadily turned up the Trojans' intensity
And softened the Greeks' resolve to win.   625
Hector would win all the glory for now,
Priam's son would burn the beaked ships
With fire from heaven, and so fulfill
The last syllable of Thetis' prayer.
It was for this that Zeus waited,   630
The glare from a burning ship. From then on
He would will the Trojans back from the ships

And shift glory to the Greeks. With this intent
He roused Hector against the hollow ships,
And Hector needed no urging. Hector   635
Raged like the War God, the Spear Wielder,

    Fire that consumes a wooded mountainside,

Foam flecking his mouth, eyes burning
Under fierce brows, and the helmet
Encasing his face a sinister glitter   640
As Hector fought, as Zeus himself
Shed a cone of light from the aether
Around the solitary warrior, but only
For this brief moment. Pallas Athena
Was hastening his doom under Achilles' hands.   645
Yes, Hector was eager, but for all his efforts,
Probing the Greek lines where he saw
The greatest concentration of fine weapons,
He could not break their ranks.
They were as solid as a wall,   650

    Or an iron cliff that drops sheer
    Into the grey sea and withstands
    Whistling winds and swollen waves
    That break against its rock face.

The Greeks were not going to budge,   655
So Hector, with a nimbus of fire about him,
Leapt high and fell upon their bulk.

[Lines 658–711 are omitted. The fighting continues.]

A̲jax decided it was time to make his move.
Separating himself from the rest of the Greeks
He boarded a ship and strode along its deck
Wielding a long pike made for naval warfare,   715
Some forty feet in length, jointed with iron rings.
And then,

as skillfully as a stunt rider
Jumps from horse to horse as his chariot,
Drawn by a team of hand-picked thoroughbreds,   720
Speeds from plain to city down a highway
Lined with spectators, who cheer him on,

Ajax leapt from ship to ship, and his voice,
Like a shock wave from the wide, blue sky,
Admonished the Greeks to defend their ships   725
And the huts clutched beneath them. Hector
Reacted quickly, a streak of bronze armor
Flashing out from the general sea of bronze

Like a golden eagle dive-bombing down
To a river bank where a flock of wild geese,   730
Or cranes, or long-necked swans are feeding.

Hector made like that for a dark-prowed ship,
And a great hand reached down from Ida
And pushed him on, and his army with him.

The fighting began again beside the ships,   735
So keenly you would have thought the troops
On both sides were fresh and had just entered battle.
Their minds were different, though. The Greeks fought
As if they would never get out of this battle alive,
While every Trojan heart beat with the hope   740
Of burning the ships and killing Greek heroes.
Such were their thoughts as they faced off in battle.

Hector laid hold of the stern of a ship,
A beautiful vessel that had brought Protesilaus
Over to Troy, but would not bring him back home.   745
It was about this ship that the Greeks and Trojans
Fought in close combat. Instead of withstanding
Assaults from arrows and javelins in flight,
They fought toe to toe here, of one heart in battle,
Hacking at each other with axes and hatchets,   750
Enormous swords and double-edged spears.

Many fine blades with black leather ferrules
Fell to the ground, some from the hands,
Others from the shoulders of men as they fought.
The earth flowed black with their blood. Hector,   755
Once he had grasped the horn of the ship's stern,
Would not let go, and he called to the Trojans:

"Fire! Bring fire! And raise the war cry
All together! Zeus has given us this day
As payment for everything—to seize the ships   760
That came here against the gods' will
And have brought us endless trouble
Because of the cowardice of our elders,
Who, when I wanted to bring the fight here,
Kept me back and withheld the army.   765
But if Zeus clouded our minds then,
There is no doubt he is urging us on now."

At this, the Trojans intensified their attack.
Ajax, battered by everything they could throw,
And sensing death if he stayed where he was,   770
Inched back along the seven-foot cross-plank
He had been standing on and jumped from the deck.
He took up a position guarding the ship,
His spearpoint menacing any Trojan
Who tried to bring up fire, and his voice   775
Kept booming out alarms to his compatriots:

"Soldiers of Greece—be men, my friends!
We have to dig in on defense now.
Do you think we have allies to back us up,
Or some stronger wall that will protect us?   780
There's no fortified city behind us now,
With reinforcements there to turn the tide.
We're out here on the plain of Troy
With the sea at our backs, far from home,
Surrounded by armed men. If there's a way out,   785
It's in our own hands, not in slacking off."

And as Ajax spoke his spear carved holes
In the various Trojans who thought that they
Might please Hector by bringing fire to the ship.
He mangled a good dozen at close range like this.   790

ILIAD 16

   While they fought for this ship, Patroclus
Came to Achilles and stood by him weeping,
His face like a sheer rock where the goat trails end
And dark springwater washes down the stone.
Achilles pitied him and spoke these feathered words: 5

"What are all these tears about, Patroclus?
You're like a little girl, pestering her mother
To pick her up, pulling at her hem
As she tries to hurry off and looking up at her
With tears in her eyes until she gets her way.   10
That's just what you look like, you know.
You have something to tell the Myrmidons?
Or myself? Bad news from back home?
Last I heard, Menoetius, your father,
And Peleus, mine, were still alive and well.   15
Their deaths would indeed give us cause to grieve.
Or are you broken-hearted because some Greeks
Are being beaten dead beside our ships?
They had it coming. Out with it, Patroclus—
Don't try to hide it. I have a right to know."   20

And with a deep groan you said to him,
Patroclus:

          "Achilles, great as you are,

Don't be vengeful. They are dying out there,
All of our best—or who used to be our best—   *25*
They've all been hit and are lying
Wounded in camp. Diomedes is out,
And Odysseus, a good man with a spear,
Even Agamemnon has taken a hit.
Eurypylus, too, an arrow in his thigh.   *30*
The medics are working on them right now,
Stitching up their wounds. But you are incurable,
Achilles. God forbid I ever feel the spite
You nurse in your heart. You and your damned
Honor! What good will it do future generations   *35*
If you let us go down to this defeat
In cold blood? Peleus was never your father
Or Thetis your mother. No, the grey sea spat you out
Onto crags in the surf, with an icy scab for a soul.

   What is it? If some secret your mother   *40*
Has learned from Zeus is holding you back,
At least send *me* out, let *me* lead a troop
Of Myrmidons and light the way for our army.
And let me wear your armor. If the Trojans think
I am you, they'll back off and give the Greeks   *45*
Some breathing space, what little there is in war.
Our rested men will turn them with a shout
And push them back from our ships to Troy."

   That was how Patroclus, like a child
Begging for a toy, begged for death.   *50*

And Achilles, angry and deeply troubled:

"Ah, my noble friend, what a thing to say.
No, I'm not in on any divine secret,
Nor has my mother told me anything from Zeus.
But I take it hard when someone in power   *55*
Uses his authority to rob his equal
And strip him of his honor. I take it hard.
The girl the Greeks chose to be my prize—
After I demolished a walled city to get her—

Lord Agamemnon, son of Atreus, just took   *60*
From my hands, as if I were some tramp.
   But we'll let that be. I never meant
To hold my grudge forever. But I did say
I would not relent from my anger until
The noise of battle lapped at my own ships' hulls.   *65*
So it's on your shoulders now. Wear my armor
And lead our Myrmidons into battle,
If it is true that a dark cloud of Trojans
Has settled in over the ships and the Greeks
Are hemmed in on a narrow strip of beach.   *70*
The Trojans have become cocky, the whole city,
Because they do not see my helmeted face
Flaring close by. They would retreat so fast
They would clog the ditches with their dead—
If Lord Agamemnon knew how to respect me.   *75*
As it is they have brought the war to our camp.
So Diomedes is out, eh? It was his inspired
Spear work that kept the Trojans at arm's length.
And I haven't been hearing Agamemnon's battle cry,
As much as I hate the throat it comes from—only   *80*
Hector's murderous shout breaking like the sea
Over the Trojans, urging them on. The whole plain
Is filled with their whooping as they rout the Greeks.
   Hit them hard, Patroclus, before they burn the ships
And leave us stranded here. But before you go,   *85*
Listen carefully to every word I say.
Win me my honor, my glory and my honor
From all the Greeks, and, as their restitution,
The girl Briseis, and many other gifts.
But once you've driven the Trojans from the ships,   *90*
You come back, no matter how much
Hera's thundering husband lets you win.
Any success you have against the Trojans
Will be at the expense of my honor.
And if you get so carried away   *95*
With killing the Trojans that you press on to Troy,
One of the immortals may intervene.
Apollo, for one, loves them dearly.

So once you have made some daylight for the ships,
You come back where you belong.   100
The others can fight it out on the plain.
  O Patroclus, I wish to Father Zeus
  And to Athena and Apollo
That all of them, Greeks and Trojans alike,
Every last man on Troy's dusty plain,   105
Were dead, and only you and I were left
  To rip Ilion down, stone by sacred stone."

And while they talked, Ajax retreated.

Zeus saw to it that everything the Trojans threw
At Ajax hit him, and his helmet tickered and rang   110
From all the metal points its bronze deflected
From his temples and cheeks. His left arm was sore
From holding up his shield, but the Trojans could not,
For all their pressure, force it aside.
Gulping in air, sweat pouring down his limbs,   115
He could scarcely breathe and had nowhere to turn.

Tell me now, Muses, who dwell on Olympus,
How fire first fell on the Achaean ships.

It was Hector who forced his way
To Ajax's side, and with his heavy sword   120
Lopped through the ash-wood shaft of his spear
At the socket's base, sending the bronze point
Clanging onto the ground far behind him
And leaving in Ajax's hands a blunted stick.
Ajax knew that this was the work of the gods,   125
That Zeus had cancelled Ajax's battle plans
And planned instead a Trojan victory.
No one could blame him for getting out of range,
And when he did, the Trojans threw their firebrands
Onto the ship, and she went up in flames.   130

Achilles slapped his thighs and said:

"Hurry, Patroclus! I see fire from the ships.
Don't let them take the fleet and cut off our escape.
Put on the armor while I gather the troops."

And so Patroclus armed, putting on   *135*
The bronze metalwork tailored to the body
Of Aeacus' swift grandson: the greaves
Trimmed with silver at the ankles, the corselet
Spangled with stars, the silver-studded sword,
The massive shield, and the crested helmet   *140*
That made every nod a threat.
He took two spears of the proper heft,
But left behind the massive battle pike
Of Aeacus' incomparable grandson.
No one but Achilles could handle this spear,   *145*
Made of ash, which the centaur Chiron
Had brought down from Mount Pelion and given
To Achilles' father to be the death of heroes.
Patroclus left the horses to Automedon,
The warrior he trusted most, after Achilles,   *150*
To be at his side in the crush of battle.
Automedon led beneath the yoke
The windswift horses Xanthus and Balius,
Immortal horses the gods gave to Peleus
When he married silver Thetis.   *155*
The Harpy Podarge had conceived them
When the West Wind blew through her
As she grazed in a meadow near Ocean's stream.
As trace horse Automedon brought up Pedasus,
Whom Achilles had acquired in the raid   *160*
On Eëtion's city. This faultless animal,
Though mortal, kept pace with immortal horses.

Achilles toured the rows of huts
That composed the Myrmidons' camp
And saw to it the men got armed.   *165*

Think of wolves
Ravenous for meat. It is impossible

To describe their savage strength in the hunt,
But after they have killed an antlered stag
Up in the hills and torn it apart, they come down   170
With gore on their jowls, and in a pack
Go to lap the black surface water in a pool
Fed by a dark spring, and as they drink,
Crimson curls float off from their slender tongues.
But their hearts are still, and their bellies gorged.   175

So too the Myrmidon commanders
Flanking Achilles' splendid surrogate,
And in their midst stood Achilles himself,
Urging on the horses and the men.

Achilles had brought fifty ships to Troy.   180
Each ship held fifty men, and the entire force
Was divided into five battalions
Whose five commanders answered to Achilles.
    Menesthius led the first battalion.
His mother, Polydore, a daughter of Peleus,   185
Had lain with the river god Spercheius,
Whose sky-swollen waters engendered the child.
His nominal father was a man called Boros,
Who gave many gifts to marry Polydore.
    The second battalion was led by Eudorus,   190
Polymele's bastard son. This woman
Once caught Hermes' eye as she danced
In Artemis' choir, and the god later
Went up to her bedroom and slept with her.
The son she bore shone like silver in battle.   195
After childbirth Actor's son Echecles
Led her to his house in marriage,
And her father, Phylas, kept the boy
And brought him up as if he were his own.
    Peisander led the third contingent.   200
He was, next to Patroclus, the best
Of all the Myrmidons with a spear.
    Old Phoenix led the fourth contingent,
And Alcimedon, Laerces' son, the fifth.

When Achilles had the troops assembled   *205*
By battalions, he spoke to them bluntly:

"Myrmidons! I would not have a man among you forget
The threats you have been issuing against the Trojans—
From the safety of our camp—while I was in my rage.
All this time you have been calling me   *210*
The hard-boiled son of Peleus and saying to my face
That my mother must have weaned me on gall
Or I wouldn't keep my friends from battle.
That, together with hints you'd sail back home
If all I was going to do was sit and sulk. Now, however,   *215*
That there *is* a major battle to hold your interest,
I hope that each of you remembers what it means to fight."

The speech steeled their spirit. The Myrmidons
Closed ranks until there was no more space between them
Than between the stones a mason sets in the wall   *220*
Of a high house when he wants to seal it from the wind.
Helmet on helmet, shield overlapping shield, man on man,
So close the horsehair plumes on their bright crests
Rubbed each other as their heads bobbed up and down.
And in front of them all, two men with one heart,   *225*
Patroclus and Automedon made their final preparations
To lead the Myrmidons into war.
                     But Achilles
Went back to his hut and opened the lid
Of a beautiful, carved chest his mother Thetis   *230*
Had put aboard his ship when he sailed for Troy,
Filled with tunics and cloaks and woolen rugs.
And in it too was a chalice that no one else
Ever drank from, and that he alone used for libation
To no other god but Zeus. This chalice   *235*
He now took from the chest, purified it
With sulfur crystals, washed it with clear water,
Then cleansed his hands and filled it with bright red wine.
And then he prayed, standing in his courtyard
Pouring out the wine as he looked up to heaven.   *240*
And as he prayed, Zeus in his thunderhead listened.

"Lord Zeus, God of Dodona, Pelasgian God
Who dwells afar in the snows of Dodona
With your barefoot priests who sleep
On the ground around your sacred oak: 245
As you have heard my prayer before
And did honor me and smite the Achaeans,
So now too fulfill my prayer.
As I wait in the muster of the ships
And send my Patroclus into battle with my men,   250
Send forth glory with him.
Make bold the heart in his breast
So that Hector will see that my comrade
Knows how to fight and win without me.
And when he has driven the noise of battle   255
Away from our ships, may he come back to me
Unharmed, with all his weapons and men."

Zeus in his wisdom heard Achilles' prayer
And granted half of it. Yes, Patroclus
Would drive the Trojans back from the ships,   260
But he would not return from battle unharmed.

Achilles placed the chalice back in the chest
And stood outside his hut. He still longed to see
The grim struggle on Troy's windswept plain.

The Myrmidons under Patroclus   265
Filed out and swarmed up to the Trojans.

Boys will sometimes disturb a hornets' nest
By the roadside, jabbing at it and infuriating
The hive—the little fools—
Until the insects become a menace to all   270
And attack any traveller who happens by,
Swarming out in defense of their brood.

So too the Myrmidons.
Patroclus called to them over their shouts:

"Remember whose men you are   *275*
And for whose honor you are fighting.
And fight so that even wide-ruling Agamemnon
Will recognize his blind folly
In not honoring the best of the Achaeans.
    FOR ACHILLES!"   *280*

This raised their spirits even higher.
They were all over the Trojans,
And the ships' hulls reverberated
With the sounds of their battle cries.
The Trojans, when they saw Patroclus   *285*
Gleaming in his armor, fell apart,
Convinced that Achilles had come out at last,
His wrath renounced and solidarity restored.
Each of them looked for a way to save his skin.

Patroclus' spear shot out like stabbing light   *290*
To where the Trojans were clustered
Around the stern of Protesilaus' ship
And hit a certain chariot commander
Named Pyraechmes, a Paeonian
Who had led a contingent of chariots   *295*
From the Axius river in Amydon.
He went down now, groaning in the dust
With Patroclus' spear in his right shoulder.
Having lost their leader and best fighter
The Paeonians panicked, and Patroclus   *300*
Drove them from the ships and doused the fire.

The half-burnt ship was left there.

          The Trojans,
Frantic and screaming, were on the run,
And the Greeks poured in with an answering roar.   *305*

Zeus will at times rein in his lightning
And remove a dense cloud from a mountain top,
And all the crests and headlands and high glades

Break into view, and brightness falls from the air.

The Greeks had repelled the enemy fire   310
From the ships and could catch their breath,
But only for a while. The battle was not over.
The Trojans had withdrawn from the black ships,
But were not giving up. They had taken a stand
And would have to be pushed back by force.   315
The fighting was scattered at first, as heroes
Killed each other in individual combat.

[Lines 318–80 are omitted. The fighting continues.]

All this time big Ajax was trying
To get a shot off at Hector, who,
Knowing the ways of war, kept his shoulders
Under his oxhide shield and listened
For the whistling of arrows and thud of spears.   385
He knew the fight was not going his way,
But he held his ground and tried to save his friends.

> *A cloud detaches itself from Olympus*
> *And moves across the clear blue sky*
> *When Zeus is about to unleash a storm.*   390

The rout from the ships had begun,
And in no good order. Hector's horses
Got him across the trench, but he left
His army behind it. The Trojans drove
Team after team into the trench   395
Only to see the horses break their poles,
Struggle free, and leave their lords
Stranded in their chariots. Patroclus
Called his men in for the kill. The Trojans
Were screaming and running   400
In every direction, while a cloud of dust
Rose high over their horses as they left
The ships behind and strained for the city.

Patroclus drove his chariot to wherever
The routed Trojans were thickest, 405
Shouting as he plowed over broken chariots
And the drivers who fell beneath his wheels.
The horses the gods had given to Peleus
Jumped the trench in one immortal leap,
And Patroclus steered them after Hector, 410
In whose back he longed to plant his spear,
But Hector's horses had too big a lead.

> *When the storm finally breaks, on a day*
> *During harvest, the black earth is soaked*
> *Until it can hold no more, and still the rain* 415
> *Comes down in sheets as Zeus' judgment*
> *On men who govern by violence*
> *And drive Justice out with their crooked verdicts,*
> *As if they have never heard of an Angry God.*
> *All the rivers flood their banks, and every hill* 420
> *Is rutted with torrents that feed the rivers,*
> *And down from the mountains the waters roar*
> *And sweep men's tillage into the shining sea.*

The Trojan mares were thundering down the plain.

Patroclus let them go. But when he had cut off 425
The foremost battalions, he hemmed them back
Toward the ships, blocking their frantic retreat
Toward the city, and in the space defined
By the ships, the river, and Troy's high wall,
He made them pay in blood. 430

[Lines 431–54 are omitted. Patroclus routs the Lycians.]

Sarpedon saw his comrades running 455
With their tunics flapping loose around their waists
And being swatted down like flies by Patroclus.
He called out, appealing to their sense of shame:

"Why this sudden burst of speed, Lycian heroes?
Slow down a little, while I make the acquaintance   460
Of this nuisance of a Greek who seems by now
To have hamstrung half the Trojan army."

And he stepped down from his chariot in his bronze
As Patroclus, seeing him, stepped down from his.

> *High above a cliff vultures are screaming*   465
> *In the air as they savage each other's craws*
> *With their hooked beaks and talons.*

　　And higher still,
Zeus watched with pity as the two heroes closed
And said to his wife Hera, who is his sister too: 470

"Fate has it that Sarpedon, whom I love more
Than any man, is to be killed by Patroclus.
Shall I take him out of battle while he still lives
And set him down in the rich land of Lycia,
Or shall I let him die under Patroclus' hands?"   475

And Hera, his lady, her eyes soft and wide:

"Son of Cronus, what a thing to say!
A mortal man, whose fate has long been fixed,
And you want to save him from rattling death?
Do it. But don't expect all of us to approve.   480
Listen to me. If you send Sarpedon home alive,
You will have to expect other gods to do the same
And save their own sons—and there are many of them
In this war around Priam's great city.
Think of the resentment you will create.   485
But if you love him and are filled with grief,
Let him fall in battle at Patroclus' hands,
And when his soul and life have left him,
Send Sleep and Death to bear him away
To Lycia, where his people will give him burial   490
With mound and stone, as befits the dead."

The Father of Gods and Men agreed
Reluctantly, but shed drops of blood as rain
Upon the earth in honor of his own dear son
Whom Patroclus was about to kill   *495*
On Ilion's rich soil, far from his native land.
When they were close, Patroclus cast, and hit
Not Prince Sarpedon, but his lieutenant
Thrasymelus, a good man—a hard throw
Into the pit of his belly. He collapsed in a heap.   *500*
Sarpedon countered and missed. His bright spear
Sliced instead through the right shoulder
Of Pedasus, who gave one pained, rasping whinny,
Then fell in the dust. His spirit fluttered off.
With the trace horse down, the remaining two   *505*
Struggled in the creaking yoke, tangling the reins.
Automedon remedied this by drawing his sword
And cutting loose the trace horse. The other two
Righted themselves and pulled hard at the reins,
And the two warriors closed again in mortal combat.   *510*
Sarpedon cast again. Another miss. The spearpoint
Glinted as it sailed over Patroclus' left shoulder
Without touching him at all. Patroclus came back,
Leaning into his throw, and the bronze point
Caught Sarpedon just below the rib cage   *515*
Where it protects the beating heart. Sarpedon fell

As a tree falls, oak, or poplar, or spreading pine,
When carpenters cut it down in the forest
With their bright axes, to be the beam of a ship,

And he lay before his horses and chariot,   *520*
Groaning heavily and clawing the bloody dust,

Like some tawny, spirited bull a lion has killed
In the middle of the shambling herd, groaning
As it dies beneath the predator's jaws.

Thus beneath Patroclus the Lycian commander   *525*
Struggled in death. And he called his friend:

"Glaucus, it's time to show what you're made of
And be the warrior you've always been,
Heart set on evil war—if you're fast enough.
Hurry, rally our best to fight for my body,   530
All the Lycian leaders. Shame on you,
Glaucus, until your dying day, if the Greeks
Strip my body bare beside their ships.
Be strong and keep the others going."

The end came as he spoke, and death settled   535
On his nostrils and eyes. Patroclus put his heel
On Sarpedon's chest and pulled out his spear.
The lungs came out with it, and Sarpedon's life.
The Myrmidons steadied his snorting horses.
They did not want to leave their master's chariot.   540

Glaucus could hardly bear to hear Sarpedon's voice,
He was so grieved that he could not save him.
He pressed his arm with his hand. His wound
Tormented him, the wound he got when Teucer
Shot him with an arrow as he attacked the wall.   545
He prayed to Apollo, Lord of bright distances:

"Hear me, O Lord, wherever you are
In Lycia or Troy, for everywhere you hear
Men in their grief, and grief has come to me.
I am wounded, Lord, my arm is on fire,   550
And the blood can't be staunched. My shoulder
Is so sore I cannot hold a steady spear
And fight the enemy. Sarpedon is dead,
My Lord, and Zeus will not save his own son.
Heal my wound and deaden my pain,   555
And give me the strength to call the Lycians
And urge them on to fight, and do battle myself
About the body of my fallen comrade."

Thus Glaucus' prayer, and Apollo heard him.
He stilled his pain and staunched the dark blood   560
That flowed from his wound. Glaucus felt

The god's strength pulsing through him,
Glad that his prayers were so quickly answered.
He rounded up the Lycian leaders
And urged them to fight for Sarpedon's body,   565
Then went with long strides to the Trojans,
To Polydamas, Agenor, Aeneas,
And then saw Hector's bronze-strapped face,
Went up to him and said levelly:

"Hector, you have abandoned your allies.   570
We have been putting our lives on the line for you
Far from our homes and loved ones,
And you don't care enough to lend us aid.
Sarpedon is down, our great warlord,
Whose word in Lycia was Lycia's law,   575
Killed by Patroclus under Ares' prodding.
Show some pride and fight for his body,
Or the Myrmidons will strip off the armor
And defile his corpse, in recompense
For all the Greeks we have killed by the ships."   580

This was almost too much for the Trojans.
Sarpedon, though a foreigner, had been
A mainstay of their city, the leader
Of a large force and its best fighter.
Hector led them straight at the Greeks,   585
    "For Sarpedon!"

[Lines 587–666 are omitted. The fighting continues.]

The plain of Troy thrummed with the sound
Of bronze and hide stretched into shields,
And of swords and spears knifing into these.
Sarpedon's body was indistinguishable   670
From the blood and grime and splintered spears
That littered his body from head to foot.

    But if you have ever seen how flies

Cluster about the brimming milk pails
On a dairy farm in early summer,   675

You will have some idea of the throng
Around Sarpedon's corpse.

                        And not once did Zeus
Avert his luminous eyes from the combatants.
All this time he looked down at them and pondered   680
When Patroclus should die, whether
Shining Hector should kill him then and there
In the conflict over godlike Sarpedon
And strip the armor from his body, or whether
He should live to destroy even more Trojans.   685
And as he pondered it seemed preferable
That Achilles' spendid surrogate should once more
Drive the Trojans and bronze-helmed Hector
Back to the city, and take many lives.
And Hector felt it, felt his blood turn milky,   690
And mounted his chariot, calling to the others
To begin the retreat, that Zeus' scales were tipping.
Not even the Lycians stayed, not with Sarpedon
Lying at the bottom of a pile of bodies
That had fallen upon him in this node of war.   695

The Greek stripped at last the glowing bronze
From Sarpedon's shoulders, and Patroclus gave it
To some of his comrades to take back to the ships.

Then Zeus turned to Apollo and said:

"Sun God, take our Sarpedon out of range.   700
Cleanse his wounds of all the clotted blood,
And wash him in the river far away
And anoint him with our holy chrism
And wrap the body in a deathless shroud
And give him over to be taken swiftly   705
   By Sleep and Death to Lycia,
Where his people shall give him burial

With mound and stone, as befits the dead."

And Apollo went down from Ida
Into the howling dust of war,   710
And cleansed Sarpedon's wounds of all the blood,
And washed him in the river far away
And anointed him with holy chrism
And wrapped the body in a deathless shroud
And gave him over to be taken swiftly   715
   By Sleep and Death to Lycia.

Patroclus called to his horses and charioteer
And pressed on after the Trojans and Lycians,
Forgetting everything Achilles had said
And mindless of the black fates gathering above.   720
Even then you might have escaped them,
Patroclus, but Zeus' mind is stronger than men's,
And Zeus now put fury in your heart.

Do you remember it, Patroclus, all the Trojans
You killed as the gods called you to your death?   725
Adrastus was first, then Autonous, and Echeclus,
Perimas, son of Megas, Epistor, Melanippus,
Elasus, Mulius, and last, Pylartes,
And it would have been more, but the others ran,
Back to Troy, which would have fallen that day   730
By Patroclus' hands.

         But Phoebus Apollo
Had taken his stand on top of Troy's wall.

Three times Patroclus
Reached the parapet, and three times   735
Apollo's fingers flicked against the human's shield
And pushed him off. But when he came back
A fourth time, like a spirit from beyond,
Apollo's voice split the daylight in two:

"Get back, Patroclus, back where you belong.   740

Troy is fated to fall, but not to you,
Nor even to Achilles, a better man by far."

And Patroclus was off, putting distance
Between himself and that wrathful voice.

Hector had halted his horses at the Western Gate   745
And was deciding whether to drive back into battle
Or call for a retreat to within the walls.
While he pondered this, Phoebus Apollo
Came up to him in the guise of Asius.
This man was Hector's uncle on his mother's side,   750
And Apollo looked just like him as he spoke:

"Why are you out of action, Hector? It's not right.
If I were as much stronger than you as I am weaker,
You'd pay dearly for withdrawing from battle.
Get in that chariot and go after Patroclus.   755
Who knows? Apollo may give you the glory."

Hector commanded Cebriones, his charioteer,
To whip the horses into battle. Apollo melted
Into the throng, a god into the toil of men.
The Greeks felt a sudden chill,   760
While Hector and the Trojans felt their spirits lift.
Hector was not interested in the other Greeks.
He drove through them and straight for Patroclus,
Who leapt down from his own chariot
With a spear in one hand and in the other   765
A jagged piece of granite he had scooped up
And now cupped in his palm. He got set,
And without more than a moment of awe
For who his opponent was, hurled the stone.
The throw was not wasted. He hit Hector's   770
Charioteer, Cebriones, Priam's bastard son,
As he stood there holding the reins. The sharp stone
Caught him right in the forehead, smashing
His brows together and shattering the skull
So that his eyeballs spurted out and dropped   775

Into the dirt before his feet. He flipped backward
From the chariot like a diver, and his soul
Dribbled away from his bones. And you,
Patroclus, you, my horseman, mocked him:

"What a spring the man has! Nice dive!   780
Think of the oysters he could come up with
If he were out at sea, jumping off the boat
In all sorts of weather, to judge by the dive
He just took from his chariot onto the plain."

And with that he rushed at the fallen warrior   785

> *Like a lion who has been wounded in the chest*
> *As he ravages a farmstead, and his own valor*
> *Destroys him.*

             Yes, Patroclus, that is how you leapt
Upon Cebriones.   790
               Hector vaulted from his chariot,
And the two of them fought over Cebriones

> *Like a pair of lions fighting over a slain deer*
> *In the high mountains, both of them ravenous,*
> *Both high of heart,*   795

             very much like these two
Human heroes hacking at each other with bronze.
Hector held Cebriones' head and would not let go.
Patroclus had hold of a foot, and around them
Greeks and Trojans squared off and fought.   800

> *Winds sometimes rise in a deep mountain wood*
> *From different directions, and the trees—*
> *Beech, ash, and cornelian cherry—*
> *Batter each other with their long, tapered branches,*
> *And you can hear the sound from a long way off,*   805
> *The unnerving splintering of hardwood limbs.*

The Trojans and Greeks collided in battle,
And neither side thought of yielding ground.

Around Cebriones many spears were stuck,
Many arrows flew singing from the string,   810
And many stones thudded onto the shields
Of men fighting around him. But there he lay
In the whirling dust, one of the great,
    Forgetful of his horsemanship.

While the sun still straddled heaven's meridian,   815
Soldiers on both sides were hit and fell.
But when the sun moved down the sky and men
All over earth were unyoking their oxen,
The Greeks' success exceeded their destiny.
They pulled Cebriones from the Trojan lines   820
And out of range, and stripped his armor.

And then Patroclus unleashed himself.

Three times he charged into the Trojan ranks
With the raw power of Ares, yelling coldly,
And on each charge he killed nine men.   825
But when you made your fourth, demonic charge,
Then—did you feel it, Patroclus?—out of the mist,
Your death coming to meet you. It was
Apollo, whom you did not see in the thick of battle,
Standing behind you, and the flat of his hand   830
Found the space between your shoulder blades.
The sky's blue disk went spinning in your eyes
As Achilles' helmet rang beneath the horses' hooves,
And rolled in the dust—no, that couldn't be right—
Those handsome horsehair plumes grimed with blood,   835
The gods would never let that happen to the helmet
That had protected the head and graceful brow
Of divine Achilles. But the gods did
Let it happen, and Zeus would now give the helmet
To Hector, whose own death was not far off.   840

Nothing was left of Patroclus' heavy battle spear
But splintered wood, his tasselled shield and baldric
Fell to the ground, and Apollo, Prince of the Sky,
Split loose his breastplate. And he stood there, naked,
Astounded, his silvery limbs floating away,   845
Until one of the Trojans slipped up behind him
And put his spear through, a boy named Euphorbus,
The best his age with a spear, mounted or on foot.
He had already distinguished himself in this war
By knocking twenty warriors out of their cars   850
The first time he went out for chariot lessons.
It was this boy who took his chance at you,
Patroclus, but instead of finishing you off,
He pulled his spear out and ran back where he belonged,
Unwilling to face even an unarmed Patroclus,   855
Who staggered back toward his comrades, still alive,
But overcome by the god's stroke, and the spear.

Hector was watching this, and when he saw
Patroclus withdrawing with a wound, he muscled
His way through to him and rammed his spearhead   860
Into the pit of his belly and all the way through.
Patroclus fell heavily. You could hear the Greeks wince.

> *A boar does not wear out easily, but a lion*
> *Will overpower it when the two face off*
> *Over a trickling spring up in the mountains*   865
> *They both want to drink from. The boar*
> *Pants hard, but the lion comes out on top.*

So too did Hector, whose spear was draining the life
From Menoetius' son, who had himself killed many.

His words beat down on Patroclus like dark wings: 870

"So, Patroclus, you thought you could ransack my city
And ship our women back to Greece to be your slaves.
You little fool. They are defended by me,
By Hector, by my horses and my spear. I am the one,

Troy's best, who keeps their doom at bay. But you,   *875*
Patroclus, the vultures will eat you
On this very spot. Your marvelous Achilles
Has done you no good at all. I can just see it,
Him sitting in his tent and telling you as you left:
'Don't bother coming back to the ships,   *880*
Patroclus, until you have ripped Hector's heart out
Through his bloody shirt.' That's what he said,
Isn't it? And you were stupid enough to listen."

And Patroclus, barely able to shake the words out:

"Brag while you can, Hector. Zeus and Apollo   *885*
Have given you an easy victory this time.
If they hadn't knocked off my armor,
I could have made mincemeat of twenty like you.
It was Fate, and Leto's son, who killed me.
Of men, Euphorbus. You came in third at best.   *890*
And one more thing for you to think over.
You're not going to live long. I see Death
Standing at your shoulder, and you going down
Under the hands of Peleus' perfect son."

Death's veil covered him as he said these things,   *895*
And his soul, bound for Hades, fluttered out
Resentfully, forsaking manhood's bloom.
He was dead when Hector said to him:

"Why prophesy my death, Patroclus?
Who knows? Achilles, son of Thetis,   *900*
May go down first under my spear."

And propping his heel against the body,
He extracted his bronze spear and took off
After Automedon. But Automedon was gone,
Pulled by immortal horses, the splendid gifts   *905*
The gods once gave to Peleus.

[Book 17 is omitted. There is a desperate struggle over the corpse of Patroclus. The Greeks send Antilochus to bring the news to Achilles.]

ILIAD 18

The fight went on, like wildfire burning.
Antilochus, running hard like a herald,
Found Achilles close to his upswept hulls,
His great heart brooding with premonitions
Of what had indeed already happened.   5

"This looks bad,
All these Greeks with their hair in the wind
Stampeding off the plain and back to the ships.
God forbid that what my mother told me
Has now come true, that while I'm still alive   10
Trojan hands would steal the sunlight
From the best of all the Myrmidons.
Patroclus, Menoetius' brave son, is dead.
Damn him! I told him only to repel
The enemy fire from our ships,   15
And not to take on Hector in a fight."

Antilochus was in tears when he reached him
And delivered his unendurable message:

"Son of wise Peleus, this is painful news
For you to hear, and I wish it were not true.   20
Patroclus is down, and they are fighting
For his naked corpse. Hector has the armor."

A mist of black grief enveloped Achilles.
He scooped up fistfuls of sunburnt dust

And poured it on his head, fouling   *25*
His beautiful face. Black ash grimed
His finespun cloak as he stretched his huge body
Out in the dust and lay there,
Tearing out his hair with his hands.
The women, whom Achilles and Patroclus   *30*
Had taken in raids, ran shrieking out of the tent
To be with Achilles, and they beat their breasts
Until their knees gave out beneath them.
Antilochus, sobbing himself, stayed with Achilles
And held his hands—he was groaning   *35*
From the depths of his soul—for fear
He would lay open his own throat with steel.

The sound of Achilles' grief stung the air.

Down in the water his mother heard him,
Sitting in the sea-depths beside her old father,
And she began to wail.   *40*
                         And the saltwater women
Gathered around her, all the deep-sea Nereids,
Glaucê and Thaleia and Cymodocê,
Neseia and Speio, Thoê and ox-eyed Haliê,   *45*
Cymothoê, Actaeê, and Limnoeira,
Melitê and Iaera, Amphithoê and Agauê,
Doris, Panopê, and milk-white Galateia,
Nemertes, Apseudes, and Callianassa,
Clymenê, Ianeira, Ianassa, and Maera,   *50*
Oreithyia and Amatheia, hair streaming behind her,
And all of the other deep-sea Nereids.
They filled the silver, shimmering cave,
And they all beat their breasts.

                              Thetis led the lament: *55*

"Hear me, sisters, hear the pain in my heart.
I gave birth to a son, and that is my sorrow,
My perfect son, the best of heroes.
He grew like a sapling, and I nursed him

As I would a plant on the hill in my garden,   60
And I sent him to Ilion on a sailing ship
To fight the Trojans. And now I will never
Welcome him home again to Peleus' house.
As long as he lives and sees the sunlight
He will be in pain, and I cannot help him.   65
But I'll go now to see and hear my dear son,
Since he is suffering while he waits out the war."

She left the cave, and they went with her,
Weeping, and around them a wave
Broke through the sea, and they came to Troy.   70
They emerged on the beach where the Myrmidons' ships
Formed an encampment around Achilles.
He was groaning deeply, and his mother
Stood next to him and held her son's head.
Her lamentation hung sharp in the air,   75
And then she spoke in low, sorrowful tones:

"Child, why are you crying? What pain
Has come to your heart? Speak, don't hide it.
Zeus has granted your prayer. The Greeks
Have all been beaten back to their ships   80
And suffered horribly. They can't do without you."

Achilles answered her:

"Mother, Zeus may have done all this for me,
But how can I rejoice? My friend is dead,
Patroclus, my dearest friend of all. I loved him,   85
And I killed him. And the armor—
Hector cut him down and took off his body
The heavy, splendid armor, beautiful to see,
That the gods gave to Peleus as a gift
On the day they put you to bed with a mortal.   90
You should have stayed with the saltwater women,
And Peleus should have married a mortal.
But now—it was all so you would suffer pain
For your ravaged son. You will never again

Welcome me home, since I no longer have the will   95
To remain alive among men, not unless Hector
Loses his life on the point of my spear
And pays for despoiling Menoetius' son."

And Thetis, in tears, said to him:

"I won't have you with me for long, my child,   100
If you say such things. Hector's death means yours."

From under a great weight, Achilles answered:

"Then let me die now. I was no help
To him when he was killed out there. He died
Far from home, and he needed me to protect him.   105
But now, since I'm not going home, and wasn't
A light for Patroclus or any of the rest
Of my friends who have been beaten by Hector,
But just squatted by my ships, a dead weight on the earth . . .
I stand alone in the whole Greek army   110
When it comes to war—though some do speak better.
I wish all strife could stop, among gods
And among men, and anger too—it sends
Sensible men into fits of temper,
It drips down our throats sweeter than honey   115
And mushrooms up in our bellies like smoke.
Yes, the warlord Agamemnon angered me.
But we'll let that be, no matter how it hurts,
And conquer our pride, because we must.
But I'm going now to find the man who destroyed   120
My beloved—Hector.
                              As for my own fate,
I'll accept it whenever it pleases Zeus
And the other immortal gods to send it.
Not even Heracles could escape his doom.   125
He was dearest of all to Lord Zeus, but fate
And Hera's hard anger destroyed him.
If it is true that I have a fate like his, then I too
Will lie down in death.

But now to win glory 130
And make some Trojan woman or deep-breasted
Dardanian matron wipe the tears
From her soft cheeks, make her sob and groan.
Let them feel how long I've been out of the war.
Don't try, out of love, to stop me. I won't listen." 135

And Thetis, her feet silver on the sand:

"Yes, child. It's not wrong to save your friends
When they are beaten to the brink of death.
But your beautiful armor is in the hands of the Trojans,
The mirrored bronze. Hector himself 140
Has it on his shoulders. He glories in it.
Not for long, though. I see his death is near.
But you, don't dive into the red dust of war
Until with your own eyes you see me returning.
Tomorrow I will come with the rising sun 145
Bearing beautiful armor from Lord Hephaestus."

Thetis spoke, turned away
From her son, and said to her saltwater sisters:

"Sink now into the sea's wide lap
And go down to our old father's house 150
And tell him all this. I am on my way
Up to Olympus to visit Hephaestus,
The glorious smith, to see if for my sake
He will give my son glorious armor."

As she spoke they dove into the waves, 155
And the silver-footed goddess was gone
Off to Olympus to fetch arms for her child.

And while her feet carried her off to Olympus,
Hector yelled, a yell so bloodcurdling and loud
It stampeded the Greeks all the way back 160
To their ships beached on the Hellespont's shore.
They could not pull the body of Patroclus

Out of javelin range, and soon Hector,
With his horses and men, stood over it again.
Three times Priam's resplendent son   *165*
Took hold of the corpse's heels and tried
To drag it off, bawling commands to his men.
Three times the two Ajaxes put their heads down,
Charged, and beat him back. Unshaken, Hector
Sidestepped, cut ahead, or held his ground   *170*
With a shout, but never yielded an inch.

   It was like shepherds against a starving lion,
   Helpless to beat it back from a carcass,

The two Ajaxes unable to rout
The son of Priam from Patroclus' corpse.   *175*
And Hector would have, to his eternal glory,
Dragged the body off, had not Iris stormed
Down from Olympus with a message for Achilles,
Unbeknownst to Zeus and the other gods.
Hera had sent her, and this was her message: *180*

"Rise, son of Peleus, most formidable of men.
Rescue Patroclus, for whom a terrible battle
Is pitched by the ships, men killing each other,
Some fighting to save the dead man's body,
The Trojans trying to drag it back   *185*
To windy Ilion. Hector's mind especially
Is bent on this. He means to impale the head
On Troy's palisade after he strips off its skin.
And you just lie there? Think of Patroclus
Becoming a ragbone for Trojan dogs. Shame   *190*
To your dying day if his corpse is defiled."

The shining sprinter Achilles answered her:

"Iris, which god sent you here?"

And Iris, whose feet are wind, responded:

"None other than Hera, Zeus' glorious wife.   *195*
But Zeus on high does not know this, nor do
Any of the immortals on snow-capped Olympus."

And Achilles, the great runner:

"How can I go to war? They have my armor.
And my mother told me not to arm myself   *200*
Until with my own eyes I see her come back
With fine weapons from Hephaestus.
I don't know any other armor that would fit,
Unless maybe the shield of Telamonian Ajax.
But he's out there in the front ranks, I hope,   *205*
Fighting with his spear over Patroclus dead."

Windfoot Iris responded:

"We know very well that they have your armor.
Just go to the trench and let the Trojans see you.
One look will be enough. The Trojans will back off   *210*
Out of fear of you, and this will give the Greeks
Some breathing space, what little there is in war."

Iris spoke and was gone. And Achilles,
Whom the gods loved, rose. Around
His mighty shoulders Athena threw   *215*
Her tasselled aegis, and the shining goddess
Haloed his head with a golden cloud
That shot flames from its incandescent glow.

Smoke is rising through the pure upper air
From a besieged city on a distant island.   *220*
Its soldiers have fought hard all day,
But at sunset they light innumerable fires
So that their neighbors in other cities
Might see the glare reflected off the sky
And sail to their help as allies in war.   *225*

So too the radiance that flared

From Achilles' head and up to the sky.
He went to the trench—away from the wall
And the other Greeks, out of respect
For his mother's tense command. Standing there,   *230*
He yelled, and behind him Pallas Athena
Amplified his voice, and shock waves
Reverberated through the Trojan ranks.

> *You have heard the piercing sound of horns*
> *When squadrons come to destroy a city.*   *235*

The Greek's voice was like that,
Speaking bronze that made each Trojan heart
Wince with pain.
                    And the combed horses
Shied from their chariots, eyes wide with fear,   *240*
And their drivers went numb when they saw
The fire above Achilles' head
Burned into the sky by the Grey-Eyed One.
Three times Achilles shouted from the trench;
Three times the Trojans and their confederates   *245*
Staggered and reeled, twelve of their best
Lost in the crush of chariots and spears.
But the Greeks were glad to pull Patroclus' body
Out of range and placed it on a litter. His comrades
Gathered around, weeping, and with them Achilles,   *250*
Shedding hot tears when he saw his loyal friend
Stretched out on the litter, cut with sharp bronze.
He had sent him off to war with horses and chariot,
But he never welcomed him back home again.

And now the ox-eyed Lady Hera   *255*
Sent the tireless, reluctant sun
Under the horizon into Ocean's streams,
Its last rays touching the departing Greeks with gold.
It had been a day of brutal warfare.

[Lines 260–503 are omitted. The Trojans hold an assembly. Hector, reject-
ing the advice of his brother Polydamas, keeps the troops out on the plain.
The Greeks mourn Patroclus. Thetis goes to Hephaestus and asks him to
make a new set of armor for her son.]

Hephaestus left her there and went to his bellows,
Turned them toward the fire and ordered them to work.   *505*
And the bellows, all twenty, blew on the crucibles,
Blasting out waves of heat in whatever direction
Hephaestus wanted as he hustled here and there
Around his forge and the work progressed.
He cast durable bronze onto the fire, and tin,   *510*
Precious gold and silver. Then he positioned
His enormous anvil up on its block
And grasped his mighty hammer
In one hand, and in the other his tongs.

He made a shield first, heavy and huge,   *515*
Every inch of it intricately designed.
He threw a triple rim around it, glittering
Like lightning, and he made the strap silver.
The shield itself was five layers thick, and he
Crafted its surface with all of his genius.   *520*

    On it he made the earth, the sky, the sea,
    The unwearied sun, and the moon near full,
    And all the signs that garland the sky,
    Pleiades, Hyades, mighty Orion,
    And the Bear they also call the Wagon,   *525*
    Which pivots in place and looks back at Orion
        And alone is aloof from the wash of Ocean.

    On it he made two cities, peopled
    And beautiful. Weddings in one, festivals,
    Brides led from their rooms by torchlight   *530*
    Up through the town, bridal song rising,
    Young men reeling in dance to the tune
    Of lyres and flutes, and the women
    Standing in their doorways admiring them.

There was a crowd in the market-place   *535*
And a quarrel arising between two men
Over blood money for a murder,
One claiming the right to make restitution,
The other refusing to accept any terms.
They were heading for an arbitrator   *540*
And the people were shouting, taking sides,
But heralds restrained them. The elders sat
On polished stone seats in the sacred circle
And held in their hands the staves of heralds.
The pair rushed up and pleaded their cases,   *545*
And between them lay two ingots of gold
    For whoever spoke straightest in judgment.

    Around the other city two armies
Of glittering soldiery were encamped.
Their leaders were at odds—should they   *550*
Move in for the kill or settle for a division
Of all the lovely wealth the citadel held fast?
The citizens wouldn't surrender, and armed
For an ambush. Their wives and little children
Were stationed on the wall, and with the old men   *555*
Held it against attack. The citizens moved out,
Led by Ares and Pallas Athena,
Both of them gold, and their clothing was gold,
Beautiful and larger than life in their armor, as befits
Gods in their glory, and all the people were smaller.   *560*
They came to a position perfect for an ambush,
A spot on the river where stock came to water,
And took their places, concealed by fiery bronze.
Farther up they had two lookouts posted
Waiting to sight shambling cattle and sheep,   *565*
Which soon came along, trailed by two herdsmen
Playing their panpipes, completely unsuspecting.
When the townsmen lying in ambush saw this
They ran up, cut off the herds of cattle and fleecy
Silver sheep, and killed the two herdsmen.   *570*
When the armies sitting in council got wind
Of the ruckus with the cattle, they mounted

Their high-stepping horses and galloped to the scene.
They took their stand and fought along the river banks,
Throwing bronze-tipped javelins against each other.   575
Among them were Hate and Din and the Angel of Death,
Holding a man just wounded, another unwounded,
And dragging one dead by his heels from the fray,
And the cloak on her shoulders was red with human blood.
They swayed in battle and fought like living men,   580
   And each side salvaged the bodies of their dead.

   On it he put a soft field, rich farmland
Wide and thrice-tilled, with many plowmen
Driving their teams up and down rows.
Whenever they came to the end of the field   585
And turned, a man would run up and hand them
A cup of sweet wine. Then they turned again
Back up the furrow pushing on through deep soil
To reach the other end. The field was black
Behind them, just as if plowed, and yet   590
   It was gold, all gold, forged to a wonder.

   On it he put land sectioned off for a king,
Where reapers with sharp sickles were working.
Cut grain lay deep where it fell in the furrow,
And binders made sheaves bound with straw bands.   595
Three sheaf-binders stood by, and behind them children
Gathered up armfuls and kept passing them on.
The king stood in silence near the line of reapers,
Holding his staff, and his heart was happy.
Under an oaktree nearby heralds were busy   600
Preparing a feast from an ox they had slaughtered
In sacrifice, and women were sprinkling it
   With abundant white barley for the reapers' dinner.

   On it he put a vineyard loaded with grapes,
Beautiful in gold. The clusters were dark,   605
And the vines were set everywhere on silver poles.
Around he inlaid a blue enamel ditch
And a fence of tin. A solitary path led to it,

And vintagers filed along it to harvest the grapes.
Girls, all grown up, and light-hearted boys   *610*
Carried the honey-sweet fruit in wicker baskets.
Among them a boy picked out on a lyre
A beguiling tune and sang the Linos song
In a low, light voice, and the harvesters
    Skipped in time and shouted the refrain.   *615*

    On it he made a herd of straight-horn cattle.
The cows were wrought of gold and tin
And rushed out mooing from the farmyard dung
To a pasture by the banks of a roaring river,
Making their way through swaying reeds.   *620*
Four golden herdsmen tended the cattle,
And nine nimble dogs followed along.
Two terrifying lions at the front of the herd
Were pulling down an ox. Its long bellows alerted
The dogs and the lads, who were running on up,   *625*
But the two lions had ripped the bull's hide apart
And were gulping down the guts and black blood.
The shepherds kept trying to set on the dogs,
But they shied away from biting the lions
    And stood there barking just out of harm's way.   *630*

    On it the renowned lame god made a pasture
In a lovely valley, wide, with silvery sheep in it,
    And stables, roofed huts, and stone animal pens.

    On it the renowned lame god embellished
A dancing ground, like the one Daedalus   *635*
Made for ringleted Ariadne in wide Cnossus.
Young men and girls in the prime of their beauty
Were dancing there, hands clasped around wrists.
The girls wore delicate linens, and the men
Finespun tunics glistening softly with oil.   *640*
Flowers crowned the girls' heads, and the men
Had golden knives hung from silver straps.
They ran on feet that knew how to run
With the greatest ease, like a potter's wheel

When he stoops to cup it in the palms of his hands   *645*
And gives it a spin to see how it runs. Then they
Would run in lines that weaved in and out.
A large crowd stood round the beguiling dance,
Enjoying themselves, and two acrobats
    Somersaulted among them on cue to the music.   *650*

On it he put the great strength of the River Ocean,
Lapping the outermost rim of the massive shield.

And when he had wrought the shield, huge and heavy,
He made a breastplate gleaming brighter than fire
And a durable helmet that fit close at the temples,   *655*
Lovely and intricate, and crested with gold.
And he wrought leg-armor out of pliant tin.
And when the renowned lame god had finished this gear,
He set it down before Achilles' mother,
And she took off like a hawk from snow-capped Olympus,   *660*
Carrying armor through the sky like summer lightning.

ILIAD 19

Dawn shrouded in saffron
Rose out of the deep water with light
For immortals and humans alike.
                                    And Thetis
Came to the ships with Hephaestus' gifts.   5
She found her son lying beside
His Patroclus, wailing,
And around him his many friends,
Mourning. The silvery goddess
Stood in their midst, took his hand,   10
Whispered his name, and said to him:

"Achilles, you must let him rest,
No matter our grief. This man was gentled
By the gods. But you, my son, my darling,
Take this glorious armor from Hephaestus,   15
So very beautiful, no man has ever worn
Anything like it."

                    She spoke,
And when she set the armor down before Achilles,
All of the metalwork clattered and chimed.   20
The Myrmidons shuddered, and to a man
Could not bear to look at it. But Achilles,
When he saw it, felt his rage seep
Deeper into his bones, and his lids narrowed
And lowered over eyes that glared   25
Like a white-hot steel flame. He turned
The polished weapons the god had given him
Over and over in his hands, and felt
Pangs of joy at all its intricate beauty.
And his words rose on wings   30
To meet his mother:
                    "My mother,

A god has given me these weapons—no
Mortal could have made them—and it is time
I arm myself in them. But I am afraid   *35*
For Patroclus, afraid that flies
Will infest his wounds and breed worms
In his body, now the life is gone,
And his flesh turn foul and rotten."

The silver-footed goddess answered: *40*

"Do not let that trouble you, child.
I will protect him from the swarming flies
That infest humans slain in war.
Even if he should lie out for a full year
His flesh would still be as firm, or better.   *45*
But call an assembly now. Renounce
Your rage against Agamemnon.
Arm yourself for war and put on your strength."

Saying this, she multiplied his heroic temper.
Then she dripped ambrosia and ruby nectar   *50*
Through Patroclus' nostrils, to keep his flesh firm.

And then Achilles went along the shore
Etched in sunlight, and shouted so loud
That not only the heroes came out, but all those too
Who had spent the war among the encamped ships,   *55*
All the pilots and oarsmen and stewards and cooks—
They all came to the assembly then, because Achilles,
Who had abstained a long time, was back.
Limping along were the two veterans,
Battle-scarred Diomedes and brilliant Odysseus,   *60*
Badly wounded, using their spears as crutches.
They came in and sat at the front of the assembly,
And behind them came the warlord, Agamemnon,
Wounded himself (that spear thrust by Coön,
Son of Antenor, in a hard-fought battle).   *65*
When all of the Greeks were gathered together,
Swift-footed Achilles rose and addressed them:

"Well, son of Atreus, are either of us better off
For this anger that has eaten our hearts away
Like acid, this bitter quarrel over a girl?   70
Artemis should have shot her aboard my ship
The day I pillaged Lyrnessus and took her.
Far fewer Greeks would have gone down in the dust
Under Trojan hands, while I nursed my grudge.
Hector and the Trojans are better off. But the Greeks?   75
I think they will remember our quarrel forever.
But we'll let all that be, no matter how it hurts,
And conquer our pride, because we must.
I hereby end my anger. There is no need for me
To rage relentlessly. But let's move quickly now   80
To get our troops back into battle
So I can confront the Trojans and test their will
To bivouac among our ships. They will more likely
Be thankful to rest their knees at day's end,
If any of them gets out of this alive."   85

He spoke, and the Greeks cheered.
Peleus' great son had renounced his rage.

[Lines 88–293 are omitted. Agamemnon and Achilles are reconciled.]

T he assembly broke up and the men scattered,
Each to his own ship. The Myrmidons got busy   295
With the gifts, bringing them to Achilles' ship.
They stored it all in his huts, left the women there,
And proudly drove the horses to the herd.

Briseis stood there like golden Aphrodite.

But when she saw Patroclus' mangled body   300
She threw herself upon him and wailed
In a high, piercing voice, and with her nails
She tore her breast and soft neck and lovely face.
And this woman, so like a goddess, cried in anguish:

"My poor Patroclus. You were so dear to me.   *305*
When I left this hut you were alive,
And now I find you, the army's leader, dead
When I come back. So it is for me always,
Evil upon evil. I have seen my husband,
The man my father and mother gave me to,   *310*
Mangled with sharp bronze before my city,
And my three brothers, all from the same mother,
Brothers I loved—they all died that day.
But you wouldn't let me cry when Achilles
Killed my husband and destroyed Mynes' city,   *315*
Wouldn't let me cry. You told me you'd make me
Achilles' bride, told me you'd take me on a ship
To Phthia, for a wedding among the Myrmidons.
I will never stop grieving for you, forever sweet."

Thus Briseis, and the women mourned with her,   *320*
For Patroclus, yes, but each woman also
For her own private sorrows.

                         Around Achilles
The Achaean elders gathered, begging him to eat,
But he refused them, groaning: *325*

                         "I beg you, my friends—
Aren't any of you listening? Don't keep asking me
To satisfy my heart with food or drink
Before it is time. My grief is too great.
I will stay as I am and endure until sunset."   *330*

And he waved them off. Only Atreus' two sons
Remained with him, along with Odysseus,
Nestor, and the old charioteer, Phoenix,
Trying to comfort him in his grief's extremity.
But he could not be comforted. His heart would ache   *335*
Until he lost himself in war's blood-stained mouth.
Memories welled up and caught in his throat:

"There was a time, my ill-fated, beloved friend,

You would serve me a fine dinner in this hut,
Deftly and quickly, while the army hurried   *340*
To bring war's sorrow to the horse-breaking Trojans.
Now you lie here a mangled corpse, and my heart
Fasts from the food and drink that are here
Out of grief for you. I could not suffer worse,
Not even if I learned my father were dead,   *345*
Who perhaps is weeping back in Phthia right now
Because he misses his son who is off fighting
On Trojan soil—for Helen, at whom we all shudder.
Not even if it were my son, Neoptolemus,
Who is being reared for me in Scyrus, if indeed   *350*
My dear child is still alive. I had hoped,
Until now, that I alone would perish at Troy,
And that you would return, and take my boy
In your swift black ship away from Scyrus
And show him all my things back home in Phthia.   *355*
For Peleus by now must be dead and gone,
Or if he does still live he draws his breath in pain,
Clinging to a shred of life and always expecting
The grim message that will tell him I am dead."

He wept, and the elders added their laments to his,   *360*
Each remembering what he had left at home.

Zeus saw them in their grief and, pitying them,
Spoke to Athena these feathered words:

"My child, have you deserted your warrior?
Do you no longer have any thought for Achilles?   *365*
He is mourning his friend, sitting there
In front of his upswept hulls. Everyone else
Has gone off to dinner, but he refuses to eat.
Go drip some nectar and savory ambrosia
Into his breast, so he will not weaken with hunger."   *370*

Athena needed no encouragement. She flew
From the crystal sky like a shrill raptor
And pounced on Achilles. The other Achaeans

Were busy arming for battle. Athena distilled
Nectar and ambrosia into Achilles' chest   375
So that grim hunger would not weaken his knees,
And then was gone, back to her father's house,
While the Greeks poured out from their beached ships.

> *Snow flurries can come so thick and fast*
> *From the cold northern sky that the wind*   380
> *That bears them becomes an icy, blinding glare.*

So too the gleaming, polished weaponry—
The helmets, shields, spears, and plated corselets—
All the bronze paraphernalia of war
That issued from the ships. The rising glare   385
Reflected off the coppery sky, and the land beneath
Laughed under the arcing metallic glow.
A deep bass thrumming rose from the marching feet.
And, like a bronze bolt in the center, Achilles,
Who now began to arm.   390
              His eyes glowed
Like white-hot steel, and he gritted his teeth
Against the grief that had sunk into his bones,
And every motion he made in putting on the armor
Forged for him in heaven was an act of passion   395
Directed against the Trojans: clasping on his shins
The greaves trimmed in silver at the ankles,
Strapping the corselet onto his chest, slinging
The silver-studded bronze sword around a shoulder,
And then lifting the massive, heavy shield   400
That spilled light around it as if it were the moon.

> *Or a fire that has flared up in a lonely settlement*
> *High in the hills of an island, reflecting light*
> *On the faces of men who have put out to sea*
> *And must watch helplessly as rising winds*   405
> *Bear them away from their dear ones.*

So too the terrible beauty of Achilles' shield,
A fire in the sky.

He lifted the helmet
And placed it on his head, and it shone like a star,   *410*
With the golden horsehair Hephaestus had set
Thickly on the crest rippling in waves.
He tested the fit and flex of the armor,
Sprinting on the sand, and found that the metal
Lifted him like wings. He pulled from its case   *415*
His father's spear, the massive, heavy
Spear that only Achilles could handle,
Made of Pelian ash, which the centaur Chiron
Had brought down from Mount Pelion and given
To Achilles' father to be the death of heroes.   *420*
Automedon and Alcimus harnessed the horses,
Cinched the leather straps, fit the bits in their jaws
And drew the reins back to the jointed chariot.
Automedon picked up the bright lash
And jumped into the car, and behind him   *425*
Achilles stepped in, shining in his war gear
Like an amber Sun, and in a cold voice
He cried to his father's horses:

"Xanthus and Balius, Podarge's famous colts,
See that you bring your charioteer back   *430*
Safe this time when we have had enough of war
And not leave him for dead, as you left Patroclus."
And from beneath the yoke Xanthus spoke back,
Hooves shimmering, his head bowed so low
That his mane swept the ground, as Hera,   *435*
The white-armed goddess, gave him a voice:

"This time we will save you, mighty Achilles,
This time—but your hour is near. We
Are not to blame, but a great god and strong Fate.
Nor was it slowness or slackness on our part   *440*
That allowed the Trojans to despoil Patroclus.
No, the best of gods, fair-haired Leto's son,
Killed him in the front lines and gave Hector the glory.
As for us, we could outrun the West Wind,

Book 20

Which men say is the swiftest, but it is your destiny   *445*
To be overpowered by a mortal and a god."

Xanthus said this; then the Furies stopped his voice.
And Achilles, greatly troubled, answered him:

"I don't need you to prophesy my death,
Xanthus. I know in my bones I will die here   *450*
Far from my father and mother. Still, I won't stop
Until I have made the Trojans sick of war."

And with a cry he drove his horses to the front.

ILIAD 20

While the Greeks armed themselves by their ships
Around you, Achilles, the vortex of war,
And while the Trojans waited for them on the high plain,
Zeus ordered Themis to call the gods to assembly.
She ranged far along Olympus' ridgeline,   *5*
Commanding them to come to the house of Zeus.
They all came—every last river (except Ocean)
And every last spirit-woman who ever haunted
A pretty copse, spring, or meadow—
They all came to the house of Zeus in the clouds   *10*
And sat in the stone colonnades that Hephaestus,
The master architect, had built for his father.
They were all inside when Poseidon came up
From the sea. Not even he could ignore
The goddess' call. He took a seat   *15*
In the middle and asked Zeus his purpose:

"Lord of Lightning,

Why have you assembled the gods?
Are you pondering the Greek-Trojan issue
Now that the fighting has flared up again?"   20

And Zeus, who masses the clouds:

"Earthshaker, you know my purpose.
I care for them, even though they die.
Even so, I will stay in a crevice of Olympus
And sit and watch and take my pleasure.   25
   The rest of you
Can go out among the Greeks and Trojans
And help whichever side you please.
If Achilles is the only one fighting out there,
The Trojans won't last a minute against him.   30
The very sight of him used to make them tremble,
And now he is in his passion. I fear
He may exceed his fate and demolish the wall."

With these words Zeus unleashed the war,
And the gods joined the battle on different sides.   35

On the Greek side were Hera and Pallas Athena,
And Poseidon Earthshaker and Hermes
The Helper, his mind sharp as needles,
And Hephaestus, who exuded strength
Though he limped along on his spindly legs.   40

The Trojans got Ares, his helmet flashing,
Apollo and the archer goddess Artemis,
Leto, Xanthus, and smiling Aphrodite.

As long as the gods had been on the sidelines,
The Greeks kept on winning: Achilles'   45
Reappearance after his absence from the war
Had reduced the Trojans to spineless jelly.
They quivered helplessly when they saw the hero
Glowing in metal like the War God himself.
But when the Olympians joined the human fray,   50

Strife, who drives armies on, lifted her head,
And Athena shouted, now by the trench,
Then long cries from the beach where the surf pounded in.
On the other side Ares responded,
Roaring to the Trojans like a dark whirlwind 55
On the city's height, then swooping down
Along the Simois' banks and across Callicolonê.

In this way the gods prompted the two armies
To clash in combat. Strife exploded in each camp.
Overhead, the Father of gods and men thundered, 60
And Poseidon shook all the ground underneath,
And the tremors climbed the steep mountain slopes.
Ida shuddered from her roots to her peaks,
Along with Troy herself and the Achaean ships.
And in the world below the Lord of the Shades, 65
Unseen Hades, leapt from his throne and shrieked,
Terrified that Poseidon would crack open the earth
And his halls would lie open to immortals and men,
The moldering horror loathed even by the gods.

Such was the force of the gods in collision. 70

       Opposite Lord Poseidon
Stood Phoebus Apollo with fletched arrows.
Taking on Ares was grey-eyed Athena.
Up against Hera went Apollo's sister,
Golden Artemis, the huntress with her bow. 75
Leto was countered by Hermes the Ally,
And against Hephaestus rolled the deep river
The gods call Xanthus, and men Scamander.

So god went up against god.

*[Lines 80–510 are omitted. Achilles, looking for Hector, faces off with
Aeneas, who is saved by Poseidon. Achilles then goes on a rampage, killing
fourteen Trojans in quick succession. Hector at first avoids Achilles, but
when Achilles kills his youngest brother, Polydorus, Hector faces Achilles.
Apollo intervenes and saves Hector from Achilles' spear.]*

> *Fire raging through a parched forest*
> *In a mountain valley, when the wind rises*
> *And spirals the flames in every direction*

Will give you some idea of Achilles' presence
As the black earth ran with blood.   515

> *A team of broad-browed oxen has been yoked*
> *And is now treading white barley*
> *On a solid threshing floor. It does not take long*
> *For the bellowing bulls to tread out the grain.*

So the hooves of Achilles' horses trampled   520
Dead bodies, shields. The chariot's axle
And rails were splashed with blood
Kicked up by the wheels and horses' hooves.
But the son of Peleus pressed on to glory,
His invincible hands spattered with gore.

ILIAD 21

When they came to the ford of Xanthus,
The eddying river that Zeus begot,
Achilles split the Trojans.

               Half he chased
Toward the city, across the plain where yesterday   5
The Greeks had fled from Hector's shining rage.
Hera, to slow this stampede of Trojans,
Spread a curtain of fog before them.

                    The others swerved—
And found themselves herded into the river.   10
They crashed down into the deep, silver water
As it tumbled and roared through its banks.
You could hear their screams as they floundered
And were whirled around in the eddies.

    Fire will sometimes cause a swarm of locusts   15
    To rise in the air and fly to a river. The fire
    Keeps coming, burning them instantly,
    And the insects shrink down into the water.

Just so Achilles. And Xanthus' noisy channel
Was clogged with chariots, horses, and men.   20

Achilles wasted no time. Leaving his spear
Propped against a tamarisk
And holding only his sword, he leapt from the bank
Like a spirit from hell bent on slaughter.
He struck over and over, in a widening spiral.   25
Hideous groans rose from the wounded,
And the river water turned crimson with blood.

    Fish fleeing a dolphin's huge maw

Hide by the hundreds in the harbor's crannies,
But the dolphin devours whatever it catches.   30

Likewise the Trojans beneath the river banks.

When Achilles' hands were sore from killing,
He culled twelve boys live from the river
To pay for the blood of dead Patroclus.
They were dazed as fawns when he led them out,   35
Their hands bound behind them with the leather belts
They had been wearing around their corded tunics.
Achilles' men led them back to the ships
And Achilles returned to his killing frenzy.

On the way back he met a son of Priam,   40
Lycaon by name, running from the river.
This boy Achilles had captured once before
In his father's orchard, where he had come one night
To cut fig saplings for chariot rails
But found Achilles' iron mask in his face.   45
That time Achilles sold him, for a good price,
To Jason's son on Lemnos, where he had shipped him.
A family friend, Eëtion of Imbros, had ransomed him
For even more money and sent him to Arisbe.
From there he managed to make his way home.   50
For eleven days he celebrated with friends
His escape from Lemnos. On the twelfth day Zeus
Gave him back to Achilles, who would send him now
Off again against his will, this time to Hades.
He was all but naked when Achilles noticed him,   55
Having discarded helmet, spear, and shield
Because they made him sweat as he clambered
Up from the river, and his knees were giving out.
Achilles was indignant and said to himself:

"What's this I see? The Trojan princes I've killed   60
Are going to start rising from the moldering gloom,
Judging from how this one has escaped his fate
After being shipped off to Lemnos and sold.

All that grey sea couldn't keep him back.
Let's give him a taste of my spearhead 65
And see whether he comes back from that
Or stays put in the teeming earth."

And he waited. Lycaon aproached in a daze,
Intent on grasping his knees. All he wanted
Was to wriggle away from death and black fate. 70
All Achilles wanted was to run him through.
His spear flashed out, but Lycaon, stooping
To touch his knees, ducked under it. The spear
Passed over his back and stuck in the earth,
Quivering with desire for a man's flesh. 75
Lycaon caught Achilles' knees with one hand
And held the pointed spear with the other
And would not let go of either as he begged:

"I am at your knees, Achilles. Pity me.
You have to respect me as your suppliant 80
For I tasted Demeter's holy grain with you
On that day you took me captive in the orchard
And sent me far from my father and friends,
Sold into sacred Lemnos for a hundred oxen.
I ransomed myself for three times that. This morning 85
Was my twelfth since getting back to Ilion
After many hard turns. And now Fate
Has put me in your hands again. Father Zeus
Must hate me to give me to you twice.
My mother bore me for a shortened life, 90
Laothoë, old Altes' daughter, Altes,
Lord of the Leleges, whose stronghold
Is steep Pedasus on the Satnioeis.
Priam had his daughter as one of his wives,
And we're her two sons, and you'll butcher us both. 95
Godlike Polydorus you've already killed,
Got him with your spear as he led the charge.
And now this is it for me. I doubt I can escape,
Since it was some god who put me in your hands.
But I'll say this too, and you can think it over: 100

Don't kill me, since I'm not from the same womb
As Hector, who killed your gentle, valiant friend."

Priam's glorious son spoke words of entreaty,
But heard a voice without a trace of softness say:

"Shut up, fool, and stop talking ransom.   105
Before Patroclus met his destiny
It was more to my taste to spare Trojan lives,
Capture them, and sell them overseas.
But now they all die, every last Trojan
God puts into my hands before Ilion's walls,   110
All of them, and especially Priam's children.
You die too, friend. Don't take it hard.
Patroclus died, and he was far better than you.
Take a look at me. Do you see how huge I am,
How beautiful? I have a noble father,   115
My mother was a goddess, but I too
Am in death's shadow. There will come a time,
Some dawn or evening or noon in this war,
When someone will take my life from me
With a spear thrust or an arrow from a string."   120

He spoke. Lycaon's knees and heart went slack.
He let go the spear and sat there, both hands
Outstretched. Achilles drew his honed sword
And struck near the collar bone. The whole blade
Sank into his trunk, and he fell prone to the ground,   125
Black blood trickling out and wetting the dirt.
Achilles slung him into the river by his foot
And crowed over him as the current bore him off:

"Lie there with the fish. They will lick the blood
From your wound, your cold funeral rites. Your mother   130
Will not lay you on a bier and lament. No,
Eddying Scamander will roll you out to sea,
And fish will dart up under the black ripples
And nibble at Lycaon's shining fat.
All of you Trojans will die like that,   135

Die all the way back to Troy's sacred town
As I whittle you down from behind!
Your river won't help you with his silver eddies,
The water you've sanctified no doubt with bulls
And with live horses thrown into his pools.   *140*
No, you'll all die, die ugly deaths, until you have paid
For the Greeks' loss, for Patroclus dead,
Killed by the ships while I was away."

As he spoke the river roiled in wrath
And pondered how to foil Achilles' efforts   *145*
And save the Trojans from this pestilence.

*[Lines 147–542 are omitted. The River Xanthus rises in rage against Achilles
and nearly overwhelms him. Hera has Hephaestus fight the river with fire,
and the river god begs for mercy. The gods battle each other. Achilles con-
tinues on to Troy.]*

Old Priam stood on Troy's sacred wall.
He saw Achilles as a prodigious force
Before whom the Trojans were being driven   *545*
Helplessly. Groaning, he climbed down to the ground
And called to the gatekeepers along the wall:

"Hold the gates wide open until the army
Can run inside the city. Achilles is here
Driving them on, and I fear the worst.   *550*
When they are all inside and can rest,
Close the double doors tight. I dread the thought
Of that monster leaping inside the wall."

He spoke, they thrust back the bars,
And light poured from the gates. Apollo   *555*
Leapt out to keep Achilles from Troy.

The Trojans were streaming toward the city's high walls,
Parched with thirst and white with dust from the plain,
With Achilles at their backs with his spear,

Maniacal in his rage and lust for glory.   560

The Greeks would have taken Troy right then
Had not Apollo lifted Antenor's son,
Agenor, to one bright, peerless moment.
He put into his heart the fortitude
To defend himself from Death's heavy hands,   565
Then stood nearby, leaning on the oak tree
And enfolded in mist.

[Lines 568–623 are omitted. Agenor faces Achilles.]

Then, with a ruse, Apollo got the son of Peleus
Away from the Trojan army. Likening himself   625
To Agenor in every detail, he stood
Just before Achilles, who gave chase,
Pursuing him across the plain, then turning him
Along the banks of the swirling Scamander.
All the while Apollo, beguiling him,   630
Stayed just out of reach, and Achilles,
With his footspeed, thought he would catch him.

This bought time for the panicked Trojans
To swarm gratefully into the city.
They no longer had the will to wait for each other   635
Outside the city walls to see who had made it
And who had died in battle. Everyone
Whose legs could carry him stampeded in.

ILIAD 22

Everywhere you looked in Troy, exhausted
Soldiers, glazed with sweat like winded deer,
Leaned on the walls, cooling down
And slaking their thirst.

Outside, the Greeks   5

Formed up close to the wall, locking their shields.
In the dead air between the Greeks
And Troy's Western Gate, Destiny
Had Hector pinned, waiting for death.

Then Apollo called back to Achilles: 10

"Son of Peleus, you're fast on your feet,
But you'll never catch me, man chasing god.
Or are you too raging mad to notice
I'm a god? Don't you care about fighting
The Trojans any more? You've chased them back   15
Into their town, but now you've veered off here.
You'll never kill me. You don't hold my doom."

And the shining sprinter, Achilles:

"That was a dirty trick, Apollo,
Turning me away from the wall like that!   20
I could have ground half of Troy face down
In the dirt! Now you've robbed me
Of my glory and saved them easily
Because you have no retribution to fear.
I swear, I'd make you pay if I could!"   25

His mind opened to the clear space before him,
And he was off toward the town, moving

Like a thoroughbred stretching it out
Over the plain for the final sprint home—

Achilles, lifting his knees as he lengthened his stride.   30

Priam saw him first, with his old man's eyes,
A single point of light on Troy's dusty plain.

> *Sirius rises late in the dark, liquid sky*
> *On summer nights, star of stars,*
> *Orion's Dog they call it, brightest*   35
> *Of all, but an evil portent, bringing heat*
> *And fevers to suffering humanity.*

Achilles' bronze gleamed like this as he ran.

And the old man groaned, and beat his head
With his hands, and stretched out his arms   40
To his beloved son, Hector, who had
Taken his stand before the Western Gate,
Determined to meet Achilles in combat.

Priam's voice cracked as he pleaded:

"Hector, my boy, you can't face Achilles   45
Alone like that, without any support—
You'll go down in a minute. He's too much
For you, son, he won't stop at anything!
O, if only the gods loved him as I do:
Vultures and dogs would be gnawing his corpse.   50
Then some grief might pass from my heart.
So many fine sons he's taken from me,
Killed or sold them as slaves in the islands.
Two of them now, Lycaon and Polydorus,
I can't see with the Trojans safe in town,   55
Laothoë's boys. If the Greeks have them
We'll ransom them with the gold and silver
Old Altes gave us. But if they're dead
And gone down to Hades, there will be grief
For myself and the mother who bore them.   60
The rest of the people won't mourn so much
Unless *you* go down at Achilles' hands.

So come inside the wall, my boy.
Live to save the men and women of Troy.
Don't just hand Achilles the glory   65
And throw your life away. Show some pity for me
Before I go out of my mind with grief
And Zeus finally destroys me in my old age,
After I have seen all the horrors of war—
My sons butchered, my daughters dragged off,   70
Raped, bedchambers plundered, infants
Dashed to the ground in this terrible war,
My sons' wives abused by murderous Greeks.
And one day some Greek soldier will stick me
With cold bronze and draw the life from my limbs,   75
And the dogs that I fed at my table,
My watchdogs, will drag me outside and eat
My flesh raw, crouched in my doorway, lapping
My blood.
            When a young man is killed in war,   80
Even though his body is slashed with bronze,
He lies there beautiful in death, noble.
But when the dogs maraud an old man's head,
Griming his white hair and beard and private parts,
There's no human fate more pitiable."   85

And the old man pulled the white hair from his head,
But did not persuade Hector.

                        His mother then,
Wailing, sobbing, laid open her bosom
And holding out a breast spoke through her tears: 90

"Hector, my child, if ever I've soothed you
With this breast, remember it now, son, and
Have pity on me. Don't pit yourself
Against that madman. Come inside the wall.
If Achilles kills you I will never   95
Get to mourn you laid out on a bier, O
My sweet blossom, nor will Andromache,
Your beautiful wife, but far from us both

Dogs will eat your body by the Greek ships."

So the two of them pleaded with their son,   100
But did not persuade him or touch his heart.
Hector held his ground as Achilles' bulk
Loomed larger. He waited as a snake waits,

> *Tense and coiled*
> *As a man approaches*   105
> *Its lair in the mountains,*
> *Venom in its fangs*
> *And poison in its heart,*
> *Glittering eyes*
> *Glaring from the rocks:*   110

So Hector waited, leaning his polished shield
Against one of the towers in Troy's bulging wall,
But his heart was troubled with brooding thoughts:

"Now what? If I take cover inside,
Polydamas will be the first to reproach me.   115
He begged me to lead the Trojans back
To the city on that black night when Achilles rose.
But I wouldn't listen, and now I've destroyed
Half the army through my recklessness.
I can't face the Trojan men and women now,   120
Can't bear to hear some lesser man say,
'Hector trusted his strength and lost the army.'
That's what they'll say. I'll be much better off
Facing Achilles, either killing him
Or dying honorably before the city.   125
    But what if I lay down all my weapons,
Bossed shield, heavy helmet, prop my spear
Against the wall, and go meet Achilles,
Promise him we'll surrender Helen
And everything Paris brought back with her   130
In his ships' holds to Troy—that was the beginning
Of this war—give all of it back
To the sons of Atreus and divide

Everything else in the town with the Greeks,
And swear a great oath not to hold   *135*
Anything back, but share it all equally,
All the treasure in Troy's citadel.
    But why am I talking to myself like this?
I can't go out there unarmed. Achilles
Will cut me down in cold blood if I take off   *140*
My armor and go out to meet him
Naked like a woman. This is no time
For talking, the way a boy and a girl
Whisper to each other from oak tree or rock,
A boy and a girl with all their sweet talk.   *145*
Better to lock up in mortal combat
As soon as possible and see to whom
God on Olympus grants the victory."

Thus Hector.
                And Achilles closed in   *150*
Like the helmeted God of War himself,
The ash-wood spear above his right shoulder
Rocking in the light that played from his bronze
In gleams of fire and the rising sun.
And when Hector saw it he lost his nerve,   *155*
Panicked, and ran, leaving the gates behind,
With Achilles on his tail, confident in his speed.

> *You have seen a falcon*
> *In a long, smooth dive*
> *Attack a fluttering dove*   *160*
> *Far below in the hills.*
> *The falcon screams,*
> *Swoops, and plunges*
> *In its lust for prey.*

So Achilles swooped and Hector trembled   *165*
In the shadow of Troy's wall.
                        Running hard,
They passed Lookout Rock and the windy fig tree,
Following the loop of the wagon road.

They came to the wellsprings of eddying   *170*
Scamander, two beautiful pools, one
Boiling hot with steam rising up,
The other flowing cold even in summer,
Cold as freezing sleet, cold as tundra snow.
There were broad basins there, lined with stone,   *175*
Where the Trojan women used to wash their silky clothes
In the days of peace, before the Greeks came.

They ran by these springs, pursuer and pursued—
A great man out front, a far greater behind—
And they ran all out. This was not a race   *180*
For such a prize as athletes compete for,
An oxhide or animal for sacrifice, but a race
For the lifeblood of Hector, breaker of horses.

> *But champion horses wheeling round the course,*
> *Hooves flying, pouring it on in a race for a prize—*   *185*
> *A woman or tripod—at a hero's funeral games*

Will give you some idea of how these heroes looked
As they circled Priam's town three times running
    While all the gods looked on.

Zeus, the gods' father and ours, spoke: *190*

"I do not like what I see, a man close
To my heart chased down around Troy's wall.
Hector has burned many an ox's thigh
To me, both on Ida's peaks and in the city's
High holy places, and now Achilles   *195*
Is running him down around Priam's town.
Think you now, gods, and take counsel whether
We should save him from death or deliver him
Into Achilles' hands, good man though he be."

The grey-eyed goddess Athena answered: *200*

    "O Father,
You may be the Lord of Lightning and the Dark Cloud,

But what a thing to say, to save a mortal man,
With his fate already fixed, from rattling death!
Do it. But don't expect us all to approve."   *205*

Zeus loomed like a thunderhead, but answered gently:

"There, there, daughter, my heart wasn't in it.
I did not mean to displease you, my child. Go now,
Do what you have in mind without delay."

Athena had been longing for action   *210*
And at his word shot down from Olympus,
As Achilles bore down on Hector.

> *A hunting hound starts a fawn in the hills,*
> *Follows it through brakes and hollows,*
> *And if it hides in a thicket, circles,*   *215*
> *Picks up the trail, and renews the chase.*

No more could Hector elude Achilles.
Every time Hector surged for the Western Gate
Under the massive towers, hoping for
Trojan archers to give him some cover,   *220*
Achilles cut him off and turned him back
Toward the plain, keeping the inside track.

> *Running in a dream, you can't catch up,*
> *You can't catch up and you can't get away.*

No more could Achilles catch Hector   *225*
Or Hector escape.
               And how could Hector
Have ever escaped death's black birds
If Apollo had not stood by his side
This one last time and put life in his knees?   *230*

Achilles shook his head at his soldiers:
He would not allow anyone to shoot
At Hector and win glory with a hit,
Leaving him only to finish him off.

But when they reached the springs the fourth time,   *235*
Father Zeus stretched out his golden scales
And placed on them two agonizing deaths,
One for Achilles and one for Hector.
When he held the beam, Hector's doom sank down
Toward Hades. And Phoebus Apollo left him.   *240*

By now the grey-eyed goddess Athena
Was at Achilles' side, and her words flew fast:

"There's nothing but glory on the beachhead
For us now, my splendid Achilles,
Once we take Hector out of action, and   *245*
There's no way he can escape us now,
Not even if my brother Apollo has a fit
And rolls on the ground before the Almighty.
You stay here and catch your breath while I go
To persuade the man to put up a fight."   *250*

Welcome words for Achilles. He rested,
Leaning on his heavy ash and bronze spear,
While the goddess made her way to Hector,
The spitting image of Deïphobus.
And her voice sounded like his as she said: *255*

"Achilles is pushing you hard, brother,
In this long footrace around Priam's town.
Why don't we stand here and give him a fight?"

Hector's helmet flashed as he turned and said:

"Deïphobus, you've always been my favorite   *260*
Brother, and again you've shown me why,
Having the courage to come out for me,
Leaving the safety of the wall, while all
Priam's other sons are cowering inside."

And Athena, her eyes as grey as winter moons: *265*

"Mother and father begged me by my knees
To stay inside, and so did all my friends.
That's how frightened they are, Hector. But I
Could not bear the pain in my heart, brother.
Now let's get tough and fight and not spare   270
Any spears. Either Achilles kills us both
And drags our blood-soaked gear to the ships,
Or he goes down with your spear in his guts."

That's how Athena led him on, with guile.
And when the two heroes faced each other,   275
Great Hector, helmet shining, spoke first:

"I'm not running any more, Achilles.
Three times around the city was enough.
I've got my nerve back. It's me or you now.
But first we should swear a solemn oath.   280
With all the gods as witnesses, I swear:
If Zeus gives me the victory over you,
I will not dishonor your corpse, only
Strip the armor and give the body back
To the Greeks. Promise you'll do the same."   285

And Achilles, fixing his eyes on him:

"Don't try to cut any deals with me, Hector.
Do lions make peace treaties with men?
Do wolves and lambs agree to get along?
No, they hate each other to the core,   290
And that's how it is between you and me,
No talk of agreements until one of us
Falls and gluts Ares with his blood.
By God, you'd better remember everything
You ever knew about fighting with spears.   295
But you're as good as dead. Pallas Athena
And my spear will make you pay in a lump
For the agony you've caused by killing my friends."

With that he pumped his spear arm and let fly.

Hector saw the long flare the javelin made, and ducked.   *300*
The bronze point sheared the air over his head
And rammed into the earth. But Athena
Pulled it out and gave it back to Achilles
Without Hector noticing. And Hector,
Prince of Troy, taunted Achilles: *305*

"Ha! You missed! Godlike Achilles! It looks like
You didn't have my number after all.
You said you did, but you were just trying
To scare me with big words and empty talk.
Did you think I'd run and you'd plant a spear   *310*
In my back? It'll take a direct hit in my chest,
Coming right at you, that and a god's help too.
Now see if you can dodge this piece of bronze.
Swallow it whole! The war will be much easier
On the Trojans with you dead and gone."   *315*

And Hector let his heavy javelin fly,
A good throw, too, hitting Achilles' shield
Dead center, but it only rebounded away.
Angry that his throw was wasted, Hector
Fumbled about for a moment, reaching   *320*
For another spear. He shouted to Deïphobus,
But Deïphobus was nowhere in sight.
It was then that Hector knew in his heart
What had happened, and said to himself:

"I hear the gods calling me to my death.   *325*
I thought I had a good man here with me,
Deïphobus, but he's still on the wall.
Athena tricked me. Death is closing in
And there's no escape. Zeus and Apollo
Must have chosen this long ago, even though   *330*
They used to be on my side. My fate is here,
But I will not perish without some great deed
That future generations will remember."

And he drew the sharp broadsword that hung

By his side and gathered himself for a charge.   *335*

   A high-flying eagle dives
   Through ebony clouds down
   To the sun-scutched plain to claw
   A lamb or a quivering hare.

Thus Hector's charge, and the light   *340*
That played from his blade's honed edge.

Opposite him, Achilles exploded forward, fury
Incarnate behind the curve of his shield,
A glory of metalwork, and the plumes
Nodded and rippled on his helmet's crest,   *345*
Thick golden horsehair set by Hephaestus,
And his spearpoint glinted like the Evening Star

   In the gloom of night,
   Star of perfect splendor,

A gleam in the air as Achilles poised   *350*
His spear with murderous aim at Hector,
Eyes boring into the beautiful skin,
Searching for the weak spot. Hector's body
Was encased in the glowing bronze armor
He had stripped from the fallen Patroclus,   *355*
But where the collarbones join at the neck
The gullet offered swift and certain death.
It was there Achilles drove his spear through
As Hector charged. The heavy bronze apex
Pierced the soft neck but did not slit the windpipe,   *360*
So that Hector could speak still.
He fell back in the dust.

         And Achilles exulted:

"So you thought you could get away with it
Didn't you, Hector? Killing Patroclus   *365*
And ripping off his armor, *my* armor,
Thinking I was too far away to matter.

You fool. His avenger was far greater—
And far closer—than you could imagine,
Biding his time back in our beachhead camp.   *370*
And now I have laid you out on the ground.
Dogs and birds are going to draw out your guts
While the Greeks give Patroclus burial."

And Hector, barely able to shake the words out:

"I beg you, Achilles, by your own soul   *375*
And by your parents, do not
Allow the dogs to mutilate my body
By the Greek ships. Accept the gold and bronze
Ransom my father and mother will give you
And send my body back home to be burned   *380*
In honor by the Trojans and their wives."

And Achilles, fixing him with a stare:

"Don't whine to me about my parents,
You dog! I wish my stomach would let me
Cut off your flesh in strips and eat it raw   *385*
For what you've done to me. There is no one
And no way to keep the dogs off your head,
Not even if they bring ten or twenty
Ransoms, pile them up here and promise more,
Not even if Dardanian Priam weighs your body   *390*
Out in gold, not even then will your mother
Ever get to mourn you laid out on a bier.
No, dogs and birds will eat every last scrap."

Helmet shining, Hector spoke his last words:

"So this is Achilles. There was no way   *395*
To persuade you. Your heart is a lump
Of iron. But the gods will not forget this,
And I will have my vengeance on that day
When Paris and Apollo destroy you
In the long shadow of Troy's Western Gate."   *400*

Death's veil covered him as he said these things,
And his soul, bound for Hades, fluttered out
Resentfully, forsaking manhood's bloom.

He was dead when Achilles spoke to him:

"Die and be done with it. As for my fate,   *405*
I'll accept it whenever Zeus sends it."

And he drew the bronze spear out of the corpse,
Laid it aside, then stripped off the blood-stained armor.
The other Greeks crowded around
And could not help but admire Hector's   *410*
Beautiful body, but still they stood there
Stabbing their spears into him, smirking.

"Hector's a lot softer to the touch now
Than he was when he was burning our ships,"

One of them would say, pulling out his spear.   *415*

After Achilles had stripped the body
He rose like a god and addressed the Greeks:

"Friends, Argive commanders and counsellors,
The gods have granted us this man's defeat,
Who did us more harm than all the rest   *420*
Put together. What do you say we try
Laying a close siege on the city now
So we can see what the Trojans intend—
Whether they will give up the citadel
With Hector dead, or resolve to fight on?   *425*
    But what am I thinking of? Patroclus' body
Still lies by the ships, unmourned, unburied,
Patroclus, whom I will never forget
As long as I am among the living,
Until I rise no more; and even if   *430*
In Hades the dead do not remember,
Even there I will remember my dear friend.

Now let us chant the victory paean, sons
Of the Achaeans, and march back to our ships
With this hero in tow. The power and the glory   *435*
Are ours. We have killed great Hector,
Whom all the Trojans honored as a god."

But it was shame and defilement Achilles
Had in mind for Hector. He pierced the tendons
Above the heels and cinched them with leather thongs   *440*
To his chariot, letting Hector's head drag.
He mounted, hoisted up the prize armor,
And whipped his team to a willing gallop
Across the plain. A cloud of dust rose
Where Hector was hauled, and the long black hair   *445*
Fanned out from his head, so beautiful once,
As it trailed in the dust. In this way Zeus
Delivered Hector into his enemies' hands
To be defiled in his own native land.

Watching this from the wall, Hector's mother   *450*
Tore off her shining veil and screamed,
And his old father groaned pitifully,
And all through town the people were convulsed
With lamentation, as if Troy itself,
The whole towering city, were in flames.   *455*
They were barely able to restrain
The old man, frantic to run through the gates,
Imploring them all, rolling in the dung,
And finally making this desperate appeal:

"Please let me go, alone, to the Greek ships.   *460*
I don't care if you're worried. I want to see
If that monster will respect my age, pity me
For the sake of his own father, Peleus,
Who is about my age, old Peleus
Who bore him and bred him to be a curse   *465*
For the Trojans, but he's caused me more pain
Than anyone, so many of my sons,
Beautiful boys, he's killed. I miss them all,

But I miss Hector more than all of them.
My grief for him will lay me in the earth.   *470*
Hector! You should have died in my arms, son!
Then we could have satisfied our sorrow,
Mourning and weeping, your mother and I."

The townsmen moaned as Priam was speaking.
Then Hecuba raised the women's lament: *475*

"Hector, my son, I am desolate!
How can I live with suffering like this,
With you dead? You were the only comfort
I had, day and night, wherever you were
In the town, and you were the only hope   *480*
For Troy's men and women. They honored you
As a god when you were alive, Hector.
Now death and doom have overtaken you."

   And all this time Andromache had heard
Nothing about Hector—news had not reached her   *485*
That her husband was caught outside the walls.
She was working the loom in an alcove
Of the great hall, embroidering flowers
Into a purple cloak, and had just called
To her serving women, ordering them   *490*
To put a large cauldron on the fire, so
A steaming bath would be ready for Hector
When he came home from battle. Poor woman,
She had little idea how far from warm baths
Hector was, undone by the Grey-Eyed One   *495*
And delivered into the hands of the Greeks.

Then she heard the lamentation from the tower.

She trembled, and the shuttle fell
To the floor. Again she called her women:

"Two of you come with me. I must see   *500*
What has happened. That was Hecuba's voice.

My heart is in my throat, my knees are like ice.
Something terrible has happened to one
Of Priam's sons. O God, I'm afraid
Achilles has cut off my brave Hector   505
Alone on the plain outside the city
And has put an end to my husband's
Cruel courage. Hector never held back
Safe in the ranks; he always charged ahead,
Second to no one in fighting spirit."   510

With these words on her lips Andromache
Ran outdoors like a madwoman, heart racing,
Her two waiting-women following behind.
She reached the tower, pushed through the crowd,
And looking out from the wall saw her husband   515
As the horses dragged him disdainfully
Away from the city to the hollow Greek ships.

Black night swept over her eyes.
She reeled backward, gasping, and her veil
And glittering headbands flew off,   520
And the diadem golden Aphrodite
Gave her on that day when tall-helmed Hector
Led her from her father's house in marriage.
And now her womenfolk were around her,
Hector's sisters and his brother's wives,   525
Holding her as she raved madly for death,
Until she caught her breath and her distraught
Spirit returned to her breast. She moaned then
And, surrounded by Trojan women, spoke:

"Hector, you and I have come to the grief   530
We were both born for, you in Priam's Troy
And I in Thebes in the house of Eëtion
Who raised me there beneath wooded Plakos
Under an evil star. Better never to have been born.
And now you are going to Hades' dark world,   535
Underground, leaving me in sorrow,
A widow in the halls, with an infant,

The son you and I bore but cannot bless.
You can't help him now you are dead, Hector,
And he can never help you. Even if   *540*
He lives through this unbearable war,
There's nothing left for him in life but pain
And deprivation, all his property
Lost to others. An orphan has no friends.
He hangs his head, his cheeks are wet with tears.   *545*
He has to beg from his dead father's friends,
Tugging on one man's cloak, another's tunic,
And if they pity him he gets to sip
From someone's cup, just enough to moisten
His lips but not enough to quench his thirst.   *550*
Or a child with both parents still alive
Will push him away from a feast, taunting him,
'Go away, your father doesn't eat with us.'
And the boy will go to his widowed mother
In tears, Astyanax, who used to sit   *555*
In his father's lap and eat nothing but
Mutton and marrow. When he got sleepy
And tired of playing he would take a nap
In a soft bed nestled in his nurse's arms
His dreaming head filled with blossoming joy.   *560*
But now he'll suffer, now he's lost his father.
The Trojans called him Astyanax
Because you alone were Troy's defender,
You alone protected their walls and gates.
Now you lie by the curved prows of the ships,   *565*
Far from your parents. The dogs will glut
On your naked body, and shiny maggots
Will eat what's left.
                    Your clothes are stored away,
Beautiful, fine clothes made by women's hands—   *570*
I'll burn them all now in a blazing fire.
They're no use to you, you'll never lie
On the pyre in them. Burning them will be
Your glory before Trojan men and women."

And the women's moans came in over her lament.   *575*

ILIAD 23

While the Trojans lamented throughout the city,
The Greeks came to their beachhead camp
On the Hellespont and dispersed, each man
To his own ship.
     But Achilles   5
Did not dismiss the Myrmidons.
He addressed his troops, men who lived for war:

"Myrmidons! I know you love your horses,
But before we unhitch them from the chariots
Let us all stay in armor and drive up close   10
And weep for Patroclus. We owe it to the dead.
After we've indulged in grief and sorrow
We can loosen our horses and eat together."

He spoke, and led them in their lamentation.
Three times they drove their horses round the corpse,   15
Wailing as they went. Thetis was with them,
And she honed their desire for grief. The sand
Was wet, and the warriors' armor, wet with tears.
They missed him. God, how he could fight!
Achilles' voice rose through their choked sobbing,   20
As he placed his man-slaying hands on his friend's breast:

"I hail you, Patroclus, even in Hades!
I am fulfilling all that I promised before,
To drag Hector here and feed him raw to the dogs,
And to cut the throats of twelve fine Trojan boys   25
Before your pyre, in my rage at your murder."

He spoke, and treated glorious Hector foully,
Stretching him out in the dust before the bier
Of Menoetius' son.

      The men took off their armor,   30
Bronze gleaming in the dusk, and unhitched

Their whinnying horses, and sat down by the ship
Of Aeacus' swift grandson, too many to count.
And he made a funeral feast to satisfy their hearts.
Many sleek bulls bellowed beneath the knife   35
As they were slaughtered, many sheep, bleating goats,
And white-tusked boars, rich with fat,
Were skewered to roast over the fire's flame.
The ground around the corpse ran cup-deep with blood.

The other Greek leaders had come for Achilles   40
And were now escorting him to Agamemnon.
It had not been easy to convince him to come—
His heart raged for his friend. When they reached
Agamemnon's hut, they ordered the heralds
To put a cauldron on the fire, hoping to persuade   45
Achilles to bathe and wash off the gore.
He refused outright and swore this oath:

"By Zeus on high, there will not be
Any washing of my head until I have laid
Patroclus on the fire, and heaped his barrow,   50
And shorn my hair, for never will I grieve
Like this again, while I am among the living.
Now let's force ourselves to eat this feast.
But at the break of dawn, Agamemnon,
Order your men to bring wood and make ready   55
All that is fit for a dead man to have
When he goes beneath the murky gloom,
So that the fire may burn him quickly out of sight
And the men return to what they have to do."

He spoke, they listened, and they did as he said.   60
They prepared a meal and each man feasted,
And when they all had enough of food and drink,
They went to their huts and took their rest.
But the son of Peleus lay groaning heavily
Among his Myrmidons on the open beach   65
Where the waves crashed and seethed.
When sleep finally took him, unknotting his heart

And enveloping his shining limbs—so fatigued
From chasing Hector to windy Ilion—
Patroclus' sad spirit came, with his same form   70
And with his beautiful eyes and his voice
And wearing the same clothes. He stood
Above Achilles' head, and said to him:

"You're asleep and have forgotten me, Achilles.
You never neglected me when I was alive,   75
But now, when I am dead! Bury me quickly
So I may pass through Hades' gates.
The spirits keep me at a distance, the phantoms
Of men outworn, and will not yet allow me
To join them beyond the River. I wander   80
Aimlessly through Hades' wide-doored house.
And give me your hand, for never again
Will I come back from Hades, once you burn me
In my share of fire. Never more in life
Shall we sit apart from our comrades and talk.   85
The Fate I was born to has swallowed me,
And it is your destiny, though you are like the gods,
Achilles, to die beneath the wall of Troy.
And one thing more, Achilles. Do not lay my bones
Apart from yours, but let them lie together,   90
Just as we were reared together in your house
After Menoetius brought me, still just a boy,
From Opoeis to your land because I had killed
Amphidamas' son on that day we played dice
And I foolishly became angry. I didn't mean to.   95
Peleus took me into his house then and reared me
With kindness, and he named me your comrade.
So let one coffer enfold the bones of us both,
The two-handled gold one your mother gave you."

And Achilles answered him, saying: 100

"Why have you come to me here, dear heart,
With all these instructions? I promise you
I will do everything just as you ask.

But come closer. Let us give in to grief,
However briefly, in each other's arms."   *105*

Saying this, Achilles reached out with his hands
But could not touch him. His spirit vanished like smoke,
Gone under the earth, with a last, shrill cry.
Awestruck, Achilles leapt up, clapping
His palms together, and said lamenting: *110*

"Ah, so there is something in Death's house,
A phantom spirit, although not in a body.
All night long poor Patroclus' spirit
Stood over me, weeping and wailing,
And giving me detailed instructions   *115*
About everything. He looked so like himself."

His words aroused in them a longing for grief,
And they were still wailing around the corpse
When Dawn's roselight touched them.

                              Then Lord Agamemnon   *120*
Sent out from all over the camp a contingent
Of mules and men to gather wood,
Putting a good man in charge, Meriones,
Idomeneus' henchman. The men went out
With axes and ropes, and the mules before them,   *125*
Upward, downward, sideways, and slantwise,
Until they came to the spurs of spring-dotted Ida.
There they set to work felling high-crowned oaks
With bronze axes. The trees kept crashing down.
They split the trunks and bound them together   *130*
Behind the mules, who tore up the ground
As they tramped through underbrush toward the plain.
Meriones ordered the whole crew of woodcutters
To carry back logs, and they cast them down
On the shore in order, where Achilles planned   *135*
A great mound for Patroclus and for himself.

When they had laid out an immense amount of wood,

The crowd sat down and waited. Then Achilles
Ordered the Myrmidons to put on their armor
And yoke the horses to the chariots. They armed   *140*
And mounted, charioteers and warriors both,
And the chariots rolled out, with foot soldiers
Following behind in an endless cloud.
In the middle his comrades bore Patroclus,
Covering his body, as if with a garment,   *145*
With hair they sheared off and cast upon it.
Behind them Achilles cradled his head, grieving
For the peerless friend he was sending to Hades.

When they came to the place Achilles had told them,
They put the body down and quickly heaped up   *150*
Enough wood and plenty. Then Achilles,
Acting on impulse, stood apart from the pyre
And sheared off his hair, the tawny hair
He had been growing long for the River Spercheius.
Brooding, he turned toward the open sea,   *155*
The water glinting like wine, and said:

"Spercheius, my father Peleus vowed in vain
That when I had come home to my native land
I would shear my hair for you and sacrifice
Bulls by the hundred and fifty rams unblemished   *160*
Into your springs, where your precinct is
And your smoking altar. An old man's prayer,
Which you did not fulfill. Since I will never
Return home to my native land, I would give
To the hero Patroclus this lock to bear with him."   *165*

And he placed it in his beloved friend's hands.
This started them all weeping, and the sun
Would have set on their lamentation
Had not Achilles said to Agamemnon:

"Son of Atreus—you have the widest command—   *170*
These men can mourn all they want, but for now
Disperse them from the pyre and have them

Prepare their dinner. Those of us who are
Closest to the dead will do everything here.
And we would have all the leaders stay too."   *175*

The warlord Agamemnon heard him
And dismissed the troops to the ships.
The funeral party stayed and heaped up wood,
Building a pyre a hundred feet on each side,
And with heavy hearts they set the corpse on top.   *180*
Then they flayed many fine sheep and oxen
And laid them dressed out before the pyre.
Achilles gathered the fat from them all
And enfolded the body from head to foot,
Then heaped around it the flayed carcasses.   *185*
Next he set amphoras of honey and oil
Against the bier, and with heavy groans
Quickly cast on the pyre four high-necked horses.
Nine dogs once fed under the prince's table.
Achilles cut the throats of two and cast them on,   *190*
And twelve Trojans also, sons from good families,
Slashing them with bronze in a vengeful spirit.
Then he kindled the fire and let its iron will rage.
With a groan he called his beloved friend's name:

"Hear me, Patroclus, even from Hades.   *195*
All that I promised you I am completing now.
Twelve Trojans, sons of good families,
The fire consumes with you. Hector, though,
I will not give to the fire to eat, but to dogs."

Thus went his threat, but no dogs would eat Hector.   *200*
Aphrodite kept the dogs from his corpse
By day and by night, and she anointed him
With ambrosial oil of rose, so that when Achilles
Dragged his body it would not be torn.
And Phoebus Apollo drew a dark blue cloud   *205*
From the sky to the plain, covering the spot
Where the body lay, so that the sun's heat
Would not shrivel the flesh on his bones.

But Patroclus' pyre would not kindle.
Achilles thought of something else to try.   210
Standing apart from the pyre, he prayed
To the North Wind and West Wind, promising
Fine offerings, pouring libations from a gold cup,
And earnestly beseeching them to come and blow
So the wood would kindle and the body burn.   215
Iris heard his prayer and was off to the Winds
With the message. They were all in the house
Of the brisk West Wind, eating a banquet,
And Iris swooped to a stop on the stone threshold.
When they saw her there, they all whooshed up,   220
And each Wind invited her to sit next to him.
But she refused to sit, and made this speech:

"No seat for me. I'm off to Ocean's streams,
To the Ethiopians. They are offering sacrifices
To the immortals, and I want to get my share.   225
But Achilles is praying for the Winds to come—
The North Wind and the howling West—
And he is promising fine offerings
If you will raise the fire on Patroclus' pyre,
For whom all the Achaeans are groaning aloud."   230

She spoke and was gone. And the Winds rose
With an eerie noise, driving clouds before them.
They reached the sea quickly, and the waves swelled
Under their whistling blast. When they came to Troy
They fell on the pyre, and the flames roared to life.   235
The whole night long the shrill winds blew steadily
On the funeral fire, and all the long night Achilles
Drew wine from a golden bowl and poured it out
From a two-handled cup, wetting the earth,
Ever summoning the spirit of forlorn Patroclus.   240

> *A father wails for his son as he burns*
> *His bones, a son newly wed, a son whose death*
> *Has brought his parents inconsolable grief.*

Achilles wailed for his friend as he burned his bones,
Moving slowly about the pyre, groaning heavily.   *245*

   The morning star rose, speaking light to the earth,
And dawn opened over the sea like a crocus.
The flames died down and the fire subsided.
The Winds left and returned to their home
Over the Thracian sea, and it moaned beneath them.   *250*
Then the son of Peleus left the pyre
And lay down exhausted. He was soon asleep,
But the men with Agamemnon gathered around,
And the sound of their tramping woke him.
He sat up and spoke to them, saying: *255*

"Son of Atreus and princes of Greece,
First quench the funeral fire with wine,
Wherever it burned. Then gather the bones
Of Patroclus, son of Menoetius. Pick them out
Carefully. They are easily recognized,   *260*
For he lay in the middle, while the others burned
Off to the sides, men and horses jumbled.
Then let us wrap the bones in fat and keep them
In a golden bowl, until I am hidden in Hades.
You need not labor over a huge barrow for him,   *265*
But only what is seemly. Later the Achaeans
Can build it broad and high, all of you still left
Amid our thwarted ships when I am gone."

Thus Peleus' swift son, and they obeyed him.
First they doused the pyre with wine   *270*
Wherever it had burned and the embers were thick.
Then they gathered the bones of their gentle comrade
Into a golden bowl, wrapping them twice in fat,
And they placed the bowl in the hut and covered it
With a soft linen cloth. Then they traced a circle   *275*
For a mound and laid a foundation around the pyre
And piled up earth to form a tumulus over it.
Then they started to go back. But Achilles
Kept all the people there and had them sit down.

Then he brought prizes from his ship: *280*
Cauldrons, tripods, horses, mules, oxen,
Silken-waisted women, and grey iron.

*[The rest of Book 23 (lines 283–923) is omitted. Achilles hosts funeral
games for Patroclus.]*

ILIAD 24

*[Lines 1–496 are omitted. Achilles continues to desecrate Hector's body,
which is preserved by Apollo. Apollo convinces the other gods to order
Achilles to allow the body to be ransomed. Thetis goes to Achilles and per-
suades him to do so. Iris tells Priam to go to Achilles with ransom. Priam is
guided by Hermes to Achilles' hut.]*

And with that Hermes left and returned
To high Olympus. Priam jumped down
And left Idaeus to hold the horses and mules.
The old man went straight to the house   *500*
Where Achilles, dear to Zeus, sat and waited.

He found him inside. His companions sat
Apart from him, and a solitary pair,
Automedon and Alcimus, warriors both,
Were busy at his side. He had just finished   *505*
His evening meal. The table was still set up.
Great Priam entered unnoticed. He stood
Close to Achilles, and touching his knees,
He kissed the dread and murderous hands
That had killed so many of his sons.   *510*

Passion sometimes blinds a man so completely
That he kills one of his own countrymen.

In exile, he comes into a wealthy house,
And everyone stares at him with wonder.

So Achilles stared in wonder at Priam.   515
Was he a god?
                    And the others there stared
And wondered and looked at each other.
But Priam spoke, a prayer of entreaty:

"Remember your father, godlike Achilles.   520
He and I both are on the doorstep
Of old age. He may well be now
Surrounded by enemies wearing him down
And have no one to protect him from harm.
But then he hears that you are still alive   525
And his heart rejoices, and he hopes all his days
To see his dear son come back from Troy.
But what is left for me? I had the finest sons
In all wide Troy, and not one of them is left.
Fifty I had when the Greeks came over,   530
Nineteen out of one belly, and the rest
The women in my house bore to me.
It doesn't matter how many they were,
The god of war has cut them down at the knees.
And the only one who could save the city   535
You've just now killed as he fought for his country,
My Hector. It is for him I have come to the Greek ships,
To get him back from you. I've brought
A fortune in ransom. Respect the gods, Achilles.
Think of your own father, and pity me.   540
I am more pitiable. I have borne what no man
Who has walked this earth has ever yet borne.
I have kissed the hand of the man who killed my son."

He spoke, and sorrow for his own father
Welled up in Achilles. He took Priam's hand   545
And gently pushed the old man away.
The two of them remembered. Priam,
Huddled in grief at Achilles' feet, cried

And moaned softly for his man-slaying Hector.
And Achilles cried for his father and   *550*
For Patroclus. The sound filled the room.

When Achilles had his fill of grief
And the aching sorrow left his heart,
He rose from his chair and lifted the old man
By his hand, pitying his white hair and beard.   *555*
And his words enfolded him like wings:

"Ah, the suffering you've had, and the courage.
To come here alone to the Greek ships
And meet my eye, the man who slaughtered
Your many fine sons! You have a heart of iron.   *560*
But come, sit on this chair. Let our pain
Lie at rest a while, no matter how much we hurt.
There's nothing to be gained from cold grief.
Yes, the gods have woven pain into mortal lives,
While they are free from care.   *565*
                              Two jars
Sit at the doorstep of Zeus, filled with gifts
That he gives, one full of good things,
The other of evil. If Zeus gives a man
A mixture from both jars, sometimes   *570*
Life is good for him, sometimes not.
But if all he gives you is from the jar of woe,
You become a pariah, and hunger drives you
Over the bright earth, dishonored by gods and men.
Now take Peleus. The gods gave him splendid gifts   *575*
From the day he was born. He was the happiest
And richest man on earth, king of the Myrmidons,
And although he was a mortal, the gods gave him
An immortal goddess to be his wife.
But even to Peleus the god gave some evil: *580*
He would not leave offspring to succeed him in power,
Just one child, all out of season. I can't be with him
To take care of him now that he's old, since I'm far
From my fatherland, squatting here in Troy,
Tormenting you and your children. And you, old sir,   *585*

We hear that you were prosperous once.
From Lesbos down south clear over to Phrygia
And up to the Hellespont's boundary,
No one could match you in wealth or in sons.
But then the gods have brought you trouble,   *590*
This constant fighting and killing around your town.
You must endure this grief and not constantly grieve.
You will not gain anything by torturing yourself
Over the good son you lost, not bring him back.
Sooner you will suffer some other sorrow."   *595*

And Priam, old and godlike, answered him:

"Don't sit me in a chair, prince, while Hector
Lies uncared for in your hut. Deliver him now
So I can see him with my own eyes, and you—
Take all this ransom we bring, take pleasure in it,   *600*
And go back home to your own fatherland,
Since you've taken this first step and allowed me
To live and see the light of day."

Achilles glowered at him and said:

"Don't provoke me, old man. It's my own decision   *605*
To release Hector to you. A messenger came to me
From Zeus—my own natural mother,
Daughter of the old sea god. And I know you,
Priam, inside out. You don't fool me one bit.
Some god escorted you to the Greek ships.   *610*
No mortal would have dared come into our camp,
Not even your best young hero. He couldn't have
Gotten past the guards or muscled open the gate.
So just stop stirring up grief in my heart,
Or I might not let you out of here alive, old man—   *615*
Suppliant though you are—and sin against Zeus."

The old man was afraid and did as he was told.

The son of Peleus leapt out the door like a lion,

Followed by Automedon and Alcimus, whom Achilles
Honored most now that Patroclus was dead.   *620*
They unyoked the horses and mules, and led
The old man's herald inside and seated him on a chair.
Then they unloaded from the strong-wheeled cart
The endless ransom that was Hector's blood price,
Leaving behind two robes and a finespun tunic   *625*
For the body to be wrapped in and brought inside.
Achilles called the women and ordered them
To wash the body well and anoint it with oil,
Removing it first for fear that Priam might see his son
And in his grief be unable to control his anger   *630*
At the sight of his child, and that this would arouse
Achilles' passion and he would kill the old man
And so sin against the commandments of Zeus.

After the female slaves had bathed Hector's body
And anointed it with olive, they wrapped it 'round   *635*
With a beautiful robe and tunic, and Achilles himself
Lifted him up and placed him on a pallet
And with his friends raised it onto the polished cart.
Then he groaned and called out to Patroclus:

"Don't be angry with me, dear friend, if somehow   *640*
You find out, even in Hades, that I have released
Hector to his father. He paid a handsome price,
And I will share it with you, as much as is right."

Achilles reentered his hut and sat down again
In his ornately decorated chair   *645*
Across the room from Priam, and said to him:

"Your son is released, sir, as you ordered.
He is lying on a pallet. At dawn's first light
You will go see him yourself.
    Now let's think about supper.   *650*
Even Niobe remembered to eat
Although her twelve children were dead in her house,
Six daughters and six sturdy sons.

Apollo killed them with his silver bow,
And Artemis, showering arrows, angry with Niobe 655
Because she compared herself to beautiful Leto.
Leto, she said, had borne only two, while she
Had borne many. Well, these two killed them all.
Nine days they lay in their gore, with no one
To bury them, because Zeus had turned 660
The people to stone. On the tenth day
The gods buried them. But Niobe remembered
She had to eat, exhausted from weeping.
Now she is one of the rocks in the lonely hills
Somewhere in Sipylos, a place they say is haunted 665
By nymphs who dance on the Achelous' banks,
And although she is stone she broods on the sorrows
The gods gave her.
                    Well, so should we, old sir,
Remember to eat. You can mourn your son later 670
When you bring him to Troy. You owe him many tears."

A moment later Achilles was up and had slain
A silvery sheep. His companions flayed it
And prepared it for a meal, sliced it, spitted it,
Roasted the morsels and drew them off the spits. 675
Automedon set out bread in exquisite baskets
While Achilles served the meat. They helped themselves
And satisfied their desire for food and drink.
Then Priam, son of Dardanus, gazed for a while
At Achilles, so big, so much like one of the gods, 680
And Achilles returned his gaze, admiring
Priam's face, his words echoing in his mind.

When they had their fill of gazing at each other,
Priam, old and godlike, broke the silence:

"Show me to my bed now, prince, and quickly, 685
So that at long last I can have the pleasure of sleep.
My eyes have not closed since my son lost his life
Under your hands. I have done nothing but groan
And brood over my countless sorrows,

Rolling in the dung of my courtyard stables. 690
Finally I have tasted food and let flaming wine
Pass down my throat. I had eaten nothing till now."

Achilles ordered his companions and women
To set bedsteads on the porch and pad them
With fine, dyed rugs, spread blankets on top, 695
And cover them over with fleecy cloaks.
The women went out with torches in their hands
And quickly made up two beds. And Achilles,
The great sprinter, said in a bitter tone:

"You will have to sleep outside, dear Priam. 700
One of the Achaean counsellors may come in,
As they always do, to sit and talk with me,
As well they should. If one of them saw you here
In the dead of night, he would tell Agamemnon,
And that would delay releasing the body. 705
But tell me this, as precisely as you can.
How many days do you need for the funeral?
I will wait that long and hold back the army."

And the old man, godlike Priam, answered:

"If you really want me to bury my Hector, 710
Then you could do this for me, Achilles.
You know how we are penned in the city,
Far from any timber, and the Trojans are afraid.
We would mourn him for nine days in our halls,
And bury him on the tenth, and feast the people. 715
On the eleventh we would heap a barrow over him,
And on the twelfth day fight, if fight we must."

And Achilles, strong, swift, and godlike:

"You will have your armistice."

And he clasped the old man's wrist 720
So he would not be afraid.
                    And so they slept,

Priam and his herald, in the covered courtyard,
Each with a wealth of thoughts in his breast.
But Achilles slept inside his well-built hut,   725
And by his side lay lovely Briseis.
Gods and heroes slept the night through,
Wrapped in soft slumber. Only Hermes
Lay awake in the dark, pondering how
To spirit King Priam away from the ships   730
And elude the strong watchmen at the camp's gates.
He hovered above Priam's head and spoke:

"Well, old man, you seem to think it's safe
To sleep on and on in the enemy camp
Since Achilles spared you. Think what it cost you   735
To ransom your son. Your own life will cost
Three times that much to the sons you have left
If Agamemnon and the Greeks know you are here."

Suddenly the old man was afraid. He woke up the herald.
Hermes harnessed the horses and mules   740
And drove them through the camp. No one noticed.
And when they reached the ford of the Xanthus,
The beautiful, swirling river that Zeus begot,
Hermes left for the long peaks of Olympus.

   Dawn spread her saffron light over earth,   745
And they drove the horses into the city
With great lamentation. The mules pulled the corpse.

No one in Troy, man or woman, saw them before
Cassandra, who stood like golden Aphrodite
On Pergamum's height. Looking out she saw   750
Her dear father standing in the chariot
With the herald, and then she saw Hector
Lying on the stretcher in the mule cart.
And her cry went out through all the city:

"Come look upon Hector, Trojan men and women,   755
If ever you rejoiced when he came home alive
From battle, a joy to the city and all its people."

She spoke. And there was not a man or woman
Left in the city, for an unbearable sorrow
Had come upon them. They met Priam by the gates   760
As he brought the body through, and in the front
Hector's dear wife and queenly mother threw themselves
On the rolling cart and pulled out their hair
As they clasped his head amid the grieving crowd.
They would have mourned Hector outside the gates   765
All the long day until the sun went down,
Had not the old man spoken from his chariot:

"Let the mules come through. Later you will have
Your fill of grieving, after I have brought him home."

He spoke, and the crowd made way for the cart.   770
And they brought him home and laid him
On a corded bed, and set around him singers
To lead the dirge and chant the death song.
They chanted the dirge, and the women with them.
White-armed Andromache led the lamentation   775
As she cradled the head of her man-slaying Hector:

"You have died young, husband, and left me
A widow in the halls. Our son is still an infant,
Doomed when we bore him. I do not think
He will ever reach manhood. No, this city   780
Will topple and fall first. You were its savior,
And now you are lost. All the solemn wives
And children you guarded will go off soon
In the hollow ships, and I will go with them.
And you, my son, you will either come with me   785
And do menial labor for a cruel master,
Or some Greek will lead you by the hand
And throw you from the tower, a hideous death,
Angry because Hector killed his brother,
Or his father, or son. Many, many Greeks   790
Fell in battle under Hector's hands.
Your father was never gentle in combat.
And so all the townspeople mourn for him,

And you have caused your parents unspeakable
Sorrow, Hector, and left me endless pain.   *795*
You did not stretch your hand out to me
As you lay dying in bed, nor did you whisper
A final word I could remember as I weep
All the days and nights of my life."

The women's moans washed over her lament,   *800*
And from the sobbing came Hecuba's voice:

"Hector, my heart, dearest of all my children,
The gods loved you when you were alive for me,
And they have cared for you also in death.
My other children Achilles sold as slaves   *805*
When he captured them, shipped them overseas
To Samos, Imbros, and barren Lemnos.
After he took your life with tapered bronze
He dragged you around Patroclus' tomb, his friend
Whom you killed, but still could not bring him back.   *810*
And now you lie here for me as fresh as dew,
Although you have been slain, like one whom Apollo
Has killed softly with his silver arrows."

The third woman to lament was Helen.

"Oh, Hector, you were the dearest to me by far   *815*
Of all my husband's brothers. Yes, Paris
Is my husband, the godlike prince
Who led me to Troy. I should have died first.
This is now the twentieth year
Since I went away and left my home,   *820*
And I have never had an unkind word from you.
If anyone in the house ever taunted me,
Any of my husband's brothers or sisters,
Or his mother—my father-in-law was kind always—
You would draw them aside and calm them   *825*
With your gentle heart and gentle words.
And so I weep for you and for myself,
And my heart is heavy, because there is no one left

In all wide Troy who will pity me
Or be my friend. Everyone shudders at me."   830

And the people's moan came in over her voice.

Then the old man, Priam, spoke to his people:

"Men of Troy, start bringing wood to the city,
And have no fear of an Argive ambush.
When Achilles sent me from the black ships,   835
He gave his word he would not trouble us
Until the twelfth day should dawn."

He spoke, and they yoked oxen and mules
To wagons, and gathered outside the city.
For nine days they hauled in loads of timber.   840
When the tenth dawn showed her mortal light,
They brought out their brave Hector
And all in tears lifted the body high
Onto the bier, and threw on the fire.

Light blossomed like roses in the eastern sky.   845

The people gathered around Hector's pyre,
And when all of Troy was assembled there
They drowned the last flames with glinting wine.
Hector's brothers and friends collected
His white bones, their cheeks flowered with tears.   850
They wrapped the bones in soft purple robes
And placed them in a golden casket, and laid it
In the hollow of the grave, and heaped above it
A mantle of stones. They built the tomb
Quickly, with lookouts posted all around   855
In case the Greeks should attack early.
When the tomb was built, they all returned
To the city and assembled for a glorious feast
In the house of Priam, Zeus' cherished king.

That was the funeral of Hector, breaker of horses.   860

ODYSSEY 1

S<small>PEAK</small>, M<small>EMORY</small>—

        O<small>f</small> the cunning hero,
The wanderer, blown off course time and again
After he plundered Troy's sacred heights.

        S<small>peak</small>
Of all the cities he saw, the minds he grasped,
The suffering deep in his heart at sea   5
As he struggled to survive and bring his men home
But could not save them, hard as he tried—
The fools—destroyed by their own recklessness
When they ate the oxen of Hyperion the Sun,
And that god snuffed out their day of return.   10

        O<small>f</small> these things,
S<small>peak</small>, I<small>mmortal</small> O<small>ne</small>,
And tell the tale once more in our time.

  B<small>y</small> now, all the others who had fought at Troy—
At least those who had survived the war and the sea—
Were safely back home. Only Odysseus   15
Still longed to return to his home and his wife.
The nymph Calypso, a powerful goddess—
And beautiful—was clinging to him
In her caverns and yearned to possess him.
The seasons rolled by, and the year came   20
In which the gods spun the thread
For Odysseus to return home to Ithaca,
Though not even there did his troubles end,
Even with his dear ones around him.
All the gods pitied him, except Poseidon,   25

Who stormed against the godlike hero
Until he finally reached his own native land.

But Poseidon was away now, among the Ethiopians,
Those burnished people at the ends of the earth—
Some near the sunset, some near the sunrise—   *30*
To receive a grand sacrifice of rams and bulls.
There he sat, enjoying the feast.
                                    The other gods
Were assembled in the halls of Olympian Zeus,
And the Father of Gods and Men was speaking.
He couldn't stop thinking about Aegisthus,   *35*
Whom Agamemnon's son, Orestes, had killed:

"Mortals! They are always blaming the gods
For their troubles, when their own witlessness
Causes them more than they were destined for!
Take Aegisthus now. He marries Agamemnon's   *40*
Lawful wife and murders the man on his return
Knowing it meant disaster—because we did warn him,
Sent our messenger, quicksilver Hermes,
To tell him not to kill the man and marry his wife,
Or Agamemnon's son, Orestes, would pay him back   *45*
When he came of age and wanted his inheritance.
Hermes told him all that, but his good advice
Meant nothing to Aegisthus. Now he's paid in full."

Athena glared at him with her owl-grey eyes:

"Yes, O our Father who art most high—   *50*
That man got the death he richly deserved,
And so perish all who would do the same.
But it's Odysseus I'm worried about,
That discerning, ill-fated man. He's suffered
So long, separated from his dear ones,   *55*
On an island that lies in the center of the sea,
A wooded isle that is home to a goddess,
The daughter of Atlas, whose dread mind knows
All the depths of the sea and who supports

The tall pillars that keep earth and heaven apart. 60
His daughter detains the poor man in his grief,
Sweet-talking him constantly, trying to charm him
Into forgetting Ithaca. But Odysseus,
Longing to see even the smoke curling up
From his land, simply wants to die. And yet you 65
Never think of him, Olympian. Didn't Odysseus
Please you with sacrifices beside the Greek ships
At Troy? Why is Odysseus so odious, Zeus?"

Zeus in his thunderhead had an answer for her:

"Quite a little speech you've let slip through your teeth, 70
Daughter. How could I forget godlike Odysseus?
No other mortal has a mind like his, or offers
Sacrifice like him to the deathless gods in heaven.
But Poseidon is stiff and cold with anger
Because Odysseus blinded his son, the Cyclops 75
Polyphemus, the strongest of all the Cyclopes,
Nearly a god. The nymph Thoösa bore him,
Daughter of Phorcys, lord of the barren brine,
After mating with Poseidon in a scalloped sea-cave.
The Earthshaker has been after Odysseus 80
Ever since, not killing him, but keeping him away
From his native land. But come now,
Let's all put our heads together and find a way
To bring Odysseus home. Poseidon will have to
Put aside his anger. He can't hold out alone 85
Against the will of all the immortals."

And Athena, the owl-eyed goddess, replied:

"Father Zeus, whose power is supreme,
If the blessed gods really do want
Odysseus to return to his home, 90
We should send Hermes, our quicksilver herald,
To the island of Ogygia without delay
To tell that nymph of our firm resolve
That long-suffering Odysseus gets to go home.

I myself will go to Ithaca   *95*
To put some spirit into his son—
Have him call an assembly of the long-haired Greeks
And rebuke the whole lot of his mother's suitors.
They have been butchering his flocks and herds.
I'll escort him to Sparta and the sands of Pylos   *100*
So he can make inquiries about his father's return
And win for himself a name among men."

    Athena spoke, and she bound on her feet
The beautiful sandals, golden, immortal,
That carry her over landscape and seascape   *105*
On a puff of wind. And she took the spear,
Bronze-tipped and massive, that the Daughter uses
To level battalions of heroes in her wrath.
She shot down from the peaks of Olympus
To Ithaca, where she stood on the threshold   *110*
Of Odysseus' outer porch. Holding her spear,
She looked like Mentes, the Taphian captain,
And her eyes rested on the arrogant suitors.

They were playing dice in the courtyard,
Enjoying themselves, seated on the hides of oxen   *115*
They themselves had slaughtered. They were attended
By heralds and servants, some of whom were busy
Blending water and wine in large mixing bowls,
Others wiping down the tables with sponges
And dishing out enormous servings of meat.   *120*

Telemachus spotted her first.
He was sitting with the suitors, nursing
His heart's sorrow, picturing in his mind
His noble father, imagining he had returned
And scattered the suitors, and that he himself,   *125*
Telemachus, was respected at last.
Such were his reveries as he sat with the suitors.
And then he saw Athena.
                He went straight to the porch,
Indignant that a guest had been made to wait so long.

Going up to her he grasped her right hand in his   *130*
And took her spear, and his words had wings:

"Greetings, stranger. You are welcome here.
After you've had dinner, you can tell us what you need."

Telemachus spoke, and Pallas Athena
Followed him into the high-roofed hall.   *135*
When they were inside he placed her spear
In a polished rack beside a great column
Where the spears of Odysseus stood in a row.
Then he covered a beautifully wrought chair
With a linen cloth and had her sit on it   *140*
With a stool under her feet. He drew up
An intricately painted bench for himself
And arranged their seats apart from the suitors
So that his guest would not lose his appetite
In their noisy and uncouth company—   *145*
And so he could inquire about his absent father.
A maid poured water from a silver pitcher
Into a golden basin for them to wash their hands
And then set up a polished table nearby.
Another serving woman, grave and dignified,   *150*
Set out bread and generous helpings
From the other dishes she had. A carver set down
Cuts of meat by the platter and golden cups.
Then a herald came by and poured them wine.

Now the suitors swaggered in. They sat down   *155*
In rows on benches and chairs. Heralds
Poured water over their hands, maidservants
Brought around bread in baskets, and young men
Filled mixing bowls to the brim with wine.
The suitors helped themselves to all this plenty,   *160*
And when they had their fill of food and drink,
They turned their attention to the other delights,
Dancing and song, that round out a feast.
A herald handed a beautiful zither
To Phemius, who sang for the suitors,   *165*

Though against his will. Sweeping the strings
He struck up a song. And Telemachus,
Putting his head close to Pallas Athena's
So the others wouldn't hear, said this to her:

"Please don't take offense if I speak my mind.   170
It's easy for them to enjoy the harper's song,
Since they are eating another man's stores
Without paying anything—the stores of a man
Whose white bones lie rotting in the rain
On some distant shore, or still churn in the waves.   175
If they ever saw him make landing on Ithaca
They would pray for more foot speed
Instead of more gold or fancy clothes.
But he's met a bad end, and it's no comfort to us
When some traveler tells us he's on his way home.   180
The day has long passed when he's coming home.
But tell me this, and tell me the truth:
Who are you, and where do you come from?
Who are your parents? What kind of ship
Brought you here? How did your sailors   185
Guide you to Ithaca, and how large is your crew?
I don't imagine you came here on foot.
And tell me this, too. I'd like to know,
Is this your first visit here, or are you
An old friend of my father's, one of the many   190
Who have come to our house over the years?"

Athena's seagrey eyes glinted as she said:

"I'll tell you nothing but the unvarnished truth.
I am Mentes, son of Anchialus, and proud of it.
I am also captain of the seafaring Taphians.   195
I just pulled in with my ship and my crew,
Sailing the deep purple to foreign ports.
We're on our way to Cyprus with a cargo of iron
To trade for copper. My ship is standing
Offshore of wild country away from the city,   200
In Rheithron harbor under Neion's woods.

You and I have ties of hospitality,
Just as our fathers did, from a long way back.
Go and ask old Laertes. They say he never
Comes to town any more, lives out in the country,   205
A hard life with just an old woman to help him.
She gets him his food and drink when he comes in
From the fields, all worn out from trudging across
The ridge of his vineyard plot.
                                    I have come
Because they say your father has returned,   210
But now I see the gods have knocked him off course.
He's not dead, though, not godlike Odysseus,
No way in the world. No, he's alive all right.
It's the sea keeps him back, detained on some island
In the middle of the sea, held captive by savages.   215
And now I will prophesy for you, as the gods
Put it in my heart and as I think it will be,
Though I am no soothsayer or reader of birds.
Odysseus will not be gone much longer
From his native land, not even if iron chains   220
Hold him. He knows every trick there is
And will think of some way to come home.
But now tell me this, and I want the truth:
Tall as you are, are you Odysseus' son?
You bear a striking resemblance to him,   225
Especially in the head and those beautiful eyes.
We used to spend quite a bit of time together
Before he sailed for Troy with the Argive fleet.
Since then, we haven't seen each other at all."

Telemachus took a deep breath and said: 230

"You want the truth, and I will give it to you.
My mother says that Odysseus is my father.
I don't know this myself. No one witnesses
His own begetting. If I had my way, I'd be the son
Of a man fortunate enough to grow old at home.   235
But it's the man with the most dismal fate of all
They say I was born from—since you want to know."

Athena's seagrey eyes glinted as she said:

"Well, the gods have made sure your family's name
Will go on, since Penelope has borne a son like you.   240
But there is one other thing I want you to tell me.
What kind of a party is this? What's the occasion?
Some kind of banquet? A wedding feast?
It's no neighborly potluck, that's for sure,
The way this rowdy crowd is carrying on   245
All through the house. Any decent man
Would be outraged if he saw this behavior."

Telemachus breathed in the salt air and said:

"Since you ask me these questions as my guest—
This, no doubt, was once a perfect house,   250
Wealthy and fine, when its master was still home.
But the gods frowned and changed all that
When they whisked him off the face of the earth.
I wouldn't grieve for him so much if he were dead,
Gone down with his comrades in the town of Troy,   255
Or died in his friends' arms after winding up the war.
The entire Greek army would have buried him then,
And great honor would have passed on to his son.
But now the whirlwinds have snatched him away
Without a trace. He's vanished, gone, and left me   260
Pain and sorrow. And he's not the only cause
I have to grieve. The gods have given me other trials.
All of the nobles who rule the islands—
Doulichium, Samê, wooded Zacynthus—
And all those with power on rocky Ithaca   265
Are courting my mother and ruining our house.
She refuses to make a marriage she hates
But can't stop it either. They are eating us
Out of house and home, and will kill me someday."

And Pallas Athena, with a flash of anger: 270

"Damn them! You really do need Odysseus back.

Just let him lay his hands on these mangy dogs!
If only he would come through that door now
With a helmet and shield and a pair of spears,
Just as he was when I saw him first,   275
Drinking and enjoying himself in our house
On his way back from Ephyre. Odysseus
Had sailed there to ask Mermerus' son, Ilus,
For some deadly poison for his arrowheads.
Ilus, out of fear of the gods' anger,   280
Would not give him any, but my father
Gave him some, because he loved him dearly.
That's the Odysseus I want the suitors to meet.
They wouldn't live long enough to get married!
But it's on the knees of the gods now   285
Whether he comes home and pays them back
Right here in his halls, or doesn't.
                                    So it's up to you
To find a way to drive them out of your house.
Now pay attention and listen to what I'm saying.
Tomorrow you call an assembly and make a speech   290
To these heroes, with the gods as witnesses.
The suitors you order to scatter, each to his own.
Your mother—if in her heart she wants to marry—
Goes back to her powerful father's house.
Her kinfolk and he can arrange the marriage,   295
And the large dowry that should go with his daughter.
And my advice for you, if you will take it,
Is to launch your best ship, with twenty oarsmen,
And go make inquiries about your long-absent father.
Someone may tell you something, or you may hear   300
A rumor from Zeus, which is how news travels best.
Sail to Pylos first and ask godly Nestor,
Then go over to Sparta and red-haired Menelaus.
He was the last home of all the bronzeclad Greeks.
If you hear your father's alive and on his way home,   305
You can grit your teeth and hold out one more year.
If you hear he's dead, among the living no more,
Then come home yourself to your ancestral land,
Build him a barrow and celebrate the funeral

Your father deserves. Then marry off your mother.   *310*
After you've done all that, think up some way
To kill the suitors in your house either openly
Or by setting a trap. You've got to stop
Acting like a child. You've outgrown that now.
Haven't you heard how Orestes won glory   *315*
Throughout the world when he killed Aegisthus,
The shrewd traitor who murdered his father?
You have to be aggressive, strong—look at how big
And well-built you are—so you will leave a good name.
Well, I'm off to my ship and my men,   *320*
Who are no doubt wondering what's taking me so long.
You've got a job to do. Remember what I said."

And Telemachus, in his clear-headed way:

"My dear guest, you speak to me as kindly
As a father to his son. I will not forget your words.   *325*
I know you're anxious to leave, but please stay
So you can bathe and relax before returning
To your ship, taking with you a costly gift,
Something quite fine, a keepsake from me,
The sort of thing a host gives to his guest."   *330*

And Athena, her eyes grey as saltwater:

"No, I really do want to get on with my journey.
Whatever gift you feel moved to make,
Give it to me on my way back home,
Yes, something quite fine. It will get you as good."   *335*

With these words the Grey-eyed One was gone,
Flown up and away like a seabird. And as she went
She put courage in Telemachus' heart
And made him think of his father even more than before.
Telemachus' mind soared. He knew it had been a god,   *340*
And like a god himself he rejoined the suitors.

They were sitting hushed in silence, listening

To the great harper as he sang the tale
Of the hard journeys home that Pallas Athena
Ordained for the Greeks on their way back from Troy.   *345*

His song drifted upstairs, and Penelope,
Wise daughter of Icarius, took it all in.
She came down the steep stairs of her house—
Not alone, two maids trailed behind—
And when she had come among the suitors   *350*
She stood shawled in light by a column
That supported the roof of the great house,
Hiding her cheeks behind her silky veils,
Grave handmaidens standing on either side.
And she wept as she addressed the brilliant harper: *355*

"Phemius, you know many other songs
To soothe human sorrows, songs of the exploits
Of gods and men. Sing one of those
To your enraptured audience as they sit
Sipping their wine. But stop singing this one,   *360*
This painful song that always tears at my heart.
I am already sorrowful, constantly grieving
For my husband, remembering him, a man
Renowned in Argos and throughout all Hellas."

And Telemachus said to her coolly: *365*

"Mother, why begrudge our singer
Entertaining us as he thinks best?
Singers are not responsible; Zeus is,
Who gives what he wants to every man on earth.
No one can blame Phemius for singing the doom   *370*
Of the Danaans: it's always the newest song
An audience praises most. For yourself,
You'll just have to endure it and listen.
Odysseus was not the only man at Troy
Who didn't come home. Many others perished.   *375*
You should go back upstairs and take care of your work,
Spinning and weaving, and have the maids do theirs.

Speaking is for men, for all men, but for me
Especially, since I am the master of this house."

Penelope was stunned and turned to go,   *380*
Her son's masterful words pressed to her heart.
She went up the stairs to her room with her women
And wept for Odysseus, her beloved husband,
Until grey-eyed Athena cast sleep on her eyelids.

All through the shadowy halls the suitors   *385*
Broke into an uproar, each of them praying
To lie in bed with her. Telemachus cut them short:

"Suitors of my mother—you arrogant pigs—
For now, we're at a feast. No shouting, please!
There's nothing finer than hearing   *390*
A singer like this, with a voice like a god's.
But in the morning we will sit in the meeting ground,
So that I can tell all of you in broad daylight
To get out of my house. Fix yourselves feasts
In each others' houses, use up your own stockpiles.   *395*
But if it seems better and more profitable
For one man to be eaten out of house and home
Without compensation—then eat away!
For my part, I will pray to the gods eternal
That Zeus grant me requital: Death for you   *400*
Here in my house. With no compensation."

Thus Telemachus. And they all bit their lips
And marveled at how boldly he had spoken to them.
Then Antinous, son of Eupeithes, replied:

"Well, Telemachus, it seems the gods, no less,   *405*
Are teaching you how to be a bold public speaker.
May the son of Cronus never make you king
Here on Ithaca, even if it is your birthright."

And Telemachus, taking in a breath:

"It may make you angry, Antinous,   410
But I'll tell you something. I wouldn't mind a bit
If Zeus granted me this—if he made me king.
You think this is the worst fate a man can have?
It's not so bad to be king. Your house grows rich,
And you're held in great honor yourself. But,   415
There are many other lords on seawashed Ithaca,
Young and old, and any one of them
Could get to be king, now that Odysseus is dead.
But I will be master of my own house
And of the servants that Odysseus left me."   420

Then Eurymachus, Polybus' son, responded:

"It's on the knees of the gods, Telemachus,
Which man of Greece will rule this island.
But you keep your property and rule your house,
And may no man ever come to wrest them away   425
From you by force, not while men live in Ithaca.
But I want to ask you, sir, about your visitor.
Where did he come from, what port
Does he call home, where are his ancestral fields?
Did he bring news of your father's coming   430
Or was he here on business of his own?
He sure up and left in a hurry, wouldn't stay
To be known. Yet by his looks he was no tramp."

And Telemachus, with a sharp response:

"Eurymachus, my father is not coming home.   435
I no longer trust any news that may come,
Or any prophecy my mother may have gotten
From a seer she has summoned up to the house.
My guest was a friend of my father's from Taphos.
He says he is Mentes, son of Anchialus   440
And captain of the seafaring Taphians."

Thus Telemachus. But in his heart he knew
It was an immortal goddess.

                                    And now
The young men plunged into their entertainment,
Singing and dancing until the twilight hour.   *445*
They were still at it when the evening grew dark,
Then one by one went to their own houses to rest.

Telemachus' room was off the beautiful courtyard,
Built high and with a surrounding view.
There he went to his bed, his mind teeming,   *450*
And with him, bearing blazing torches,
Went true-hearted Eurycleia, daughter of Ops
And Peisenor's grandaughter. Long ago,
Laertes had bought her for a small fortune
When she was still a girl. He paid twenty oxen   *455*
And honored her in his house as he honored
His wedded wife, but he never slept with her
Because he would rather avoid his wife's wrath.
Of all the women, she loved Telemachus the most
And had nursed him as a baby. Now she bore   *460*
The blazing torches as Telemachus opened
The doors to his room and sat on his bed.
He pulled off his soft tunic and laid it
In the hands of the wise old woman, and she
Folded it and smoothed it and hung it on a peg   *465*
Beside the corded bed. Then she left the room,
Pulled the door shut by its silver handle,
And drew the bolt home with the strap.

                                    There Telemachus
Lay wrapped in a fleece all the night through,
Pondering the journey Athena had shown him.   *470*

*[Books 2 and 3 are omitted. Telemachus calls an assembly and announces
his intention to sail abroad in search of news of his father. Athena, now dis-
guised as Mentor, an old family friend, helps him procure a ship and a
crew. They sail to Pylos, where they are entertained by Nestor, who then
sends Telemachus, accompanied by his son Peisistratus, overland by char-
iot to Sparta to visit Menelaus.]*

ODYSSEY 4

[Lines 1–124 are omitted. Menelaus welcomes Telemachus and entertains him but does not yet know his identity. When Menelaus mentions Odysseus, Telemachus begins to weep.]

While Menelaus pondered this,   125
Helen came from her fragrant bedroom
Like gold-spindled Artemis. Adraste,
Her attendant, drew up a beautiful chair for her,
And Alcippe brought her a soft wool rug.
Another maid, Phylo, brought a silver basket—   130
A gift from Alcandre, wife of Polybus,
Who lived in Thebes, the city in Egypt
That has the wealthiest houses in the world.
Polybus had given Menelaus two silver baths,
Two tripods, and ten bars of gold.   135
And his wife, Alcandre, gave to Helen
Beautiful gifts of her own—a golden spindle
And a silver basket with gold-rimmed wheels.
This basket Phylo now placed beside her,
Filled with fine-spun yarn, and across it   140
Was laid the spindle, twirled with violet wool.
Helen sat upon the chair, a footstool
Under her feet, and questioned her husband:

"Do we know, Menelaus, who our guests
Claim to be? Shall I speak my mind or not?   145
My heart urges me to speak. I have never seen
Such a resemblance between any two people,
Man or woman, as between this man
And Odysseus' son—as I imagine him now—
Telemachus, who was a newborn baby   150
When for my sake, shameless thing that I was,
The Greeks came to Troy with war in their hearts."

And Menelaus, the red-haired king:

"Now that you mention it, I see
The resemblance myself—the feet, the hands,   *155*
The way he looks at you, that head of hair.
And just now when I was talking about Odysseus,
Saying how much he went through for my sake,
Tears welled up in his eyes, bitter tears,
And he covered his face with his purple cloak."   *160*

At this Nestor's son Peisistratus spoke up:

"Menelaus, son of Atreus, Zeus-bred king,
This is indeed, as you say, Odysseus' son.
But he is prudent and would not think it proper,
When he just got here, to make a big speech   *165*
Before you—whose voice delights us as a god's.
Nestor of Gerenia sent me with him as a guide,
For he was eager to see you, hoping that
You could suggest something he could do or say.
A son has many problems to face at home   *170*
When his father is gone and there is no one else
To help him. So it is now with Telemachus,
Whose father is gone, and there is no one else
Among the people to keep him from harm."

And Menelaus, the red-haired king: *175*

"What's this? Here in my house, the son
Of my dear friend who did so much for me!
I used to think that if he came back
I would give him a welcome no other Greek
Could ever hope to have—if Olympian Zeus   *180*
Had brought us both home from over the sea
In our swift ships. I would have given him
A city of his own in Argos, built him a house,
Brought him over from Ithaca with his goods,
His son and all of his people—a whole city   *185*
Cleared out just for him! We would have been together,

Enjoying each other's company, and nothing
Would have parted us until death's black cloud
Finally enfolded us. But I suppose Zeus himself
Begrudged us this, for Odysseus alone,   *190*
That unlucky man, was never brought home."

His words aroused in all of them
A longing for lamentation. Argive Helen,
A child of Zeus, wept; Telemachus wept;
And Menelaus wept, the son of Atreus.   *195*
Nor could Nestor's son keep his eyes dry,
For he remembered Antilochus,
His flawless brother, who had been killed
By Memnon, Dawn's resplendent son,
And this memory gave wings to his words: *200*

"Son of Atreus, old Nestor used to say,
Whenever we talked about things like this,
That no one could match your understanding.
So please understand me when I say
That I do not enjoy weeping after supper—   *205*
And it will be dawn before we know it.
Not that I think it's wrong to lament the dead.
This is all we can do—cut our hair
And shed some tears. I lost someone myself
At Troy, my brother, not the least hero there.   *210*
You probably knew him. I am too young
Ever to have seen him, but men say Antilochus
Could run and fight as well as any man alive."

And Menelaus, the red-haired king:

"No one could have put that better, my friend,   *215*
Not even someone much older. Your speech,
Wise and clear, shows the sort of father you have.
It's easy to spot a man for whom Zeus
Has spun out happiness in marriage and children,
As he has done for Nestor throughout his life.   *220*
And now he has reached a sleek old age in his halls,

And his sons are wise and fight with the best.
So we will stop this weeping, and once more
Think of supper. Let the servants pour water
Over our hands. Telemachus and I will have   225
Much to say to each other come morning."

So he spoke, and Asphalion,
Menelaus' attendant, poured water
Over their hands, and they reached out
For all the good cheer spread out before them.   230

But Helen, child of Zeus, had other ideas.
She threw a drug into the wine bowl
They were drinking from, a drug
That stilled all pain, quieted all anger
And brought forgetfulness of every ill.   235
Whoever drank wine laced with this drug
Would not be sad or shed a tear that day,
Not even if his own father and mother
Should lie there dead, or if someone killed
His brother, or son, before his eyes.   240
Helen had gotten this potent, cunning drug
From Polydamna, the wife of Thon,
A woman in Egypt, where the land
Proliferates with all sorts of drugs,
Many beneficial, many poisonous.   245
Men there know more about medicines
Than any other people on earth,
For they are of the race of Paeeon, the Healer.
When she had slipped the drug into the wine,
Helen ordered another round to be poured,   250
And then she turned to the company and said:

"Menelaus, son of Atreus in the line of Zeus,
And you sons of noble fathers, it is true
That Zeus gives easy lives to some of us
And hard lives to others—he can do anything, after all—   255
But you should sit now in the hall and feast
And entertain yourselves by telling stories.

I'll start you off. I couldn't begin to tell you
All that Odysseus endured and accomplished,
But listen to what that hero did once   260
In the land of Troy, where the Achaeans suffered.
First, he beat himself up—gave himself some nasty bruises—
Then put on a cheap cloak so he looked like a slave,
And in this disguise he entered the wide streets
Of the enemy city. He looked like a beggar,   265
Far from what he was back in the Greek camp,
And fooled everyone when he entered Troy.
I alone recognized him in his disguise
And questioned him, but he cleverly put me off.
It was only after I had bathed him   270
And rubbed him down with oil and clothed him
And had sworn a great oath not to tell the Trojans
Who he really was until he got back to the ships,
That he told me, at last, what the Achaeans planned.
He killed many Trojans before he left   275
And arrived back at camp with much to report.
The other women in Troy wailed aloud,
But I was glad inside, for my heart had turned
Homeward, and I rued the infatuation
Aphrodite gave me when she led me away   280
From my native land, leaving my dear child,
My bridal chamber, and my husband,
A man who lacked nothing in wisdom or looks."

And Menelaus, the red-haired king:

"A very good story, my wife, and well told.   285
By now I have come to know the minds
Of many heroes, and have traveled far and wide,
But I have never laid eyes on anyone
Who had an enduring heart like Odysseus.
Listen to what he did in the wooden horse,   290
Where all we Argive chiefs sat waiting
To bring slaughter and death to the Trojans.
You came there then, with godlike Deiphobus.
Some god who favored the Trojans

Must have lured you on. Three times you circled   *295*
Our hollow hiding place, feeling it
With your hands, and you called out the names
Of all Argive leaders, making your voice
Sound like each of our wives' in turn.
Diomedes and I, sitting in the middle   *300*
With Odysseus, heard you calling
And couldn't take it. We were frantic
To come out, or answer you from inside,
But Odysseus held us back and stopped us.
Then everyone else stayed quiet also,   *305*
Except for Anticlus, who wanted to answer you,
But Odysseus saved us all by clamping
His strong hands over Anticlus' mouth
And holding them there until Athena led you off."

Then Telemachus said in his clear-headed way: *310*

"Menelaus, son of Atreus in the line of Zeus,
It is all the more unbearable then, isn't it?
My father may have had a heart of iron,
But it didn't do him any good in the end.
Please send us to bed now. It is time   *315*
We rested and enjoyed some sweet sleep."

He spoke, and Helen of Argos told her maids
To place beds on the porch and spread upon them
Beautiful purple blankets and fleecy cloaks.
The maids went out of the hall with torches   *320*
And made up the beds, and a herald
Led the guests out to them. So they slept there
On the palace porch, the hero Telemachus
And Nestor's glorious son. But Menelaus slept
In the innermost chamber of that high house   *325*
Next to Helen, Zeus' brightness upon her.

Dawn brushed her pale rose fingers across the sky,
And Menelaus got out of bed and dressed.
He slung his sharp sword around his shoulder,

Tied oiled leather sandals onto his feet,   *330*
And walked out of the bedroom like a god.
Then he sat down next to Telemachus and said:

"Tell me, Telemachus, what has brought you here
To gleaming Sparta over the sea's broad back?
Public business or private? Tell me the truth."   *335*

Telemachus took a deep breath and said:

"Menelaus, son of Atreus in the line of Zeus,
I came to see if you could tell me anything
About my father. My land is in ruin.
I'm being eaten out of house and home   *340*
By hostile men who constantly throng my halls
Slaughtering my sheep and horned cattle
In their arrogant courtship of my mother.
And so I am at your knees. Tell me
How my father, Odysseus, met his end,   *345*
Whether you saw it with your own eyes,
Or heard about it from someone else,
Some wanderer. He was born to sorrow,
More than any man on earth. And do not,
Out of pity, spare me the truth, but tell me   *350*
Whatever you have seen, whatever you know.
I beseech you, if my father, noble Odysseus,
Ever fulfilled a promise he made to you
In the land of Troy, where the Achaeans suffered,
Remember it now, and tell me the truth."   *355*

And Menelaus, deeply troubled by this:

"Those dogs! Those puny weaklings,
Wanting to sleep in the bed of a hero!
A doe might as well bed her suckling fawns
In the lair of a lion, leaving them there   *360*
In the bush and then going off over the hills
Looking for grassy fields. When the lion
Comes back, the fawns die an ugly death.

That's the kind of death these men will die
When Odysseus comes back. O Father Zeus,   *365*
And Athena and Apollo, bring Odysseus back
With the strength he showed in Lesbos once
When he wrestled a match with Philomeleides
And threw him hard, making all of us cheer—
That's the Odysseus I want the suitors to meet!   *370*
They'd get married all right—to bitter death.
But, as to what you ask me about,
I will not stray from the point or deceive you.
No, I will tell you all that the infallible
Old Man of the Sea told me, and hide nothing.   *375*
    I was in Egypt, held up by the gods
Because I failed to offer them sacrifice.
The gods never allow us to forget them.
There is an island in the whitecapped sea
Just north of Egypt. Men call it Pharos,   *380*
And it lies one hard day's sailing offshore.
There is a good harbor there where ships
Take on fresh water before heading out to sea.
The gods kept me stuck in that harbor
For twenty days. A good sailing breeze   *385*
Never rose up, and all my supplies
Would have been exhausted, and my crew spent,
Had not one of the gods taken pity on me
And saved me. This was Eidothea,
Daughter of Proteus, the Old Man of the Sea.   *390*
Somehow I had moved her heart. She met me
As I wandered alone, apart from my crew,
Who roamed the island continually, fishing
With bent hooks, their bellies cramped with hunger.
She came close to me and spoke: *395*

'Are you completely out of your mind, stranger,
Or do you actually like suffering like this?
You've been marooned on this island a long time
With no end in sight, and your crew's fading fast.'

"She spoke like this, and I answered her: *400*

'I tell you, goddess—whichever goddess you are—
That I am not stranded here of my own free will.
I must have offended one of the immortals.
But you tell me—for gods know everything—
Which of the immortals is pinning me down here   *405*
And won't let me go. And tell me how
I can sail back home over the teeming sea.'

"And the shining goddess answered me:

'Well, all right, stranger, since you ask.
This is the haunt of an unerring immortal,   *410*
Egyptian Proteus, the Old Man of the Sea,
Who serves Poseidon and knows all the deeps.
They say he's my father. If you can
Somehow catch him in ambush here,
He will tell you the route, and the distance too,   *415*
Of your journey home over the teeming sea.
And he will tell you, prince, if you so wish,
What has been done in your house for better or worse
While you have been gone on your long campaign.'

"So she spoke, and I answered her: *420*

'Show me yourself how to ambush
The old god, or he may give me the slip.
It's hard for a mortal to master a god.'

"And the shining goddess answered me:

'I'll tell you exactly what you need to know.   *425*
When the sun is at high noon, the unerring
Old Man of the Sea comes from the saltwater,
Hidden in dark ripples the West Wind stirs up,
And then lies down to sleep in the scalloped caves.
All around him seals, the brine-spirit's brood,   *430*
Sleep in a herd. They come out of the grey water
With breath as fetid as the depths of the sea.
I will lead you there at break of day

And lay you in a row, you and three comrades
Chosen by you as the best on your ship.   *435*
Now I'll tell you all the old man's wiles.
First, he will go over the seals and count them,
And when he has counted them off by fives,
He will lie down like a shepherd among them.
As soon as you see him lying down to rest,   *440*
Screw up your courage to the sticking point
And pin him down, no matter how he struggles
And tries to escape. He will try everything,
And turn into everything that moves on the earth,
And into water also, and a burning flame.   *445*
Just hang on and grip him all the more tightly.
When he finally speaks to you of his own free will
In the shape you saw him in when he lay down to rest,
Then ease off, hero, and let the old man go,
And ask him which of the gods is angry with you,   *450*
And how you can sail home over the teeming sea.'

"And with that she slipped into the surging sea.
I headed for my ships where they stood on the sand
And brooded on many things as I went.
When I had come down to the ships and the sea,   *455*
We made supper, and when night came on,
We lay down to take our rest on the beach.
When dawn came, a palmetto of rose,
I went along the shore of the open sea
Praying over and over to the immortal gods,   *460*
Taking with me the three of my crew
I trusted the most for any adventure.

"The goddess, meanwhile, dove underwater
And now came back with the skins of four seals,
All newly flayed. She was out to trick her father.   *465*
She scooped out hiding places for us in the sand
And sat waiting as we cautiously drew near.
Then she had us lie down in a row, and threw
A seal skin over each of us. It would have been
A gruesome ambush—the stench of the seals   *470*

Was unbearable—but the goddess saved us
By putting ambrosia under each man's nose,
Drowning out the stench with its immortal fragrance.
So we waited patiently all morning long,
And then the seals came from the water in throngs.   *475*
They lay down in rows along the seashore,
And at noon the Old One came from the sea.
He found the fat seals and went over the herd,
Counting them up. He counted us first,
Never suspecting any kind of trick,   *480*
And then he lay down. We rushed him
With a shout and got our hands on him,
And the Old One didn't forget his wiles,
Turning first into a bearded lion,
Then a serpent, a leopard, and a huge boar.   *485*
He even turned into flowing water,
And into a high, leafy tree. But we
Held on, gritting our teeth, and at last
The wily Old One grew weary, and said to me:

'Which god have you plotted with, son of Atreus,   *490*
To catch me off-guard? What do you want?'

"He spoke, and I answered him:

'You know, old man—don't try to put me off—
How long I have been stuck on this island
With no end in sight. I'm losing heart.   *495*
Just tell me this—you gods know everything—
Which of the immortals has marooned me here?
How can I sail home over the teeming sea?'

"When I said this, he answered:

'You should have offered noble sacrifice to Zeus   *500*
And the other gods before embarking
If you wanted a speedy journey home
Over the deep purple sea. It is not your fate
To come home to your friends and native land

Until you go once more to the waters of the Aegyptus,   *505*
The sky-fed river, and offer holy hecatombs
To the immortal gods who hold high heaven.
Only then will they grant the journey you desire.'

"When he said this my spirit was crushed.
It was a long, hard pull over the misty deep   *510*
Back to the Aegyptus. Still, I answered:

'I will do all these things, just as you say.
But tell me this, and tell me the truth:
Did all the Achaeans make it home in their ships,
All those whom Nestor and I left at Troy?   *515*
Or did any die on shipboard, or in their friends' arms,
After winding up the war?'

                    "To which Proteus said:

'Why, son of Atreus, ask me about this?
You don't need to know. Nor do I think
You will be free from tears once you have heard it.   *520*
Many were killed in the war. You were there
And know who they were. Many, too, survived.
On the homeward journey two heroes died.
Another still lives, perhaps, held back by the sea.

'Ajax went down among his long-oared ships.   *525*
Poseidon had driven him onto Gyrae's rocks
But saved him from the sea. He would have escaped,
Despite Athena's hatred, but he lost his wits
And boasted loudly that he had survived the deep
In spite of the gods. Poseidon heard this boast,   *530*
And with his trident he struck Gyrae's rock
And broke it asunder. One part held firm,
But the other part, upon which Ajax sat
In his blind arrogance, fell into the gulf
And took Ajax with it. And so he perished,   *535*
His lungs full of saltwater.
                              Your brother, though,

Outran the fates in his hollow ships,
With the help of Hera. But when he was nearing
Malea's heights, a stormwind caught him
And carried him groaning over the teeming sea   540
To the frontier of the land where Thyestes once lived
And after him Thyestes' son, Aegisthus.
Then the gods gave him a following wind
And safe passage homeward. Agamemnon
Rejoiced to set foot on his ancestral land.   545
He fell to the ground and kissed the good earth
And hot tears of joy streamed from his eyes,
So glad was he to see his homeland again.
But from a high lookout a watchman saw him.
Aegisthus had treacherously posted him there   550
And promised a reward of two bars of gold.
He had been keeping watch for a year by then
So that Agamemnon would not slip by unseen
And unleash his might, and now he reported
His news to Aegisthus, who acted quickly   555
And set a trap. He chose his twenty best men
And had them wait in ambush. Opposite them,
On the hall's farther side, he had a feast prepared,
And then he drove off in his chariot,
Brooding darkly, to invite Agamemnon.   560
So he brought Agamemnon up to the palace
Unaware of his doom and slaughtered him
The way an ox is slaughtered at the stall.
None of Agamemnon's men was left alive,
Nor any of Aegisthus'. All were slain in the hall.'   565

"Proteus spoke, and my heart was shattered.
I wept and wept as I sat on the sand, losing
All desire to live and see the light of the sun.
When I could not weep or flail about any more,
The unerring Old Man of the Sea addressed me: 570

'Weep no more, son of Atreus. We gain nothing
By such prolonged bouts of grief. Instead,
Go as quickly as you can to your native land.

Either Aegisthus will still be alive, or
Orestes may have beat you to it and killed him,   575
And you may happen to arrive during his funeral.'

"These words warmed my heart, although
I was still in shock. Then I asked him:

'I know now what became of these two,
But who is the third man, the one who's alive,   580
But held back by the sea, or perhaps is dead.
I want to hear about him, despite my grief.'

"Proteus answered me without hesitation:

'It is Laertes' son, whose home is in Ithaca.
I saw him on an island, shedding salt tears,   585
In the halls of Calypso, who keeps him there
Against his will. He has no way to get home
To his native land. He has no ships left,
No crew to row him over the sea's broad back.
As for you, Menelaus, Zeus' cherished king,   590
You are not destined to die and to meet your fate
In bluegrass Argos. The immortals will take you
To the ends of the earth and the Elysian Fields,
Where Rhadamanthus lives and life is easiest.
No snow, nor storm, nor heavy rain comes there,   595
But a sighing wind from the West always blows
Off the Ocean, a cooling breeze for men.
For Helen is your wife, and in the gods' eyes
You are the son-in-law of great Zeus himself.'

"And with that he dove into the surging sea.   600
I went back to the ships with my godlike companions
And brooded on many things as I went.
When we had come down to the ships and the sea,
And had made supper, immortal night came on,
And we lay down to take our rest on the beach.   605
When dawn came with palmettoes of rose,
We hauled our ships down to the shining water,

And set up the masts and sails in the hulls.
The crews came aboard, and sitting in rows
They beat the sea white with their churning oars.   610
And so I sailed back to the rain-fed Aegyptus,
Moored my ships, and offered perfect sacrifice.
When I had appeased the everlasting gods
I heaped up a barrow for Agamemnon
So that his memory would not fade. Only then   615
Did I set sail for home, and the gods gave me
A following wind that brought me back swiftly."

[The rest of Book 4 (lines 618–907) is omitted. The suitors discover that Telemachus has set sail, and they prepare an ambush for him at sea.]

ODYSSEY 5

D awn reluctantly
Left Tithonus in her rose-shadowed bed,
Then shook the morning into flakes of fire.

Light flooded the halls of Olympus
Where Zeus, high Lord of Thunder,   5
Sat with the other gods, listening to Athena
Reel off the tale of Odysseus' woes.
It galled her that he was still in Calypso's cave:

"Zeus, my father—and all you blessed immortals—
Kings might as well no longer be gentle and kind   10
Or understand the correct order of things.
They might as well be tryannical butchers
For all that any of Odysseus' people
Remember him, a godly king as kind as a father.
No, he's still languishing on that island, detained   15

Against his will by that nymph Calypso,
No way in the world for him to get back to his land.
His ships are all lost, he has no crew left
To row him across the sea's crawling back.
And now the islanders are plotting to kill his son   20
As he heads back home. He went for news of his father
To sandy Pylos and white-bricked Sparta."

Storm Cloud Zeus had an answer for her:

"Quite a little speech you've let slip through your teeth,
Daughter. But wasn't this exactly your plan   25
So that Odysseus would make them pay for it later?
You know how to get Telemachus
Back to Ithaca and out of harm's way
With his mother's suitors sailing in a step behind."

Zeus turned then to his son Hermes and said: 30

"Hermes, you've been our messenger before.
Go tell that ringleted nymph it is my will
To let that patient man Odysseus go home.
Not with an escort, mind you, human or divine,
But on a rickety raft—tribulation at sea—   35
Until on the twentieth day he comes to Schería
In the land of the Phaeacians, our distant relatives,
Who will treat Odysseus as if he were a god
And take him on a ship to his own native land
With gifts of bronze and clothing and gold,   40
More than he ever would have taken back from Troy
Had he come home safely with his share of the loot.
That's how he's destined to see his dear ones again
And return to his high-gabled Ithacan home."

Thus Zeus, and the quicksilver messenger   45
Laced on his feet the beautiful sandals,
Golden, immortal, that carry him over
Landscape and seascape on a puff of wind.
And he picked up the wand he uses to charm

Mortal eyes to sleep and make sleepers awake.   *50*

Holding this wand the tough quicksilver god
Took off, bounded onto Pieria
And dove through the ether down to the sea,

> *Skimming the waves like a cormorant,*
> *The bird that patrols the saltwater billows*   *55*
> *Hunting for fish, seaspume on its plumage,*

Hermes flying low and planing the whitecaps.

When he finally arrived at the distant island
He stepped from the violet-tinctured sea
On to dry land and proceeded to the cavern   *60*
Where Calypso lived. She was at home.
A fire blazed on the hearth, and the smell
Of split cedar and arbor vitae burning
Spread like incense across the whole island.
She was seated inside, singing in a lovely voice   *65*
As she wove at her loom with a golden shuttle.
Around her cave the woodland was in bloom,
Alder and poplar and fragrant cypress.
Long-winged birds nested in the leaves,
Horned owls and larks and slender-throated shorebirds   *70*
That screech like crows over the bright saltwater.
Tendrils of ivy curled around the cave's mouth,
The glossy green vine clustered with berries.
Four separate springs flowed with clear water, criss-
Crossing channels as they meandered through meadows   *75*
Lush with parsley and blossoming violets.
It was enough to make even a visiting god
Enraptured at the sight. Quicksilver Hermes
Took it all in, then turned and entered
The vast cave.
        Calypso knew him at sight.   *80*
The immortals have ways of recognizing each other,
Even those whose homes are in outlying districts.
But Hermes didn't find the great hero inside.

Odysseus was sitting on the shore,
As ever those days, honing his heart's sorrow,   *85*
Staring out to sea with hollow, salt-rimmed eyes.

Calypso, sleek and haloed, questioned Hermes
Politely, as she seated him on a lacquered chair:

"My dear Hermes, to what do I owe
The honor of this unexpected visit? Tell me   *90*
What you want, and I'll oblige you if I can."

The goddess spoke, and then set a table
With ambrosia and mixed a bowl of rosy nectar.
The quicksilver messenger ate and drank his fill,
Then settled back from dinner with heart content   *95*
And made the speech she was waiting for:

"You ask me, goddess to god, why I have come.
Well, I'll tell you exactly why. Remember, you asked.
Zeus ordered me to come here; I didn't want to.
Who would want to cross this endless stretch   *100*
Of deserted sea? Not a single city in sight
Where you can get a decent sacrifice from men.
But you know how it is: Zeus has the aegis,
And none of us gods can oppose his will.
He says you have here the most woebegone hero   *105*
Of the whole lot who fought around Priam's city
For nine years, sacked it in the tenth, and started home.
But on the way back they offended Athena,
And she swamped them with hurricane winds and waves.
His entire crew was wiped out, and he   *110*
Drifted along until he was washed up here.
Anyway, Zeus wants you to send him back home. Now.
The man's not fated to rot here far from his friends.
It's his destiny to see his dear ones again
And return to his high-gabled Ithacan home."   *115*

He finished, and the nymph's aura stiffened.
Words flew from her mouth like screaming hawks:

"You gods are the most jealous bastards in the universe—
Persecuting any goddess who ever openly takes
A mortal lover to her bed and sleeps with him. *120*
When Dawn caressed Orion with her rosy fingers,
You celestial layabouts gave her nothing but trouble
Until Artemis finally shot him on Ortygia—
Gold-throned, holy, gentle-shafted assault goddess!
When Demeter followed her heart and unbound *125*
Her hair for Iasion and made love to him
In a late-summer field, Zeus was there taking notes
And executed the man with a cobalt lightning blast.
And now you gods are after me for having a man.
Well, I was the one who saved his life, unprying him *130*
From the spar he came floating here on, sole survivor
Of the wreck Zeus made of his streamlined ship,
Slivering it with lightning on the wine-dark sea.
I loved him, I took care of him, I even told him
I'd make him immortal and ageless all of his days. *135*
But you said it, Hermes: Zeus has the aegis
And none of us gods can oppose his will.
So all right, he can go, if it's an order from above,
Off on the sterile sea. How I don't know.
I don't have any oared ships or crewmen *140*
To row him across the sea's broad back.
But I'll help him. I'll do everything I can
To get him back safely to his own native land."

The quicksilver messenger had one last thing to say:

"Well send him off now and watch out for Zeus' temper. *145*
Cross him and he'll really be rough on you later."

With that the tough quicksilver god made his exit.

Calypso composed herself and went to Odysseus,
Zeus' message still ringing in her ears.
She found him sitting where the breakers rolled in. *150*
His eyes were perpetually wet with tears now,
His life draining away in homesickness.

The nymph had long since ceased to please.
He still slept with her at night in her cavern,
An unwilling lover mated to her eager embrace.   *155*
Days he spent sitting on the rocks by the breakers,
Staring out to sea with hollow, salt-rimmed eyes.
She stood close to him and started to speak:

"You poor man. You can stop grieving now
And pining away. I'm sending you home.   *160*
Look, here's a bronze axe. Cut some long timbers
And make yourself a raft fitted with topdecks,
Something that will get you across the sea's misty spaces.
I'll stock it with fresh water, food, and red wine—
Hearty provisions that will stave off hunger—and   *165*
I'll clothe you well and send you a following wind
To bring you home safely to your own native land,
If such is the will of the gods of high heaven,
Whose minds and powers are stronger than mine."

Odysseus' eyes shone with weariness. He stiffened,   *170*
And shot back at her words fletched like arrows:

"I don't know what kind of send-off you have in mind,
Goddess, telling me to cross all that open sea on a raft,
Painful, hard sailing. Some well-rigged vessels
Never make it across with a stiff wind from Zeus.   *175*
You're not going to catch me setting foot on any raft
Unless you agree to swear a solemn oath
That you're not planning some new trouble for me."

Calypso's smile was like a shower of light.
She touched him gently, and teased him a little: *180*

"Blasphemous, that's what you are—but nobody's fool!
How do you manage to say things like that?
All right. I swear by Earth and Heaven above
And the subterranean water of Styx—the greatest
Oath and the most awesome a god can swear—   *185*
That I'm not planning more trouble for you, Odysseus.

I'll put my mind to work for you as hard as I would
For myself, if ever I were in such a fix.
My heart is in the right place, Odysseus,
Nor is it a cold lump of iron in my breast."   *190*

With that the haloed goddess walked briskly away
And the man followed in the deity's footsteps.
The two forms, human and divine, came to the cave
And he sat down in the chair which moments before
Hermes had vacated, and the nymph set out for him   *195*
Food and drink such as mortal men eat.
She took a seat opposite godlike Odysseus
And her maids served her ambrosia and nectar.
They helped themselves to as much as they wanted,
And when they had their fill of food and drink   *200*
Calypso spoke, an immortal radiance upon her:

"Son of Laertes in the line of Zeus, my wily Odysseus,
Do you really want to go home to your beloved country
Right away? Now? Well, you still have my blessings.
But if you had any idea of all the pain   *205*
You're destined to suffer before getting home,
You'd stay here with me, deathless—
Think of it, Odysseus!—no matter how much
You missed your wife and wanted to see her again.
You spend all your daylight hours yearning for her.   *210*
I don't mind saying she's not my equal
In beauty, no matter how you measure it.
Mortal beauty cannot compare with immortal."

Odysseus, always thinking, answered her this way:

"Goddess and mistress, don't be angry with me.   *215*
I know very well that Penelope,
For all her virtues, would pale beside you.
She's only human, and you are a goddess,
Eternally young. Still, I want to go back.
My heart aches for the day I return to my home.   *220*
If some god hits me hard as I sail the deep purple,

I'll weather it like the sea-bitten veteran I am.
God knows I've suffered and had my share of sorrows
In war and at sea. I can take more if I have to."

The sun set on his words, and the shadows darkened.　　225
They went to a room deep in the cave, where they made
Sweet love and lay side by side through the night.

D awn came early, touching the sky with rose.

Odysseus put on a shirt and cloak,
And the nymph slipped on a long silver robe　　230
Shimmering in the light, cinched it at the waist
With a golden belt and put a veil on her head.
What to do about sending Odysseus off?
She handed him an axe, bronze, both edges honed.
The olive-wood haft felt good in his palms.　　235
She gave him a sharp adze, too, then led the way
To the island's far side where the trees grew tall,
Alder and poplar and silver fir, sky-topping trees
Long-seasoned and dry that would keep him afloat.
Calypso showed him where the trees grew tall　　240
Then went back home, a glimmer in the woods,
While Odysseus cut timber.
　　　　　　　　　　　　Working fast,
He felled twenty trees, cut them to length,
Smoothed them skillfully and trued them to the line.
The glimmer returned—Calypso with an auger—　　245
And he drilled the beams through, fit them up close
And hammered them together with joiners and pegs.
About the size of a deck a master shipwright
Chisels into shape for a broad-bowed freighter
Was the size Odysseus made his wide raft.　　250
He fit upright ribs close-set in the decking
And finished them with long facing planks.
He built a mast and fit in a yardarm,
And he made a rudder to steer her by.
Then he wove a wicker-work barrier　　255
To keep off the waves, plaiting it thick.

Calypso brought him a large piece of cloth
To make into a sail, and he fashioned that, too.
He rigged up braces and halyards and lines,
Then levered his craft down to the glittering sea.   260

Day four, and the job was finished.
Day five, and Calypso saw him off her island,
After she had bathed him and dressed him
In fragrant clothes. She filled up a skin
With wine that ran black, another large one   265
With water, and tucked into a duffel
A generous supply of hearty provisions.
And she put a breeze at his back, gentle and warm.

   Odysseus' heart sang as he spread sail to the wind,
And he steered with the rudder, a master mariner   270
Aboard his craft. Sleep never fell on his eyelids
As he watched the Pleiades and slow-setting Boötes
And the Bear (also known as the Wagon)
That pivots in place and chases Orion
And alone is aloof from the wash of Ocean.   275
Calypso, the glimmering goddess, had told him
To sail with the stars of the Bear on his left.
Seventeen days he sailed the deep water,
And on the eighteenth day the shadowy mountains
Of the Phaeacians' land loomed on the horizon,   280
To his eyes like a shield on the misty sea.

And Poseidon saw him.
                 From the far Solymi Mountains
The Lord of Earthquake, returning from Ethiopia,
Saw him, an image in his mind bobbing on the sea.
Angrier than ever, he shook his head   285
And cursed to himself:

          "Damn it all, the gods
Must have changed their minds about Odysseus
While I was away with the Ethiopians.
He's close to Phaeacia, where he's destined to escape

The great ring of sorrow that has closed around him.   *290*
But I'll bet I can still blow some trouble his way."

He gathered the clouds, and gripping his trident
He stirred the sea. And he raised all the blasts
Of every wind in the world and covered with clouds
Land and sea together. Night rose in the sky.   *295*
The winds blew hard from every direction,
And lightning-charged Boreas rolled in a big wave.
Odysseus felt his knees and heart weaken.
Hunched over, he spoke to his own great soul:

"Now I'm in for it.   *300*
I'm afraid that Calypso was right on target
When she said I would have my fill of sorrow
On the open sea before I ever got home.
It's all coming true. Look at these clouds
Zeus is piling like flowers around the sky's rim,   *305*
And he's roughened the sea, and every wind
In the world is howling around me.
Three times, four times luckier than I
Were the Greeks who died on Troy's wide plain!
If only I had gone down on that day   *310*
When the air was whistling with Trojan spears
In the desperate fight for Achilles' dead body.
I would have had burial then, honored by the army.
As it is I am doomed to a wretched death at sea."

His words weren't out before a huge cresting wave   *315*
Crashed on his raft and shivered its timbers.
He was pitched clear of the deck. The rudder flew
From his hands, the mast cracked in two
Under the force of the hurricane winds,
And the yardarm and sail hove into the sea.   *320*
He was under a long time, unable to surface
From the heaving swell of the monstrous wave,
Weighed down by the clothes Calypso had given him.
At last he came up, spitting out saltwater,
Seabrine gurgling from his nostrils and mouth.   *325*

For all his distress, though, he remembered his raft,
Lunged through the waves, caught hold of it
And huddled down in its center shrinking from death.

An enormous wave rode the raft into cross-currents.

> *The North Wind in autumn sweeps through a field*   330
> *Rippling with thistles and swirls them around.*

So the winds swirled the raft all over the sea,
South Wind colliding at times with the North,
East Wind shearing away from the West.

And the White Goddess saw him, Cadmus' daughter   335
Ino, once a human girl with slim, beautiful ankles
Who had won divine honors in the saltwater gulfs.
She pitied Odysseus his wandering, his pain,
And rose from the water like a flashing gull,
Perched on his raft, and said this to him: 340

"Poor man. Why are you so odious to Poseidon,
Odysseus, that he sows all this grief for you?
But he'll not destroy you, for all of his fury.
Now do as I say—you're in no way to refuse:
Take off those clothes and abandon your raft   345
To the winds' will. Swim for your life
To the Phaeacians' land, your destined safe harbor.
Here, wrap this veil tightly around your chest.
It's immortally charmed: Fear no harm or death.
But when with your hands you touch solid land   350
Untie it and throw it into the deep blue sea
Clear of the shore so it can come back to me."

With these words the goddess gave him the veil
And slipped back into the heavy seas
Like a silver gull. The black water swallowed her.   355
Godlike Odysseus brooded on his trials
And spoke these words to his own great soul:

"Not this. Not another treacherous god
Scheming against me, ordering me to abandon my raft.
I will not obey. I've seen with my own eyes   360
How far that land is where she says I'll be saved.
I'll play it the way that seems best to me.
As long as the timbers are still holding together
I'll hang on and gut it out right here where I am.
When and if a wave shatters my raft to pieces,   365
Then I'll swim for it. What else can I do?"

As he churned these thoughts in the pit of his stomach
Poseidon Earthshaker raised up a great wave—
An arching, cavernous, cresting tsunami—
And brought it crashing down on him.   370

   As storm winds blast into a pile of dry chaff
   And scatter the stuff all over the place,

So the long beams of Odysseus' raft were scattered.
He went with one beam and rode it like a stallion,
Stripping off the clothes Calypso had given him   375
And wrapping the White Goddess's veil round his chest.
Then he dove into the sea and started to swim
A furious breaststroke. The Lord of Earthquake saw him
And said to himself with a slow toss of his head:

"That's right. Thrash around in misery on the open sea   380
Until you come to human society again.
I hope that not even then will you escape from evil."

With these words he whipped his sleek-coated horses
And headed for his fabulous palace on Aegae.

But Zeus' daughter Athena had other ideas.   385
She barricaded all the winds but one
And ordered them to rest and fall asleep.
Boreas, though, she sent cracking through the waves,
A tailwind for Odysseus until he was safe on Phaeacia,
And had beaten off the dark birds of death.   390

Two nights and two days the solid, mitered waves
Swept him on, annihilation all his heart could foresee.
But when Dawn combed her hair in the third day's light,
The wind died down and there fell
A breathless calm. Riding a swell   *395*
He peered out and saw land nearby.

> *You know how precious a father's life is*
> *To children who have seen him through a long disease,*
> *Gripped by a malevolent spirit and melting away,*
> *But then released from suffering in a spasm of joy.*   *400*

The land and woods were that welcome a sight
To Odysseus. He kicked hard for the shoreline,
But when he was as close as a shout would carry
He heard the thud of waves on the rocks,
Thundering surf that pounded the headland   *405*
And bellowed eerily. The sea churned with foam.
There were no harbors for ships, no inlets or bays,
Only jutting cliffs and rocks and barnacled crags.
Odysseus' heart sank and his knees grew weak.
With a heavy sigh he spoke to his own great soul: *410*

"Ah, Zeus has let me see land I never hoped to see
And I've cut my way to the end of this gulf,
But there's no way to get out of the grey saltwater.
Only sharp rocks ahead, laced by the breakers,
And beyond them slick stone rising up sheer   *415*
Right out of deep water, no place for a foothold,
No way to stand up and wade out of trouble.
If I try to get out here a wave might smash me
Against the stone cliff. Some mooring that would be!
If I swim around farther and try to find   *420*
A shelving shore or an inlet from the sea,
I'm afraid that a squall will take me back out
Groaning deeply on the teeming dark water,
Or some monster will attack me out of the deep
From the swarming brood of great Amphitrîtê.   *425*
I know how odious I am to the Earthshaker."

As these thoughts welled up from the pit of his stomach
A breaker bore him onto the rugged coast.
He would have been cut to ribbons and his bones crushed
But grey-eyed Athena inspired him.   *430*
Slammed onto a rock he grabbed it with both hands
And held on groaning until the breaker rolled by.
He had no sooner ducked it when the backwash hit him
And towed him far out into open water again.

> *It was just like an octopus pulled out of its hole*   *435*
> *With pebbles stuck to its tentacles,*

Odysseus' strong hands clinging to the rocks
Until the skin was ripped off. The wave
Pulled him under, and he would have died
Then and there. But Athena was with him.   *440*
He surfaced again: the wave spat him up landwards,
And he swam along parallel to the coast, scanning it
For a shelving beach, an inlet from the sea,
And when he swam into the current of a river delta
He knew he had come to the perfect spot,   *445*
Lined with smooth rocks and sheltered from the wind.
He felt the flowing of the rivergod, and he prayed:

"Hear me, Riverlord, whoever you are
And however men pray to you:
I am a fugitive from the sea   *450*
And Poseidon's persecution,
A wandering mortal, pitiful
To the gods, I come to you,
To your water and your knees.
I have suffered much, O Lord,   *455*
Lord, hear my prayer."

At these words the god stopped his current,
Made his waters calm and harbored the man
In his river's shallows. Odysseus crawled out
On hands and knees. The sea had broken his spirit.   *460*
His whole body was swollen, and saltwater trickled

From his nose and mouth. Breath gone, voice gone,
He lay scarcely alive, drained and exhausted.
When he could breathe again and his spirit returned
He unbound the goddess' veil from his body   *465*
And threw it into the sea-melding river
Where it rode the crest of a wave down the current
And into Ino's own hands. He turned away from the river,
Sank into a bed of rushes, and kissed the good earth.
Huddled over he spoke to his own great soul: *470*

"What am I in for now? How will this end?
If I keep watch all night here by the river
I'm afraid a hard frost—or even a gentle dew—
Will do me in, as weak as I am.
The wind blows cold from a river toward dawn.   *475*
But if I climb the bank to the dark woods up there
And fall asleep in a thicket, even if I survive
Fatigue and cold and get some sweet sleep,
I'm afraid I'll fall prey to some prowling beast."

He thought it over and decided it was better   *480*
To go to the woods. They were near the water
On an open rise. He found two olive trees there,
One wild, one planted, their growth intertwined,
Proof against blasts of the wild, wet wind,
The sun unable to needle light through,   *485*
Impervious to rain, so thickly they grew
Into one tangle of shadows. Odysseus burrowed
Under their branches and scraped out a bed.
He found a mass of leaves there, enough to keep warm
Two or three men on the worst winter day.   *490*
The sight of these leaves was a joy to Odysseus,
And the godlike survivor lay down in their midst
And covered himself up.

            A solitary man
    Who lives on the edge of the wilderness
    And has no neighbors, will hide a charred log   *495*
    Deep in the black embers and so keep alive

The fire's seed and not have to rekindle it
From who knows where.

                    So Odysseus buried
Himself in the leaves. And Athena sprinkled
His eyes with sleep for quickest release   500
From pain and fatigue.
                  And she closed his eyelids.

ODYSSEY 6

So Odysseus slept, the godlike survivor
Overwhelmed with fatigue.
                    But the goddess Athena
Went off to the land of the Phaeacians,
A people who had once lived in Hypereia,
Near to the Cyclopes, a race of savages   5
Who marauded their land constantly. One day
Great Nausithous led his people
Off to Schería, a remote island,
Where he walled off a city, built houses
And shrines, and parceled out fields.   10
After he died and went to the world below,
Alcinous ruled, wise in the gods' ways.
Owl-eyed Athena now came to his house
To devise a passage home for Odysseus.
She entered a richly decorated bedroom   15
Where a girl as lovely as a goddess was sleeping,
Nausicaa, daughter of noble Alcinous.
Two maids, blessed with the beauty of Graces,
Slept on either side of the closed, polished doors.
Athena rushed in like a breath of wind,   20
Stood over Nausicaa's head, and spoke to her

In the guise of her friend, the daughter
Of the famed mariner Dymas. Assuming
This girl's form, the owl-eyed goddess spoke:

"Nausicaa, how could your mother have raised   25
Such a careless child? Your silky clothes
Are lying here soiled, and your wedding is near!
You'll have to dress yourself and your party well,
If you want the people to speak highly of you
And make your mother and father glad.   30
We'll wash these clothes at the break of dawn.
I'll go with you and help so you'll get it done quickly.
You're not going to be a virgin for long, you know!
All the best young men in Phaeacia are eager
To marry you—as well they should be.   35
Wake up now, and at dawn's first blush
Ask your father if he will hitch up the mulecart
To carry all these sashes and robes and things.
It'll be much more pleasant than going on foot.
The laundry pools are a long way from town."   40

The grey-eyed goddess spoke and was gone,
Off to Olympus, which they say is forever
The unmoving abode of the gods, unshaken
By winds, never soaked by rain, and where the snow
Never drifts, but the brilliant sky stretches   45
Cloudless away, and brightness streams through the air.
There, where the gods are happy all the world's days,
Went the Grey-eyed One after speaking to the girl.

Dawn came throned in light, and woke Nausicaa,
Who wondered at the dream as it faded away.   50
She went through the house to tell her parents,
Her dear father and mother. She found them within,
Her mother sitting by the hearth with her women,
Spinning sea-blue yarn. Her father she met
As he headed for the door accompanied by elders   55
On his way to a council the nobles had called.
She stood very close to her father and said:

"Daddy, would you please hitch up a wagon for me—
A high one that rolls well—so I can go to the river
And wash our good clothes that are all dirty now.   60
You yourself should wear clean clothes
When you sit among the first men in council.
And you have five sons who live in the palace,
Two married and three still bachelors.
They always want freshly washed clothes   65
To wear to the dances. This has been on my mind."

She was too embarrassed to mention marriage
To her father, but he understood and said:

"Of course you can have the mules, child,
And anything else. Go on. The servants will rig up   70
A high, smooth-rolling wagon fitted with a trunk."

He called the servants, and they got busy
Rolling out a wagon and hitching up mules.
Nausicaa brought out a pile of laundry
And loaded it into the polished cart,   75
While her mother packed a picnic basket
With all sorts of food and filled a goatskin with wine.
The girl put these up on the cart, along with
A golden flask of oil her mother gave her
For herself and her maids to rub on their skin.   80
She took the lash and the glossy reins
And had the mules giddyup. They jangled along
At a steady pace, pulling the clothes and the girl,
While the other girls, her maids, ran alongside.

They came to the beautiful, running river   85
And the laundry pools, where the clear water
Flowed through strongly enough to clean
Even the dirtiest clothes. They unhitched the mules
And shooed them out along the swirling river's edge
To munch the sweet clover. Then they unloaded   90
The clothes, brought them down to the water,
And trod them in the trenches, working fast

And making a game of it. When the clothes were washed
They spread them out neatly on the shore of the sea
Where the waves scoured the pebbled beach clean.   *95*
Then they bathed themselves and rubbed rich olive oil
Onto their skin, and had a picnic on the river's banks
While they waited for the sun to dry the clothes.
When the princess and her maids had enough to eat
They began to play with a ball, their hair streaming free.   *100*

> *Artemis sometimes roams the mountains—*
> *Immense Taygetus, or Erymanthus—*
> *Showering arrows upon boars or fleet antelope,*
> *And with her play the daughters of Zeus*
> *Who range the wild woods—and Leto is glad*   *105*
> *That her daughter towers above them all*
> *With her shining brow, though they are beautiful all—*

So the unwed princess among her attendants.

But when she was about to fold the clothes,
Yoke the mules, and head back home,   *110*
The Grey-eyed One sprung her plan:
Odysseus would wake up, see the lovely girl,
And she would lead him to the Phaeacians' city.
The princess threw the ball to one of the girls,
But it sailed wide into deep, swirling water.   *115*
The girls screamed, and Odysseus awoke.
Sitting up, he tried to puzzle it out:

"What kind of land have I come to now?
Are the natives wild and lawless savages,
Or godfearing men who welcome strangers?   *120*
That sounded like girls screaming, or the cry
Of the spirit women who hold the high peaks,
The river wells, and the grassy meadows.
Can it be I am close to human voices?
I'll go have a look and see for myself."   *125*

With that Odysseus emerged from the bushes.

He broke off a leafy branch from the undergrowth
And held it before him to cover himself.

> *A weathered mountain lion steps into a clearing,*
> *Confident in his strength, eyes glowing.*   130
> *The wind and rain have let up, and he's hunting*
> *Cattle, sheep, or wild deer, but is hungry enough*
> *To jump the stone walls of the animal pens.*

So Odysseus advanced upon these ringleted girls,
Naked as he was. What choice did he have?   135
He was a frightening sight, disfigured with brine,
And the girls fluttered off to the jutting beaches.
Only Alcinous' daughter stayed. Athena
Put courage in her heart and stopped her trembling.
She held her ground, and Odysseus wondered   140
How to approach this beautiful girl. Should he
Fall at her knees, or keep his distance
And ask her with honeyed words to show him
The way to the city and give him some clothes?
He thought it over and decided it was better   145
To keep his distance and not take the chance
Of offending the girl by touching her knees.
So he started this soft and winning speech:

"I implore you, Lady: Are you a goddess
Or mortal? If you are one of heaven's divinities   150
I think you are most like great Zeus' daughter
Artemis. You have her looks, her stature, her form.
If you are a mortal and live on this earth,
Thrice blest is your father, your queenly mother,
Thrice blest your brothers! Their hearts must always   155
Be warm with happiness when they look at you,
Just blossoming as you enter the dance.
And happiest of all will be the lucky man
Who takes you home with a cartload of gifts.
I've never seen anyone like you,   160
Man or woman. I look upon you with awe.
Once, on Delos, I saw something to compare—

A palm shoot springing up near Apollo's altar.
I had stopped there with the troops under my command
On what would prove to be a perilous campaign.   165
I marveled long and hard when I saw that tree,
For nothing like it had ever grown from the earth.
And I marvel now, Lady, and I am afraid
To touch your knees. Yet my pain is great.
Yesterday, after twenty days, I pulled myself out   170
Of the wine-dark sea. All that time, wind and wave
Bore me away from Ogygia Island,
And now some spirit has cast me up here
To suffer something new. I do not think
My trials will end soon. The gods have much more   175
In store for me before that ever happens.
Pity me, mistress. After all my hardships
It is to you I have come first. I don't know
A soul who lives here, not a single one.
Show me the way to town, and give me   180
A rag to throw over myself, some piece of cloth
You may have brought along to bundle the clothes.
And for yourself, may the gods grant you
Your heart's desire, a husband and a home,
And the blessing of a harmonious life.   185
For nothing is greater or finer than this,
When a man and woman live together
With one heart and mind, bringing joy
To their friends and grief to their foes."

And white-armed Nausicaa answered him: 190

"Stranger, you do not seem to be a bad man
Or a fool. Zeus himself, the Olympian god,
Sends happiness to good men and bad men both,
To each as he wills. To you he has given these troubles,
Which you have no choice but to bear. But now,   195
Since you have come to our country,
You shall not lack clothing, nor anything needed
By a sore-tried suppliant who presents himself.
I will show you where the city is and tell you

That the people here are called Phaeacians.   *200*
This is their country, and I am the daughter
Of great-hearted Alcinous, the Phaeacians' lord."

Then the princess called to the ringleted girls:

"Stop this now. Running away at the sight of a man!
Do you think he is part of an enemy invasion?   *205*
There is no man on earth, nor will there ever be,
Slippery enough to invade Phaeacia,
For we are very dear to the immortal gods,
And we live far out in the surging sea,
At the world's frontier, out of all human contact.   *210*
This poor man comes here as a wanderer,
And we must take care of him now. All strangers,
All beggars, are under the protection of Zeus,
And even small gifts are welcome. So let's feed
This stranger, give him something to drink,   *215*
And bathe him in the river, out of the wind."

The girls stopped, turned, and urged each other on.
They took Odysseus to a sheltered spot,
As Nausicaa, Alcinous' daughter, had ordered.
They set down a mantle and a tunic,   *220*
Gave him a golden flask of olive oil,
And told him to wash in the river.
Then sunlit Odysseus said to them:

"Stay off a ways there, girls, and let me
Wash the brine off my shoulders myself   *225*
And rub myself down. It's been a long time
Since my skin has felt oil. But I don't want
To wash in front of you. I'd be ashamed
To come out naked in front of young girls."

The girls went off and talked with Nausicaa,   *230*
And Odysseus rinsed off with river water
All the brine that caked his shoulders and back,
And he scrubbed the salty scurf from his scalp.

He finished his bath, rubbed himself down with oil,
And put on the clothes the maiden had given him.   235
Then Athena, born from Zeus, made him look
Taller and more muscled, and made his hair
Tumble down his head like hyacinth flowers.

> *Imagine a craftsman overlaying silver*
> *With pure gold. He has learned his art*   240
> *From Pallas Athena and Lord Hephaestus,*
> *And creates works of breathtaking beauty.*

So Athena herself made Odysseus' head and shoulders
Shimmer with grace. He walked down the beach
And sat on the sand. The princess was dazzled,   245
And she said to her white-armed serving girls:

"Listen, this man hasn't come to Phaeacia
Against the will of the Olympian gods.
Before, he was a terrible sight, but now,
He's like one of the gods who live in the sky.   250
If only such a man would be called my husband,
Living here, and content to stay here.
Well, go on, give him something to eat and drink."

They were only too glad to do what she said.
They served Odysseus food and drink,   255
And the long-suffering man ate and drank
Ravenously. It had been a long fast.

Nausicaa had other things on her mind.
She folded the clothes and loaded the wagon,
Hitched up the mules and climbed aboard.   260
Then she called to Odysseus and said:

"Get ready now, stranger, to go to the city,
So I can show you the way to my father's house,
Where I promise you will meet the best of the Phaeacians.
Now this is what you must do—and I think you understand: 265
As long as we're going through countryside and farms,

Keep up with my handmaidens behind the wagon.
Just jog along with them. I'll lead the way,
And we'll soon come to the city. It has a high wall
Around it, and a harbor on each side.   *270*
The isthmus gets narrow, and the upswept hulls
Are drawn up to the road. Every citizen
Has his own private slip. The market's there, too,
Surrounding Poseidon's beautiful temple
And bounded by stones set deep in the earth.   *275*
There men are always busy with their ships' tackle,
With cables and sails, and with planing their oars.
Phaeacians don't care for quivers and bows
But for oars and masts and streamlined ships
In which they love to cross the grey, salt sea.   *280*
It's their rude remarks I would rather avoid.
There are some insolent louts in this town,
And I can just hear one of them saying:
'Well, who's this tall, handsome stranger trailing along
Behind Nausicaa? Where'd she pick him up?   *285*
She'll probably marry him, some shipwreck she's taken in
From parts unknown. He's sure not local.
Maybe a god has come to answer her prayers,
Dropped out of the sky for her to have and to hold.
It's just as well she's found herself a husband   *290*
From somewhere else, since she turns her nose up
At the many fine Phaeacians who woo her.'
That's what they'll say, and it will count against me.
I myself would blame anyone who acted like this,
A girl who, with her father and mother to tell her better,   *295*
Kept the company of men before her wedding day.
No, stranger, be quick to understand me,
So that you can win from my father an escort home,
And soon at that.
                          Close by the road you will find
A grove of Athena, beautiful poplars   *300*
Surrounded by a meadow. A spring flows through it.
Right there is my father's estate and vineyard,
About as far from the city as a shout would carry.
Sit down there and wait for a while, until

We reach the city and arrive at my house.   *305*
When you think we've had enough time to get there,
Go into the city and ask any Phaeacian
For the house of my father, Lord Alcinous.
It's very easy to spot, and any child
Can lead you there. There's no other house   *310*
In all Phaeacia built like the house
Of the hero Alcinous. Once you're safely within
The courtyard, go quickly though the hall
Until you come to my mother. She'll be sitting
By the hearth in the firelight, spinning   *315*
Sea-blue yarn—a sight worth seeing—
As she leans against a column, her maids behind her.
Right beside her my father sits on his throne,
Sipping his wine like an immortal god.
Pass him by and throw your arms   *320*
Around my mother's knees, if you want to see
Your homeland soon, however far it may be.
If she smiles upon you, there is hope that you will
Return to your home and see your loved ones again."

And she smacked the mules with the shining lash.   *325*
They trotted on smartly, leaving the river behind.
She drove so that Odysseus and the girls
Could keep up, and used the lash with care.
The sun had set when they reached the grove
Sacred to Athena. Odysseus sat down there   *330*
And said this prayer to great Zeus' daughter:

"Hear me, mystic child of the Storm God,
O hear me now, as you heard me not
When I was shattered by the Earthshaker's blows.
Grant that I come to Phaeacia pitied and loved."   *335*

Thus his prayer, and Pallas Athena heard it
But did not appear to him face to face, not yet,
Out of respect for her uncle, who would rage against
Godlike Odysseus until he reached home.

ODYSSEY 8

*[Book 7 and lines 1–489 of Book 8 are omitted. Odysseus is welcomed by
Queen Arete and King Alcinous, who entertain him with feasting, dancing,
and athletic competitions. Challenged by a young Phaeacian and aided by
Athena, Odysseus throws the discus much farther than anyone else. The
bard Demodocus sings a bawdy tale about Ares and Aphrodite. Then
Odysseus, who has not yet told the Phaeacians his name, is given a bath.]*

When the women had bathed him, rubbed him with oil,   490
And clothed him in a beautiful tunic and cloak,
Odysseus strode from the bath and was on his way
To join the men drinking wine.
                                   Nausicaa,
Beautiful as only the gods could make her,
Stood by the doorpost of the great hall.   495
Her eyes went wide when she saw Odysseus,
And her words beat their way to him on wings:

"Farewell, stranger, and remember me
In your own native land. I saved your life."

And Odysseus, whose thoughts ran deep: 500

"Nausicaa, daughter of great Alcinous,
So may Zeus, Hera's thundering lord,
Grant that I see my homeland again.
There I will pray to you, as to a god,
All of my days. I owe you my life."   505

And he took his seat next to Lord Alcinous.
They were serving food and mixing the wine
When the herald came up leading the bard,
Honored Demodocus, and seated him on a chair
Propped against a tall pillar in the middle of the hall.   510
Odysseus, with his great presence of mind,

Cut off part of a huge chine of roast pork
Glistening with fat, and said to the herald:

"Herald, take this cut of meat to Demodocus
For him to eat. And I will greet him   *515*
Despite my grief. Bards are revered
By all men upon earth, for the Muse
Loves them well and has taught them the songways."

The herald brought the cut of meat to Demodocus
And placed it in his hands, much to the bard's delight. *520*
Then everyone reached out to the feast before them,
And when they had eaten and drunk to their hearts' content,
Odysseus spoke to Demodocus:

"I don't know whether it was the Muse
Who taught you, or Apollo himself,   *525*
But I praise you to the skies, Demodocus.
When you sing about the fate of the Greeks
Who fought at Troy, you have it right,
All that they did and suffered, all they endured.
It's as if you had been there yourself,   *530*
Or heard a first-hand account. But now,
Switch to the building of the wooden horse
Which Epeius made with Athena's help,
The horse which Odysseus led up to Troy
As a trap, filled with men who would   *535*
Destroy great Ilion. If you tell me this story
Just as it happened, I will tell the whole world
That some god must have opened his heart
And given to you the divine gift of song."

So he spoke, and the bard, moved by the god,   *540*
Began to sing. He made them see it happen,
How the Greeks set fire to their huts on the beach
And were sailing away, while Odysseus
And the picked men with him sat in the horse,
Which the Trojans had dragged into their city.   *545*
There the horse stood, and the Trojans sat around it

And could not decide what they should do.
There were three ways of thinking:
Hack open the timbers with pitiless bronze,
Or throw it from the heights to the rocks below,   *550*
Or let it stand as an offering to appease the gods.
The last was what would happen, for it was fated
That the city would perish once it enclosed
The great wooden horse, in which now sat
The Greek heroes who would spill Troy's blood.   *555*
The song went on. The Greeks poured out
Of their hollow ambush and sacked the city.
He sang how one hero here and another there
Ravaged tall Troy, but how Odysseus went,
Like the War God himself, with Menelaus   *560*
To the house of Deiphobus, and there, he said,
Odysseus fought his most daring battle
And won with the help of Pallas Athena.

This was his song. And Odysseus wept. Tears
Welled up in his eyes and flowed down his cheeks.   *565*

> *A woman wails as she throws herself upon*
> *Her husband's body. He has fallen in battle*
> *Before the town walls, fighting to the last*
> *To defend his city and protect his children.*
> *As she sees him dying and gasping for breath*   *570*
> *She clings to him and shrieks, while behind her*
> *Soldiers prod their spears into her shoulders and back,*
> *And as they lead her away into slavery*
> *Her tear-drenched face is a mask of pain.*

So too Odysseus, pitiful in his grief.   *575*
He managed to conceal his tears from everyone
Except Alcinous, who sat at his elbow
And could not help but hear his heavy sighs.
Alcinous acted quickly and said to his guests:

"Hear me, Phaeacian counselors and lords—   *580*
Demodocus should stop playing his lyre.

His song is not pleasing to everyone here.
Ever since dinner began and the divine bard
Rose up to sing, our guest has not ceased
From lamentation. He is overcome with grief.   585
Let the lyre stop. It is better if we all,
Host and guest alike, can enjoy the feast.
All that we are doing we are doing on behalf
Of the revered stranger, providing him
With passage home and gifts of friendship.   590
A stranger and suppliant is as dear as a brother
To anyone with even an ounce of good sense.
So there is no need, stranger, for you to withhold
What I am about to ask for, no need to be crafty
Or think of gain. Better to speak the plain truth.   595
Tell me your name, the one you were known by
To your mother and father and your people back home.
No one is nameless, rich man or poor.
Parents give names to all of their children
When they are born. And tell me your country,   600
Your city, and your land, so that our ships
May take you there, finding their way by their wits.
For Phaeacian ships do not have pilots,
Nor steering oars, as other ships have.
They know on their own their passengers' thoughts,   605
And know all the cities and rich fields in the world,
And they cross the great gulfs with the greatest speed,
Hidden in mist and fog, with never a fear
Of damage or shipwreck.
                         But I remember hearing
My father, Nausithous, say how Poseidon   610
Was angry with us because we always give
Safe passage to men. He said that one day
Poseidon would smite a Phaeacian ship
As it sailed back home over the misty sea,
And would encircle our city within a mountain.   615
The old man used to say that, and either the god
Will bring it to pass or not, as suits his pleasure.
But tell me this, and tell me the truth.
Where have you wandered, to what lands?

Tell me about the people and cities you saw,   *620*
Which ones are cruel and without right and wrong,
And which are godfearing and kind to strangers.
And tell me why you weep and grieve at heart
When you hear the fate of the Greeks and Trojans.
This was the gods' doing. They spun that fate   *625*
So that in later times it would turn into song.
Did some kinsman of yours die at Troy,
A good, loyal man, your daughter's husband
Or your wife's father, someone near and dear,
Or perhaps even a relative by blood?   *630*
Or was it a comrade, tried and true?
A friend like that is no less than a brother."

ODYSSEY 9

And Odysseus, his great mind teeming:

"My Lord Alcinous, what could be finer
Than listening to a singer of tales
Such as Demodocus, with a voice like a god's?
Nothing we do is sweeter than this—   *5*
A cheerful gathering of all the people
Sitting side by side throughout the halls,
Feasting and listening to a singer of tales,
The tables filled with food and drink,
The server drawing wine from the bowl   *10*
And bringing it around to fill our cups.
For me, this is the finest thing in the world.
But you have a mind to draw out of me
My pain and sorrow, and make me feel it again.
Where should I begin, where end my story?   *15*
Heaven has sent me many tribulations.

I will tell you my name first, so that you, too,
Will know who I am, and when I escape
The day of my doom, I will always be
Your friend and host, though my home is far.   20
I am Odysseus, great Laertes' son,
Known for my cunning throughout the world,
And my fame reaches even to heaven.
My native land is Ithaca, a sunlit island
With a forested peak called Neriton,   25
Visible for miles. Many other islands
Lie close around her—Doulichion, Samê,
And wooded Zacynthus—off toward the sunrise,
But Ithaca lies low on the evening horizon,
A rugged place, a good nurse of men.   30
No sight is sweeter to me than Ithaca. Yes,
Calypso, the beautiful goddess, kept me
In her caverns, yearning to possess me;
And Circe, the witch of Aeaea, held me
In her halls and yearned to possess me;   35
But they could not persuade me or touch my heart.
Nothing is sweeter than your own country
And your own parents, not even living in a rich house—
Not if it's far from family and home.
But let me tell you of the hard journey homeward   40
Zeus sent me on when I sailed from Troy.

   From Ilion the wind took me to the Cicones
In Ismaros. I pillaged the town and killed the men.
The women and treasure that we took out
I divided as fairly as I could among all hands   45
And then gave the command to pull out fast.
That was my order, but the fools wouldn't listen.
They drank a lot of wine and slaughtered
A lot of sheep and cattle on the shore.
Some of the town's survivors got away inland   50
And called their kinsmen. There were more of them,
And they were braver, too, men who knew how to fight
From chariots and on foot. They came on as thick
As leaves and flowers in spring, attacking

At dawn. We were out of luck, cursed by Zeus   55
To suffer heavy losses. The battle-lines formed
Along our beached ships, and bronze spears
Sliced through the air. As long as the day's heat
Climbed toward noon, we held our ground
Against superior numbers. But when the sun   60
Dipped down, the Cicones beat us down, too.
We lost six fighting men from each of our ships.
The rest of us cheated destiny and death.

We sailed on in shock, glad to get out alive
But grieving for our lost comrades.   65
I wouldn't let the ships get under way
Until someone had called out three times
For each mate who had fallen on the battlefield.
And then Zeus hit us with a norther,
A freak hurricane. The clouds blotted out   70
Land and sea, and night climbed up the sky.
The ships pitched ahead. When their sails
Began to shred in the gale-force winds,
We lowered them and stowed them aboard,
Fearing the worst, and rowed hard for the mainland. 75
We lay offshore two miserable days and nights.
When Dawn combed her hair in the third day's light,
We set up the masts, hoisted the white sails,
And took our seats. The wind and the helmsmen
Steered the ships, and I would have made it home   80
Unscathed, but as I was rounding Cape Malea
The waves, the current, and wind from the North
Drove me off course past Cythera Island.

Nine days of bad winds blew us across
The teeming seas. On the tenth day we came   85
To the land of the Lotus-Eaters.
                                  We went ashore,
And the crews lost no time in drawing water
And preparing a meal beside their ships.
After they had filled up on food and drink,
I sent out a team—two picked men and a herald—   90

To reconnoiter and sound out the locals.
They headed out and made contact with the Lotus-Eaters,
Who meant no harm but did give my men
Some lotus to eat. Whoever ate that sweet fruit
Lost the will to report back, preferring instead   95
To stay there, munching lotus, oblivious of home.
I hauled them back wailing to the ships,
Bound them under the benches, then ordered
All hands to board their ships on the double
Before anyone else tasted the lotus.   100
They were aboard in no time and at their benches,
Churning the sea white with their oars.

   We sailed on, our morale sinking,
And we came to the land of the Cyclopes,
Lawless savages who leave everything   105
Up to the gods. These people neither plow nor plant,
But everything grows for them unsown:
Wheat, barley, and vines that bear
Clusters of grapes, watered by rain from Zeus.
They have no assemblies or laws but live   110
In high mountain caves, ruling their own
Children and wives and ignoring each other.

A fertile island slants across the harbor's mouth,
Neither very close nor far from the Cyclopes' shore.
It's well-wooded and populated with innumerable   115
Wild goats, uninhibited by human traffic.
Not even hunters go there, tramping through the woods
And roughing it on the mountainsides.
It pastures no flocks, has no tilled fields—
Unplowed, unsown, virgin forever, bereft   120
Of men, all it does is support those bleating goats.
The Cyclopes do not sail and have no craftsmen
To build them benched, red-prowed ships
That could supply all their wants, crossing the sea
To other cities, visiting each other as other men do.   125
These same craftsmen would have made this island
Into a good settlement. It's not a bad place at all

And would bear everything in season. Meadows
Lie by the seashore, lush and soft,
Where vines would thrive. It has level plowland   *130*
With deep, rich soil that would produce bumper crops
Season after season. The harbor's good, too,
No need for moorings, anchor-stones, or tying up.
Just beach your ship until the wind is right
And you're ready to sail. At the harbor's head   *135*
A spring flows clear and bright from a cave
Surrounded by poplars.
                          There we sailed in,
Some god guiding us through the murky night.
We couldn't see a thing. A thick fog
Enveloped the ships, and the moon   *140*
Wasn't shining in the cloud-covered sky.
None of us could see the island, or the long waves
Rolling toward the shore, until we ran our ships
Onto the sandy beach. Then we lowered sail,
Disembarked, and fell asleep on the sand.   *145*

Dawn came early, with palmettoes of rose,
And we explored the island, marveling at it.
The spirit-women, daughters of Zeus,
Roused the mountain goats so that my men
Could have a meal. We ran to the ships,   *150*
Got our javelins and bows, formed three groups
And started to shoot. The god let us bag our game,
Nine goats for each of the twelve ships,
Except for my ship, which got ten.

So all day long until the sun went down   *155*
We feasted on meat and sweet wine.
The ships had not yet run out of the dark red
Each crew had taken aboard in large jars
When we ransacked the Cicones' sacred city.
And we looked across at the Cyclopes' land.   *160*
We could see the smoke from their fires
And hear their voices, and their sheep and goats.
When the sun set, and darkness came on

We went to sleep on the shore of the sea.
As soon as dawn brightened in the rosy sky,   *165*
I assembled all the crews and spoke to them:

'The rest of you will stay here while I go
With my ship and crew on reconnaissance.
I want to find out what those men are like,
Wild savages with no sense of right or wrong   *170*
Or hospitable folk who fear the gods.'

With that, I boarded ship and ordered my crew
To get on deck and cast off. They took their places
And were soon whitening the sea with their oars.
As we pulled in over the short stretch of water,   *175*
There on the shoreline we saw a high cave
Overhung with laurels. It was a place
Where many sheep and goats were penned at night.
Around it was a yard fenced in by stones
Set deep in the earth, and by tall pines and crowned oaks.   *180*
This was the lair of a huge creature, a man
Who pastured his flocks off by himself,
And lived apart from others and knew no law.
He was a freak of nature, not like men who eat bread,
But like a lone wooded crag high in the mountains.   *185*

I ordered part of my crew to stay with the ship
And counted off the twelve best to go with me.
I took along a goatskin filled with red wine,
A sweet vintage I had gotten from Maron,
Apollo's priest on Ismaros, when I spared both him   *190*
And his wife and child out of respect for the god.
He lived in a grove of Phoebus Apollo
And gave me splendid gifts: seven bars of gold,
A solid-silver bowl, and twelve jars of wine,
Sweet and pure, a drink for the gods.   *195*
Hardly anyone in his house, none of the servants,
Knew about this wine—just Maron, his wife,
And a single housekeeper. Whenever he drank
This sweet dark red wine, he would fill one goblet

And pour it into twenty parts of water,   *200*
And the bouquet that spread from the mixing bowl
Was so fragrant no one could hold back from drinking.
I had a large skin of this wine, a sack
Of provisions—and a strong premonition
That we had a rendezvous with a man of great might,   *205*
A savage with no notion of right and wrong.

We got to the cave quickly. He was out,
Tending his flocks in the rich pastureland.
We went inside and had a good look around.
There were crates stuffed with cheese, and pens   *210*
Crammed with lambs and kids—firstlings,
Middlings, and newborns in separate sections.
The vessels he used for milking—pails and bowls
Of good workmanship—were brimming with whey.
My men thought we should make off with some cheese   *215*
And then come back for the lambs and kids,
Load them on board, and sail away on the sea.
But I wouldn't listen. It would have been far better
If I had! But I wanted to see him, and see
If he would give me a gift of hospitality.   *220*
When he did come he was not a welcome sight.

We lit a fire and offered sacrifice
And helped ourselves to some of the cheese.
Then we sat and waited in the cave
Until he came back, herding his flocks.   *225*
He carried a huge load of dry wood
To make a fire for his supper and heaved it down
With a crash inside the cave. We were terrified
And scurried back into a corner.
He drove his fat flocks into the wide cavern,   *230*
At least those that he milked, leaving the males—
The rams and the goats—outside in the yard.
Then he lifted up a great doorstone,
A huge slab of rock, and set it in place.
Two sturdy wagons—twenty sturdy wagons—   *235*
Couldn't pry it from the ground—that's how big

The stone was he set in the doorway. Then,
He sat down and milked the ewes and bleating goats,
All in good order, and put the sucklings
Beneath their mothers. Half of the white milk   240
He curdled and scooped into wicker baskets,
The other half he let stand in the pails
So he could drink it later for his supper.
He worked quickly to finish his chores,
And as he was lighting the fire he saw us and said: 245

'Who are you strangers? Sailing the seas, huh?
Where from, and what for? Pirates, probably,
Roaming around causing people trouble.'

He spoke, and it hit us like a punch in the gut—
His booming voice and the sheer size of the monster—   250
But even so I found the words to answer him:

'We are Greeks, blown off course by every wind
In the world on our way home from Troy, traveling
Sea routes we never meant to, by Zeus' will no doubt.
We are proud to be the men of Agamemnon,   255
Son of Atreus, the greatest name under heaven,
Conquerer of Troy, destroyer of armies.
Now we are here, suppliants at your knees,
Hoping you will be generous to us
And give us the gifts that are due to strangers.   260
Respect the gods, sir. We are your suppliants,
And Zeus avenges strangers and suppliants,
Zeus, god of strangers, who walks at their side.'

He answered me from his pitiless heart:

'You're dumb, stranger, or from far away,   265
If you ask me to fear the gods. Cyclopes
Don't care about Zeus or his aegis
Or the blessed gods, since we are much stronger.
I wouldn't spare you or your men
Out of fear of Zeus. I would spare them only   270

If I myself wanted to. But tell me,
Where did you leave your ship? Far
Down the coast, or close? I'd like to know.'

Nice try, but I knew all the tricks and said:

'My ship? Poseidon smashed it to pieces   275
Against the rocks at the border of your land.
He pushed her in close and the wind did the rest.
These men and I escaped by the skin of our teeth.'

This brought no response from his pitiless heart
But a sudden assault upon my men. His hands   280
Reached out, seized two of them, and smashed them
To the ground like puppies. Their brains spattered out
And oozed into the dirt. He tore them limb from limb
To make his supper, gulping them down
Like a mountain lion, leaving nothing behind—   285
Guts, flesh, or marrowy bones.
Crying out, we lifted our hands to Zeus
At this outrage, bewildered and helpless.
When the Cyclops had filled his huge belly
With human flesh, he washed it down with milk,   290
Then stretched out in his cave among his flocks.
I crept up close and was thinking about
Drawing my sharp sword and driving it home
Into his chest where the lungs hide the liver.
I was feeling for the spot when another thought   295
Checked my hand: we would die to a man in that cave,
Unable to budge the enormous stone
He had set in place to block the entrance. And so,
Groaning through the night, we waited for dawn.

As soon as dawn came, streaking the sky red,   300
He rekindled the fire and milked his flocks,
All in good order, and placing the sucklings
Beneath their mothers. His chores done,
He seized two of my men and made his meal.
After he had fed he drove his flocks out,   305

Easily lifting the great stone, which he then set
Back in place as lightly as if he were setting
A lid upon a quiver. And then, with loud whistling,
The Cyclops turned his fat flocks toward the mountain,
And I was left there, brooding on how   310
I might make him pay and win glory from Athena.

This was the best plan I could come up with:
Beside one of the sheep pens lay a huge pole
Of green olive which the Cyclops had cut
To use as a walking stick when dry. Looking at it   315
We guessed it was about as large as the mast
Of a black ship, a twenty-oared, broad-beamed
Freighter that crosses the wide gulfs.
That's how long and thick it looked. I cut off
About a fathom's length from this pole   320
And handed it over to my men. They scraped it
And made it smooth, and I sharpened the tip
And took it over to the fire and hardened it.
Then I hid it, setting it carefully in the dung
That lay in piles all around the cave.   325
And I told my men to draw straws to decide
Which of them would have to share the risk with me—
Lift that stake and grind it in his eye
While he was asleep. They drew straws and came up with
The very men I myself would have chosen.   330
There were four of them, and I made five.

At evening he came, herding his fleecy sheep.
He drove them straight into the cave, drove in
All his flocks in fact. Maybe he had some
Foreboding, or maybe some god told him to.   335
Then he lifted the doorstone and set it in place,
And sat down to milk the goats and bleating ewes,
All in good order, and setting the sucklings
Beneath their mothers. His chores done,
Again he seized two of my men and made his meal.   340
Then I went up to the Cyclops and spoke to him,
Holding an ivy-wood bowl filled with dark wine.

'Cyclops, have some wine, now that you have eaten
Your human flesh, so you can see what kind of drink
Was in our ship's hold. I was bringing it to you   345
As an offering, hoping you would pity me
And help me get home. But you are a raving
Maniac! How do you expect any other man
Ever to visit you after acting like this?'

He took the bowl and drank it off, relishing   350
Every last, sweet drop. And he asked me for more:

'Be a pal and give me another drink. And tell me
Your name, so I can give you a gift you'll like.
Wine grapes grow in the Cyclopes' land, too.
Rain from the sky makes them grow from the earth.   355
But this—this is straight ambrosia and nectar.'

So I gave him some more of the ruby-red wine.
Three times the fool drained the bowl dry,
And when the wine had begun to work on his mind,
I spoke these sweet words to him:

                          'Cyclops,   360
You ask me my name, my glorious name,
And I will tell it to you. Remember now,
To give me the gift just as you promised.
Noman is my name. They call me Noman—
My mother, my father, and all my friends, too.'   365

He answered me from his pitiless heart:

'Noman I will eat last after his friends.
Friends first, him last. That's my gift to you.'

He listed as he spoke and then fell flat on his back,
His thick neck bent sideways. He was sound asleep,   370
Belching out wine and bits of human flesh
In his drunken stupor. I swung into action,
Thrusting the stake deep in the embers,

Heating it up, and all the while talking to my men
To keep up their morale. When the olive-wood stake   375
Was about to catch fire, green though it was,
And was really glowing, I took it out
And brought it right up to him. My men
Stood around me, and some god inspired us.
My men lifted up the olive-wood stake   380
And drove the sharp point right into his eye,
While I, putting my weight behind it, spun it around
The way a man bores a ship's beam with a drill,
Leaning down on it while other men beneath him
Keep it spinning and spinning with a leather strap.   385
That's how we twirled the fiery-pointed stake
In the Cyclops' eye. The blood formed a whirlpool
Around its searing tip. His lids and brow
Were all singed by the heat from the burning eyeball
And its roots crackled in the fire and hissed   390
Like an axe-head or adze a smith dips into water
When he wants to temper the iron—that's how his eye
Sizzled and hissed around the olive-wood stake.
He screamed, and the rock walls rang with his voice.
We shrank back in terror while he wrenched   395
The blood-grimed stake from his eye and flung it
Away from him, blundering about and shouting
To the other Cyclopes, who lived around him
In caverns among the windswept crags.
They heard his cry and gathered from all sides   400
Around his cave and asked him what ailed him:

'Polyphemus, why are you hollering so much
And keeping us up the whole blessed night?
Is some man stealing your flocks from you,
Or killing you, maybe, by some kind of trick?'   405

And Polyphemus shouted out to them:

'Noman is killing me by some kind of trick!'

They sent their words winging back to him:

'If no man is hurting you, then your sickness
Comes from Zeus and can't be helped.   *410*
You should pray to your father, Lord Poseidon.'

They left then, and I laughed in my heart
At how my phony name had fooled them so well.
Cyclops meanwhile was groaning in agony.
Groping around, he removed the doorstone   *415*
And sat in the entrance with his hands spread out
To catch anyone who went out with the sheep—
As if I could be so stupid. I thought it over,
Trying to come up with the best plan I could
To get us all out from the jaws of death.   *420*
I wove all sorts of wiles, as a man will
When his life is on the line. My best idea
Had to do with the sheep that were there, big,
Thick-fleeced beauties with wool dark as violets.
Working silently, I bound them together   *425*
With willow branches the Cyclops slept on.
I bound them in threes. Each middle sheep
Carried a man underneath, protected by
The two on either side: three sheep to a man.
As for me, there was a ram, the best in the flock.   *430*
I grabbed his back and curled up beneath
His shaggy belly. There I lay, hands twined
Into the marvelous wool, hanging on for dear life.
And so, muffling our groans, we waited for dawn.

When the first streaks of red appeared in the sky,   *435*
The rams started to bolt toward the pasture.
The unmilked females were bleating in the pens,
Their udders bursting. Their master,
Worn out with pain, felt along the backs
Of all of the sheep as they walked by, the fool,   *440*
Unaware of the men under their fleecy chests.
The great ram headed for the entrance last,
Heavy with wool—and with me thinking hard.
Running his hands over the ram, Polyphemus said:

'My poor ram, why are you leaving the cave   *445*
Last of all? You've never lagged behind before.
You were always the first to reach the soft grass
With your big steps, first to reach the river,
First to want to go back to the yard
At evening. Now you're last of all. Are you sad   *450*
About your master's eye? A bad man blinded me,
Him and his nasty friends, getting me drunk,
Noman—but he's not out of trouble yet!
If only you understood and could talk,
You could tell me where he's hiding. I would   *455*
Smash him to bits and spatter his brains
All over the cave. Then I would find some relief
From the pain this no-good Noman has caused me.'

He spoke, and sent the ram off through the door.
When we had gone a little way from the cave,   *460*
I first untangled myself from the ram
And then untied my men. Then, moving quickly,
We drove those fat, long-shanked sheep
Down to the ship, keeping an eye on our rear.
We were a welcome sight to the rest of the crew,   *465*
But when they started to mourn the men we had lost
I forbade it with an upward nod of my head,
Signaling each man like that and ordering them
To get those fleecy sheep aboard instead,
On the double, and get the ship out to sea.   *470*
Before you knew it they were on their benches
Beating the sea to white froth with their oars.
When we were offshore but still within earshot,
I called out to the Cyclops, just to rub it in:

'So, Cyclops, it turns out it wasn't a coward   *475*
Whose men you murdered and ate in your cave,
You savage! But you got yours in the end,
Didn't you? You had the gall to eat the guests
In your own house, and Zeus made you pay for it.'

He was even angrier when he heard this.   *480*

Breaking off the peak of a huge crag
He threw it toward our ship, and it carried
To just in front of our dark prow. The sea
Billowed up where the rock came down,
And the backwash pushed us to the mainland again,   485
Like a flood tide setting us down at the shore.
I grabbed a long pole and shoved us off,
Nodding to the crew to fall on the oars
And get us out of there. They leaned into it,
And when we were twice as far out to sea as before   490
I called to the Cyclops again, with my men
Hanging all over me and begging me not to:

'Don't do it, man! The rock that hit the water
Pushed us in and we thought we were done for.
If he hears any sound from us, he'll heave   495
Half a cliff at us and crush the ship and our skulls
With one throw. You know he has the range.'

They tried, but didn't persuade my hero's heart—
I was really angry—and I called back to him:

'Cyclops, if anyone, any mortal man,   500
Asks you how you got your eye put out,
Tell him that Odysseus the marauder did it,
Son of Laertes, whose home is on Ithaca.'

He groaned, and had this to say in response:

'Oh no! Now it's coming to me, the old prophecy.   505
There was a seer here once, a tall handsome man,
Telemos Eurymides. He prophesied well
All his life to the Cyclopes. He told me
That all this would happen some day,
That I would lose my sight at Odysseus' hands.   510
I always expected a great hero
Would come here, strong as can be.
Now this puny, little, good-for-nothing runt
Has put my eye out—because he got me drunk.

But come here, Odysseus, so I can give you a gift,   515
And ask Poseidon to help you on your way.
I'm his son, you know. He claims he's my father.
He will heal me, if he wants. But none
Of the other gods will, and no mortal man will.'

He had his say and then prayed to Poseidon,   520
Stretching his arms out to starry heaven:

'Hear me, Poseidon, blue-maned Earth-Holder,
If you are the father you claim to be.
Grant that Odysseus, son of Laertes,
May never reach his home on Ithaca.   525
But if he is fated to see his family again,
And return to his home and own native land,
May he come late, having lost all companions,
In another's ship, and find trouble at home.'

He prayed, and the blue-maned sea-god heard him.   530
Then he broke off an even larger chunk of rock,
Pivoted, and threw it with incredible force.
It came down just behind our dark-hulled ship,
Barely missing the end of the rudder. The sea
Billowed up where the rock hit the water,   535
And the wave pushed us forward all the way
To the island where our other ships waited
Clustered on the shore, ringed by our comrades
Sitting on the sand, anxious for our return.
We beached the ship and unloaded the Cyclops' sheep,   540
Which I divided up as fairly as I could
Among all hands. The veterans gave me the great ram,
And I sacrificed it on the shore of the sea
To Zeus in the dark clouds, who rules over all.
I burnt the thigh pieces, but the god did not accept   545
My sacrifice, brooding over how to destroy
All my benched ships and my trusty crews.

So all the long day until the sun went down
We sat feasting on meat and drinking sweet wine.

When the sun set and darkness came on   550
We lay down and slept on the shore of the sea.
Early in the morning, when the sky was streaked red,
I roused my men and ordered the crews
To get on deck and cast off. They took their places
And were soon whitening the sea with their oars.   555

We sailed on in shock, glad to get away alive
But grieving for the comrades we had lost."

ODYSSEY 10

"We came next to the island of Aeolia,
Home of Aeolus, son of Hippotas,
Dear to the immortals. Aeolia
Is a floating island surrounded by a wall
Of indestructible bronze set on sheer stone.   5
Aeolus' twelve children live there with him,
Six daughters and six manly sons.
He married his daughters off to his boys,
And they all sit with their father and mother
Continually feasting on abundant good cheer   10
Spread out before them. Every day
The house is filled with steamy savor
And the courtyard resounds. Every night
The men sleep next to their high-born wives
On blankets strewn on their corded beds.   15
We came to their city and their fine palace,
And for a full month he entertained me.
He questioned me in great detail about Troy,
The Greek fleet, and the Greeks' return home.
I told him everything, from beginning to end.   20
And when I, in turn, asked if I might leave

And requested him to send me on my way,
He did not refuse, and this was his send-off:
He gave me a bag made of the hide of an ox
Nine years old, which he had skinned himself,   25
And in this bag he bound the wild winds' ways,
For Zeus had made him keeper of the winds,
To still or to rouse whichever he will.
He tied this bag down in the hold of my ship
With a bright silver cord, so that not a puff   30
Could escape. But he let the West Wind out
To blow my ships along and carry us home.
It was not to be. Our own folly undid us.

For nine days and nights we sailed on.
On the tenth day we raised land, our own   35
Native fields, and got so close we saw men
Tending their fires. Then sleep crept up on me,
Exhausted from minding the sail the whole time
By myself. I wouldn't let any of my crew
Spell me, because I wanted to make good time.   40
As soon as I fell asleep, the men started to talk,
Saying I was bringing home for myself
Silver and gold as gifts from great Aeolus.
You can imagine the sort of things they said:

'This guy gets everything wherever he goes.   45
First, he's freighting home his loot from Troy,
Beautiful stuff, while we, who made the same trip,
Are coming home empty-handed. And now
Aeolus has lavished these gifts upon him.
Let's have a quick look, and see what's here,   50
How much gold and silver is stuffed in this bag.'

All malicious nonsense, but it won out in the end,
And they opened the bag. The winds rushed out
And bore them far out to sea, weeping
As their native land faded on the horizon.   55
When I woke up and saw what had happened
I thought long and hard about whether I should

Just go over the side and end it all in the sea
Or endure in silence and remain among the living.
In the end I decided to bear it and live.   60
I wrapped my head in my cloak and lay down on the deck
While an evil wind carried the ships
Back to Aeolia. My comrades groaned.

We went ashore and drew water
And the men took a meal beside the swift ships.   65
When we had tasted food and drink
I took a herald and one man
And went to Aeolus' glorious palace.
I found him feasting with his wife and children,
And when we came in and sat on the threshold   70
They were amazed and questioned me:

'What happened, Odysseus? What evil spirit
Abused you? Surely we sent you off
With all you needed to get back home
Or anywhere else your heart desired.'   75

I answered them from the depths of my sorrow:

'My evil crew ruined me, that and stubborn sleep.
But make it right, friends, for you have the power.'

I made my voice soft and tried to persuade them,
But they were silent. And then their father said: 80

'Begone from this island instantly!
You are the most cursed of all living things.
It would go against all that is right
For me to help or send on his way
A man so despised by the blessed gods.   85
Begone! You are cursed by heaven!'

And with that he sent me from his house,
Groaning heavily. We sailed on from there
With grief in our hearts. Because of our folly

There was no breeze to push us along,   *90*
And our morale sank because the rowing was hard.
We sailed on for six solid days and nights,
And on the seventh we came to Lamus,
The lofty city of Telepylus
In the land of the Laestrygonians,   *95*
Where a herdsman driving in his flocks at dusk
Calls to another driving his out at dawn.
A man could earn a double wage there
If he never slept, one by herding cattle
And another by pasturing white sheep,   *100*
For night and day make one twilight there.
The harbor we came to is a glorious place,
Surrounded by sheer cliffs. Headlands
Jut out on either side to form a narrow mouth,
And there all the others steered in their ships   *105*
And moored them close together in the bay.
No wave, large or small, ever rocks a boat
In that silvery calm. I alone moored my black ship
Outside the harbor, tying her up
On the rocks that lie on the border of the land.   *110*
Then I climbed to a rugged lookout point
And surveyed the scene. There was no sign
Of plowed fields, only smoke rising up from the land.

I sent out a team—two picked men and a herald—
To reconnoiter and find out who lived there.   *115*
They went ashore and followed a smooth road
Used by wagons to bring wood from the mountains
Down to the city. In front of the city
They met a girl drawing water. Her father
Was named Antiphates, and she had come down   *120*
To the flowing spring Artacia,
From which they carried water to the town.
When my men came up to her and asked her
Who the people there were and who was their king,
She showed them her father's high-roofed house.   *125*
They entered the house and found his wife inside,
A woman, to their horror, as huge as a mountain top.

At once she called her husband, Antiphates,
Who meant business when he came. He seized
One of my men and made him into dinner.   130
The other two got out of there and back to the ships,
But Antiphates had raised a cry throughout the city,
And when they heard it, the Laestrygonians
Came up on all sides, thousands of them,
Not like men but like the Sons of the Earth,   135
The Giants. They pelted us from the cliffs
With rocks too large for a man to lift.
The sounds that came from the ships were sickening,
Sounds of men dying and boats being crushed.
The Laestrygonians speared the bodies like fish,   140
And carried them back for their ghastly meal.
While this was happening I drew my sword
And cut the cables of my dark-prowed ship,
Barking out orders for the crew to start rowing
And get us out of there. They rowed for their lives,   145
Ripping the sea, and my ship sped joyfully
Out and away from the beetling rocks,
But all of the others were destroyed as they lay.

W e sailed on in shock, glad to get out alive
But grieving for the comrades we'd lost.   150
And we came to Aeaea, the island that is home
To Circe, a dread goddess with richly coiled hair
And a human voice. She is the sister
Of dark-hearted Aeetes, and they are both sprung
From Helios and Perse, daughter of Ocean.   155
Some god guided us into a harbor
And we put in to shore without a sound.
We disembarked and lay there for two days and nights,
Eating our hearts out with weariness and grief.
But when Dawn combed her hair in the third day's light,   160
I took my sword and spear and went up
From the ship to open ground, hoping to see
Plowed fields, and to hear human voices.
So I climbed to a rugged lookout point
And surveyed the scene. What I saw was smoke   165

Rising up from Circe's house. It curled up high
Through the thick brush and woods, and I wondered
Whether I should go and have a closer look.
I decided it was better to go back to the ship
And give my crew their meal, and then   *170*
Send out a party to reconnoiter.
I was on my way back and close to the ship
When some god took pity on me,
Walking there alone, and sent a great antlered stag
Right into my path. He was on his way   *175*
Down to the river from his pasture in the woods,
Thirsty and hot from the sun beating down,
And as he came out I got him right on the spine
In the middle of his back. The bronze spear bored
All the way through, and he fell in the dust   *180*
With a groan, and his spirit flew away.
Planting my foot on him, I drew the bronze spear
Out of the wound and laid it down on the ground.
Then I pulled up a bunch of willow shoots
And twisted them together to make a rope   *185*
About a fathom long. I used this to tie
The stag's feet together so I could carry him
Across my back, leaning on my spear
As I went back to the ship. There was no way
An animal that large could be held on one shoulder.   *190*
I flung him down by the ship and roused my men,
Going up to each in turn and saying to them:

'We're not going down to Hades, my friends,
Before our time. As long as there is still
Food and drink in our ship, at least   *195*
We don't have to starve to death.'

When they heard this, they drew their cloaks
From their faces, and marveled at the size
Of the stag lying on the barren seashore.
When they had seen enough, they washed their hands
And prepared a glorious feast. So all day long
Until the sun went down we sat there feasting

On all that meat, washing it down with wine.
When the sun set and darkness came on,
We lay down to sleep on the shore of the sea.   *205*

When Dawn brushed the eastern sky with rose,
I called my men together and spoke to them:

'Listen to me, men. It's been hard going.
We don't know east from west right now,
But we have to see if we have any good ideas left.   *210*
We may not. I climbed up to a lookout point.
We're on an island, ringed by the endless sea.
The land lies low, and I was able to see
Smoke rising up through the brushy woods.'

This was too much for them. They remembered   *215*
What Antiphates, the Laestrygonian, had done,
And how the Cyclops had eaten their comrades.
They wailed and cried, but it did them no good.
I counted off the crew into two companies
And appointed a leader for each. Eurylochus   *220*
Headed up one group and I took the other,
And then we shook lots in a bronze helmet.
Out jumped the lot of Eurylochus, brave heart,
And so off he went, with twenty-two men,
All in tears, leaving us behind in no better mood.   *225*

They went through the woods and found Circe's house
In an upland clearing. It was built of polished stone
And surrounded by mountain lions and wolves,
Creatures Circe had drugged and bewitched.
These beasts did not attack my men, but stood   *230*
On their hind legs and wagged their long tails,
Like dogs fawning on their master who always brings
Treats for them when he comes home from a feast.
So these clawed beasts were fawning around my men,
Who were terrified all the same by the huge animals.   *235*
While they stood like this in the gateway
They could hear Circe inside, singing in a lovely voice

As she moved about weaving a great tapestry,
The unfading handiwork of an immortal goddess,
Finely woven, shimmering with grace and light.   240
Polites, a natural leader, and of all the crew
The one I loved and trusted most, spoke up then:

'Someone inside is weaving a great web,
And singing so beautifully the floor thrums with the sound.
Whether it's a goddess or a woman, let's call her out now.'   245

And so they called to her, and she came out
And flung open the bright doors and invited them in.
They all filed in naively behind her,
Except Eurylochus, who suspected a trap.
When she had led them in and seated them   250
She brewed up a potion of Pramnian wine
With cheese, barley, and pale honey stirred in,
And she laced this potion with insidious drugs
That would make them forget their own native land.
When they had eaten and drunk, she struck them   255
With her wand and herded them into the sties outside.
Grunting, their bodies covered with bristles,
They looked just like pigs, but their minds were intact.
Once in the pens, they squealed with dismay,
And Circe threw them acorns and berries—   260
The usual fare for wallowing swine.

Eurylochus at once came back to the ship
To tell us of our comrades' unseemly fate,
But, hard as he tried, he could not speak a word.
The man was in shock. His eyes welled with tears,   265
And his mind was filled with images of horror.
Finally, under our impatient questioning,
He told us how his men had been undone:

'We went through the woods, as you told us to,
Glorious Odysseus, and found a beautiful house   270
In an upland clearing, built of polished stone.
Someone inside was working a great loom

And singing in a high, clear voice, some goddess
Or a woman, and they called out to her,
And she came out and opened the bright doors   275
And invited them in, and they naively
Filed in behind her. But I stayed outside,
Suspecting a trap. And they all disappeared,
Not one came back. I sat and watched
For a long, long time, and not one came back.'   280

He spoke, and I threw my silver-studded sword
Around my shoulders, slung on my bow,
And ordered Eurylochus to retrace his steps
And lead me back there. But he grabbed me by the knees
And pleaded with me, wailing miserably: 285

'Don't force me to go back there. Leave me here,
Because I know that you will never come back yourself
Or bring back the others. Let's just get out of here
With those that are left. We might still make it.'

Those were his words, and I answered him: 290

'All right, Eurylochus, you stay here by the ship.
Get yourself something to eat and drink.
I'm going, though. We're in a really tight spot.'

And so I went up from the ship and the sea
Into the sacred woods. I was closing in   295
On Circe's house, with all its bewitchment,
When I was met by Hermes. He had a golden wand
And looked like a young man, a hint of a moustache
Above his lip—youth at its most charming.
He clasped my hand and said to me: 300

'Where are you off to now, unlucky man,
Alone, and in rough, uncharted terrain?
Those men of yours are up in Circe's house,
Penned like pigs into crowded little sties.
And you've come to free them? I don't think so.   305

You'll never return; you'll have to stay there, too.
Oh well, I will keep you out of harm's way.
Take this herb with you when you go to Circe,
And it will protect you from her deadly tricks.
She'll mix a potion and spike it with drugs,   *310*
But she won't be able to cast her spell
Because you'll have a charm that works just as well—
The one I'll give you—and you'll be forewarned.
When Circe strikes you with her magic wand,
Draw your sharp sword from beside your thigh   *315*
And rush at her with murder in your eye.
She'll be afraid and invite you to bed.
Don't turn her down—that's how you'll get
Your comrades freed and yourself well loved.
But first make her swear by the gods above   *320*
She will not unsex you when you are nude,
Or drain you of your manly fortitude.'

So saying, Hermes gave me the herb,
Pulling it out of the ground, and showed it to me.
It was black at the root, with a milk-white flower.   *325*
Moly, the gods call it, hard for mortal men to dig up,
But the gods can do anything. Hermes rose
Through the wooded island and up to Olympus,
And I went on to Circe's house, brooding darkly
On many things. I stood at the gates   *330*
Of the beautiful goddess's house and gave a shout.
She heard me call and came out at once,
Opening the bright doors and inviting me in.
I followed her inside, my heart pounding.
She seated me on a beautiful chair   *335*
Of finely wrought silver, and prepared me a drink
In a golden cup, and with evil in her heart
She laced it with drugs. She gave me the cup
And I drank it off, but it did not bewitch me.
So she struck me with her wand and said: *340*

'Off to the sty, with the rest of your friends.'

At this, I drew the sharp sword that hung by my thigh
And lunged at Circe as if I meant to kill her.
The goddess shrieked and, running beneath my blade,
Grabbed my knees and said to me wailing: *345*

'Who are you, and where do you come from?
What is your city and who are your parents?
I am amazed that you drank this potion
And are not bewitched. No other man
Has ever resisted this drug once it's past his lips.   *350*
But you have a mind that cannot be beguiled.
You must be Odysseus, the man of many wiles,
Who Quicksilver Hermes always said would come here
In his swift black ship on his way home from Troy.
Well then, sheath your sword and let's   *355*
Climb into my bed and tangle in love there,
So we may come to trust each other.'

She spoke, and I answered her:

'Circe, how can you ask me to be gentle to you
After you turned my men into swine?   *360*
And now you have me here and want to trick me
Into going to bed with you, so that you can
Unman me when I am naked. No, Goddess,
I'm not getting into any bed with you
Unless you agree first to swear a solemn oath   *365*
That you're not planning some new trouble for me.'

Those were my words, and she swore an oath at once
Not to do me any harm, and when she finished
I climbed into Circe's beautiful bed.

   Meanwhile, her serving women were busy,   *370*
Four maidens who did all the housework,
Spirit women born of the springs and groves
And of the sacred rivers that flow to the sea.
One of them brought rugs with a purple sheen
And strewed them over chairs lined with fresh linen.   *375*

Another drew silver tables up to the chairs
And set golden baskets upon them. The third
Mixed honey-hearted wine in a silver bowl
And set out golden cups. The fourth
Filled a cauldron with water and lit a great fire 380
Beneath it, and when the water was boiling
In the glowing bronze, she set me in a tub
And bathed me, mixing in water from the cauldron
Until it was just how I liked it, and pouring it over
My head and shoulders until she washed from my limbs 385
The weariness that had consumed my soul.
When she had bathed me and rubbed me
With rich olive oil, and had thrown about me
A beautiful cloak and tunic, she led me to the hall
And had me sit on a silver-studded chair, 390
Richly wrought and with a matching footstool.
A maid poured water from a silver pitcher
Over a golden basin for me to wash my hands
And then set up a polished table nearby.
And the housekeeper, grave and dignified, 395
Set out bread and generous helpings
From all the dishes she had. She told me to eat,
But nothing appealed. I sat there with other thoughts
Occupying my mind, and my mood was dark.
When Circe noticed I was just sitting there, 400
Depressed, and not reaching out for food,
She came up to me and spoke winged words:

'Why are you just sitting there, Odysseus,
Eating your heart out and not touching your food?
Are you afraid of some other trick? You need not be. 405
I have already sworn I will do you no harm.'

So she spoke, and I answered her:

'Circe, how could anyone bring himself—
Any decent man—to taste food and drink
Before seeing his comrades free? 410
If you really want me to eat and drink,

Set my men free and let me see them.'

So I spoke, and Circe went outside
Holding her wand and opened the sty
And drove them out. They looked like swine   415
Nine or ten years old. They stood there before her
And she went through them and smeared each one
With another drug. The bristles they had grown
After Circe had given them the poisonous drug
All fell away, and they became men again,   420
Younger than before, taller and far handsomer.
They knew me, and they clung to my hands,
And the house rang with their passionate sobbing.
The goddess herself was moved to pity.

Then she came to my side and said: 425

'Son of Laertes in the line of Zeus,
My wily Odysseus, go to your ship now
Down by the sea and haul it ashore.
Then stow all the tackle and gear in caves
And come back here with the rest of your crew.' 430

So she spoke, and persuaded my heart.
I went to the shore and found my crew there
Wailing and crying beside our sailing ship.
When they saw me they were like farmyard calves
Around a herd of cows returning to the yard.   435
The calves bolt from their pens and run friskily
Around their mothers, lowing and mooing.
That's how my men thronged around me
When they saw me coming. It was as if
They had come home to their rugged Ithaca,   440
And wailing miserably they said so to me:

'With you back, Zeus-born, it is just as if
We had returned to our native Ithaca.
But tell us what happened to the rest of the crew.'

So they spoke, and I answered them gently: *445*

'First let's haul our ship onto dry land
And then stow all the tackle and gear in caves.
Then I want all of you to come along with me
So you can see your shipmates in Circe's house,
Eating and drinking all they could ever want.' *450*

They heard what I said and quickly agreed.
Eurylochus, though, tried to hold them back,
Speaking to them these winged words:

'Why do you want to do this to yourselves,
Go down to Circe's house? She will turn all of you *455*
Into pigs, wolves, lions, and make you guard her house.
Remember what the Cyclops did when our shipmates
Went into his lair? It was this reckless Odysseus
Who led them there. It was his fault they died.'

When Eurylochus said that, I considered *460*
Drawing my long sword from where it hung
By my thigh and lopping off his head,
Close kinsman though he was by marriage.
But my crew talked me out of it, saying things like:

'By your leave, let's station this man here *465*
To guard the ship. As for the rest of us,
Lead us on to the sacred house of Circe.'

And so the whole crew went up from the sea,
And Eurylochus did not stay behind with the ship
But went with us, in mortal fear of my temper. *470*

Meanwhile, back in Circe's house, the goddess
Had my men bathed, rubbed down with oil,
And clothed in tunics and fleecy cloaks.
We found them feasting well in her halls.
When they recognized each other, they wept openly *475*
And their cries echoed throughout Circe's house.

Then the shining goddess stood near me and said:

'Lament no more. I myself know
All that you have suffered on the teeming sea
And the losses on land at your enemies' hands.   *480*
Now you must eat, drink wine, and restore the spirit
You had when you left your own native land,
Your rugged Ithaca. You are skin and bones now
And hollow inside. All you can think of
Is your hard wandering, no joy in your heart,   *485*
For you have, indeed, suffered many woes.'

She spoke, and I took her words to heart.
So we sat there day after day for a year,
Feasting on abundant meat and sweet wine.
But when a year had passed, and the seasons turned,   *490*
And the moons waned and the long days were done,
My trusty crew called me out and said:

'Good god, man, at long last remember your home,
If it is heaven's will for you to be saved
And return to your house and your own native land.'   *495*

They spoke, and I saw what they meant.
So all that long day until the sun went down
We sat feasting on meat and sweet red wine.
When the sun set and darkness came on,
My men lay down to sleep in the shadowy hall,   *500*
But I went up to Circe's beautiful bed
And touching her knees I beseeched the goddess:

'Circe, fulfill now the promise you made
To send me home. I am eager to be gone
And so are my men, who are wearing me out   *505*
Sitting around whining and complaining
Whenever you happen not to be present.'

So I spoke, and the shining goddess answered:

'Son of Laertes in the line of Zeus,
My wily Odysseus—you need not stay   510
Here in my house any longer than you wish.
But there is another journey you must make first—
To the house of Hades and dread Persephone,
To consult the ghost of Theban Tiresias,
The blind prophet, whose mind is still strong.   515
To him alone Persephone has granted
Intelligence even after his death.
The rest of the dead are flitting shadows.'

This broke my spirit. I sat on the bed
And wept. I had no will to live, nor did I care   520
If I ever saw the sunlight again.
But when I had my fill of weeping and writhing,
I looked at the goddess and said:

'And who will guide me on this journey, Circe?
No man has ever sailed his black ship to Hades.'   525

And the goddess, shining, answered at once:

'Son of Laertes in the line of Zeus,
My wily Odysseus—do not worry about
A pilot to guide your ship. Just set up the mast,
Spread the white sail, and sit yourself down.   530
The North Wind's breath will bear her onwards.
But when your ship crosses the stream of Ocean
You will see a shelving shore and Persephone's groves,
Tall poplars and willows that drop their fruit.
Beach your ship there by Ocean's deep eddies,   535
And go yourself to the dank house of Hades.
There into Acheron flow Pyriphlegethon
And Cocytus, a branch of the water of Styx.
And there is a rock where the two roaring rivers
Flow into one. At that spot, hero, gather yourself   540
And do as I say.
            Dig an ell-square pit,
And around it pour libation to all the dead,

First with milk and honey, then with sweet wine,
And a third time with water. Then sprinkle barley
And pray to the looming, feeble death-heads,   545
Vowing sacrifice on Ithaca, a barren heifer,
The herd's finest, and rich gifts on the altar,
And to Tiresias alone a great black ram.
After these supplications to the spirits,
Slaughter a ram and a black ewe, turning their heads   550
Toward Erebus, yourself turning backward
And leaning toward the streams of the river.
Then many ghosts of the dead will come forth.
Call to your men to flay the slaughtered sheep
And burn them as a sacrifice to the gods below,   555
To mighty Hades and dread Persephone.
You yourself draw your sharp sword and sit there,
Keeping the feeble death-heads from the blood
Until you have questioned Tiresias.
Then, and quickly, the great seer will come.   560
He will tell you the route and how long it will take
For you to reach home over the teeming deep.'

Dawn rose in gold as she finished speaking.
Circe gave me a cloak and tunic to wear
And the nymph slipped on a long silver robe   565
Shimmering in the light, cinched it at the waist
With a golden belt and put a veil on her head.
I went through the halls and roused my men,
Going up to each with words soft and sweet:

'Time to get up! No more sleeping late.   570
We're on our way. Lady Circe has told me all.'

So I spoke, and persuaded their heroes' hearts.
But not even from Circe's house could I lead my men
Unscathed. One of the crew, Elpenor, the youngest,
Not much of a warrior nor all that smart,   575
Had gone off to sleep apart from his shipmates,
Seeking the cool air on Circe's roof
Because he was heavy with wine.

He heard the noise of his shipmates moving around
And sprang up suddenly, forgetting to go   *580*
To the long ladder that led down from the roof.
He fell headfirst, his neck snapped at the spine,
And his soul went down to the house of Hades.

As my men were heading out I spoke to them:

'You think, no doubt, that you are going home,   *585*
But Circe has plotted another course for us,
To the house of Hades and dread Persephone,
To consult the ghost of Theban Tiresias.'

This broke their hearts. They sat down
Right where they were and wept and tore their hair,   *590*
But no good came of their lamentation.

While we were on our way to our swift ship
On the shore of the sea, weeping and crying,
Circe had gone ahead and tethered a ram and a black ewe
By our tarred ship. She had passed us by   *595*
Without our ever noticing. Who could see
A god on the move against the god's will?"

ODYSSEY 11

"When we reached our black ship
We hauled her onto the bright saltwater,
Set up the mast and sail, loaded on
The sheep, and boarded her ourselves,
Heartsick and weeping openly by now.   5
The dark prow cut through the waves
And a following wind bellied the canvas,
A good sailing breeze sent by Circe,
The dread goddess with a human voice.
We lashed everything down and sat tight,   10
Leaving the ship to the wind and helmsman.
All day long she surged on with taut sail;
Then the sun set, and the sea grew dark.

The ship took us to the deep, outermost Ocean
And the land of the Cimmerians, a people   15
Shrouded in mist. The sun never shines there,
Never climbs the starry sky to beam down at them,
Nor bathes them in the glow of its last golden rays;
Their wretched sky is always racked with night's gloom.
We beached our ship there, unloaded the sheep,   20
And went along the stream of Ocean
Until we came to the place spoken of by Circe.

There Perimedes and Eurylochus held the victims
While I dug an ell-square pit with my sword,
And poured libation to all the dead,   25
First with milk and honey, then with sweet wine,
And a third time with water. Then I sprinkled
White barley and prayed to the looming dead,
Vowing sacrifice on Ithaca—a barren heifer,
The herd's finest, and rich gifts on the altar,   30
And to Tiresias alone a great black ram.
After these supplications to the spirits,

I cut the sheeps' throats over the pit,
And the dark blood pooled there.
                                     Then out of Erebus
The souls of the dead gathered, the ghosts   *35*
Of brides and youths and worn-out old men
And soft young girls with hearts new to sorrow,
And many men wounded with bronze spears,
Killed in battle, bearing blood-stained arms.
They drifted up to the pit from all sides   *40*
With an eerie cry, and pale fear seized me.
I called to my men to flay the slaughtered sheep
And burn them as a sacrifice to the gods,
To mighty Hades and dread Persephone.
Myself, I drew my sharp sword and sat,   *45*
Keeping the feeble death-heads from the blood
Until I had questioned Tiresias.

First to come was the ghost of Elpenor,
Whose body still lay in Circe's hall,
Unmourned, unburied, since we'd been hard pressed.   *50*
I wept when I saw him, and with pity in my heart
Spoke to him these feathered words:

'Elpenor, how did you get to the undergloom
Before me, on foot, outstripping our black ship?'

I spoke, and he moaned in answer: *55*

'Bad luck and too much wine undid me.
I fell asleep on Circe's roof. Coming down
I missed my step on the long ladder
And fell headfirst. My neck snapped
At the spine and my ghost went down to Hades.   *60*
Now I beg you—by those we left behind,
By your wife and the father who reared you,
And by Telemachus, your only son,
Whom you left alone in your halls—
When you put the gloom of Hades behind you   *65*
And beach your ship on the Isle of Aeaea,

As I know you will, remember me, my lord.
Do not leave me unburied, unmourned,
When you sail for home, or I might become
A cause of the gods' anger against you.   70
Burn me with my armor, such as I have,
Heap me a barrow on the grey sea's shore,
In memory of a man whose luck ran out.
Do this for me, and fix in the mound the oar
I rowed with my shipmates while I was alive.'   75

Thus Elpenor, and I answered him:

'Pitiful spirit, I will do this for you.'

Such were the sad words we exchanged
Sitting by the pit, I on one side holding my sword
Over the blood, my comrade's ghost on the other.   80

Then came the ghost of my dead mother,
Anticleia, daughter of the hero Autolycus.
She was alive when I left for sacred Ilion.
I wept when I saw her, and pitied her,
But even in my grief I would not allow her   85
To come near the blood until I had questioned Tiresias.

And then he came, the ghost of Theban Tiresias,
Bearing a golden staff. He knew me and said:

'Odysseus, son of Laertes, master of wiles,
Why have you come, leaving the sunlight   90
To see the dead and this joyless place?
Move off from the pit and take away your sword,
So I may drink the blood and speak truth to you.'

I drew back and slid my silver-studded sword
Into its sheath. After he had drunk the dark blood   95
The flawless seer rose and said to me:

'You seek a homecoming sweet as honey,

Shining Odysseus, but a god will make it bitter,
For I do not think you will elude the Earthshaker,
Who has laid up wrath in his heart against you,   *100*
Furious because you blinded his son. Still,
You just might get home, though not without pain,
You and your men, if you curb your own spirit,
And theirs, too, when you beach your ship
On Thrinacia. You will be marooned on that island   *105*
In the violet sea, and find there the cattle
Of Helios the Sun, and his sheep, too, grazing.
Leave these unharmed, keep your mind on your homecoming,
And you may still reach Ithaca, though not without pain.
But if you harm them, I foretell doom for you,   *110*
Your ship, and your crew. And even if you
Yourself escape, you will come home late
And badly, having lost all companions
And in another's ship. And you shall find
Trouble in your house, arrogant men   *115*
Devouring your wealth and courting your wife.
Yet vengeance will be yours, and when you have slain
The suitors in your hall, by ruse or by sword,
Then you must go off again, carrying a broad-bladed oar,
Until you come to men who know nothing of the sea,   *120*
Who eat their food unsalted, and have never seen
Red-prowed ships or oars that wing them along.
And I will tell you a sure sign that you have found them,
One you cannot miss. When you meet another traveler
Who thinks you are carrying a winnowing fan,   *125*
Then you must fix your oar in the earth
And offer sacrifice to Lord Poseidon,
A ram, a bull, and a boar in its prime.
Then return to your home and offer
Perfect sacrifice to the immortal gods   *130*
Who hold high heaven, to each in turn.
And death will come to you off the sea,
A death so gentle, and carry you off
When you are worn out in sleek old age,
Your people prosperous all around you.   *135*
All this will come true for you as I have told.'

Thus Tiresias. And I answered him:

'All that, Tiresias, is as the gods have spun it.
But tell me this: I see here the ghost
Of my dead mother, sitting in silence   140
Beside the blood, and she cannot bring herself
To look her son in the eye or speak to him.
How can she recognize me for who I am?'

And Tiresias, the Theban prophet:

'This is easy to tell you. Whoever of the dead   145
You let come to the blood will speak truly to you.
Whoever you deny will go back again.'

With that, the ghost of Lord Tiresias
Went back into Hades, his soothsaying done.
But I stayed where I was until my mother   150
Came up and drank the dark blood. At once
She knew me, and her words reached me on wings:

'My child, how did you come to the undergloom
While you are still alive? It is hard for the living
To reach these shores. There are many rivers to cross, 155
Great bodies of water, nightmarish streams,
And Ocean itself, which cannot be crossed on foot
But only in a well-built ship. Are you still wandering
On your way back from Troy, a long time at sea
With your ship and your men? Have you not yet come   160
To Ithaca, or seen your wife in your halls?'

So she spoke, and I answered her:

'Mother, I came here because I had to,
To consult the ghost of the prophet Tiresias.
I have not yet come to the coast of Achaea   165
Or set foot on my own land. I have had nothing
But hard travels from the day I set sail
With Lord Agamemnon to go to Ilion,

Famed for its horses, to fight the Trojans.
But tell me truly, how did you die? 170
Was it a long illness, or did Artemis
Shoot you suddenly with her gentle arrows?
And tell me about my father and my son,
Whom I left behind. Does the honor I had
Still remain with them, or has it passed 175
To some other man, and do they all say
I will never return? And what about my wife?
What has she decided, what does she think?
Is she still with my son, keeping things safe?
Or has someone already married her, 180
Whoever is now the best of the Achaeans?'

So I spoke, and my mother answered at once:

'Oh, yes indeed, she remains in your halls,
Her heart enduring the bitter days and nights.
But the honor that was yours has not passed 185
To any man. Telemachus holds your lands
Unchallenged, and shares in the feasts
To which all men invite him as the island's lawgiver.
Your father, though, stays out in the fields
And does not come to the city. He has no bed 190
Piled with bright rugs and soft coverlets
But sleeps in the house where the slaves sleep,
In the ashes by the fire, and wears poor clothes.
In summer and autumn his vineyard's slope
Is strewn with beds of leaves on the ground, 195
Where he lies in his sorrow, nursing his grief,
Longing for your return. His old age is hard.
I died from the same grief. The keen-eyed goddess
Did not shoot me at home with her gentle shafts,
Nor did any long illness waste my body away. 200
No, it was longing for you, my glorious Odysseus,
For your gentle heart and your gentle ways,
That robbed me of my honey-sweet life.'

So she spoke, and my heart yearned

To embrace the ghost of my dead mother.   *205*
Three times I rushed forward to hug her,
And three times she drifted out of my arms
Like a shadow or a dream. The pain
That pierced my heart grew ever sharper,
And my words rose to my mother on wings: *210*

'Mother, why do you slip away when I try
To embrace you? Even though we are in Hades,
Why can't we throw our arms around each other
And console ourselves with chill lamentation?
Are you a phantom sent by Persephone   *215*
To make me groan even more in my grief?'

And my mother answered me at once:

'O my child, most ill-fated of men,
It is not that Persephone is deceiving you.
This is the way it is with mortals.   *220*
When we die, the sinews no longer hold
Flesh and bones together. The fire destroys these
As soon as the spirit leaves the white bones,
And the ghost flutters off and is gone like a dream.
Hurry now to the light, and remember these things,   *225*
So that later you may tell them all to your wife.'

That was the drift of our talk.

                              Then the women came,
Sent by Persephone, all those who had been
The wives and daughters of the heroes of old.
They flocked together around the dark blood,   *230*
But I wanted to question them one at a time.
The best way I could think of to question them
Was to draw the sharp sword from beside my thigh,
And keep them from drinking the blood all at once.
They came up in procession then, and one by one   *235*
They declared their birth, and I questioned them all.

The first one I saw was highborn Tyro,
Who said she was born of flawless Salmoneus
And was wed to Cretheus, a son of Aeolus.
She fell in love with a river, divine Enipeus,   240
The most beautiful of all the rivers on earth,
And she used to play in his lovely streams.
But the Earthshaker took Enipeus' form
And lay with her in the swirling eddies
Near the river's mouth. And an indigo wave,   245
Towering like a mountain, arched over them
And hid the god and the mortal woman from view.
He unbound the sash that had kept her virgin
And shed sleep upon her. And when the god
Had finished his lovemaking, he took her hand   250
And called her name softly and said to her:

'Be happy in this love, woman. As the year turns
You will bear glorious children, for a god's embrace
Is never barren. Raise them and care for them.
Now go to your house and say nothing of this,   255
But I am Poseidon, who makes the earth tremble.'

With that he plunged into the surging sea.
And Tyro conceived and bore Pelias and Neleus,
Who served great Zeus as strong heroes both,
Pelias with his flocks in Iolcus' grasslands,   260
And Neleus down in sandy Pylos.
She bore other children to Cretheus: Aeson,
Pheres, and the charioteer Amythaon.

Then I saw Antiope, daughter of Asopus,
Who boasted she had slept in the arms of Zeus   265
And bore two sons, Amphion and Zethus,
Who founded seven-gated Thebes and built its walls,
Since they could not live in the wide land of Thebes
Without walls and towers, mighty though they were.

Next I saw Alcmene, Amphitryon's wife,   270
Who bore Heracles, the lionhearted battler,

After lying in Zeus' almighty embrace.
And I saw Megara, too, wife of Heracles,
The hero whose strength never wore out.

I saw Oedipus' mother, beautiful Epicaste,   275
Who unwittingly did a monstrous deed,
Marrying her son, who had killed his father.
The gods soon brought these things to light;
Yet, for all his misery, Oedipus still ruled
In lovely Thebes, by the gods' dark designs.   280
But Epicaste, overcome by her grief,
Hung a deadly noose from the ceiling rafters
And went down to implacable Hades' realm,
Leaving behind for her son all of the sorrows
A mother's avenging spirits can cause.   285

And then I saw Chloris, the great beauty
Whom Neleus wedded after courting her
With myriad gifts. She was the youngest daughter
Of Amphion, king of Minyan Orchomenus.
As queen of Pylos, she bore glorious children,   290
Nestor, Chromius, and lordly Periclymenus,
And magnificent Pero, a wonder to men.
Everyone wanted to marry her, but Neleus
Would only give her to the man who could drive
The cattle of mighty Iphicles to Pylos,   295
Spiral-horned, broad-browed, stubborn cattle,
Difficult to drive. Only Melampus,
The flawless seer, rose to the challenge,
But he was shackled by Fate. Country herdsmen
Put him in chains, and months went by   300
And the seasons passed and the year turned
Before he was freed by mighty Iphicles,
After he had told him all of his oracles,
And so the will of Zeus was fulfilled.

I saw Leda also, wife of Tyndareus,   305
Who bore to him two stout-hearted sons,
Castor the horseman and the boxer Polydeuces.

They are under the teeming earth though alive,
And have honor from Zeus in the world below,
Living and dying on alternate days.   *310*
Such is the honor they have won from the gods.

After her I saw Iphimedeia,
Aloeus' wife. She made love to Poseidon
And bore two sons, who did not live long,
Godlike Otus and famed Ephialtes,   *315*
The tallest men ever reared upon earth
And the handsomest after gloried Orion.
At nine years old they measured nine cubits
Across the chest, and were nine fathoms tall.
They threatened to wage a furious war   *320*
Against the immortal Olympian gods,
And were bent on piling Ossa on Olympus,
And forested Pelion on top of Ossa
And so reach the sky. And they would have done it,
But the son of Zeus and fair-haired Leto   *325*
Destroyed them both before the down blossomed
Upon their cheeks and their beards had come in.

And I saw Phaedra and Procnis
And lovely Ariadne, whom Theseus once
Tried to bring from Crete to sacred Athens   *330*
But had no joy of her. Artemis first
Shot her on Dia, the seagirt island,
After Dionysus told her he saw her there.

And I saw Maera and Clymene
And hateful Eriphyle, who valued gold   *335*
More than her husband's life.
                              But I could not tell you
All the wives and daughters of heroes I saw.
It would take all night. And it is time
To sleep now, either aboard ship with the crew
Or here in this house. My journey home   *340*
Is up to you, and to the immortal gods."

He paused, and they sat hushed in silence,
Spellbound throughout the shadowy hall.
And then white-armed Arete began to speak:

"Well, Phaeacians, does this man impress you   *345*
With his looks, stature, and well-balanced mind?
He is my guest, moreover, though each of you
Shares in that honor. Do not send him off, then,
Too hastily, and do not stint your gifts
To one in such need. You have many treasures   *350*
Stored in your halls by grace of the gods."

Then the old hero Echeneus spoke up:

"Friends, the words of our wise queen
Are not wide of the mark. Give them heed.
But upon Alcinous depend both word and deed."   *355*

And Alcinous answered:

"Arete's word will stand, as long as I live
And rule the Phaeacians who love the oar.
But let our guest, though he longs to go home,
Endure until tomorrow, until I have time   *360*
To make our gift complete. We all have a stake
In getting him home, but mine is greatest,
For mine is the power throughout the land."

And Odysseus, who missed nothing:

"Lord Alcinous, most renowned of men,   *365*
You could ask me to stay for even a year
While you arranged a send-off with glorious gifts,
And I would assent. Better far to return
With a fuller hand to my own native land.
I would be more respected and loved by all   *370*
Who saw me come back to Ithaca."

Alcinous answered him:

"Odysseus, we do not take you
For the sort of liar and cheat the dark earth breeds
Among men everywhere, telling tall tales   *375*
No man could ever test for himself.
Your words have outward grace and wisdom within,
And you have told your tale with the skill of a bard—
All that the Greeks and you yourself have suffered.
But tell me this, as accurately as you can: *380*
Did you see any of your godlike comrades
Who went with you to Troy and met their fate there?
The night is young—and magical. It is not yet time
To sleep in the hall. Tell me these wonders.
Sit in our hall and tell us of your woes   *385*
For as long as you can bear. I could listen until dawn."

And Odysseus, his mind teeming:

"Lord Alcinous, most glorious of men,
There is a time for words and a time for sleep.
But if you still yearn to listen, I will not refuse   *390*
To tell you of other things more pitiable still,
The woes of my comrades who died after the war,
Who escaped the Trojans and their battle-cry
But died on their return through a woman's evil.

When holy Persephone had scattered   *395*
The women's ghosts, there came the ghost
Of Agamemnon, son of Atreus,
Distraught with grief. Around him were gathered
Those who died with him in Aegisthus' house.
He knew me as soon as he drank the dark blood.   *400*
He cried out shrilly, tears welling in his eyes,
And he stretched out his hands, trying to touch me,
But he no longer had anything left of the strength
He had in the old days in those muscled limbs.
I wept when I saw him, and with pity in my heart   *405*
I spoke to him these winged words:

'Son of Atreus, king of men, most glorious

Agamemnon—what death laid you low?
Did Poseidon sink your fleet at sea,
After hitting you hard with hurricane winds?   410
Or were you killed by enemy forces on land,
As you raided their cattle and flocks of sheep
Or fought to capture their city and women?'

And Agamemnon answered at once:

'Son of Laertes in the line of Zeus,   415
My crafty Odysseus—No,
Poseidon did not sink my fleet at sea
After hitting us hard with hurricane winds,
Nor was I killed by enemy forces on land.
Aegisthus was the cause of my death.   420
He killed me with the help of my cursed wife
After inviting me to a feast in his house,
Slaughtered me like a bull at a manger.
So I died a most pitiable death,
And all around me my men were killed   425
Relentlessly, like white-tusked swine
For a wedding banquet or dinner party
In the house of a rich and powerful man.
You have seen many men cut down, both
In single combat and in the crush of battle,   430
But your heart would have grieved
As never before at the sight of us lying
Around the wine-bowl and the laden tables
In that great hall. The floor steamed with blood.
But the most piteous cry I ever heard   435
Came from Cassandra, Priam's daughter.
She had her arms around me down on the floor
When Clytemnestra ran her through from behind.
I lifted my hands and beat the ground
As I lay dying with a sword in my chest,   440
But that bitch, my wife, turned her back on me
And would not shut my eyes or close my lips
As I was going down to Death. Nothing
Is more grim or more shameless than a woman

Who sets her mind on such an unspeakable act   *445*
As killing her own husband. I was sure
I would be welcomed home by my children
And all my household, but she, with her mind set
On stark horror, has shamed not only herself
But all women to come, even the rare good one.'   *450*

Thus Agamemnon, and I responded:

'Ah, how broad-browed Zeus has persecuted
The house of Atreus from the beginning,
Through the will of women. Many of us died
For Helen's sake, and Clytemnestra   *455*
Set a snare for you while you were far away.'

And Agamemnon answered me at once:

'So don't go easy on your own wife either,
Or tell her everything you know.
Tell her some things, but keep some hidden.   *460*
But your wife will not bring about your death,
Odysseus. Icarius' daughter,
Your wise Penelope, is far too prudent.
She was newly wed when we went to war.
We left her with a baby boy still at the breast,   *465*
Who must by now be counted as a man,
And prosperous. His father will see him
When he comes, and he will embrace his father,
As is only right. But my wife did not let me
Even fill my eyes with the sight of my son.   *470*
She killed me before I could do even that.
But let me tell you something, Odysseus:
Beach your ship secretly when you come home.
Women just can't be trusted any more.
And one more thing. Tell me truthfully   *475*
If you've heard anything about my son
And where he is living, perhaps in Orchomenus,
Or in sandy Pylos, or with Menelaus in Sparta.
For Orestes has not yet perished from the earth.'

So he spoke, and I answered him: *480*

'Son of Atreus, why ask me this?
I have no idea whether he is alive or dead,
And it is not good to speak words empty as wind.'

Such were the sad words we had for each other
As we stood there weeping, heavy with grief.   *485*

Then came the ghost of Achilles, son of Peleus,
And those of Patroclus and peerless Antilochus
And Ajax, who surpassed all the Danaans,
Except Achilles, in looks and build.
Aeacus' incomparable grandson, Achilles, knew me,   *490*
And when he spoke his words had wings:

'Son of Laertes in the line of Zeus,
Odysseus, you hard rover, not even you
Can ever top this, this bold foray
Into Hades, home of the witless dead   *495*
And the dim phantoms of men outworn.'

So he spoke, and I answered him:

'Achilles, by far the mightiest of the Achaeans,
I have come here to consult Tiresias,
To see if he has any advice for me   *500*
On how I might get back to rugged Ithaca.
I've had nothing but trouble, and have not yet set foot
On my native land. But no man, Achilles,
Has ever been as blessed as you, or ever will be.
While you were alive the army honored you   *505*
Like a god, and now that you are here
You rule the dead with might. You should not
Lament your death at all, Achilles.'

I spoke, and he answered me at once:

'Don't try to sell me on death, Odysseus.   *510*

I'd rather be a hired hand back up on earth,
Slaving away for some poor dirt farmer,
Than lord it over all these withered dead.
But tell me about that boy of mine.
Did he come to the war and take his place   *515*
As one of the best? Or did he stay away?
And what about Peleus? What have you heard?
Is he still respected among the Myrmidons,
Or do they dishonor him in Phthia and Hellas,
Crippled by old age in hand and foot?   *520*
And I'm not there for him up in the sunlight
With the strength I had in wide Troy once
When I killed Ilion's best and saved the army.
Just let me come with that kind of strength
To my father's house, even for an hour,   *525*
And wrap my hands around his enemies' throats.
They would learn what it means to face my temper.'

Thus Achilles, and I answered him:

'I have heard nothing of flawless Peleus,
But as for your son, Neoptolemus,   *530*
I'll tell you all I know, just as you ask.
I brought him over from Scyros myself,
In a fine vessel, to join the Greek army
At Troy, and every time we held council there,
He was always the first to speak, and his words   *535*
Were never off the mark. Godlike Nestor and I
Alone surpassed him. And every time we fought
On Troy's plain, he never held back in the ranks
But charged ahead to the front, yielding
To no one, and he killed many in combat.   *540*
I could not begin to name them all,
All the men he killed when he fought for us,
But what a hero he dismantled in Telephus' son,
Eurypylus, dispatching him and a crowd
Of his Ceteian compatriots. Eurypylus   *545*
Came to Troy because Priam bribed his mother.
After Memnon, I've never seen a handsomer man.

And then, too, when all our best climbed
Into the wooden horse Epeius made,
And I was in command and controlled the trapdoor,   550
All the other Danaan leaders and counselors
Were wiping away tears from their eyes
And their legs shook beneath them, but I never saw
Neoptolemus blanch or wipe away a tear.
No, he just sat there handling his sword hilt   555
And heavy bronze spear, and all he wanted
Was to get out of there and give the Trojans hell.
And after we had sacked Priam's steep city,
He boarded his ship with his share of the loot
And more for valor. And not a scratch on him.   560
He never took a hit from a spear or sword
In close combat, where wounds are common.
When Ares rages anyone can be hit.'

So I spoke, and the ghost of swift-footed Achilles
Went off with huge strides through the fields of asphodel, 565
Filled with joy at his son's preeminence.

The other ghosts crowded around in sorrow,
And each asked about those who were dear to him.
Only the ghost of Telamonian Ajax
Stood apart, still furious with me   570
Because I had defeated him in the contest at Troy
To decide who would get Achilles' armor.
His goddess mother had put it up as a prize,
And the judges were the sons of the Trojans
And Pallas Athena. I wish I had never won.   575
That contest buried Ajax, that brave heart,
The best of the Danaans in looks and deeds,
After the incomparable son of Peleus.
I tried to win him over with words like these:

'Ajax, son of flawless Telamon,   580
Are you to be angry with me even in death
Over that accursed armor? The gods
Must have meant it to be the ruin of the Greeks.

We lost a tower of strength to that armor.
We mourn your loss as we mourn the loss   *585*
Of Achilles himself. Zeus alone
Is to blame. He persecuted the Greeks
Terribly, and he brought you to your doom.
No, come back, Lord Ajax, and listen!
Control your wrath and rein in your proud spirit.'   *590*

I spoke, but he said nothing. He went his way
To Erebus, to join the other souls of the dead.
He might yet have spoken to me there, or I
Might yet have spoken to him, but my heart
Yearned to see the other ghosts of the dead.   *595*

There I saw Minos, Zeus' glorious son,
Scepter in hand, judging the dead
As he sat in the wide-gated house of Hades;
And the dead sat, too, and asked him for judgments.

And then Orion loomed up before me,   *600*
Driving over the fields of asphodel
The beasts he had slain in the lonely hills,
In his hands a bronze club, forever unbroken.

And I saw Tityos, a son of glorious Earth,
Lying on the ground, stretched over nine acres,   *605*
And two vultures sat on either side of him
And tore at his liver, plunging their beaks
Deep into his guts, and he could not beat them off.
For Tityos had raped Leto, a consort of Zeus,
As she went to Pytho through lovely Panopeus.   *610*

And I saw Tantalus there in his agony,
Standing in a pool with water up to his chin.
He was mad with thirst, but unable to drink,
For every time the old man bent over
The water would drain away and vanish,   *615*
Dried up by some god, and only black mud
Would be left at his feet. Above him dangled

Treetop fruits, pears and pomegranates,
Shiny apples, sweet figs, and luscious olives.
But whenever Tantalus reached up for them,   620
The wind tossed them high to the shadowy clouds.

And I saw Sisyphus there in his agony,
Pushing a monstrous stone with his hands.
Digging in hard, he would manage to shove it
To the crest of a hill, but just as he was about   625
To heave it over the top, the shameless stone
Would teeter back and bound down to the plain.
Then he would strain every muscle to push it back up,
Sweat pouring from his limbs and dusty head.

And then mighty Heracles loomed up before me—   630
His phantom that is, for Heracles himself
Feasts with the gods and has as his wife
Beautiful Hebe, daughter of great Zeus
And gold-sandaled Hera. As he moved
A clamor arose from the dead around him,   635
As if they were birds flying off in terror.
He looked like midnight itself. He held his bow
With an arrow on the string, and he glared around him
As if he were always about to shoot. His belt,
A baldric of gold crossing his chest,   640
Was stark horror, a phantasmagoria
Of Bears, and wild Boars, and green-eyed Lions,
Of Battles, and Bloodshed, Murder and Mayhem.
May this be its maker's only masterpiece,
And may there never again be another like it.   645
Heracles recognized me at once,
And his words beat down on me like dark wings:

'Son of Laertes in the line of Zeus,
Crafty Odysseus—poor man, do you too
Drag out a wretched destiny   650
Such as I once bore under the rays of the sun?
I was a son of Zeus and grandson of Cronus,
But I had immeasurable suffering,

Enslaved to a man who was far less than I
And who laid upon me difficult labors.   655
Once he even sent me here, to fetch
The Hound of Hell, for he could devise
No harder task for me than this. That hound
I carried out of the house of Hades,
With Hermes and grey-eyed Athena as guides.'   660

And Heracles went back into the house of Hades.
But I stayed where I was, in case any more
Of the heroes of yesteryear might yet come forth.
And I would have seen some of them—
Heroes I longed to meet, Theseus and Peirithous,   665
Glorious sons of the gods—but before I could,
The nations of the dead came thronging up
With an eerie cry, and I turned pale with fear
That Persephone would send from Hades' depths
The pale head of that monster, the Gorgon.   670

I went to the ship at once and called to my men
To get aboard and untie the stern cables.
They boarded quickly and sat at their benches.
The current bore the ship down the River Ocean.
We rowed at first, and then caught a good tailwind."   675

ODYSSEY 12

"Our ship left the River Ocean
And came to the swell of the open sea
And the Island of Aeaea,
Where Dawn has her dancing grounds
And the Sun his risings. We beached our ship   5
On the sand, disembarked, and fell asleep
On the shore, waiting for daybreak.

Light blossomed like roses in the eastern sky,
And I sent some men to the house of Circe
To bring back the body of Elpenor.   10
We cut wood quickly, and on the headland's point
We held a funeral, shedding warm tears.
When the body was burned, and the armor with it,
We heaped up a mound, dragged a stone onto it,
And on the tomb's very top we planted his oar.   15

While we were busy with these things,
Circe, aware that we had come back
From the Underworld, put on her finest clothes
And came to see us. Her serving women
Brought meat, bread, and bright red wine,   20
And the goddess shone with light as she spoke:

'So you went down alive to Hades' house.
Most men die only once, but you twice.
Come, though, eat and drink wine
The whole day through. You sail at dawn.   25
I will tell you everything on your route,
So that you will not come to grief
In some web of evil on land or sea.'

She spoke, and our proud hearts consented.
All day long until the sun went down   30

We sat feasting on meat and good red wine.
When the sun set and darkness came on
My men went to sleep beside the ship's stern-cables.
But Circe took me by the hand and had me sit
Away from my men. And she lay down beside me 35
And asked me about everything. I told her all
Just as it happened, and then the goddess spoke:

'So all that is done. But now listen
To what I will tell you. One day a god
Will remind you of it. First, you will come 40
To the Sirens, who bewitch all men
Who come near. Anyone who approaches
Unaware and hears their voice will never again
Be welcomed home by wife and children
Dancing with joy at his return— 45
Not after the Sirens bewitch him with song.
They loll in a meadow, and around them are piled
The bones of shriveled and moldering bodies.
Row past them, first kneading sweet wax
And smearing it into the ears of your crew 50
So they cannot hear. But if you yourself
Have a mind to listen, have them bind you
Hand and foot upright in the mast-step
And tie the ends of the rope to the mast.
Then you can enjoy the song of the Sirens. 55
If you command your crew and plead with them
To release you, they should tie you up tighter.
After your men have rowed past the Sirens,
I will not prescribe which of two ways to go.
You yourself must decide. I will tell you both. 60

'One route takes you past beetling crags
Pounded by blue-eyed Amphitrítê's seas.
The blessed gods call these the Wandering Rocks.
Not even birds can wing their way through.
Even the doves that bring ambrosia to Zeus 65
Crash and perish on that slick stone,
And the Father has to replenish their numbers.

Ships never get through. Whenever one tries,
The sea is awash with timbers and bodies
Blasted by the waves and the fiery winds.   70
Only one ship has ever passed through,
The famous Argo as she sailed from Aeetes,
And even she would have been hurled onto those crags
Had not Hera loved Jason and sent his ship through.

'On the other route there are two rocks.   75
One stabs its peak into the sky
And is ringed by a dark blue cloud. This cloud
Never melts, and the air is never clear
During summer or autumn. No mortal man
Could ever scale this rock, not even if he had   80
Twenty hands and feet. The stone is as smooth
As if it were polished. Halfway up the cliff
Is a misty cave facing the western gloom.
It is there you will sail your hollow ship
If you listen to me, glorious Odysseus.   85
The strongest archer could not shoot an arrow
Up from his ship all the way to the cave,
Which is the lair of Scylla. She barks and yelps
Like a young puppy, but she is a monster,
An evil monster that not even a god   90
Would be glad to see. She has—listen to this—
Twelve gangly legs and six very long necks,
And on each neck is perched a bloodcurdling head,
Each with three rows of close-set teeth
Full of black death. Up to her middle   95
She is concealed in the cave, but her heads dangle
Into the abyss, and she fishes by the rock
For dolphins and seals or other large creatures
That the moaning sea breeds in multitudes.
No crew can boast to have sailed past Scylla   100
Unscathed. With each head she carries off a man,
Snatching him out of his dark-prowed vessel.

'The other rock, as you will see, Odysseus,
Lies lower—the two are close enough

That you could shoot an arrow across—   *105*
And on this rock is a large, leafy fig tree.
Beneath this tree the divine Charybdis
Sucks down the black water. Three times a day
She belches it out and three times a day
She sucks it down horribly. Don't be there   *110*
When she sucks it down. No one could save you,
Not even Poseidon, who makes the earth tremble.
No, stay close to Scylla's rock, and push hard.
Better to mourn six than the whole crew at once.'

Thus Circe. And I, in a panic: *115*

'I beg you, goddess, tell me, is there
Any way I can escape from Charybdis
And still protect my men from the other?'

And the goddess, in a nimbus of light:

'There you go again, always the hero.   *120*
Won't you yield even to the immortals?
She's not mortal, she's an immortal evil,
Dread, dire, ferocious, unfightable.
There is no defense. It's flight, not fight.
If you pause so much as to put on a helmet   *125*
She'll attack again with just as many heads
And kill just as many men as before.
Just row past as hard as you can. And call upon
Crataïïs, the mother who bore her as a plague to men.
She will stop her from attacking a second time.   *130*

'Then you will come to Thrinacia,
An island that pastures the cattle of the Sun,
Seven herds of cattle and seven flocks of sheep,
Fifty in each. They are immortal.
They bear no young and they never die off,   *135*
And their shepherds are goddesses,
Nymphs with gorgeous hair, Phaethusa
And Lampetiê, whom gleaming Neaera

Bore to Helios, Hyperion the Sun.
When she had borne them and reared them   *140*
She sent them to Thrinacia, to live far away
And keep their father's spiral-horned cattle.
If you leave these unharmed and keep your mind
On your journey, you might yet struggle home
To Ithaca. But if you harm them, I foretell   *145*
Disaster for your ship and crew, and even if you
Escape yourself, you shall come home late
And badly, having lost all your companions.'

D awn rose in gold as she finished speaking,
And light played about her as she disappeared   *150*
Up the island.
                    I went to the ship
And got my men going. They loosened
The stern cables and were soon in their benches,
Beating the water white with their oars.
A following wind rose in the wake   *155*
Of our dark-prowed ship, a sailor's breeze
Sent by Circe, that dread, beautiful goddess.
We tied down the tackling and sat tight,
Letting the wind and the helmsman take over.

Then I made a heavy-hearted speech to my men: *160*

'Friends, it is not right that one or two alone
Should know what the goddess Circe foretold.
Better we should all know, live or die.
We may still beat death and get out of this alive.
First, she told us to avoid the eerie voices   *165*
Of the Sirens and sail past their soft meadows.
She ordered me alone to listen. Bind me
Hand and foot upright in the mast-step
And tie the ends of the rope to the mast.
If I command you and plead with you   *170*
To release me, just tie me up tighter.'

Those were my instructions to the crew.

Meanwhile, our good ship was closing fast
On the Sirens' island, when the breeze we'd had
Tailed off, and we were becalmed—not a breath   *175*
Of wind left—some spirit lulled the waves.
My men got up and furled the sails,
Stowed them in the ship's hold, then sat down
At their oars and whitened the water with pine.
Myself, I got out a wheel of wax, cut it up   *180*
With my sharp knife, and kneaded the pieces
Until they were soft and warm, a quick job
With Lord Helios glaring down from above.
Then I went down the rows and smeared the wax
Into all my men's ears. They in turn bound me   *185*
Hand and foot upright to the mast,
Tied the ends of the rope to the mast, and then
Sat down and beat the sea white with their oars.
We were about as far away as a shout would carry,
Surging ahead, when the Sirens saw our ship   *190*
Looming closer, and their song pierced the air:

'Come hither, Odysseus,
  glory of the Achaeans,
Stop your ship
  so you can hear our voices.
No one has ever sailed
  his black ship past here
Without listening to the honeyed
  sound from our lips.   *195*
He journeys on delighted
  and knows more than before.
For we know everything
  that the Greeks and Trojans
Suffered in wide Troy
  by the will of the gods.
We know all that happens
  on the teeming earth.'

They made their beautiful voices carry,   *200*
And my heart yearned to listen. I ordered my men

To untie me, signaling with my brows,
But they just leaned on their oars and rowed on.
Perimedes and Eurylochus jumped up,
Looped more rope around me, and pulled tight.   *205*
When we had rowed past, and the Sirens' song
Had faded on the waves, only then did my crew
Take the wax from their ears and untie me.

We had no sooner left the island when I saw
The spray from an enormous wave   *210*
And heard its booming. The oars flew
From my men's frightened hands
And shirred in the waves, stopping the ship
Dead in the water. I went down the rows
And tried to boost the crew's morale: *215*

'Come on, men, this isn't the first time
We've run into trouble. This can't be worse
Than when the Cyclops with his brute strength
Had us penned in his cave. We got out
By my courage and fast thinking. One day   *220*
We'll look back on this. Now let's do as I say,
Every man of you! Stay on your benches
And beat the deep surf with your oars!
Zeus may yet deliver us from death.
Helmsman, here's my command to you,   *225*
And make sure you remember it, since
You're steering this vessel: Keep the ship
Away from this heavy surf. Hug the cliff,
Or before you know it she'll swerve
To starboard and you'll send us all down.'   *230*

I spoke, they obeyed. But I didn't mention
Scylla. There was nothing we could do about that,
And I didn't want the crew to freeze up,
Stop rowing, and huddle together in the hold.
Then I forgot Circe's stern warning   *235*
Not to arm myself no matter what happened.
I strapped on my bronze, grabbed two long spears

And went to the foredeck, where I thought
Scylla would first show herself from the cliff.
But I couldn't see her anywhere, and my eyes   240
Grew weary scanning the misty rock face.

We sailed on up the narrow channel, wailing,
Scylla on one side, Charybdis on the other
Sucking down saltwater. When she belched it up
She seethed and bubbled like a boiling cauldron   245
And the spray would reach the tops of the cliffs.
When she sucked it down you could see her
Churning within, and the rock bellowed
And roared, and you could see the sea floor
Black with sand. My men were pale with fear.   250
While we looked at her, staring death in the eyes,
Scylla seized six of my men from our ship,
The six strongest hands aboard. Turning my eyes
To the deck and my crew, I saw above me
Their hands and feet as they were raised aloft.   255
They cried down to me, calling me by name
That one last time in their agony.
                                        You know
How a fisherman on a jutting rock
Casts his bait with his long pole. The horned hook
Sinks into the sea, and when he catches a fish   260
He pulls it writhing and squirming out of the water.
Writhing like that my men were drawn up the cliff.
And Scylla devoured them at her door, as they shrieked
And stretched their hands down to me
In their awful struggle. Of all the things   265
That I have borne while I scoured the seas,
I have seen nothing more pitiable.

When we had fled Charybdis, the rocks,
And Scylla, we came to the perfect island
Of Hyperion the Sun, where his herds ranged   270
And his flocks browsed. While our black ship
Was still out at sea I could hear the bleating
Of the sheep and the lowing of the cattle

As they were being penned, and I remembered
The words of the blind seer, Theban Tiresias,   *275*
And of Circe, who gave me strict warnings
To shun the island of the warmth-giving Sun.
And so I spoke to my crew with heavy heart:

'Hear my words, men, for all your pain.
So I can tell you Tiresias' prophecies   *280*
And Circe's, too, who gave me strict warnings
To shun the island of the warmth-giving Sun,
For there she said was our gravest peril.
No, row our black ship clear of this island.'

This broke their spirits, and at once   *285*
Eurylochus answered me spitefully:

'You're a hard man, Odysseus, stronger
Than other men, and you never wear out,
A real iron-man, who won't allow his crew,
Dead tired from rowing and lack of sleep,   *290*
To set foot on shore, where we might make
A meal we could enjoy. No, you just order us
To wander on through the swift darkness
Over the misty deep, and be driven away
From the island. It is at night that winds rise   *295*
That wreck ships. How could we survive
If we were hit by a South Wind or a West,
Which sink ships no matter what the great gods want?
No, let's give in to black night now
And make our supper. We'll stay by the ship,   *300*
Board her in the morning, and put out to sea.'

Thus Eurylochus, and the others agreed.
I knew then that some god had it in for us,
And my words had wings:

                          'Eurylochus,
It's all of you against me alone. All right,   *305*
But swear me a great oath, every last man:

If we find any cattle or sheep on this island,
No man will kill a single cow or sheep
In his recklessness, but will be content
To eat the food immortal Circe gave us.'   *310*

They swore they would do just as I said,
And when they had finished the words of the oath,
We moored our ship in a hollow harbor
Near a sweet-water spring. The crew disembarked
And skillfully prepared their supper.   *315*
When they had their fill of food and drink,
They fell to weeping, remembering how Scylla
Had snatched their shipmates and devoured them.
Sweet sleep came upon them as they wept.
Past midnight, when the stars had wheeled around,   *320*
Zeus gathered the clouds and roused a great wind
Against us, an ungodly tempest that shrouded
Land and sea and blotted out the night sky.
At the first blush of Dawn we hauled our ship up
And made her fast in a cave where you could see   *325*
The nymphs' beautiful seats and dancing places.
Then I called my men together and spoke to them:

'Friends, there is food and drink in the ship.
Let's play it safe and keep our hands
Off those cattle, which belong to Helios,   *330*
A dread god who hears and sees all.'

So I spoke, and their proud hearts consented.

Then for a full month the South Wind blew,
And no other wind but the East and the South.
As long as my men had grain and red wine   *335*
They didn't touch the cattle—life was still worth living.
But when all the rations from the ship were gone,
They had to roam around in search of game—
Hunting for birds and whatever they could catch
With fishing hooks. Hunger gnawed at their bellies.   *340*

I went off by myself up the island
To pray to the gods to show me the way.
When I had put some distance between myself
And the crew, and found a spot
Sheltered from the wind, I washed my hands   345
And prayed to the gods, but all they did
Was close my eyelids in sleep.

                        Meanwhile,
Eurylochus was giving bad advice to the crew:

'Listen to me, shipmates, despite your distress.
All forms of death are hateful, but to die   350
Of hunger is the most wretched way to go.
What are we waiting for? Let's drive off
The prime beef in that herd and offer sacrifice
To the gods of broad heaven. If we ever
Return to Ithaca, we will build a rich temple   355
To Hyperion the Sun, and deposit there
Many fine treasures. If he becomes angry
Over his cattle and gets the other gods' consent
To destroy our ship, well, I would rather
Gulp down saltwater and die once and for all   360
Than waste away slowly on a desert island.'

Thus Eurylochus, and the others agreed.
In no time they had driven off the best
Of Helios' cattle, pretty, spiral-horned cows
That were grazing close to our dark-prowed ship.   365
They surrounded these cows and offered prayers
To the gods, plucking off tender leaves
From a high-crowned oak in lieu of white barley,
Of which there was none aboard our benched ship.
They said their prayers, cut the cows' throats,   370
Flayed the animals and carved out the thigh joints,
Wrapped these in a double layer of fat
And laid all the raw bits upon them.
They had no wine to pour over the sacrifice
And so used water as they roasted the entrails.   375

When the thighs were burned and the innards tasted,
They carved up the rest and skewered it on spits.

That's when I awoke, bolting upright.
I started down to the shore, and as I got near the ship
The aroma of sizzling fat drifted up to me.   *380*
I groaned and cried out to the undying gods:

'Father Zeus, and you other immortals,
You lulled me to sleep—and to my ruin—
While my men committed this monstrous crime!'

Lampetiê rushed in her long robes to Helios   *385*
And told him that we had killed his cattle.
Furious, the Sun God addressed the immortals:

'Father Zeus, and you other gods eternal,
Punish Odysseus' companions, who have insolently
Killed the cattle I took delight in seeing   *390*
Whenever I ascended the starry heaven
And whenever turned back from heaven to earth.
If they don't pay just atonement for the cows
I will sink into Hades and shine on the dead.'

And Zeus, who masses the clouds, said: *395*

'Helios, you go on shining among the gods
And for mortal men on the grain-giving earth.
I will soon strike their ship with sterling lightning
And shatter it to bits on the wine-purple sea.'

All this I heard from rich-haired Calypso,   *400*
Who said she heard it from Hermes the Guide.

When I reached the ship I chewed out my men,
Giving each one an earful. But there was nothing
We could do. The cattle were already dead.
Then the gods showed some portents   *405*
Directed at my men. The hides crawled,

And the meat, both roasted and raw,
Mooed on the spits, like cattle lowing.

Each day for six days my men slaughtered oxen
From Helios' herd and gorged on the meat.   410
But when Zeus brought the seventh day,
The wind tailed off from gale force.
We boarded ship at once and put out to sea
As soon as we had rigged the mast and sail.

When we left the island behind, there was   415
No other land in sight, only sea and sky.
Then Zeus put a black cloud over our ship
And the sea grew dark beneath it. She ran on
A little while, and then the howling West Wind
Blew in with hurricane force. It snapped   420
Both forestays, and the mast fell backward
Into the bilge with all of its tackle.
On its way down the mast struck the helmsman
And crushed his skull. He fell from the stern
Like a diver, and his proud soul left his bones.   425
In the same instant, Zeus thundered
And struck the ship with a lightning bolt.
She shivered from stem to stern and was filled
With sulfurous smoke. My men went overboard,
Bobbing in the waves like sea crows   430
Around the black ship, their day of return
Snuffed out by the Sun God.
I kept pacing the deck until the sea surge
Tore the sides from the keel. The waves
Drove the bare keel on and snapped the mast   435
From its socket; the leather backstay
Was still attached, and I used this to lash
The keel to the mast. Perched on these timbers
I was swept along by deathly winds.

Then the West Wind died down,   440
And, to my horror, the South Wind rose.
All that way, back to the whirlpool,

I was swept along the whole night through
And at dawn reached Scylla's cliff
And dread Charybdis. She was sucking down   *445*
Seawater, and I leapt up
To the tall fig tree, grabbed hold of it
And hung on like a bat. I could not
Plant my feet or get myself set on the tree
Because its roots spread far below   *450*
And its branches were high overhead,
Long, thick limbs that shaded Charybdis.
I just grit my teeth and hung on
Until she spat out the mast and keel again.
It seemed like forever. Finally,   *455*
About the hour a man who has spent the day
Judging quarrels that young men bring to him
Rises from the marketplace and goes to dinner,
My ship's timbers surfaced again from Charybdis.
I let go with my hands and feet   *460*
And hit the water hard beyond the spars.
Once aboard, I rowed away with my hands.
As for Scylla, Zeus never let her see me,
Or I would have been wiped out completely.

I floated on for nine days. On the tenth night   *465*
The gods brought me to Ogygia
And to Calypso, the dread, beautiful goddess,
Who loved me and took care of me.
But I have told that tale only yesterday,
Here in your hall, to yourself and your wife,   *470*
And I wouldn't bore you by telling it again."

ODYSSEY 13

Odysseus finished his story,
And they were all spellbound, hushed
To silence throughout the shadowy hall,
Until Alcinous found his voice and said:

"Odysseus, now that you have come to my house,　　　　　5
High-roofed and founded on bronze, I do not think
You will be blown off course again
Before reaching home.
　　　　　　　　　　Hear now my command,
All who drink the glowing wine of Elders
Daily in my halls and hear the harper sing:　　　　　10
Clothes for our guest lie in a polished sea-chest,
Along with richly wrought gold and all the other gifts
The Phaeacian lords have brought to the palace.
But now each man of us gives him a cauldron, too.
We will recoup ourselves later with a general tax.　　　　　15
It is hard to make such generous gifts alone."

They were all pleased with what Alcinous said.
Each man went to his own house to sleep,
And when Dawn's rosy fingers appeared in the sky
They hurried to the ship with their gifts of bronze.　　　　　20
Alcinous, the sacred king himself, went on board
And stowed them away beneath the benches
Where they would not hinder the rowers' efforts.
Then they all went back to feast in the palace.

In their honor Alcinous sacrificed an ox　　　　　25
To Zeus, the Dark Cloud, who rules over all.
They roasted the haunches and feasted gloriously
While the godlike harper, honored Demodocus,
Sang in their midst.
　　　　　　　　But Odysseus

Kept turning his head toward the shining sun,   *30*
Urging it down the sky. He longed to set forth.

   A man who has been in the fields all day
   With his wooden plow and wine-faced oxen
   Longs for supper and welcomes the sunset
   That sends him homeward with weary knees.   *35*

So welcome to Odysseus was the evening sun.
As soon as it set he addressed the Phaeacians,
Alcinous especially, and his words had wings:

"Lord Alcinous, I bid you and your people
To pour libation and send me safely on my way.   *40*
And I bid you farewell. All is now here
That my heart has desired—passage home
And cherished gifts that the gods in heaven
Have blessed me with. When I reach home
May I find my wife and loved ones unharmed.   *45*
May you enjoy your wife and children here,
May the gods send you everything good,
And may harm never come to your island people."

They all cheered this speech, and demanded
That the stranger and guest be given passage home.   *50*
Alcinous then nodded to his herald:

"Pontonous, mix a bowl of wine and serve
Cups to all, that we may pray to Lord Zeus
And send our guest to his own native land."

Thus the King, and Pontonous mixed   *55*
The mellow-hearted wine and served it to all.
Still seated, they tipped their cups to the gods
Who possess wide heaven. Then Odysseus
Stood up and placed a two-handled cup
In Arete's hands, and his words rose on wings: *60*

"Be well, my queen, all of your days, until age

And death come to you, as they come to all.
I am leaving now. But you, Lady—enjoy this house,
Your children, your people, and Lord Alcinous."

And godlike Odysseus stepped over the threshold.   65
Alcinous sent a herald along
To guide him to the shore and the swift ship there,
And Arete sent serving women with him,
One carrying a cloak and laundered shirt,
And another to bring the strong sea-chest.   70
A third brought along bread and red wine.
They came down to the sea, and the ship's crew
Stowed all these things away in the hold,
The food and drink, too. Then they spread out
A rug and a linen sheet on the stern deck   75
For Odysseus to sleep upon undisturbed.
He climbed on board and lay down in silence
While they took their places upon the benches
And untied the cable from the anchor stone.
As soon as they dipped their oars in the sea,   80
A deep sleep fell on his eyelids, a sleep
Sound, and sweet, and very much like death.

        And as four yoked stallions spring all together
        Beneath the lash, leaping high,
        And then eat up the dusty road on the plain,   85

So lifted the keel of that ship, and in her wake
An indigo wave hissed and roiled
As she ran straight ahead. Not even a falcon,
Lord of the skies, could have matched her pace,
So light her course as she cut through the waves,   90
Bearing a man with a mind like the gods',
A man who had suffered deep in his heart,
Enduring men's wars and the bitter sea—
But now he slept, his sorrows forgotten.

   The sea turned silver   95
Under the star that precedes the dawn,

And the great ship pulled up to Ithaca.

Phorcys, the Old Man of the Sea,
Has a harbor there. Two fingers of rock
Curl out from the island, steep to seaward   *100*
But sloping down to the bay they protect
From hurricane winds and high waves outside.
Inside, ships can ride without anchor
In the still water offshore.
At the harbor's head a slender-leaved olive   *105*
Stands near a cave glimmering through the mist
And sacred to the nymphs called Naiades.
Inside are bowls and jars of stone
Where bees store honey, and long stone looms
Where the nymphs weave shrouds as dark as the sea.   *110*
Waters flow there forever, and there are two doors,
One toward the North Wind, by which humans
Go down, the other toward the South Wind,
A door for the gods. No men enter there:
It is the Way of Immortals.

                The Phaeacians   *115*
Had been here before. In they rowed,
And with such force that their ship was propelled
Half of its length onto the shelving shore.
The crew disembarked, lifting Odysseus
Out of the ship—sheet, carpet, and all—   *120*
And laying him down, sound asleep, on the sand.
Then they hauled from the ship all of the goods
The Phaeacian lords had given him
As he was going home—all thanks to Athena.
They piled these together near the bole of the olive,   *125*
Away from the path, fearing that someone
Might come along before Odysseus awoke
And rob him blind. Then the Phaeacians went home.

[Lines 129–93 are omitted. Poseidon turns the Phaeacian ship to stone as it sails into the harbor and hems in the island with a mountain.]

Odysseus, meanwhile,
Awoke from sleep in his ancestral land—   195
And did not recognize it. He had been gone so long,
And Pallas Athena had spread haze all around.
The goddess wanted to explain things to him,
And to disguise him, so that his wife and dear ones
Would not know who he was until he had made   200
The arrogant suitors pay for their outrage.
So everything on Ithaca now looked different
To its lord—the winding trails, the harbors,
The towering rocks and the trees. Odysseus
Sprang to his feet and gazed at his homeland.   205
He groaned, smacked his thighs with his hands,
And in a voice choked with tears, said:

"What land have I come to now? Who knows
What kind of people live here—lawless savages,
Or godfearing men who take kindly to strangers?   210
Where am I going to take all these things? Where
Am I going to go myself? I should have stayed
With the Phaeacians until I could go on from there
To some other powerful king who would have
Entertained me and sent me off homeward bound.   215
Now I don't even know where to put this stuff.
I can't leave it here as easy pickings for a thief.
Those Phaeacian lords were not as wise
As they seemed, nor as just, bringing me here
To this strange land. They said they would bring me   220
To Ithaca's shore, but that's not what they've done.
May Zeus pay them back, Zeus, god of suppliants,
Who spots transgressors and punishes them.
Well, I'd better count my goods and go over them.
Those sailors may have made off with some in their ship." 225

And he set about counting the hammered tripods,
The cauldrons, the gold, the finely woven clothes.
Nothing was missing. It was his homeland he missed
As he paced along the whispering surf-line,
Utterly forlorn.

And then Athena was beside him   *230*
In the form of a young man out herding sheep.
She had the delicate features of a prince,
A fine-spun mantle folded over her shoulders,
Sandals on her glistening feet, a spear in her hand.
Odysseus' spirits soared when he saw her,   *235*
And he turned to her with these words on his lips:

"Friend—you are the first person I've met here—
I wish you well. Now don't turn on me.
Help me keep these things safe, and keep me safe,
I beg you at your knees as if you were a god.   *240*
And tell me this, so I will know:
What land is this, who are the people here?
Is this an island, or a rocky arm
Of the mainland shore stretching out to sea?"

Athena's eyes glinted with azure light: *245*

"Where in the world do you come from, stranger,
That you have to ask what land this is?
It's not exactly nameless! Men from all over
Know this land, sailing in from the sunrise
And from far beyond the evening horizon.   *250*
It's got rough terrain, not for driving horses,
But it's not at all poor even without wide open spaces.
There's abundant grain here, and wine-grapes,
Good rainfalls, and rich, heavy dews.
Good pasture, too, for goats and for cattle,   *255*
And all sorts of timber, and year-round springs.
That's why Ithaca is a name heard even in Troy,
Which they say is far from any Greek land."

And Odysseus, who had borne much,
Felt joy at hearing his homeland described   *260*
By Pallas Athena, Zeus' own daughter.
His words flew out as if on wings—
But he did not speak the truth. He checked that impulse,
And, jockeying for an advantage, made up this story:

"I've heard of Ithaca, of course—even in Crete, 265
Far over the sea, and now I've just come ashore
With my belongings here. I left as much
To my sons back home. I've been on the run
Since killing a man, Orsilochus,
Idomeneus' son, the great sprinter. 270
No one in all Crete could match his speed.
He wanted to rob me of all of the loot
I took out of Troy—stuff I had sweated for
In hand-to-hand combat in the war overseas—
Because I wouldn't serve under his father at Troy 275
But led my own unit instead. I ambushed him
With one of my men, got him with a spear
As he came back from the fields. It was night,
Pitch-black. No one saw us, and I got away
With a clean kill with sharp bronze. Then, 280
I found a ship, Phoenician, and made it
Worth the crew's while to take me to Pylos,
Or Elis maybe, where the Epeans are in power.
Well, the wind pushed us back from those shores—
It wasn't their fault, they didn't want to cheat me— 285
And we were driven here in the middle of the night
And rowed like hell into the harbor. Didn't even
Think of chow, though we sure could have used some,
Just got off the boat and lay down, all of us.
I slept like a baby, dead to the world, 290
And they unloaded my stuff from the ship's hold
And set it down next to me where I lay on the sand.
Then off they went to Sidonia, the big city,
And I was left here, stranded, just aching inside."

Athena smiled at him, her eyes blue as the sea, 295
And her hand brushed his cheek. She was now
A tall, beautiful woman, with an exquisite touch
For handiwork, and her words had wings:

"Only a master thief, a real con artist,
Could match your tricks—even a god 300
Might come up short. You wily bastard,

You cunning, elusive, habitual liar!
Even in your own land you weren't about
To give up the stories and sly deceits
That are so much a part of you.   *305*
Never mind about that though. Here we are,
The two shrewdest minds in the universe,
You far and away the best man on earth
In plotting strategies, and I famed among gods
For my clever schemes. Not even you   *310*
Recognized Pallas Athena, Zeus' daughter,
I who stand by you in all your troubles
And who made you dear to all the Phaeacians.
And now I've come here, ready to weave
A plan with you, and to hide the goods   *315*
The Phaeacians gave you—which was my idea—
And to tell you what you still have to endure
In your own house. And you do have to endure,
And not tell anyone, man or woman,
That you have come home from your wanderings.   *320*
No, you must suffer in silence, and take a beating."

And Odysseus, his mind teeming:

"It would be hard for the most discerning man alive
To see through all your disguises, Goddess.
I know this, though: you were always kind to me   *325*
When the army fought at Troy.
But after we plundered Priam's steep city,
And boarded our ships, and a god scattered us,
I didn't see you then, didn't sense your presence
Aboard my ship or feel you there to help me.   *330*
No, and I suffered in my wanderings
Until the gods released me from my troubles.
It wasn't until I was on Phaeacia
That you comforted me—and led me to the city.
Now I beg you, by your Father—I don't believe   *335*
I've come to sunlit Ithaca, but to some other land.
I think you're just giving me a hard time,
And trying to put one over on me. Tell me

If I've really come to my own native land."

And Athena, her eyes glinting blue: 340

"Ah, that mind of yours! That's why
I can't leave you when you're down and out:
Because you're so intelligent and self-possessed.
Any other man come home from hard travels
Would rush to his house to see his children and wife.   345
But you don't even want to hear how they are
Until you test your wife, who,
As a matter of fact, just sits in the house,
Weeping away the lonely days and nights.
I never lost faith, though. I always knew in my heart   350
You'd make it home, all your companions lost,
But I couldn't bring myself to fight my uncle,
Poseidon, who had it in for you,
Angry because you blinded his son.
And now, so you will believe, I will show you   355
Ithaca from the ground up: There is the harbor
Of Phorcys, the Old Man of the Sea, and here,
At its head, is the slender-leaved olive tree
Standing near a cave that glimmers in the mist
And is sacred to the nymphs called Naiades.   360
Under that cavern's arched roof you sacrificed
Many a perfect victim to the nymphs.
And there stands Mount Neriton, mantled in forest."

As she spoke, the goddess dispelled the mist.
The ground appeared, and Odysseus,   365
The godlike survivor, felt his mind soar
At the sight of his land. He kissed the good earth,
And with his palms to the sun, Odysseus prayed:

"Nymphs, Naiades, daughters of Zeus!
I never thought I would see you again.   370
Take pleasure in my whispered prayers
And we will give you gifts as before,
If Zeus' great daughter Athena

Allows me to live and my son to reach manhood."

And Athena, her eyes glinting blue: *375*

"You don't have to worry about that.
Right now, let's stow these things in a nook
Of the enchanted cave, where they'll be safe for you.
Then we can talk about a happy ending."

With that, the goddess entered the shadowy cave *380*
And searched out its recesses while Odysseus
Brought everything closer—the gold, the bronze,
The well-made clothes the Phaeacians had given him.
And Zeus' own daughter stored them away
And blocked the entrance to the cave with a stone. *385*
Then, sitting at the base of the sacred olive,
The two plotted death for the insolent suitors.
Athena began their discussion this way:

"Son of Laertes in the line of Zeus,
Odysseus, the master tactician—consider how *390*
You're going to get your hands on the shameless suitors,
Who for three years now have taken over your house,
Proposing to your wife and giving her gifts.
She pines constantly for your return,
But she strings them along, makes little promises, *395*
Sends messages—while her intentions are otherwise."

And Odysseus, his mind teeming:

"Ah, I'd be heading for the same pitiful death
That Agamemnon met in his house
If you hadn't told me all this, Goddess. *400*
Weave a plan so I can pay them back!
And stand by me yourself, give me the spirit I had
When we ripped down Troy's shining towers!
With you at my side, your eyes glinting
And your mind fixed on battle—I would take on *405*
Three hundred men if your power were with me."

And Athena, eyes reflecting the blue sea-light:

"Oh, I'll be there all right, and I'll keep my eye on you
When we get down to business. And I think
More than one of these suitors destroying your home   *410*
Will spatter the ground with their blood and brains.
Now let's see about disguising you. First,
I'll shrivel the skin on your gnarly limbs,
And wither that tawny hair. A piece of sail-cloth
Will make a nice, ugly cloak. Then   *415*
We'll make those beautiful eyes bleary and dim.
You'll look disgusting to all the suitors, as well as to
The wife and child you left behind in your halls.
But you should go first to your swineherd.
He may only tend your pigs, but he's devoted to you,   *420*
And he loves your son and Penelope.
You'll find him with the swine. They are feeding
By Raven's Rock and Arethusa's spring,
Gorging on acorns and drinking black water,
Which fattens swine up nicely. Stay with him,   *425*
Sit with him a while and ask him about everything,
While I go to Lacedaemon, land of lovely women,
To summon Telemachus. Your son, Odysseus,
Went to Menelaus' house in Sparta
Hoping for news that you are still alive."   *430*

And Odysseus, his mind teeming:

"You knew. Why didn't you tell him?
So he could suffer too, roving barren seas
While my wife's suitors eat him out of house and home?"

Athena answered, her eyes glinting blue: *435*

"You needn't worry too much about him.
I accompanied him in person. I wanted him
To make a name for himself by traveling there.
He's not exactly laboring as he takes his ease
In Menelaus' luxurious palace.   *440*

Sure, these young louts have laid an ambush for him
In a ship out at sea, meaning to kill him
Before he reaches home. But I don't think they will.
These suitors who have been destroying your home
Will be six feet under before that'll ever happen."   *445*

So saying, Athena touched him with a wand.
She shriveled the flesh on his gnarled limbs,
And withered his tawny hair. She wrinkled the skin
All over his body so he looked like an old man,
And she made his beautiful eyes bleary and dim.   *450*
Then she turned his clothes into tattered rags,
Dirty and smoke-grimed, and cast about him
A great deerskin cloak with the fur worn off.
And she gave him a staff and a ratty pouch
All full of holes, slung by a twisted cord.   *455*

Having laid their plans, they went their own ways,
The goddess off to Sparta to fetch Telemachus.

*[Books 14 and 15 are omitted. Odysseus spends a day and a night in the
hut of Eumaeus, the faithful servant who tends the swine. Although
Eumaeus does not know who Odysseus is, he treats him hospitably, and
Odysseus hears from him how the suitors have been ravaging the palace.
Telemachus, meanwhile, has traveled from Sparta to Pylos and sailed back
to Ithaca, having eluded the suitors' ambush. He has come ashore by him-
self near the swineherd's hut and has sent the ship on to the harbor.]*

ODYSSEY 16

Meanwhile, in the hut, Odysseus
And the noble swineherd had kindled a fire
And were making breakfast in the early light.
They had already sent the herdsmen out
With the droves of swine.

                   The dogs fawned   5
Around Telemachus and did not bark at him
As he approached. Odysseus noticed
The dogs fawning and heard footsteps.
His words flew fast to Eumaeus:

"Eumaeus, one of your men must be coming,   10
Or at least someone you know. The dogs aren't barking
And are fawning around him. I can hear his footsteps."

His words weren't out when his own son
Stood in the doorway. Up jumped the swineherd
In amazement, and from his hands fell the vessels   15
He was using to mix the wine. He went
To greet his master, kissing his head
And his shining eyes and both his hands.

   And as a loving father embraces his own son
   Come back from a distant land after ten long years,   20
   His only son, greatly beloved and much sorrowed for—

So did the noble swineherd clasp Telemachus
And kiss him all over—he had escaped from death—
And sobbing he spoke to him these winged words:

"You have come, Telemachus, sweet light!   25
I thought I would never see you again
After you left in your ship for Pylos. But come in,
Dear child, let me feast my eyes on you

Here in my house, come back from abroad!
You don't visit the farm often, or us herdsmen, 30
But stay in town. It must do your heart good
To look at that weeviling crowd of suitors."

And Telemachus, in his clear-headed way:

"Have it your way, Papa. But it's for your sake I've come,
To see you with my own eyes, and to hear from you 35
Whether my mother is still in our house,
Or someone else has married her by now,
And Odysseus' bed, with no one to sleep in it,
Has become a nest of spider webs."

The swineherd answered him: 40

"Yes, she's in your house, waiting and waiting
With an enduring heart, poor soul,
Weeping away the lonely days and nights."

He spoke, and took the young man's spear.
Telemachus went in, and as he crossed 45
The stone threshold, Odysseus stood up
To offer him his seat, but Telemachus,
From across the room, checked him and said:

"Keep your seat, stranger. We'll find another one
Around the place. Eumaeus here can do that." 50

He spoke, and Odysseus sat down again.
The swineherd piled up some green brushwood
And covered it with a fleece, and upon this
The true son of Odysseus sat down.
Then the swineherd set out platters of roast meat— 55
Leftovers from yesterday's meal—
And hurried around heaping up bread in baskets
And mixing sweet wine in an ivy-wood bowl.
Then he sat down opposite godlike Odysseus,
And they helped themselves to the fare before them. 60

When they had enough to eat and drink,
Telemachus spoke to the godlike swineherd:

"Where did this stranger come from, Papa?
What kind of sailors brought him to Ithaca?
I don't suppose he walked to our island."   65

And you answered, Eumaeus, my swineherd:

"I'll tell you everything plainly, child.
He says he was born somewhere in Crete
And that it has been his lot to be a roamer
And wander from city to city. But now   70
He has run away from a Thesprotian ship
And come to my farmstead. I put him in your hands.
Do as you wish. He declares he is your suppliant."

And Telemachus, wise beyond his years:

"This makes my heart ache, Eumaeus.   75
How can I welcome this guest in my house?
I am still young, and I don't have the confidence
To defend myself if someone picks a fight.
As for my mother, her heart is torn.
She can't decide whether to stay here with me   80
And keep the house, honoring her husband's bed
And the voice of the people, or to go away
With whichever man among her suitors
Is the best of the Achaeans, and offers the most gifts.
But as to our guest—now that he's come to your house,   85
I will give him a tunic and cloak, fine clothes,
And a two-edged sword, and sandals for his feet,
And passage to wherever his heart desires.
Or keep him here if you wish, at your farmstead
And take care of him. I'll send the clothes   90
And all of his food, so it won't be a hardship
For you or your men. What I won't allow
Is for him to come up there among the suitors.
They are far too reckless and arrogant,

And I fear they will make fun of him, mock him, 95
And it would be hard for me to take that.
But what could I do? One man, however powerful,
Can't do much against superior numbers."

Then Odysseus, who had borne much, said:

"My friend—surely it is right for me to speak up— 100
It breaks my heart to hear you talk about
The suitors acting like this in your house
And going against the will of a man as great as you.
It is against your will, isn't it? What happened?
Do the people up and down the land all hate you? 105
Has a god turned them against you? Or do you blame
Your brothers, whom a man has to rely upon
In a fight, especially if a big fight comes up?
I wish I were as vigorous as I am angry,
Or were a son of flawless Odysseus, or Odysseus himself! 110
Then I would put my neck on the chopping block
If I did not give them hell when I came into
The halls of Odysseus, son of Laertes!
But if they overwhelmed me with superior numbers,
I would rather be dead, killed in my own halls, 115
Than have to keep watching these disgraceful deeds,
Strangers mistreated, men dragging the women
Through the beautiful halls, wine spilled,
Bread wasted, and all with no end in sight."

Telemachus answered in his clear-headed way: 120

"Well, stranger, I'll tell you the whole story.
It's not that the people have turned against me,
Nor do I have any brothers to blame. Zeus
Has made our family run in a single line.
Laertes was the only son of Arcesius, 125
And Laertes had only one son, Odysseus,
Who only had me, a son he never knew.
And so now our house is filled with enemies,
All of the nobles who rule the islands—

Dulichium, Samê, wooded Zacynthus—   *130*
And all of those with power on rocky Ithaca
Are courting my mother and ruining our house.
She neither refuses to make a marriage she hates
Or is able to stop it. They are eating us
Out of house and home, and will come after me soon.   *135*
But all of this rests on the knees of the gods.
Eumaeus, go tell Penelope right away
That I'm safe and back from Pylos.
I'll wait for you here. Tell only her
And don't let any of the suitors find out.   *140*
Many of them are plotting against me."

And you answered him, Eumaeus, my swineherd:

"I follow you, Telemachus, I understand.
But tell me this. Should I go the same way
To Laertes also, and tell him the news?   *145*
Poor man, for a while he still oversaw the fields,
Although he was grieving greatly for Odysseus,
And would eat and drink with the slaves in the house
Whenever he had a notion. But now, since the very day
You sailed to Pylos, they say he hasn't been   *150*
Eating or drinking as before, or overseeing the fields.
He just sits and groans, weeping his heart out,
And the flesh is wasting away from his bones."

And Telemachus, in his clear-headed way:

"That's hard, but we will let him be, despite our pain.   *155*
If mortals could have all their wishes granted,
We would choose first the day of my father's return.
No, just deliver your message and come back,
And don't go traipsing all through the countryside
Looking for Laertes. But tell my mother   *160*
To send the housekeeper as soon as she can,
Secretly. She could bring the old man the message."

So the swineherd got going. He tied on his sandals

And was off to the city.
               The swineherd's departure
Was not unnoticed by Athena. She approached   *165*
The farmstead in the likeness of a woman,
Beautiful, tall, and accomplished in handiwork,
And stood in the doorway of Eumaeus' hut,
Showing herself to Odysseus. Telemachus
Did not see her before him or notice her presence,   *170*
For the gods are not visible to everyone.
But Odysseus saw her, and the dogs did, too,
And they did not bark, but slunk away whining
To the other side of the farmstead. The goddess
Lifted her brows, and Odysseus understood.   *175*
He went out of the hut, past the courtyard's great wall,
And stood before her. Athena said to him:

"Son of Laertes in the line of Zeus,
Tell your son now and do not keep him in the dark,
So that you two can plan the suitors' destruction   *180*
And then go into town. As for myself,
I will not be gone long. No, I am eager for battle."

With this, she touched him with her golden wand.
A fresh tunic and cloak replaced his rags,
And he was taller and younger, his skin tanned,   *185*
His jawline firm, and his beard glossy black.
Having worked her magic, the goddess left,
And Odysseus went back into the hut.
His son was astounded. Shaken and flustered,
He turned away his eyes for fear it was a god,   *190*
And words fell from his lips in nervous flurries:

"You look different, stranger, than you did before,
And your clothes are different, and your complexion.
You must be a god, one of the immortals
Who hold high heaven. Be gracious to us   *195*
So we can offer you acceptable sacrifice
And finely wrought gold. And spare us, please."

And godlike Odysseus, who had borne much:

"I am no god. Why liken me to the deathless ones?
No, I am your father, on whose account you have suffered   200
Many pains and endured the violence of men."

Saying this, he kissed his son, and let his tears
Fall to the ground. He had held them in until now.
But Telemachus could not believe
That this was his father, and he blurted out: 205

"You cannot be my father Odysseus.
You must be some spirit, enchanting me
Only to increase my grief and pain later.
No mortal man could figure out how to do this
All on his own. Only a god could so easily   210
Transform someone from old to young.
A while ago you were old and shabbily dressed,
And now you are like the gods who hold high heaven."

And Odysseus, from his mind's teeming depths:

"Telemachus, it does not become you to be so amazed   215
That your father is here in this house. You can be sure
That no other Odysseus will ever come.
But I am here, just as you see, home at last
After twenty years of suffering and wandering.
So you will know, this is Athena's doing.   220
She can make me look like whatever she wants:
A beggar sometimes, and sometimes a young man
Wearing fine clothes. It's easy for the gods
To glorify a man or to make him look poor."

He spoke, and sat down. And Telemachus   225
Threw his arms around his wonderful father
And wept. And a longing arose in both of them
To weep and lament, and their shrill cries
Crowded the air

like the cries of birds—
Sea-eagles or taloned vultures— 230
Whose young chicks rough farmers have stolen
Out of their nests before they were fledged.

Their tears were that piteous. And the sun,
Its light fading, would have set on their weeping,
Had not Telemachus suddenly said to his father: 235

"What ship brought you here, Father,
And where did the crew say they were from?
I don't suppose you came here on foot."

And Odysseus, the godlike survivor:

"I'll tell you the truth about this, son. 240
The Phaeacians brought me, famed sailors
Who give passage to all who come their way.
They brought me over the sea as I slept
In their swift ship, and set me ashore on Ithaca
With donations of bronze and clothing and gold, 245
Splendid treasures that are now stored in caves
By grace of the gods. I have come here now
At Athena's suggestion. You and I must plan
How to kill our enemies. List them for me now
So I can know who they are, and how many, 250
And so I can weigh the odds and decide whether
You and I can go up against them alone
Or whether we have to enlist some allies."

Telemachus took a deep breath and said:

"Father, look now, I know your great reputation, 255
How you can handle a spear and what a strategist you are,
But this is too much for me. Two men
Simply cannot fight against such superior numbers
And superior force. There are not just ten suitors,
Or twice that, but many times more. Here's the count: 260
From Dulichium there are fifty-two—

The pick of their young men—and six attendants.
From Samê there are twenty-four,
From Zacynthus there are twenty,
And from Ithaca itself, twelve, all the noblest,   265
And with them are Medon the herald,
The divine bard, and two attendants who carve.
If we go up against all of them in the hall,
I fear your vengeance will be bitter indeed.
Please try to think of someone to help us,   270
Someone who would gladly be our ally."

And Odysseus, who had borne much:

"I'll tell you who will help. Do you think
That Athena and her father, Zeus,
Would be help enough? Or should I think of more?"   275

Telemachus answered in his clear-headed way:

"You're talking about two excellent allies,
Although they do sit a little high in the clouds
And have to rule the whole world and the gods as well."

And Odysseus, who had borne much: 280

"Those two won't hold back from battle for long.
They'll be here, all right, when the fighting starts
Between the suitors and us in my high-roofed halls.
For now, go at daybreak up to the house,
And keep company with these insolent hangers-on.   285
The swineherd will lead me to the city later
Looking like an old, broken-down beggar.
If they treat me badly in the house,
Just endure it. Even if they drag me
Through the door by my feet, or throw things at me,   290
Just bear it patiently. Try to dissuade them,
Try to talk them out of their folly, sure,
But they won't listen to you at all,
Because their day of reckoning is near.

And here's something else for you to keep in mind: *295*
When Athena in her wisdom prompts me,
I'll give you a signal. When you see me nod,
Take all the weapons that are in the hall
Into the lofted storeroom and stow them there.
When the suitors miss them and ask you   *300*
Where they are, set their minds at ease, saying:
'Oh, I have stored them out of the smoke.
They're nothing like they were when Odysseus
Went off to Troy, but are all grimed with soot.
Also, a god put this thought into my head,   *305*
That when you men are drinking, you might
Start quarreling and someone could get hurt,
Which would ruin your feasting and courting.
Steel has a way of drawing a man to it.'
But leave behind a couple of swords for us,   *310*
And two spears and oxhide shields—leave them
Where we can get to them in a hurry.
Pallas Athena and Zeus in his cunning
Will keep the suitors in a daze for a while.
And one more thing before you go.   *315*
If you are really my son and have my blood
In your veins, don't let anyone know
That Odysseus is at home—not Laertes,
Not the swineherd, not anyone in the house,
Not even Penelope. You and I by ourselves   *320*
Will figure out which way the women are leaning.
We'll test more than one of the servants, too,
And see who respects us and fears us,
And who cares nothing about either one of us
And fails to honor you. You're a man now."   *325*

And Odysseus' resplendent son answered:

"You'll soon see what I'm made of, Father,
And I don't think you'll find me lacking.
But I'm not sure your plan will work
To our advantage. Think about it.   *330*
It'll take forever for you to make the rounds

Testing each man, while back in the house
The high-handed suitors are having a good time
Eating their way through everything we own.
I agree you should find out which of the women   *335*
Dishonor you, and which are innocent.
But as for testing the men in the fields,
Let's do that afterward, if indeed you know
Something from Zeus, who holds the aegis."

*[The rest of Book 16 (lines 340–517) is omitted. News is brought to Pene-
lope of Telemachus' safe return. The suitors also learn that he has escaped
their trap, but they are still plotting to kill him. Penelope angrily confronts
Antinous, the suitors' ringleader, who attempts to appease her.]*

ODYSSEY 17

*[Lines 1–210 are omitted. Telemachus goes to the palace and tells his
mother about his journey. Odysseus and Eumaeus prepare to go to the
palace.]*

Odysseus threw around his shoulders
His ratty pouch, full of holes and slung
By a twisted cord. Eumaeus gave him a staff
That suited him, and the two of them set out.
The dogs and the herdsmen stayed behind   *215*
To guard the farmstead. And so the swineherd
Led his master to the city, looking like
An old, broken-down beggar, leaning
On a staff and dressed in miserable rags.

They were well along the rugged path   *220*
And near to the city when they came to a spring
Where the townspeople got their water.

This beautiful fountain had been made
By Ithacus, and Neritus, and Polyctor.
A grove of poplars encircled it   225
And the cold water flowed from the rock above,
On top of which was built an altar to the nymphs,
Where all wayfarers made offerings.
                                                          There
Melanthius, son of Dolius, met them
As he was driving his she-goats, the best   230
In the herds, into town for the suitors' dinner.
Two herdsmen trailed along behind him.
When he saw Eumaeus and his companion,
He greeted them with language so ugly
It made Odysseus' blood boil to hear it: 235

"Well, look at this, trash dragging along trash.
Birds of a feather, as usual. Where
Are you taking this walking pile of shit,
You miserable hog-tender, this diseased beggar
Who will slobber all over our feasts?   240
How many doorposts has he rubbed with his shoulders,
Begging for scraps? You think he's ever gotten
A proper present, a cauldron or sword? Ha!
Give him to me and I'll have him sweep out the pens
And carry loads of shoots for the goats to eat,   245
Put some muscle on his thigh by drinking whey.
I'll bet he's never done a hard day's work in his life.
No, he prefers to beg his way through town
For food to stuff into his bottomless belly.
I'll tell you this, though, and you can count on it.   250
If he comes to the palace of godlike Odysseus,
He'll be pelted with footstools aimed at his head.
If he's lucky they'll only splinter on his ribs."

And as he passed Odysseus, the fool kicked him
On the hip, trying to shove him off the path.   255
Odysseus absorbed the blow without even quivering—
Only stood there and tried to decide whether
To jump the man and knock him dead with his staff

Or lift him by the ears and smash his head to the ground.
In the end, he controlled himself and just took it.   260
But the swineherd looked the man in the eye
And told him off, and lifted his hands in prayer:

"Nymphs of the spring, daughters of Zeus,
If Odysseus ever honored you by burning
Thigh bones of lambs and kids wrapped in rich fat,   265
Grant me this prayer:
                              May my master come back,
May some god guide him back!
                              Then,
He would scatter all that puffery of yours,
All the airs you put on strutting around town
While bad herdsmen destroy all the flocks."   270

Melanthius, the goatherd, came back with this:

"Listen to the dog talk, with his big, bad notions.
I'm going to take him off in a black ship someday
Far from Ithaca, and sell him for a fortune.
You want my prayer? May Apollo with his silver bow   275
Strike Telemachus dead today in his halls,
Or may the suitors kill him, as surely as Odysseus
Is lost for good in some faraway land."

He left them with that. They walked on slowly,
While the goatherd pushed ahead and came quickly   280
To the palace. He went right in and sat down
Among the suitors, opposite Eurymachus,
Whom he liked best of all. The servers
Set out for him a helping of meat,
And the grave housekeeper brought him bread.   285

Odysseus and the swineherd came up to the house
And halted. The sound of the hollow lyre
Drifted out to them, for Phemius
Was sweeping the strings as he began his song.
Odysseus took the swineherd's hand and said: 290

"Eumaeus, this beautiful house must be Odysseus'.
It would stand out anywhere. Look at all the rooms
And stories, and the court built with wall and coping,
And the well-fenced double gates. No one could scorn it.
And I can tell there are many men feasting inside   295
From the savor of meat wafting out from it,
And the sound of the lyre, which rounds out a feast."

And you answered him, swineherd Eumaeus:

"You don't miss a thing, do you? Well,
Let's figure out what we should do here.   300
Either you go in first and mingle with the suitors,
While I wait here; or you wait here,
If you'd rather, and I'll go in before you.
But don't wait long, or someone might see you
And either throw something at you or smack you.   305
Think it over. What would you like to do?"

And Odysseus, the godlike survivor:

"I understand. You don't have to prompt me.
You go in before me, and I'll wait here.
I've had things thrown at me before,   310
And I have an enduring heart, Eumaeus.
God knows I've had my share of suffering
At war and at sea. I can take more if I have to.
But no one can hide a hungry belly.
It's our worst enemy. It's why we launch ships   315
To bring war to men across the barren sea."

And as they talked, a dog that was lying there
Lifted his head and pricked up his ears.
This was Argus, whom Odysseus himself
Had patiently bred—but never got to enjoy—   320
Before he left for Ilion. The young men
Used to set him after wild goats, deer, and hare.
Now, his master gone, he lay neglected
In the dung of mules and cattle outside the doors,

A deep pile where Odysseus' farmhands   *325*
Would go for manure to spread on his fields.
There lay the hound Argus, infested with lice.
And now, when he sensed Odysseus was near,
He wagged his tail and dropped both ears
But could not drag himself nearer his master.   *330*
Odysseus wiped away a tear, turning his head
So Eumaeus wouldn't notice, and asked him:

"Eumaeus, isn't it strange that this dog
Is lying in the dung? He's a beautiful animal,
But I wonder if he has speed to match his looks,   *335*
Or if he's like the table dogs men keep for show."

And you answered him, Eumaeus, my swineherd:

"Ah yes, this dog belonged to a man who has died
Far from home. He was quite an animal once.
If he were now as he was when Odysseus   *340*
Left for Troy, you would be amazed
At his speed and strength. There's nothing
In the deep woods that dog couldn't catch,
And what a nose he had for tracking!
But he's fallen on hard times, now his master   *345*
Has died abroad. These feckless women
Don't take care of him. Servants never do right
When their masters aren't on top of them.
Zeus takes away half a man's worth
The day he loses his freedom."
                              So saying,   *350*
Eumaeus entered the great house
And the hall filled with the insolent suitors.
But the shadow of death descended upon Argus,
Once he had seen Odysseus after twenty years.

Godlike Telemachus spotted the swineherd first   *355*
Striding through the hall, and with a nod of his head
Signaled him to join him. Eumaeus looked around
And took a stool that lay near, one that the carver

Ordinarily sat on when he sliced meat for the suitors
Dining in the hall. Eumaeus took this stool   *360*
And placed it at Telemachus' table, opposite him,
And sat down. A herald came and served him
A portion of meat, and bread from the basket.

Soon after, Odysseus came in, looking like
An old, broken-down beggar, leaning   *365*
On a staff and dressed in miserable rags.
He sat down on the ashwood threshold
Just inside the doors, leaning back
On the cypress doorpost, a post planed and trued
By some skillful carpenter in days gone by.   *370*
Telemachus called the swineherd over
And taking a whole loaf from the beautiful basket
And all the meat his hands could hold, said to him:

"Take this over to the stranger, and tell him
To go around and beg from each of the suitors.   *375*
Shame is no good companion for a man in need."

Thus Telemachus. The swineherd nodded,
And going over to Odysseus, said to him:

"Telemachus gives you this, and he tells you
To go around and beg from each of the suitors.   *380*
Shame, he says, is not good for a beggar."

And Odysseus, his mind teeming:

"Lord Zeus, may Telemachus be blessed among men
And may he have all that his heart desires."

And he took the food in both his hands   *385*
And set it down at his feet on his beggar's pouch.
Odysseus ate as long as the bard sang in the hall.
When the song came to an end, and the suitors
Began to be noisy and boisterous, Athena
Drew near to him and prompted him   *390*

To go among the suitors and beg for crusts
And so learn which of them were decent men
And which were scoundrels—not that the goddess had
The slightest intention of sparing any of them.

Odysseus made his rounds from right to left,   395
Stretching his hands out to every side,
As if he had been a beggar all his life.
They all pitied him and gave him something,
And they wondered out loud who he was
And where he had come from. To which questions   400
Melanthius, the goatherd, volunteered:

"Hear me, suitors of our noble queen.
As to this stranger, I have seen him before.
The swineherd brought him here, but who he is
I have no idea, or where he claims he was born."   405

At this, Antinous tore into the swineherd:

"Swineherd! Why did you bring this man to town?
Don't we have enough tramps around here without him,
This nuisance of a beggar who will foul our feast?
I suppose you don't care that these men are eating away   410
Your master's wealth, or you wouldn't have invited him."

The swineherd Eumaeus came back with this:

"You may be a fine gentleman, Antinous,
But that's an ugly thing to say. Who, indeed,
Ever goes out of his way to invite a stranger   415
From abroad, unless it's a prophet, or healer,
Or a builder, or a singer of tales—someone like that,
A master of his craft who benefits everyone.
Men like that get invited everywhere on earth.
But who would burden himself with a beggar?   420
You're just plain mean, the meanest of the suitors
To Odysseus' servants, and especially to me.
But I don't care, as long as my lady Penelope

Lives in the hall, and godlike Telemachus."

To which Telemachus responded coolly: *425*

"Quiet! Don't waste your words on this man.
Antinous is nasty like that—provoking people
With harsh words and egging them on."

And then he had these fletched words for Antinous:

"Why, Antinous, you're just like a father to me,   *430*
Kindly advising me to kick this stranger out.
God forbid that should ever happen. No,
Go ahead and give him something. I want you to.
Don't worry about my mother or anyone else
In this house, when it comes to giving things away.   *435*
But the truth is that you're just being selfish
And would rather eat more yourself than give any away."

And Antinous answered him:

"What a high and mighty speech, Telemachus!
Look now, if only everyone gave him what I will,   *440*
It would be months before he darkened your door."

As he spoke he grabbed the stool upon which
He propped his shining feet whenever he dined
And brandished it beneath the table.
But all the rest gave the beggar something   *445*
And filled his pouch with bread and meat.
And Odysseus would have had his taste of the suitors
Free of charge, but on his way back to the threshold
He stopped by Antinous' place and said:

"Give me something, friend. You don't look like   *450*
You are the poorest man here—far from it—
But the most well off. You look like a king.
So you should give me more than the others.
If you did, I'd sing your praises all over the earth.

I, too, once had a house of my own, a rich man   *455*
In a wealthy house, and I gave freely and often
To any and everyone who wandered by.
I had slaves, too, more than I could count,
And everything I needed to live the good life.
But Zeus smashed it all to pieces one day—   *460*
Who knows why?—when he sent me out
With roving pirates all the way to Egypt
So I could meet my doom.
                                             I moored my ships
In the river Nile, and you can be sure I ordered
My trusty mates to stand by and guard them   *465*
While I sent out scouts to look around.
Then the crews got cocky and overconfident
And started pillaging the Egyptian countryside,
Carrying off the women and children
And killing the men. The cry came to the city,   *470*
And at daybreak troops answered the call.
The whole plain was filled with infantry,
War chariots, and the glint of bronze.
Thundering Zeus threw my men into a panic,
And not one had the courage to stand and fight   *475*
Against odds like that. It was bad.
They killed many of us outright with bronze
And led the rest to their city to work as slaves.
But they gave me to a friend of theirs, from Cyprus,
To take me back there and give me to Dmetor,   *480*
Son of Iasus, who ruled Cyprus with an iron hand.
From there I came here, with all my hard luck."

Antinous had this to say in reply:

"What god has brought this plague in here?
Get off to the side, away from me,   *485*
Or I'll show you Egypt and Cyprus,
You pushy panhandler! You don't know your place.
You make your rounds and everyone
Hands things out recklessly. And why shouldn't they?
It's easy to be generous with someone else's wealth."   *490*

Odysseus took a step back and answered him:

"It's too bad your mind doesn't match your good looks.
You wouldn't give a suppliant even a pinch of salt
If you had to give it from your own cupboard.
Here you sit at another man's table   *495*
And you can't bear to give me a piece of bread
From the huge pile that's right by your hand."

This made Antinous even angrier,
And he shot back with a dark scowl:

"That does it. I'm not going to let you just   *500*
Breeze out of here if you're going to insult me."

As he spoke he grabbed the footstool and threw it,
Hitting Odysseus under his right shoulderblade.
Odysseus stood there as solid as a rock
And didn't even blink. He only shook his head   *505*
In silence, and brooded darkly.
Then he went back to the threshold and sat down
With his pouch bulging and spoke to the suitors:

"Hear me, suitors of our glorious queen,
So I can speak my mind. No one regrets   *510*
Being hit while fighting for his own possessions,
His cattle or sheep. But Antinous struck me
Because of my belly, that vile growling beast
That gives us so much trouble. If there are gods
For beggars, or avenging spirits,   *515*
May death come to Antinous before marriage does."

Antinous, son of Eupeithes, answered:

"Just sit still and eat, stranger—or get the hell out.
Keep talking like this and some of the young men here
Will haul you by the feet all through the house   *520*
And strip the skin right off your back."

Thus Antinous. But the other suitors
Turned on him, one of them saying:

"That was foul, Antinous, hitting a poor beggar.
You're done for if he turns out to be a god   525
Come down from heaven, the way they do,
Disguised as strangers from abroad or whatever,
Going around to different cities
And seeing who's lawless and who lives by the rules."

Antinous paid no attention to this.   530
Telemachus took it hard that his father was struck
But he kept it inside. Not a tear
Fell from his eye. He only shook his head
In silence, and brooded darkly.

*[The rest of Book 17 (lines 535–662) is omitted. Penelope tells Eumaeus
that she would like to speak with the stranger. Odysseus agrees to speak
with her later in the evening.]*

ODYSSEY 18

And now there came the town beggar
Making his rounds, known throughout Ithaca
For his greedy belly and endless bouts
Of eating and drinking. He had no real strength
Or fighting power—just plenty of bulk.   5
Arnaeus was the name his mother had given him,
But the young men all called him Irus
Because he was always running errands for someone.
He had a mind to drive Odysseus out of his own house
And started in on him with words like this: 10

"Out of the doorway, geezer, before I throw you out
On your ear! Don't you see all these people
Winking at me to give you the bum's rush?
I wouldn't want to stoop so low, but if you don't
Get out now, I may have to lay hands on you."   15

Odysseus gave him a measured look and said:

"What's wrong with you? I'm not doing
Or saying anything to bother you. I don't mind
If someone gives you a handout, even a large one.
This doorway is big enough for both of us.   20
There's no need for you to be jealous of others.
Now look, you're a vagrant, just like I am.
Prosperity is up to the gods. But if I were you,
I'd be careful about challenging me with your fists.
I might get angry, and old man though I am,   25
I just might haul off and bust you in the mouth.
I'd have more peace and quiet tomorrow.
I don't think you'd come back a second time
To the hall of Laertes' son, Odysseus."

This got Irus angry, and he answered: 30

"Listen to the mangy glutton run on,
Like an old kitchen woman! I'll fix him good—
Hit him with a left and then a right until
I knock his teeth out onto the ground,
The way we'd do a pig caught eating the crops.   35
Put 'em up, and everybody will see how we fight.
How are you going to stand up to a younger man?"

That's how they goaded each other on
There on the great polished threshold.
Antinous took this in and said with a laugh: 40

"How about this, friends? We haven't had
This much fun in a long time. Thank God
For a little entertainment! The stranger and Irus
Are getting into a fight. Let's have them square off!"

They all jumped up laughing and crowded around   45
The two tattered beggars. And Antinous said:

"Listen, proud suitors, to my proposal.
We've got these goat paunches on the fire,
Stuffed with fat and blood, ready for supper.
Whichever of the two wins and proves himself   50
The better man, gets the stuffed paunch of his choice.
Furthermore, he dines with us in perpetuity
And to the exclusion of all other beggars."

Everyone approved of Antinous' speech.
Then Odysseus, who knew all the moves, said: 55

"Friends, there's no way a broken-down old man
Can fight with a younger. Still, my belly,
That troublemaker, urges me on. So,
I'll just have to get beat up. But all of you,
Swear me an oath that no one, favoring Irus,   60
Will foul me and beat me for him."

They all swore that they wouldn't hit him,

And then Telemachus, feeling his power, said:

"Stranger, if you have the heart for this fight,
Don't worry about the onlookers. If anyone   65
Strikes you, he will have to fight us all.
I guarantee this as your host, and I am joined
By Antinous and Eurymachus,
Lords and men of discernment both."

Everyone praised this speech.
                              Then Odysseus   70
Tied his rags around his waist, revealing
His sculpted thighs, his broad shoulders,
His muscular chest and arms. Athena
Stood near the hero, magnifying his build.
The suitors' jaws dropped open.   75
They looked at each other and said things like:

"Irus is history."
                    "Brought it on himself, too."
"Will you look at the thigh on that old man!"

So they spoke. Irus' heart was in his throat,
But some servants tucked up his clothes anyway   80
And dragged him out, his rolls of fat quivering.
Antinous laid into him, saying:

"You big slob. You'll be sorry
You were ever born, if you try to duck
This woebegone, broken-down old man.   85
I'm going to give it to you straight now.
If he gets the better of you and beats you,
I'm going to throw you on a black ship
And send you to the mainland to King Echetus,
The maimer, who will slice off your nose and ears   90
With cold bronze, and tear out your balls
And give them raw to the dogs to eat."

This made Irus tremble even more.

They shoved him out into the middle,
And both men put up their fists. Odysseus,   *95*
The wily veteran, thought it over.
Should he knock the man stone cold dead,
Or ease up on the punch and just lay him out flat?
Better to go easy and just flatten him, he thought,
So that the crowd won't get suspicious.   *100*
The fighters stood tall, circling each other,
And as Irus aimed a punch at his right shoulder,
Odysseus caught him just beneath the ear,
Crushing his jawbone. Blood ran from his mouth,
And he fell in the dust snorting like an ox   *105*
And gnashing his teeth, his heels kicking the ground.
The suitors lifted their hands and died
With laughter. Odysseus took Irus by one fat foot
And dragged him out through the doorway
All the way to the court and the portico's gates.   *110*
He propped him up against the courtyard's wall,
Stuck his staff in his hand, and said to him:

"Sit there now and scare off the pigs and dogs,
And stop lording it over the other beggars,
You sorry bastard, or things could get worse."   *115*

*[The rest of Book 18 (lines 116–466) is omitted. Melantho, one of the
maidservants, taunts Odysseus. Eurymachus, one of the suitors, mocks
Odysseus. Odysseus stands up for himself, and Eurymachus throws a foot-
stool at him. Telemachus rebukes the suitors, and they retire for the night.]*

ODYSSEY 19

Odysseus was left alone in the hall,
Planning death for the suitors with Athena's aid.
He spoke winged words to Telemachus:

"Telemachus, get all the weapons out of the hall.
When the suitors miss them and ask you   5
Where they are, set their minds at ease, saying:
'Oh, I have stored them out of the smoke.
They're nothing like they were when Odysseus
Went off to Troy, but are all grimed with soot.
Also, a god put this thought into my head,   10
That when you men are drinking, you might
Start quarreling and someone could get hurt,
Which would ruin your feasting and courting.
Steel has a way of drawing a man to it.'"

Thus Odysseus. Telemachus nodded,   15
And calling Eurycleia he said to her:

"Nurse, shut the women inside their rooms
While I put my father's weapons away,
The beautiful weapons left out in the hall
And dulled by the smoke since he went off to war.   20
I was just a child then. But now I want
To store them away, safe from the smoke."

And Eurycleia, his old nurse, said:

"Yes, child, you are right
To care for the house and guard its wealth.   25
But who will fetch a light and carry it for you,
Since you won't let any of the women do it?"

Telemachus coolly answered her:

"This stranger here. I won't let anyone
Who gets rations be idle, even a traveler   30
From a distant land."

                    Telemachus' words sank in,
And the nurse locked the doors of the great hall.
Odysseus and his illustrious son sprang up
And began storing away the helmets, bossed shields,
And honed spears. And before them Pallas Athena,   35
Bearing a golden lamp, made a beautiful light.
Telemachus suddenly blurted out to his father:

"Father, this is a miracle I'm seeing!
The walls of the house, the lovely panels,
The beams of fir, and the high columns   40
Are glowing like fire. Some god is inside,
One of the gods from the open sky."

Odysseus, his mind teeming, replied:

"Hush. Don't be too curious about this.
This is the way of the gods who hold high heaven.   45
Go get some rest. I'll remain behind here
And draw out the maids—and your mother,
Who in her grief will ask many questions."

And Telemachus went out through the hall
By the light of blazing torches. He came   50
To his room, lay down, and waited for dawn.
Odysseus again was alone in the hall,
Planning death for the suitors with Athena's aid.

  P enelope, wary and thoughtful,
Now came from her bedroom, and she was like   55
Artemis or golden Aphrodite.
They set a chair for her by the fire
Where she always sat, a chair inlaid
With spiraling ivory and silver
Which the craftsman Icmalius had made long ago.   60

It had a footstool attached, covered now
With a thick fleece.
                  Penelope sat down,
Taking everything in. White-armed maids
Came out from the women's quarters
And started to take away all of the food,   65
Clearing the tables and picking up the cups
From which the men had been drinking.
They emptied the braziers, scattering the embers
Onto the floor, and then stocked them up
With loads of fresh wood for warmth and light.   70

Then Melantho started in on Odysseus again:

"Are we going to have to put up with you all night,
Roaming though the house and spying on the women?
Go on outside and be glad you had supper,
Or you'll soon stagger out struck with a torch."   75

And Odysseus answered from his teeming mind:

"What's wrong with you, woman? Are you mean to me
Because I'm dirty and dressed in rags
And beg through the land? I do it because I have to.
That's how it is with beggars and vagabonds.   80
You know, I too once lived in a house in a city,
A rich man in a wealthy house, and I often gave
Gifts to wanderers, whatever they needed.
I had servants, too, countless servants,
And plenty of everything else a man needs   85
To live the good life and be considered wealthy.
But Zeus crushed me. Who knows why?
So be careful, woman. Someday you may lose
That glowing beauty that makes you stand out now.
Or your mistress may become fed up with you.   90
Or Odysseus may come. We can still hope for that.
But even if, as seems likely, he is dead
And will never return, his son, Telemachus,
Is now very much like him, by Apollo's grace,

And if any of the women are behaving loosely   *95*
It won't get by him. He's no longer a child."

None of this was lost on Penelope,
And she scolded the maidservant, saying:

"Your outrageous conduct does not escape me,
Shameless whore that you are, and it will be   *100*
On your own head. You knew very well,
For you heard me say it, that I intended
To question the stranger here in my halls
About my husband; for I am sick with worry."

Then to Eurynome, the housekeeper, she said: *105*

"Bring a chair here with a fleece upon it
So that the stranger can sit down and tell his tale
And listen to me. I have many questions for him."

So Eurynome brought up a polished chair
And threw a fleece over it, and upon it sat   *110*
Odysseus, patient and godlike.
Penelope, watchful, began with a question:

"First, stranger, let me ask you this:
Who are you and where are you from?"

Odysseus, his mind teeming, answered her: *115*

"Lady, no one on earth could find fault with you,
For your fame reaches the heavens above,
Just like the fame of a blameless king,
A godfearing man who rules over thousands
Of valiant men, upholding justice.   *120*
His rich, black land bears barley and wheat,
The trees are laden with fruit, the flocks
Are always with young, and the sea teems with fish—
Because he rules well, and so his people prosper.
Ask me, therefore, about anything else,   *125*

But not about my birth or my native land.
That would fill my heart with painful memories.
I have many sorrows, and it wouldn't be right
To sit here weeping in another's house,
Nor is it good to be constantly grieving.   *130*
I don't want one of your maids, or you yourself,
To be upset with me and say I am awash with tears
Because the wine has gone to my head."

And Penelope, watching, answered him:

"Stranger, the gods destroyed my beauty   *135*
On the day when the Argives sailed for Ilion
And with them went my husband, Odysseus.
If he were to come back and be part of my life,
My fame would be greater and more resplendent so.
But now I ache, so many sorrows   *140*
Has some spirit showered upon me.
All of the nobles who rule the islands—
Dulichium, Samê, wooded Zacynthus—
And all those with power on rocky Ithaca
Are courting me and ruining this house.   *145*
So I pay no attention to strangers
Or to suppliants or public heralds. No,
I just waste away with longing for Odysseus.
My suitors press on, and I weave my wiles.
First some god breathed into me the thought   *150*
Of setting up a great loom in the main hall,
And I started weaving a vast fabric
With a very fine thread, and I said to them:

'Young men—my suitors, since Odysseus is dead—
Eager as you are to marry me, you must wait   *155*
Until I finish this robe—it would be a shame
To waste my spinning—a shroud for the hero
Laertes, when death's doom lays him low.
I fear the Achaean women would reproach me
If he should lie in death shroudless for all his wealth.'   *160*

"So I spoke, and their proud hearts consented.
Every day I would weave at the great loom,
And every night unweave the web by torchlight.
I fooled them for three years with my craft.
But in the fourth year, as the seasons rolled by,   165
And the moons waned, and the days dragged on,
My shameless and headstrong serving women
Betrayed me. The men barged in and caught me at it,
And a howl went up. So I was forced to finish the shroud.
Now I can't escape the marriage. I'm at my wit's end.   170
My parents are pressing me to marry,
And my son agonizes over the fact
That these men are devouring his inheritance.
He is a man now, and able to preside
Over a household to which Zeus grants honor.   175
But tell me of your birth, for you are not sprung,
As the saying goes, from stock or stone."

And Odysseus, from his mind's teeming depths:

"Honored wife of Laertes' son, Odysseus,
Will you never stop asking about my lineage?   180
All right, I will tell you, but bear in mind
You are only adding to the sorrows I have.
For so it is when a man has been away from home
As long as I have, wandering from city to city
And bearing hardships. Still, I will tell you.   185
   Crete is an island that lies in the middle
Of the wine-dark sea, a fine, rich land
With ninety cities swarming with people
Who speak many different languages.
There are Achaeans there, and native Cretans,   190
Cydonians, Pelasgians, and three tribes of Dorians.
One of the cities is great Cnossus,
Where Minos ruled and every nine years
Conversed with great Zeus. He was the father
Of my father, the great hero Deucalion.   195
Deucalion had another son, Idomeneus,
Who sailed his beaked ships to Ilion

Following the sons of Atreus. I was the younger,
And he the better man. My name is Aethon.
It was in Crete that I saw Odysseus   200
And gave him gifts of hospitality.
He had been blown off course rounding Malea
On his way to Troy. He put in at Amnisus,
Where the cave of Eileithyia is found.
That is a difficult harbor, and he barely escaped   205
The teeth of the storm. He went up to the city
And asked for Idomeneus, claiming to be
An old and honored friend. But Idomeneus' ships
Had left for Troy ten days before, so I
Took him in and entertained him well,   210
Drawing on the ample supplies in the house.
I gathered his men and distributed to them
Barley meal, wine, and bulls for sacrifice
From the public supplies, to keep them happy.
They stayed for twelve days. A norther so strong   215
You could barely stand upright in it
Had them corralled—some evil spirit had roused it.
On the thirteenth day the wind dropped, and they left."

All lies, but he made them seem like the truth,
And as she listened, her face melted with tears.   220

> *Snow deposited high in the mountains by the wild West Wind*
> *Slowly melts under the East Wind's breath,*
> *And as it melts the rivers rise in their channels.*

So her lovely cheeks coursed with tears as she wept
For her husband, who was sitting before her.   225
Odysseus pitied her tears in his heart,
But his eyes were as steady between their lids
As if they were made of horn or iron
As he concealed his own tears through guile.
When Penelope had cried herself out,   230
She spoke to him again, saying:

"Now I feel I must test you, stranger,

To see if you really did entertain my husband
And his godlike companions, as you say you did.
Tell me what sort of clothes he wore, and tell me   *235*
What he was like, and what his men were like."

And Odysseus, from his mind's teeming depths:

"Lady, it is difficult for me to speak
After we've been apart for so long. It has been
Twenty years since he left my country.   *240*
But I have an image of him in my mind.
Odysseus wore a fleecy purple cloak,
Folded over, and it had a brooch
With a double clasp, fashioned of gold,
And on the front was an intricate design: *245*
A hound holding in his forepaws a dappled fawn
That writhed to get free. Everyone marveled
At how, though it was all made of gold,
The hound had his eye fixed on the fawn
As he was strangling it, and the fawn   *250*
Twisted and struggled to get to its feet.
And I remember the tunic he wore,
Glistening like onionskin, soft and shiny
And with a sheen like sunlight. There were
Quite a few women who admired it.   *255*
But remember, now, I do not know
Whether Odysseus wore this at home,
Or whether one of his men gave it to him
When he boarded ship, or someone else,
For Odysseus was a man with many friends.   *260*
He had few equals among the Achaeans.
I, too, gave him gifts—a bronze sword,
A beautiful purple cloak, and a fringed tunic,
And I gave him a ceremonious send-off
In his benched ship. And one more thing: *265*
He had a herald, a little older than he was,
And I will tell you what he looked like.
He was slope-shouldered, with dark skin
And curly hair. His name was Eurybates,

And Odysseus held him in higher esteem   270
Than his other men, because they thought alike."

These words stirred up Penelope's grief.
She recognized the unmistakeable tokens
Odysseus was giving her. She wept again,
And then composed herself and said to him: 275

"You may have been pitied before, stranger,
But now you will be loved and honored
Here in my halls. I gave him those clothes.
I folded them, brought them from the storeroom,
And pinned on the gleaming brooch,   280
To delight him. But I will never welcome him
Home again, and so the fates were dark
When Odysseus left in his hollow ship
For Ilion, that curse of a city."

And Odysseus, from his mind's teeming depths: 285

"Revered wife of Laertes' son, Odysseus,
Do not mar your fair skin with tears any more,
Or melt your heart with weeping for your husband.
Not that I blame you. Any woman weeps
When she has lost her husband, a man with whom   290
She has made love and whose children she has borne—
And the husband you've lost is Odysseus,
Who they say is like the immortal gods.
Stop weeping, though, and listen to my words,
For what I am about to tell you is true.   295
I have lately heard of Odysseus' return,
That he is near, in the rich land of Thesprotia,
Still alive. And he is bringing home treasures,
Seeking gifts, and getting them, throughout the land.
But he lost his trusty crew and his hollow ship   300
On the wine-dark sea. As he was sailing out
From the island of Thrinacia, Zeus and Helios
Hit him hard because his companions had killed
The cattle of the Sun. His men went under,

But he rode his ship's keel until the waves   *305*
Washed him ashore in the land of the Phaeacians,
Whose race is closely akin to the gods'.
They treated him as if he were a god,
Gave him many gifts, and were more than willing
To escort him home. And he would have been here   *310*
By now, but he thought it more profitable
To gather wealth by roaming the land.
No one is as good as Odysseus
At finding ways to gain an advantage.
I had all this from Pheidon, the Thesprotian king.   *315*
And he swore to me, as he poured libations
There in his house, that a ship was already launched,
And a crew standing by, to take him home.
He sent me off first, since a Thesprotian ship
Happened to be leaving for Dulichium,   *320*
But before I left, Pheidon showed me
All the treasure Odysseus had amassed,
Bronze, gold, and wrought iron, enough to feed
His children's children for ten generations,
All stored there for him in the halls of the king.   *325*
Odysseus, he said, had gone to Dodona
To consult the oak-tree oracle of Zeus
And ask how he should return to Ithaca—
Openly or in secret—after being gone so long.
So he is safe, and will come soon.   *330*
He is very near, and will not be away long
From his dear ones and his native land.
I will swear to this. Now Zeus on high
Be my witness, and this hospitable table,
And the hearth of flawless Odysseus himself—   *335*
That everything will happen just as I say:
Before this month is out Odysseus will come,
In the dark of the moon, before the new crescent."

And Penelope, watching him carefully:

"Ah, stranger, may your words come true.   *340*
Then you would know my kindness, and my gifts

Would make you blessed in all men's eyes.
But I know in my heart that Odysseus
Will never come home, and that you will never
Find passage elsewhere, since there is not now   *345*
Any master in the house like Odysseus—
If he ever existed—to send honored guests
Safely on their way, or to welcome them.
But still, wash our guest's feet, maidens,
And prepare a bed for him. Set up a frame   *350*
And cover it with cloaks and lustrous blankets
To keep him cozy and warm. When golden Dawn
Shows her first light, bathe him and anoint him,
So he can sit side by side with Telemachus
And share in the feast here in the hall.   *355*
And anyone who causes this man any pain
Will regret it sorely and will accomplish nothing
Here in this house, however angry he gets.
For how would you ever find out, stranger,
Whether or not I surpass all other women   *360*
In presence of mind, if you sit down to dinner
Squalid and disheveled here in my hall?
Our lives are short. A hard-hearted man
Is cursed while he lives and reviled in death.
But a good-hearted man has his fame spread   *365*
Far and wide by the guests he has honored,
And men speak well of him all over the earth."

And Odysseus, his mind teeming, answered her:

"Revered wife of Odysseus, Laertes' son,
I lost all interest in cloaks and blankets   *370*
On the day I left the snowy mountains of Crete
In my long-oared ship. I will lie down tonight,
As I have through many a sleepless night,
On a poor bed, waiting for golden-throned Dawn.
Nor do I have any taste for foot-baths,   *375*
And none of the serving women here in your hall
Will touch my feet, unless there is some old,
Trustworthy woman who has suffered as I have.

I would not mind if she touched my feet."

And Penelope, watching him carefully: *380*

"Of all the travelers who have come to my house,
None, dear guest, have been as thoughtful as you
And none as welcome, so wise are your words.
I do have an old and trustworthy woman here,
Who nursed and raised my ill-starred husband,   *385*
Taking him in her arms the day he was born.
She will wash your feet, frail as she is.
Eurycleia, rise and wash your master's—that is,
Wash the feet of this man who is your master's age.
Odysseus' feet and hands are no doubt like his now,   *390*
For men age quickly when life is hard."

At this, the old woman hid her face in her hands.
Shedding warm tears, she spoke through her sobs:

"My lost child, I can do nothing for you.
Zeus must have hated you above all other men,   *395*
Although you were always godfearing. No one
Burned more offerings to the Lord of Lightning,
So many fat thighbones, bulls by the hundreds,
With prayers that you reach a sleek old age
And raise your glorious son. And now the god has   *400*
Deprived you alone of your day of return.
    And I suppose, stranger, women mocked him, too,
When he came to some man's gloried house
In a distant land, just as these cheeky bitches
All mock you here. It is to avoid their insults   *405*
That you will not allow them to wash your feet.
But Penelope, Icarius' wise daughter,
Has asked me to do it, and I will,
For her sake and for yours,
For my heart is throbbing with sorrow.   *410*
But listen now to what I have to say.
Many road-weary strangers have come here,
But I have never seen such a resemblance

As that between you and Odysseus,
In looks, voice—even the shape of your feet." 415

And Odysseus, from his mind's teeming depths:

"Oh, everyone who has seen us both says that,
Old woman, that we are very much alike,
Just as you yourself have noticed."

And the old woman took the shining basin 420
She used for washing feet, poured
Cold water into it, and then added the hot.
Odysseus, waiting, suddenly sat down at the hearth
And turned away toward the shadows. The scar!
It flashed through his mind that his old nurse 425
Would notice his scar as soon as she touched him,
And then everything would be out in the open.
She drew near and started to wash her master,
And knew at once the scar from the wound
He had gotten long ago from a boar's white tusk 430
When he had gone to Parnassus to visit Autolycus,
His mother's father, who was the best man on earth
At thieving and lying, skills he had learned
From Hermes. He had won the god's favor
With choice burnt offerings of lambs and kids. 435

Autolycus had visited Ithaca once
When his grandson was still a newborn baby.
After he finished supper, Eurycleia
Put the child in his lap and said to him:

"Autolycus, now name the child 440
Of your own dear child. He has been much prayed for."

Then Autolycus made this response:

"Daughter and son-in-law of mine,
Give this child the name I now tell you.
I come here as one who is odious, yes, 445

Hateful to many for the pain I have caused
All over the land. Let this child, therefore,
Go by the name of Odysseus.
For my part, when he is grown up
And comes to the great house of his mother's kin   450
In Parnassus, where my possessions lie,
I will give him a share and send him home happy."

In due time, Odysseus came to get these gifts
From Autolycus. His grandfather
And his uncles all welcomed him warmly,   455
And Amphithea, his mother's mother,
Embraced Odysseus and kissed his head
And beautiful eyes. Autolycus told his sons
To prepare a meal, and they obeyed at once,
Leading in a bull, five years old,   460
Which they flayed, dressed, and butchered.
They skewered the meat, roasted it skillfully,
And then served out portions to everyone.
All day long until the sun went down
They feasted to their hearts' content.   465
But when the sun set and darkness came on
They went to bed and slept through the night.
When Dawn brushed the early sky with rose,
They went out to hunt—Autolycus' sons
Running their hounds—and with them went   470
Godlike Odysseus. They climbed the steep wooded slopes
Of Mount Parnassus and soon reached
The windy hollows. The sun was up now,
Rising from the damasked waters of Ocean
And just striking the fields, when the beaters came   475
Into a glade. The dogs were out front,
Tracking the scent, and behind the dogs
Came Autolycus' sons and noble Odysseus,
His brandished spear casting a long shadow.
Nearby, a great boar was lying in his lair,   480
A thicket that was proof against the wild wet wind
And could not be pierced by the rays of the sun,
So dense it was. Dead leaves lay deep

Upon the ground there. The sound of men and dogs
Pressing on though the leaves reached the boar's ears,   *485*
And he charged out from his lair, back bristling
And his eyes spitting fire. He stood at bay
Right before them, and Odysseus rushed him,
Holding his spear high, eager to thrust.
The boar was too quick. Slashing in,   *490*
He got Odysseus in the thigh, right above the knee,
His white tusk tearing a long gash in the muscle
Just shy of the bone. Even so, Odysseus
Did not miss his mark, angling his spear
Into the boar's right shoulder. The gleaming point   *495*
Went all the way through, and with a loud grunt
The boar went down and gasped out his life.
Autolycus' sons took care of the carcass
And tended the wound of the flawless Odysseus,
Skillfully binding it and staunching the blood   *500*
By chanting a spell. Then they quickly returned
To their father's house. When Odysseus
Had regained his strength, Autolycus and his sons
Gave him glorious gifts and sent him home happy,
Home to Ithaca. His mother and father   *505*
Rejoiced at his return and asked him all about
How he got his scar; and he told them the story
Of how a boar had gashed him with his white tusk
As he hunted on Parnassus with Autolycus' sons.

This was the scar the old woman recognized   *510*
When the palm of her hand ran over it
As she held his leg. She let the leg fall,
And his foot clanged against the bronze basin,
Tipping it over and spilling the water
All over the floor. Eurycleia's heart   *515*
Trembled with mingled joy and grief,
Tears filled her eyes, and her voice
Was choked as she reached out
And touched Odysseus' chin and said:

"You are Odysseus, dear child. I did not know you   *520*

Until I laid my hands on my master's body."

She spoke, and turned her eyes toward Penelope,
Wanting to show her that her husband was home.
But Penelope could not return her gaze
Or understand her meaning, for Athena   525
Had diverted her mind. Odysseus reached
For the old woman's throat, seized it in his right hand
And drawing her closer with his other, he said:

"Do you want to destroy me? You yourself
Nursed me at your own breast, and now   530
After twenty hard years I've come back home.
Now that some god has let you in on the secret,
You keep it to yourself, you hear? If you don't,
I'll tell you this, and I swear I'll do it:
If, with heaven's help, I subdue the suitors,   535
I will not spare you—even if you are my nurse—
When I kill the other women in the hall."

And Eurycleia, the wise old woman:

"How can you say that, my child? You know
What I'm made of. You know I won't break.   540
I'll be as steady as solid stone or iron.
And I'll tell you this, and you remember it:
If, with heaven's help, you subdue the proud suitors,
I'll list for you all the women in the house,
Those who dishonor you and those who are true."   545

And Odysseus, his mind teeming:

"Nurse, you don't have to tell me about them.
I'll keep an eye out and get to know each one.
Don't say a thing. Just leave it up to the gods."

At this, the old woman went off for more water   550
To wash his feet, since it had all been spilled.
When she had washed him and rubbed on oil,

Odysseus pulled his chair close to the fire again
To keep warm, and hid the scar with his rags.

Penelope now resumed their talk: 555

"There's one more thing I want to ask you about,
And then it will be time to get some sleep—
At least for those to whom sweet sleep comes
Despite their cares. But some god has given me
Immeasurable sorrow. By day   560
I console myself with lamentation
And see to my work and that of my women.
But at night, when sleep takes hold of others,
I lie in bed, smothered by my own anxiety,
Mourning restlessly, my heart racing.   565
Just as the daughter of Pandareus,
The pale nightingale, sings sweetly
In the greening of spring, perched in the leaves,
And trills out her song of lament for her son,
Her beloved Itylus, whom she killed unwittingly,   570
Itylus, the son of Zethus her lord—
So too my heart is torn with dismay.
Should I stay here with my son
And keep everything safe and just as it is,
My goods, my slaves, my high-gabled house,   575
Honoring my husband's bed and public opinion—
Or should I go with whoever is best
Of all my suitors, and gives me gifts past counting?
And then there's my son. While he was young
And not yet mature, he kept me from leaving   580
My husband's house and marrying another.
But now that he's grown and come into manhood,
He begs me to leave, worried because
These Achaean men are devouring his goods.
    But listen now to a dream I had   585
And tell me what it means. In my dream
I have twenty geese at home. I love to watch them
Come out of the water and eat grains of wheat.
But a huge eagle with a hooked beak comes

Down from the mountain and breaks their necks,   *590*
Killing them all. They lie strewn through the hall
While he rides the wind up to the bright sky.
I weep and wail, still in my dream,
And Achaean ladies gather around me
As I grieve because the eagle killed my geese.   *595*
Then the eagle comes back and perches upon
A jutting roofbeam and speaks to me
In a human voice, telling me not to cry:

'Take heart, daughter of famed Icarius.
This is no dream, but a true vision   *600*
That you can trust. The geese are the suitors,
And I, who was once an eagle, am now
Your husband come back, and I will deal out doom,
A grisly death for all of the suitors.'

"So he spoke, and I woke up refreshed.   *605*
Looking around I saw the geese in the house,
Feeding on wheat by the trough, as before."

And Odysseus, his mind teeming:

"Lady, there is no way to give this dream
Another slant. Odysseus himself has shown you   *610*
How he will finish this business. The suitors' doom
Is clear. Not one will escape death's black birds."

And Penelope, in her circumspect way:

"Stranger, you should know that dreams
Are hard to interpret, and don't always come true.   *615*
There are two gates for dreams to drift through,
One made of horn and the other of ivory.
Dreams that pass through the gate of ivory
Are deceptive dreams and will not come true,
But when someone has a dream that has passed   *620*
Through the gate of polished horn, that dream
Will come true. My strange dream, though,

Did not come from there. If it had,
It would have been welcome to me and my child.
    One more thing, and, please, take it to heart.   625
Dawn is coming, the accursed dawn of the day
Which will sever me from the house of Odysseus.
I will announce a contest. Odysseus
Used to line up axes inside his hall,
Twelve of them, like the curved chocks   630
That prop up a ship when it is being built,
And he would stand far off and send an arrow
Whizzing through them all. I will propose
This contest to my suitors, and whoever
Can bend that bow and slip the string on its notch   635
And shoot an arrow through all twelve axes,
With him will I go, leaving behind this house
I was married in, this beautiful, prosperous house,
Which I will remember always, even in my dreams."

And Odysseus, from the depths of his teeming mind: 640

"Revered wife of Laertes' son, Odysseus,
Do not put off this contest any longer,
For Odysseus will be here, with all his cunning,
Handling that polished bow, before these men
Could ever string it and shoot through the iron."   645

Then Penelope, still watching him:

"If you were willing, stranger, to sit here
Beside me in my halls and give me joy,
Sleep would never settle upon my eyes.
But we cannot always be sleepless,   650
For every thing there is a season, and a time
For all we do on the life-giving earth.
I will go now to my room upstairs
And lie on my bed, which has become
A sorrowful bed, wet with my tears   655
Since the day Odysseus left
For Ilion, that accursed city.

I will lie there, but you can lie here
In the hall. Spread some blankets on the floor,
Or have the maids make up a bed for you."   660

Saying this, Penelope went upstairs
To her softly lit room, not alone,
For her women went up with her.
Once in her room she wept for Odysseus,
Her beloved husband, wept until Athena   665
Let sweet sleep settle upon her eyelids.

[Book 20 is omitted. Odysseus wakes from a restless sleep and hears Penelope weeping. Servants prepare the house for another day of feasting. The herdsmen bring animals from the fields. Philoetius, the cowherd, is sympathetic to Odysseus. Ctessipus, one of the suitors, throws an ox's hoof at Odysseus, who dodges it. Theoclymenus, a seer, to whom Telemachus is showing hospitality, foretells the suitors' doom.]

ODYSSEY 21

Owl-eyed Athena now prompted Penelope
To set before the suitors Odysseus' bow
And the grey iron, implements of the contest
And of their death.
               Penelope climbed
The steep stairs to her bedroom and picked up   *5*
A beautiful bronze key with an ivory handle
And went with her maids to a remote storeroom
Where her husband's treasures lay—bronze, gold,
And wrought iron. And there lay the curved bow
And the quiver, still loaded with arrows,   *10*
Gifts which a friend of Odysseus had given him
When they met in Lacedaemon long ago.
This was Iphitus, Eurytus' son, a godlike man.
They had met in Messene, in the house of Ortilochus.
Odysseus had come to collect a debt   *15*
The Messenians owed him: three hundred sheep
They had taken from Ithaca in a sea raid,
And the shepherds with them. Odysseus
Had come to get them back, a long journey
For a young man, sent by his father and elders.   *20*
Iphitus had come to search for twelve mares
He had lost, along with the mules they were nursing.
These mares turned out to be the death of Iphitus
When he came to the house of Heracles,
Zeus' tough-hearted son, who killed him,   *25*
Guest though he was, without any regard
For the gods' wrath or the table they had shared—
Killed the man and kept the strong-hoofed mares.
It was while looking for these mares that Iphitus
Met Odysseus and gave him the bow   *30*
Which old Eurytus had carried and left to his son.
Odysseus gave him a sword and spear
To mark the beginning of their friendship

But before they had a chance to entertain each other
Zeus' son killed Iphitus, son of Eurytus,   *35*
A man like the gods. Odysseus did not take
The bow with him on his black ship to Troy.
It lay at home as a memento of his friend,
And Odysseus carried it only on Ithaca.

Penelope came to the storeroom   *40*
And stepped onto the oak threshold
Which a carpenter in the old days had planed,
Leveled, and then fitted with doorposts
And polished doors. Lovely in the half-light,
She quickly loosened the thong from the hook,   *45*
Drove home the key and shot back the bolts.
The doors bellowed like a bull in a meadow
And flew open before her. Stepping through,
She climbed onto a high platform that held chests
Filled with fragrant clothes. She reached up   *50*
And took the bow, case and all, from its peg,
Then sat down and laid the gleaming case on her knees
Her eyes welling with tears. Then she opened the case
And took out her husband's bow. When she had her fill
Of weeping, she went back to the hall   *55*
And the lordly suitors, bearing in her hands
The curved bow and the quiver loaded
With whining arrows. Two maidservants
Walked beside her, carrying a wicker chest
Filled with the bronze and iron gear her husband   *60*
Once used for this contest. When the beautiful woman
Reached the crowded hall, she stood
In the doorway flanked by her maidservants.
Then, covering her face with her shining veil,
Penelope spoke to her suitors: *65*

"Hear me, proud suitors. You have used this house
For an eternity now—to eat and drink
In its master's absence, nor could you offer
Any excuse except your lust to marry me.
Well, your prize is here, and this is the contest.   *70*

I set before you the great bow of godlike Odysseus.
Whoever bends this bow and slips the string on its notch
And shoots an arrow through all twelve axes,
With him will I go, leaving behind this house
I was married in, this beautiful, prosperous house,   75
Which I will remember always, even in my dreams."

Penelope said this, and then ordered Eumaeus
To set out for the suitors the bow and grey iron.
All in tears, Eumaeus took them and laid them down,
And the cowherd wept, too, when he saw   80
His master's bow. Antinous scoffed at them both:

"You stupid yokels! You can't see farther than your noses.
What a pair! Disturbing the lady with your bawling.
She's sad enough already because she's lost her husband.
Either sit here in silence or go outside to weep,   85
And leave the bow behind for us suitors. This contest
Will separate the men from the boys. It won't be easy
To string that polished bow. There is no man here
Such as Odysseus was. I know. I saw him myself
And remember him well, though I was still a child."   90

So Antinous said, hoping in his heart
That he would string the bow first and shoot an arrow
Through the iron. But the only arrow
He would touch first would be the one shot
Into his throat from the hands of Odysseus,   95
The man he himself was dishonoring
While inciting his comrades to do the same.

And then Telemachus, with a sigh of disgust:

"Look at me! Zeus must have robbed me of my wits.
My dear mother declares, for all her good sense,   100
That she will marry another and abandon this house,
And all I do is laugh and think it is funny.
Well, come on, you suitors, here's your prize,
A woman the likes of whom does not exist

In all Achaea, or in sacred Pylos,   *105*
Nowhere in Argos or in Mycenae,
Or on Ithaca itself or on the dark mainland.
You all know this. Why should I praise my mother?
Let's get going. Don't start making excuses
To put off stringing the bow. We'll see what happens.   *110*
And I might give that bow a try myself.
If I string it and shoot an arrow through the axeheads,
It won't bother me so much that my honored mother
Is leaving this house and going off with another,
Because I would at least be left here as someone   *115*
Capable of matching his father's prowess."

With that he took off his scarlet cloak, stood up,
And unstrapped his sword from his shoulders.
Then he went to work setting up the axeheads,
First digging a long trench true to the line   *120*
To hold them in a row, and then tamping the earth
Around each one. Everyone was amazed
That he made such a neat job of it
When he had never seen it done before.
Then he went and took his stance on the threshold   *125*
And began to try the bow. Three times
He made it quiver as he strained to string it,
And three times he eased off, although in his heart
He yearned to draw that bow and shoot an arrow
Through the iron axeheads. And on his fourth try   *130*
He would have succeeded in muscling the string
Onto its notch, but Odysseus reined him in,
Signaling him to stop with an upward nod.
So Telemachus said for all to hear:

"I guess I'm going to be a weakling forever!   *135*
Or else I'm still too young and don't have the strength
To defend myself against an enemy.
But come on, all of you who are stronger than me—
Give the bow a try and let's settle this contest."

And he set the bow aside, propping it against   *140*

The polished, jointed door, and leaning the arrow
Against the beautiful latch. Then Telemachus
Sat down on the chair from which he had risen.

Antinous, Eupeithes' son, then said:

"All right. We go in order from left to right,   *145*
Starting from where the wine gets poured."

Everyone agreed with Antinous' idea.
First up was their soothsayer, Leodes,
Oenops' son. He always sat in the corner
By the wine-bowl, and he was the only one   *150*
Who loathed the way the suitors behaved.
He now carried the bow and the arrow
Onto the threshold, took his stance,
And tried to bend the bow and string it,
But his tender, unworn hands gave out,   *155*
And he said for all the suitors to hear:

"Friends, I'm not the man to string this bow.
Someone else can take it. I foresee it will rob
Many a young hero of the breath of life.
And that will be just as well, since it is far better   *160*
To die than live on and fall short of the goal
We gather here for, with high hopes day after day.
You might hope in your heart—you might yearn—
To marry Penelope, the wife of Odysseus,
But after you've tried this bow and seen what it's like, *165*
Go woo some other Achaean woman
And try to win her with your gifts. And Penelope
Should just marry the highest bidder,
The man who is fated to be her husband."

And he set the bow aside, propping it against   *170*
The polished, jointed door, and leaning the arrow
Against the beautiful latch. Then
He sat down on the chair from which he had risen.
And Antinous heaped contempt upon him:

"What kind of thing is that to say, Leodes?   *175*
I'm not going to stand here and listen to this.
You think this bow is going rob some young heroes
Of life, just because you can't string it?
The truth is your mother didn't bear a son
Strong enough to shoot arrows from bows.   *180*
But there are others who will string it soon enough."

Then Antinous called to Melanthius, the goatherd:

"Get over here and start a fire, Melanthius,
And set by it a bench with a fleece over it,
And bring out a tub of lard from the pantry,   *185*
So we can grease the bow, and warm it up.
Then maybe we can finish this contest."

He spoke, and Melanthius quickly rekindled the fire
And placed by it a bench covered with a fleece
And brought out from the pantry a tub of lard   *190*
With which the young men limbered up the bow—
But they still didn't have the strength to string it.

Only Antinous and godlike Eurymachus,
The suitors' ringleaders—and their strongest—
Were still left in the contest.

                           Meanwhile,   *195*
Two other men had risen and left the hall—
The cowherd and swineherd—and Odysseus himself
Went out, too. When the three of them
Were outside the gates, Odysseus said softly:

"Cowherd and swineherd, I've been wondering   *200*
If I should tell you what I'm about to tell you now.
Let me ask you this. What would you do
If Odysseus suddenly showed up here
Out of the blue, just like that?
Would you side with the suitors or Odysseus?   *205*
Tell me how you stand."

And the cattle herder answered him:

"Father Zeus, if only this would come true!
Let him come back. Let some god guide him.
Then you would see what these hands could do."   210

And Eumaeus prayed likewise to all the gods
That Odysseus would return.

               When Odysseus
Was sure of both these men, he spoke to them again:

"I am back, right here in front of you.
After twenty hard years I have returned to my home.   215
I know that only you two of all my slaves
Truly want me back. I have heard
None of the others pray for my return.
So this is my promise to you. If a god
Beats these proud suitors down before me,   220
I will give you each a wife, property,
And a house built near mine. You two shall be
Friends to me and brothers to Telemachus.
And look, so you can be sure of who I am,
Here's a clear sign, that scar from the wound   225
I got from a boar's tusk when I went long ago
To Parnassus with the sons of Autolycus."

And he pulled his rags aside from the scar.
When the two men had examined it carefully,
They threw their arms around Odysseus and wept,   230
And kept kissing his head and shoulders in welcome.
Odysseus kissed their heads and hands,
And the sun would have gone down on their weeping,
Had not Odysseus stopped them, saying:

"No more weeping and wailing now. Someone might come   235
Out of the hall and see us and tell those inside.
We'll go back in now—not together, one at a time.
I'll go first, and then you. And here's what to watch for.

None of the suitors will allow the bow and quiver
To be given to me. It'll be up to you, Eumaeus,   240
To bring the bow over and place it in my hands.
Then tell the women to lock the doors to their hall,
And if they hear the sound of men groaning
Or being struck, tell them not to rush out
But to sit still and do their work in silence.   245
Philoetius, I want you to bar the courtyard gate
And secure it quickly with a piece of rope."

With this, Odysseus entered his great hall
And sat down on the chair from which he had risen.
Then the two herdsmen entered separately.   250

Eurymachus was turning the bow
Over and over in his hands, warming it
On this side and that by the fire, but even so
He was unable to string it. His pride hurt,
Shoulders sagging, he groaned and then swore: 255

"Damn it! It's not just myself I'm sorry for,
But for all of us—and not for the marriage either.
That hurts, but there are plenty of other women,
Some here in Ithaca, some in other cities.
No, it's that we fall so short of Odysseus'   260
Godlike strength. We can't even string his bow!
We'll be laughed at for generations to come!"

Antinous, son of Eupeithes, answered him:

"That'll never happen, Eurymachus,
And you know it. Now look, today is a holiday   265
Throughout the land, a sacred feast
In honor of Apollo, the Archer God.
This is no time to be bending bows.
So just set it quietly aside for now.
As for the axes, why don't we leave them   270
Just as they are? No one is going to come
Into Odysseus' hall and steal those axes.

Now let's have the cupbearer start us off
So we can forget about the bow
And pour libations. Come morning, 275
We'll have Melanthius bring along
The best she-goats in all the herds,
So we can lay prime thigh-pieces
On the altar of Apollo, the Archer God,
And then finish this business with the bow." 280

Antinous' proposal carried the day.
The heralds poured water over everyone's hands,
And boys filled the mixing bowls up to the brim
And served out the wine, first pouring
A few drops into each cup for libation. 285
When they had poured out their libations
And drunk as much as they wanted, Odysseus
Spoke among them, his heart full of cunning:

"Hear me, suitors of the glorious queen—
And I address Eurymachus most of all, 290
And godlike Antinous, since his speech
Was right on the mark when he said that for now
You should stop the contest and leave everything
Up to the gods. Tomorrow the Archer God
Will give the victory to whomever he chooses. 295
But come, let me have the polished bow.
I want to see, here in this hall with you,
If my grip is still strong, and if I still have
Any power left in these gnarled arms of mine,
Or if my hard traveling has sapped all my strength." 300

They seethed with anger when they heard this,
Afraid that he would string the polished bow,
And Antinous addressed him contemptuously:

"You don't have an ounce of sense in you,
You miserable tramp. Isn't it enough 305
That we let you hang around with us,
Undisturbed, with a full share of the feast?

You even get to listen to what we say,
Which no other stranger, much less beggar, can do.
It's wine that's screwing you up, as it does   310
Anyone who guzzles it down. It was wine
That deluded the great centaur, Eurytion,
In the hall of Peirithous, the Lapith hero.
Eurytion got blind-drunk and in his madness
Did a terrible thing in Peirithous' house.   315
The enraged Lapiths sliced off his nose and ears
And dragged him outside, and Eurytion
Went off in a stupor, mutilated and muddled.
Men and centaurs have been at odds ever since.
Eurytion hurt himself because he got drunk.   320
And you're going to get hurt, too, I predict,
Hurt badly, if you string the bow. No one
In all the land will show you any kindness.
We'll send you off in a black ship to Echetus,
Who maims them all. You'll never get out alive.   325
So just be quiet and keep on drinking,
And don't challenge men who are younger than you."

It was Penelope who answered Antinous:

"It is not good, or just, Antinous,
To cheat any of Telemachus' guests   330
Who come to this house. Do you think
That if this stranger proves strong enough
To string Odysseus' bow, he will then
Lead me to his home and make me his wife?
I can't imagine that he harbors this hope.   335
So do not ruin your feast on that account.
The very idea is preposterous."

Eurymachus responded to this:

"Daughter of Icarius, wise Penelope,
Of course it's preposterous that this man   340
Would marry you. That's not what we're worried about.
But we are embarrassed at what men—and women—will say:

'A bunch of weaklings were wooing the wife
Of a man they couldn't touch—they couldn't even string
His polished bow. Then along came a vagrant   *345*
Who strung it easily and shot through the iron.'
That's what they'll say, to our lasting shame."

And Penelope, her eyes narrowing:

"Eurymachus, men who gobble up
The house of a prince cannot expect   *350*
To have a good reputation anywhere.
So there isn't any point in bringing up honor.
This stranger is a very well-built man
And says he is the son of a noble father.
So give him the bow and let us see what happens.   *355*
And here is my promise to all of you.
If Apollo gives this man the glory
And he strings the bow, I will clothe him
In a fine cloak and tunic, and give him
A javelin to ward off dogs and men,   *360*
And a double-edged sword, and sandals
For his feet, and I will give him passage
To wherever his heart desires."

This time it was Telemachus who answered:

"As for the bow, Mother, no man alive   *365*
Has a stronger claim than I do to give it
To whomever I want, or to deny it—
No, none of the lords on rocky Ithaca
Nor on the islands over toward Elis,
None of them could force his will upon me,   *370*
Not even if I wanted to give this bow
Outright, case and arrows and all,
As a gift to the stranger.
                          Go to your rooms,
Mother, and take care of your work,
Spinning and weaving, and have the maids do theirs.   *375*
This bow is men's business, and my business

Especially, since I am the master of this house."

Penelope was stunned and turned to go,
Her son's masterful words pressed to her heart.
She went up the stairs to her room with her women   *380*
And wept for Odysseus, her beloved husband,
Until grey-eyed Athena cast sleep on her eyelids.

Downstairs, the noble swineherd was carrying
The curved bow across the hall. The suitors
Were in an uproar, and one of them called out: *385*

"Where do you think you're going with that bow,
You miserable swineherd? You're out of line.
Go back to your pigsties, where your own dogs
Will wolf you down—a nice, lonely death—
If Apollo and the other gods smile upon us."   *390*

Afraid, the swineherd stopped in his tracks
And set the bow down. Men were yelling at him
All through the hall, and now Telemachus weighed in:

"Keep going with the bow. You'll regret it
If you try to obey everyone. I may be   *395*
Younger than you, but I'll chase you back
Into the country with a shower of stones.
I am stronger than you. I wish I were as strong
When it came to the suitors. I'd throw more than one
Out of here in a sorry state. They're all up to no good."   *400*

This got the suitors laughing hilariously
At Telemachus. The tension in the room eased,
And the swineherd carried the bow
Across to Odysseus and put it in his hands.
Then he called Eurycleia aside and said: *405*

"Telemachus says you should lock the doors to the hall,
And if the women hear the sound of men groaning
Or being struck, tell them not to rush out

But to sit still and do their work in silence."

Eumaeus' words sank in, and Eurycleia   *410*
Locked the doors to the crowded hall.

Meanwhile, Philoetius left without a word
And barred the gates to the fenced courtyard.
Beside the portico there lay a ship's hawser
Made of papyrus. Philoetius used this   *415*
To secure the gates, and then he went back in,
Sat down on the chair from which he had risen,
And kept his eyes on Odysseus.

He was handling the bow, turning it over and over
And testing its flex to make sure that worms   *420*
Had not eaten the horn in its master's absence.
The suitors glanced at each other
And started to make sarcastic remarks:

"Ha! A real connoisseur, an expert in bows!"

"He must have one just like it in a case at home."   *425*

"Or plans to make one just like it, to judge by the way
The masterful tramp keeps turning it in his hands."

"May he have as much success in life
As he'll have in trying to string that bow."

Thus the suitors, while Odysseus, deep in thought,   *430*
Was looking over his bow. And then, effortlessly,

> *Like a musician stretching a string*
> *Over a new peg on his lyre, and making*
> *The twisted sheep-gut fast at either end,*

Odysseus strung the great bow. Lifting it up,   *435*
He plucked the string, and it sang beautifully
Under his touch, with a note like a swallow's.

The suitors were aghast. The color drained
From their faces, and Zeus thundered loud,
Showing his portents and cheering the heart   *440*
Of the long-enduring, godlike Odysseus.
One arrow lay bare on the table. The rest,
Which the suitors were about to taste,
Were still in the quiver. Odysseus picked up
The arrow from the table and laid it upon   *445*
The bridge of the bow, and, still in his chair,
Drew the bowstring and the notched arrow back.
He took aim and let fly, and the bronze-tipped arrow
Passed clean through the holes of all twelve axeheads
From first to last. And he said to Telemachus: *450*

"Well, Telemachus, the guest in your hall
Has not disgraced you. I did not miss my target,
Nor did I take all day in stringing the bow.
I still have my strength, and I'm not as the suitors
Make me out to be in their taunts and jeers.   *455*
But now it is time to cook these men's supper,
While it is still light outside, and after that,
We'll need some entertainment—music and song—
The finishing touches for a perfect banquet."

He spoke, and lowered his brows. Telemachus,   *460*
The true son of godlike Odysseus, slung on
His sharp sword, seized his spear, and gleaming in bronze
Took his place by his father's side.

ODYSSEY 22

And now Odysseus' cunning was revealed.
He stripped off his rags and leapt with his bow
To the great threshold. Spreading the arrows
Out before his feet, he spoke to the suitors:

"Now that we've separated the men from the boys,   5
I'll see if I can hit a mark that no man
Has ever hit. Apollo grant me glory!"

As he spoke he took aim at Antinous,
Who at that moment was lifting to his lips
A golden cup—a fine, two-eared golden goblet—   10
And was just about to sip the wine. Bloodshed
Was the farthest thing from his mind.
They were at a banquet. Who would think
That one man, however strong, would take them all on
And so ensure his own death? Odysseus   15
Took dead aim at Antinous' throat and shot,
And the arrow punched all the way through
The soft neck tissue. Antinous fell to one side,
The cup dropped from his hands, and a jet
Of dark blood spurted from his nostrils.   20
He kicked the table as he went down,
Spilling the food on the floor, and the bread
And roast meat were fouled in the dust.
                              The crowd
Burst into an uproar when they saw
Antinous go down. They jumped from their seats   25
And ran in a panic through the hall,
Scanning the walls for weapons—
A spear, a shield. But there were none to be had.
Odysseus listened to their angry jeers:

"You think you can shoot at men, you tramp?"   30

"That's your last contest—you're as good as dead!"

"You've killed the best young man in Ithaca!"

"Vultures will eat you on this very spot!"

They all assumed he had not shot to kill,
And had no idea how tightly the net   35
Had been drawn around them. Odysseus
Scowled at the whole lot of them, and said:

"You dogs! You thought I would never
Come home from Troy. So you wasted my house,
Forced the women to sleep with you,   40
And while I was still alive you courted my wife
Without any fear of the gods in high heaven
Or of any retribution from the world of men.
Now the net has been drawn tight around you."

At these words the color drained from their faces,   45
And they all looked around for a way to escape.
Only Eurymachus had anything to say:

"If you are really Odysseus of Ithaca,
Then what you say is just. The citizens
Have done many foolish things in this house   50
And many in the fields. But the man to blame
Lies here dead, Antinous. He started it all,
Not so much because he wanted a marriage
Or needed one, but for another purpose,
Which Zeus did not fulfill: he wanted to be king   55
In Ithaca, and to kill your son in ambush.
Now he's been killed, and he deserved it.
But spare your people. We will pay you back
For all we have eaten and drunk in your house.
We will make a collection; each man will put in   60
The worth of twenty oxen; we will make restitution
In bronze and gold until your heart is soothed.
Until then no one could blame you for being angry."

Odysseus fixed him with a stare and said:

"Eurymachus, not even if all of you   *65*
Gave me your entire family fortunes,
All that you have and ever will have,
Would I stay my hands from killing.
You courted my wife, and you will pay in full.
Your only choice now is to fight like men   *70*
Or run for it. Who knows, one or two of you
Might live to see another day. But I doubt it."

Their blood turned milky when they heard this.
Eurymachus now turned to them and said:

"Friends, this man is not going to stop at anything.   *75*
He's got his arrows and bow, and he'll shoot
From the threshold until he's killed us all.
We've got to fight back. Draw your swords
And use the tables as shields. If we charge him
In a mass and push him from the doorway   *80*
We can get reinforcements from town in no time.
Then this man will have shot his last shot."

With that, he drew his honed bronze sword
And charged Odysseus with an ear-splitting cry.
Odysseus in the same instant let loose an arrow   *85*
That entered his chest just beside the nipple
And spiked down to his liver. The sword fell
From Eurymachus' hand. He spun around
And fell on a table, knocking off dishes and cups,
And rolled to the ground, his forehead banging   *90*
Up and down against it and his feet kicking a chair
In his death throes, until the world went dark.

Amphinomus went for Odysseus next,
Rushing at him with his sword drawn,
Hoping to drive him away from the door.   *95*
Telemachus got the jump on him, though,
Driving a bronze-tipped spear into his back

Square between his shoulder blades
And through to his chest. He fell with a thud,
His forehead hammering into the ground.   *100*
Telemachus sprang back, leaving the spear
Right where it was, stuck in Amphinomus,
Fearing that if he tried to pull it out
Someone would rush him and cut him down
As he bent over the corpse. So he ran over   *105*
To his father's side, and his words flew fast:

"I'll bring you a shield, Father, two spears
And a bronze helmet—I'll find one that fits.
When I come back I'll arm myself
And the cowherd and swineherd. Better armed than not."   *110*

And Odysseus, the great tactician:

"Bring me what you can while I still have arrows
Or these men might drive me away from the door."

And Telemachus was off to the room
Where the weapons were stored. He took   *115*
Four shields, eight spears, and four bronze helmets
With thick horsehair plumes and brought them
Quickly to his father. Telemachus armed himself,
The two servants did likewise, and the three of them
Took their stand alongside the cunning warrior,   *120*
Odysseus. As long as the arrows held out
He kept picking off the suitors one by one,
And they fell thick as flies. But when the master archer
Ran out of arrows, he leaned the bow
Against the doorpost of the entrance hall   *125*
And slung a four-ply shield over his shoulder,
Put on his head a well-wrought helmet
With a plume that made his every nod a threat,
And took two spears tipped with heavy bronze.

Built into the higher wall of the main hall   *130*
Was a back door reached by a short flight of stairs

And leading to a passage closed by double doors.
Odysseus posted the swineherd at this doorway,
Which could be attacked by only one man at a time.
It was just then that Agelaus called to the suitors: *135*

"Let's one of us get up to the back door
And get word to the town. Act quickly
And this man will have shot his last."

But the goatherd Melanthius answered him:

"That won't work, Agelaus.   *140*
The door outside is too near the courtyard—
An easy shot from where he is standing—
And the passageway is dangerously narrow.
One good man could hold it against all of us.
Look, let me bring you weapons and armor   *145*
From the storeroom. That has to be where
Odysseus and his son have laid them away."

So saying, Melanthius clambered up
To Odysseus' storerooms. There he picked out
Twelve shields and as many spears and helmets   *150*
And brought them out quickly to give to the suitors.
Odysseus' heart sank, and his knees grew weak
When he saw the suitors putting on armor
And brandishing spears. This wasn't going to be easy.
His words flew out to Telemachus: *155*

"One of the women in the halls must be
Waging war against us—unless it's Melanthius."

And Telemachus, cool-headed under fire:

"No, it's my fault, Father, and no one else's.
I must have left the storeroom door open,   *160*
And one of them spotted it.
                          Eumaeus!
Go close the door to the storeroom,

And see whether one of the women is behind this,
Or Melanthius, son of Dolius, as I suspect."

As they were speaking, Melanthius the goatherd   165
Was making another trip to the storeroom
For more weapons. The swineherd spotted him
And was quick to point him out to Odysseus:

"There he goes, my lord Odysseus—
The sneak—just as we thought, on his way   170
To the storeroom! Tell me what to do.
Kill him if I prove to be the better man,
Or bring him to you, so he can pay in full
For all the wrongs he has done here in your house?"

Odysseus brought his mind to bear on this: 175

"Telemachus and I will keep the suitors busy
In the hall here. Don't worry about that.
Tie him up. Bend his arms and legs behind him
And lash them to a board strapped onto his back.
Then hoist him up to the rafters in the store room   180
And leave him there to twist in the wind."

This was just what Eumaeus and the cowherd
Wanted to hear. Off they went to the storeroom,
Unseen by Melanthius, who was inside
Rooting around for armor and weapons.   185
They lay in wait on either side of the door,
And when Melanthius crossed the threshold,
Carrying a beautiful helmet in one hand
And in the other a broad old shield,
Flecked with rust—a shield the hero Laertes   190
Had carried in his youth but that had long since
Been laid aside with its straps unstitched—
Eumaeus and the cowherd Philoetius
Jumped him and dragged him by the hair
Back into the storeroom. They threw him   195
Hard to the ground, knocking the wind out of him,

And tied his hands and feet behind his back,
Making it hurt, as Odysseus had ordered.
Then they attached a rope to his body
And hoisted him up along the tall pillar   *200*
Until he was up by the rafters, and you,
Swineherd Eumaeus, you mocked him:

"Now you'll really be on watch, Melanthius,
The whole night through, lying on a feather bed—
Just your style—and you're sure to see   *205*
The early dawn come up from Ocean's streams,
Couched in gold, at the hour when you drive your goats
Up to the hall to make a feast for the suitors."

So Melanthius was left there, racked with pain,
While Eumaeus and the cowherd put on their armor,   *210*
Closed the polished door, and rejoined Odysseus,
The cunning warrior. So they took their stand
There on the threshold, breathing fury,
Four of them against the many who stood in the hall.

And then Athena was with them, Zeus' daughter   *215*
Looking just like Mentor and assuming his voice.
Odysseus, glad to see her, spoke these words:

"Mentor, old friend, help me out here.
Remember all the favors I've done for you.
We go back a long way, you and I."   *220*

He figured it was Athena, the soldier's goddess.
On the other side, the suitors yelled and shouted,
Agelaus' voice rising to rebuke Athena:

"You there, Mentor, don't let Odysseus
Talk you into helping him and fighting us.   *225*
This is the way I see it turning out.
When we have killed these men, father and son,
We'll kill you next for what you mean to do
In this hall. You'll pay with your life.

And when we've taken care of all five of you,   230
We'll take everything you have, Mentor,
Everything in your house and in your fields,
And add it to Odysseus' property.
We won't let your sons stay in your house
Or let your daughters or even your wife   235
Go about freely in the town of Ithaca."

This made Athena all the more angry,
And she turned on Odysseus and snapped at him:

"I can't believe, Odysseus, that you,
Of all people, have lost the guts you had   240
When you fought the Trojans for nine long years
To get Helen back, killing so many in combat
And coming up with the plan that took wide Troy.
How is it that now, when you've come home,
You get all teary-eyed about showing your strength   245
To this pack of suitors? Get over here
Next to me and see what I can do. I'll show you
What sort of man Mentor, son of Alcimus, is,
And how he repays favors in the heat of battle."

Athena spoke these words, but she did not yet   250
Give Odysseus the strength to turn the tide.
She was still testing him, and his glorious son,
To see what they were made of. As for herself,
The goddess flew up to the roofbeam
Of the smoky hall, just like a swallow.   255

The suitors were now rallied by Agelaus
And by Damastor, Eurynomus, and Amphimedon,
As well as by Demoptolemus and Peisander,
Son of Polyctor, and the warrior Polybus.
These were the best of the suitors lucky enough   260
To still be fighting for their lives. The rest
Had been laid low by the showers of arrows.
Agelaus now made this speech to them:

"He's had it now. Mentor's abandoned him
After all that hot air, and the four of them   265
Are left alone at the outer doors.
All right, now. Don't throw your spears all at once.
You six go first, and hope that Zeus allows
Odysseus to be hit and gives us the glory.
The others won't matter once he goes down."   270

They took his advice and gave it their best,
But Athena made their shots all come to nothing,
One man hitting the doorpost, another the door,
Another's bronze-tipped ash spear sticking
Into the wall. Odysseus and his men   275
Weren't even nicked, and the great hero said to them:

"It's our turn now. I say we throw our spears
Right into the crowd. These bastards mean to kill us
On top of everything else they've done to wrong me."

He spoke, and they all threw their sharp spears   280
With deadly aim. Odysseus hit Demoptolemus;
Telemachus got Euryades; the swineherd, Elatus;
And the cattle herder took out Peisander.
They all bit the dirt at the same moment,
And the suitors retreated to the back of the hall,   285
Allowing Odysseus and his men to run out
And pull their spears from the dead men's bodies.

The suitors rallied for another volley,
Throwing their sharp spears with all they had.
This time Athena made most of them miss,   290
One man hitting the doorpost, another the door,
Another's bronze-tipped ash spear sticking
Into the wall. But Amphimedon's spear
Grazed Telemachus' wrist, breaking the skin,
And Ctessipus' spear clipped Eumaeus' shoulder   295
As it sailed over his shield and kept on going
Until it hit the ground. Then Odysseus and his men
Got off another round into the throng,

Odysseus, sacker of cities, hitting Eurydamas;
Telemachus getting Amphimedon; the swineherd, Polybus;　　300
And lastly the cattle herder striking Ctessipus
Square in the chest. And he crowed over him:

"Always picking a fight, just like your father.
Well, you can stop all your big talk now.
We'll let the gods have the last word this time.　　305
Take this spear as your host's gift, fair exchange
For the hoof you threw at godlike Odysseus
When he made his rounds begging in the hall."

Thus the herder of the spiral-horned cattle.

Odysseus, meanwhile, had skewered Damastor's son　　310
With a hard spear-thrust in hand-to-hand fighting,
And Telemachus killed Leocritus, Evenor's son,
Piercing him in the groin and driving his bronze spear
All the way through. Leocritus pitched forward,
His forehead slamming onto the ground.

　　　　　　　　　　　　　　　Only then　　315
Did Athena hold up her overpowering aegis
From her high perch, and the minds of the suitors
Shriveled with fear, and they fled through the hall

　　Like a herd of cattle that an iridescent gadfly
　　Goads along on a warm spring afternoon,　　320

With Odysseus and his men after them

　　Like vultures with crooked talons and hooked beaks
　　Descending from the mountains upon a flock
　　Of smaller birds, who fly low under the clouds
　　And over the plain. The vultures swoop down　　325
　　To pick them off; the smaller birds cannot escape,
　　And men thrill to see the chase in the sky.

Odysseus and his cohorts were clubbing the suitors

Right and left all through the hall; horrible groans
Rose from their lips as their heads were smashed in, *330*
And the floor of the great hall smoked with blood.

It was then that Leodes, the soothsayer, rushed forward,
Clasped Odysseus' knees, and begged for his life:

"By your knees, Odysseus, respect me
And pity me. I swear I have never said or done *335*
Anything wrong to any woman in your house.
I tried to stop the suitors when they did such things,
But they wouldn't listen, wouldn't keep their hands clean,
And now they've paid a cruel price for their sins.
And I, their soothsayer, who have done no wrong, *340*
Will be laid low with them. That's the gratitude I get."

Odysseus scowled down at the man and said:

"If you are really their soothsayer, as you boast you are,
How many times must you have prayed in the halls
That my sweet homecoming would never come, *345*
And that you would be the one my wife would go off with
And bear children to! You're a dead man."

As he spoke his strong hand reached for a sword
That lay nearby—a sword Agelaus had dropped
When he was killed. The soothsayer was struck *350*
Full in the neck. His lips were still forming words
When his lopped head rolled in the dust.

All this while the bard, Phemius, was busy
Trying not to be killed. This man, Terpes' son,
Sang for the suitors under compulsion. *355*
He stood now with his pure-toned lyre
Near the high back door, trying to decide
Whether he should slip out from the hall
And crouch at the altar of Zeus of the Courtyard—
The great altar on which Laertes and Odysseus *360*
Had burned many an ox's thigh—

Or whether he should rush forward
And supplicate Odysseus by his knees.
Better to fall at the man's knees, he thought.
So he laid the hollow lyre on the ground   365
Between the wine-bowl and silver-studded chair
And ran up to Odysseus and clasped his knees.
His words flew up to Odysseus like birds:

"By your knees, Odysseus, respect me
And pity me. You will regret it someday   370
If you kill a bard—me—who sings for gods and men.
I am self-taught, and a god has planted in my heart
All sorts of songs and stories, and I can sing to you
As to a god. So don't be too eager
To slit my throat. Telemachus will tell you   375
That I didn't come to your house by choice
To entertain the suitors at their feasts.
There were too many of them; they made me come."

Telemachus heard him and said to his father:

"He's innocent; don't kill him.   380
And let's spare the herald, Medon,
Who used to take care of me when I was a child,
If Philoetius hasn't already killed him—
Or the swineherd—or if he didn't run into you
As you were charging through the house."   385

Medon heard what Telemachus said.
He was under a chair, wrapped in an oxhide,
Cowering from death. Now he jumped up,
Stripped off the oxhide, ran to Telemachus
And fell at his knees. His words rose on wings: 390

"I'm here, Telemachus! Hold back, and ask your father
To hold back too, or he might kill me with cold bronze,
Strong as he is and as mad as he is at the suitors,
Who ate away his house and paid you no honor."

Odysseus smiled at this and said to him: *395*

"Don't worry, he's saved you. Now you know,
And you can tell the world, how much better
Good deeds are than evil. Go outside, now,
You and the singer, and sit in the yard
Away from the slaughter, until I finish   *400*
Everything I have to do inside the house."

So he spoke, and the two went out of the hall
And sat down by the altar of great Zeus,
Wide-eyed and expecting death at any moment.
Odysseus, too, had his eyes wide open,   *405*
Looking all through his house to see if anyone
Was still alive and hiding from death.
But everyone he saw lay in the blood and dust,
The whole lot of them,

> > *like fish that fishermen*
> > *Have drawn up in nets from the grey sea*   *410*
> > *Onto the curved shore. They lie all in heaps*
> > *On the sand beach, longing for the salt waves,*
> > *And the blazing sun drains their life away.*

So too the suitors, lying in heaps.

Then Odysseus called to Telemachus: *415*

"Go call the nurse Eurycleia for me.
I want to tell her something."

> > > So Telemachus went
To Eurycleia's room, rattled the door, and called:

"Get up and come out here, old woman—you
Who are in charge of all our women servants.   *420*
Come on. My father has something to say to you."

Eurycleia's response died on her lips.

She opened the doors to the great hall,
Came out, and followed Telemachus
To where Odysseus, spattered with blood and grime
Stood among the bodies of the slain.   425

A lion that has just fed upon an ox in a field
Has his chest and cheeks smeared with blood,
And his face is terrible to look upon.

                                        So too Odysseus,
Smeared with gore from head to foot.

                                        When Eurycleia   430
Saw all the corpses and the pools of blood,
She lifted her head to cry out in triumph—
But Odysseus stopped her cold,
Reining her in with these words:

"Rejoice in your heart, but do not cry aloud.   435
It is unholy to gloat over the slain. These men
Have been destroyed by divine destiny
And their own recklessness. They honored no one,
Rich or poor, high or low, who came to them.
And so by their folly they have brought upon themselves   440
An ugly fate.
                Now tell me, which of the women
Dishonor me and which are innocent?"

And Eurycleia, the loyal nurse:

"Yes indeed, child, I will tell you all.
There are fifty women in your house,   445
Servants we have taught to do their work,
To card wool and bear all the drudgery.
Of these, twelve have shamed this house
And respect neither me nor Penelope herself.
Telemachus has only now become a man,   450
And his mother has not allowed him
To direct the women servants.

May I go now
To the upstairs room and tell your wife?
Some god has wrapped her up in sleep."

Odysseus, his mind teeming, answered her: 455

"Don't wake her yet. First bring those women
Who have acted so disgracefully."

While the old woman went out through the hall
To tell the women the news—and to summon twelve—
Odysseus called Telemachus and the two herdsmen   460
And spoke to them words fletched like arrows:

"Start carrying out the bodies,
And have the women help you.
                              Then sponge down
All of the beautiful tables and chairs.
When you have set the whole house in order,   465
Take the women outside between the round house
And the courtyard fence. Slash them with your swords
Until they have forgotten their secret lovemaking
With the suitors. Then finish them off."

Thus Odysseus, and the women came in,   470
Huddled together and shedding salt tears.
First they carried out the dead bodies
And set them down under the courtyard's portico,
Propping them against each other. Odysseus himself
Kept them at it. Then he had them sponge down   475
All of the beautiful tables and chairs.
Telemachus, the swineherd, and the cowherd
Scraped the floor with hoes, and the women
Carried out the scrapings and threw them away.
When they had set the whole house in order,   480
They took the women out between the round house
And the courtyard fence, penning them in
With no way to escape. And Telemachus,
In his cool-headed way, said to the others:

"I won't allow a clean death for these women— 485
The suitors' sluts—who have heaped reproaches
Upon my own head and upon my mother's."

He spoke, and tied the cable of a dark-prowed ship
To a great pillar and pulled it about the round house,
Stretching it high so their feet couldn't touch the ground. 490

    Long-winged thrushes, or doves, making their way
    To their roosts, fall into a snare set in a thicket,
    And the bed that receives them is far from welcome.

So too these women, their heads hanging in a row,
The cable looped around each of their necks. 495
It was a most piteous death. Their feet fluttered
For a little while, but not for long.

Then they brought Melanthius outside,
And in their fury they sliced off
His nose and ears with cold bronze
And pulled his genitals out by the root— 500
Raw meat for the dogs—and chopped off
His hands and feet.

           This done,
They washed their own hands and feet
And went back into their master's great hall. 505

Then Odysseus said to Eurycleia:

"Bring me sulfur, old woman, and fire,
So that I can fumigate the hall.
And go tell Penelope to come down here,
And all of the women in the house as well." 510

And Eurycleia, the faithful nurse:

"As you say, child. But first let me bring you
A tunic and a cloak for you to put on.

You should not be standing here like this
With rags on your body. It's not right."   515

Odysseus, his mind teeming, answered her:

"First make a fire for me here in the hall."

He spoke, and Eurycleia did as she was told.
She brought fire and sulfur, and Odysseus
Purified his house, the halls and the courtyard.   520

Then the old nurse went through Odysseus'
Beautiful house, telling the women the news.
They came from their hall with torches in their hands
And thronged around Odysseus and embraced him.
And as they kissed his head and shoulders and hands   525
He felt a sudden, sweet urge to weep,
For in his heart he knew them all.

ODYSSEY 23

The old woman laughed as she went upstairs
To tell her mistress that her husband was home.
She ran up the steps, lifting her knees high,
And, bending over Penelope, she said:

"Wake up, dear child, so you can see for yourself   5
What you have yearned for day in and day out.
Odysseus has come home, after all this time,
And has killed those men who tried to marry you
And who ravaged your house and bullied your son."

And Penelope, alert now and wary: 10

"Dear nurse, the gods have driven you crazy.
The gods can make even the wise mad,
Just as they often make the foolish wise.
Now they have wrecked your usually sound mind.
Why do you mock me and my sorrowful heart,   15
Waking me from sleep to tell me this nonsense—
And such a sweet sleep. It sealed my eyelids.
I haven't slept like that since the day Odysseus
Left for Ilion—that accursed city.
Now go back down to the hall.   20
If any of the others had told me this
And wakened me from sleep, I would have
Sent her back with something to be sorry about!
You can thank your old age for this at least."

And Eurycleia, the loyal nurse: 25

"I am not mocking you, child. Odysseus
Really is here. He's come home, just as I say.
He's the stranger they all insulted in the great hall.
Telemachus has known all along, but had

The self-control to hide his father's plans   *30*
Until he could pay the arrogant bastards back."

Penelope felt a sudden pang of joy. She leapt
From her bed and flung her arms around the old woman,
And with tears in her eyes she said to her:

"Dear nurse, if it is true, if he really has   *35*
Come back to his house, tell me how
He laid his hands on the shameless suitors,
One man alone against all of that mob."

Eurycleia answered her:

"I didn't see and didn't ask. I only heard the groaning   *40*
Of men being killed. We women sat
In the far corner of our quarters, trembling,
With the good solid doors bolted shut
Until your son came from the hall to call me,
Telemachus. His father had sent him to call me.   *45*
And there he was, Odysseus, standing
In a sea of dead bodies, all piled
On top of each other on the hard-packed floor.
It would have warmed your heart to see him,
Spattered with blood and filth like a lion.   *50*
And now the bodies are all gathered together
At the gates, and he is purifying the house
With sulfur, and has built a great fire,
And has sent me to call you. Come with me now
So that both your hearts can be happy again.   *55*
You have suffered so much, but now
Your long desire has been fulfilled.
He has come himself, alive, to his own hearth,
And has found you and his son in the hall.
As for the suitors, who did him wrong,   *60*
He's taken his revenge on every last man."

And Penelope, ever cautious:

"Dear nurse, don't gloat over them yet.
You know how welcome the sight of him
Would be to us all, and especially to me   65
And the son he and I bore. But this story
Can't be true, not the way you tell it.
One of the immortals must have killed the suitors,
Angry at their arrogance and evil deeds.
They respected no man, good or bad,   70
So their blind folly has killed them. But Odysseus
Is lost, lost to us here, and gone forever."

And Eurycleia, the faithful nurse:

"Child, how can you say this? Your husband
Is here at his own fireside, and yet you are sure   75
He will never come home! Always on guard!
But here's something else, clear proof:
The scar he got from the tusk of that boar.
I noticed it when I was washing his feet
And wanted to tell you, but he shrewdly clamped   80
His hand on my mouth and wouldn't let me speak.
Just come with me, and I will stake my life on it.
If I am lying you can torture me to death."

Still wary, Penelope replied:

"Dear nurse, it is hard for you to comprehend   85
The ways of the eternal gods, wise as you are.
Still, let us go to my son, so that I may see
The suitors dead and the man who killed them."

And Penelope descended the stairs, her heart
In turmoil. Should she hold back and question   90
Her husband? Or should she go up to him,
Embrace him, and kiss his hands and head?
She entered the hall, crossing the stone threshold,
And sat opposite Odysseus, in the firelight
Beside the farther wall. He sat by a column,   95
Looking down, waiting to see if his incomparable wife

Would say anything to him when she saw him.
She sat a long time in silence, wondering.
She would look at his face and see her husband,
But then fail to know him in his dirty rags. 100
Telemachus couldn't take it any more:

"Mother, how can you be so hard,
Holding back like that? Why don't you sit
Next to father and talk to him, ask him things?
No other woman would have the heart 105
To stand off from her husband who has come back
After twenty hard years to his country and home.
But your heart is always colder than stone."

And Penelope, cautious as ever:

"My child, I am lost in wonder 110
And unable to speak or ask a question
Or look him in the eyes. If he really is
Odysseus come home, the two of us
Will be sure of each other, very sure.
There are secrets between us no one else knows." 115

Odysseus, who had borne much, smiled,
And his words flew to his son on wings:

"Telemachus, let your mother test me
In our hall. She will soon see more clearly.
Now, because I am dirty and wearing rags, 120
She is not ready to acknowledge who I am.
But you and I have to devise a plan.
When someone kills just one man,
Even a man who has few to avenge him,
He goes into exile, leaving country and kin. 125
Well, we have killed a city of young men,
The flower of Ithaca. Think about that."

And Telemachus, in his clear-headed way:

"You should think about it, Father. They say
No man alive can match you for cunning.   *130*
We'll follow you for all we are worth,
And I don't think we'll fail for lack of courage."

And Odysseus, the master strategist:

"Well, this is what I think we should do.
First, bathe yourselves and put on clean tunics   *135*
And tell the women to choose their clothes well.
Then have the singer pick up his lyre
And lead everyone in a lively dance tune,
Loud and clear. Anyone who hears the sound,
A passerby or neighbor, will think it's a wedding,   *140*
And so word of the suitors' killing won't spread
Down through the town before we can reach
Our woodland farm. Once there we'll see
What kind of luck the Olympian gives us."

They did as he said. The men bathed   *145*
And put on tunics, and the women dressed up.
The godlike singer, sweeping his hollow lyre,
Put a song in their hearts and made their feet move,
And the great hall resounded under the tread
Of men and silken-waisted women dancing.   *150*
And people outside would hear it and say:

"Well, someone has finally married the queen,
Fickle woman. Couldn't bear to keep the house
For her true husband until he came back."

But they had no idea how things actually stood.   *155*

Odysseus, meanwhile, was being bathed
By the housekeeper, Eurynome. She
Rubbed him with olive oil and threw about him
A beautiful cloak and tunic. And Athena
Shed beauty upon him, and made him look   *160*
Taller and more muscled, and made his hair

Tumble down his head like hyacinth flowers.

> *Imagine a craftsman overlaying silver*
> *With pure gold. He has learned his art*
> *From Pallas Athena and Lord Hephaestus,* 165
> *And creates works of breathtaking beauty.*

So Athena herself made his head and shoulders
Shimmer with grace. He came from the bath
Like a god, and sat down on the chair again
Opposite his wife, and spoke to her and said: 170

"You're a mysterious woman.
                                                    The gods
Have given to you, more than to any
Other woman, an unyielding heart.
No other woman would be able to endure
Standing off from her husband, come back 175
After twenty hard years to his country and home.
Nurse, make up a bed for me so I can lie down
Alone, since her heart is a cold lump of iron."

And Penelope, cautious and wary:

"You're a mysterious man.
                                                    I am not being proud 180
Or scornful, nor am I bewildered—not at all.
I know very well what you looked like
When you left Ithaca on your long-oared ship.
Nurse, bring the bed out from the master bedroom,
The bedstead he made himself, and spread it for him 185
With fleeces and blankets and silky coverlets."

She was testing her husband.
                                                    Odysseus
Could bear no more, and he cried out to his wife:

"By God, woman, now you've cut deep.
Who moved my bed? It would be hard 190

For anyone, no matter how skilled, to move it.
A god could come down and move it easily,
But not a man alive, however young and strong,
Could ever pry it up. There's something telling
About how that bed's built, and no one else   *195*
Built it but me.
                              There was an olive tree
Growing on the site, long-leaved and full,
Its trunk thick as a post. I built my bedroom
Around that tree, and when I had finished
The masonry walls and done the roofing   *200*
And set in the jointed, close-fitting doors,
I lopped off all of the olive's branches,
Trimmed the trunk from the root on up,
And rounded it and trued it with an adze until
I had myself a bedpost. I bored it with an auger,   *205*
And starting from this I framed up the whole bed,
Inlaying it with gold and silver and ivory
And stretching across it oxhide thongs dyed purple.
So there's our secret. But I do not know, woman,
Whether my bed is still firmly in place, or if   *210*
Some other man has cut through the olive's trunk."

At this, Penelope finally let go.
Odysseus had shown he knew their old secret.
In tears, she ran straight to him, threw her arms
Around him, kissed his face, and said: *215*

"Don't be angry with me, Odysseus. You,
Of all men, know how the world goes.
It is the gods who gave us sorrow, the gods
Who begrudged us a life together, enjoying
Our youth and arriving side by side   *220*
To the threshold of old age. Don't hold it against me
That when I first saw you I didn't welcome you
As I do now. My heart has been cold with fear
That an imposter would come and deceive me.
There are many who scheme for ill-gotten gains.   *225*
Not even Helen, daughter of Zeus,

Would have slept with a foreigner had she known
The Greeks would go to war to bring her back home.
It was a god who drove her to that dreadful act,
Or she never would have thought of doing what she did,   *230*
The horror that brought suffering to us as well.
But now, since you have confirmed the secret
Of our marriage bed, which no one has ever seen—
Only you and I and a single servant, Actor's daughter,
Whom my father gave me before I ever came here   *235*
And who kept the doors of our bridal chamber—
You have persuaded even my stubborn heart."

This brought tears from deep within him,
And as he wept he clung to his beloved wife.

> *Land is a welcome sight to men swimming*   *240*
> *For their lives, after Poseidon has smashed their ship*
> *In heavy seas. Only a few of them escape*
> *And make it to shore. They come out*
> *Of the grey water crusted with brine, glad*
> *To be alive and set foot on dry land.*   *245*

So welcome a sight was her husband to her.
She would not loosen her white arms from his neck,
And rose-fingered Dawn would have risen
On their weeping, had not Athena stepped in
And held back the long night at the end of its course   *250*
And stopped gold-stitched Dawn at Ocean's shores
From yoking the horses that bring light to men,
Lampus and Phaethon, the colts of Dawn.

Then Odysseus said to his wife:

"We have not yet come to the end of our trials.   *255*
There is still a long, hard task for me to complete,
As the spirit of Tiresias foretold to me
On the day I went down to the house of Hades
To ask him about my companions' return
And my own. But come to bed now,   *260*

And we'll close our eyes in the pleasure of sleep."

And Penelope calmly answered him:

"Your bed is ready for you whenever
You want it, now that the gods have brought you
Home to your family and native land.   265
But since you've brought it up, tell me
About this trial. I'll learn about it soon enough,
And it won't be any worse to hear it now."

And Odysseus, his mind teeming:

"You are a mystery to me. Why do you insist   270
I tell you now? Well, here's the whole story.
It's not a tale you will enjoy, and I have no joy
In telling it.
              Tiresias told me that I must go
To city after city carrying a broad-bladed oar,
Until I come to men who know nothing of the sea,   275
Who eat their food unsalted, and have never seen
Red-prowed ships or the oars that wing them along.
And he told me that I would know I had found them
When I met another traveler who thought
The oar I was carrying was a winnowing fan.   280
Then I must fix my oar in the earth
And offer sacrifice to Lord Poseidon,
A ram, a bull, and a boar in its prime.
Then at last I am to come home and offer
Grand sacrifice to the immortal gods   285
Who hold high heaven, to each in turn.
And death shall come to me from the sea,
As gentle as this touch, and take me off
When I am worn out in sleek old age,
With my people prosperous around me.   290
All this Tiresias said would come true."

Then Penelope, watching him, answered:

"If the gods are going to grant you a happy old age,
There is hope your troubles will someday be over."

While they spoke to one another,   *295*
Eurynome and the nurse made the bed
By torchlight, spreading it with soft coverlets.
Then the old nurse went to her room to lie down,
And Eurynome, who kept the bedroom,
Led the couple to their bed, lighting the way.   *300*
When she had led them in, she withdrew,
And they went with joy to their bed
And to their rituals of old.

                     Telemachus and his men
Stopped dancing, stopped the women's dance,
And lay down to sleep in the shadowy halls.   *305*

    After Odysseus and Penelope
Had made sweet love, they took turns
Telling stories to each other. She told him
All that she had to endure as the fair lady
In the palace, looking upon the loathsome throng   *310*
Of suitors, who used her as an excuse
To kill many cattle, whole flocks of sheep,
And to empty the cellar of much of its wine.
Odysseus told her of all the suffering
He had brought upon others, and of all the pain   *315*
He endured himself. She loved listening to him
And did not fall asleep until he had told the whole tale.

He began with how he overcame the Cicones
And then came to the land of the Lotus-Eaters,
And all that the Cyclops did, and how he   *320*
Paid him back for eating his comrades.
Then how he came to Aeolus,
Who welcomed him and sent him on his way,
But since it was not his destiny to return home then,
The stormwinds grabbed him and swept him off   *325*
Groaning deeply over the teeming saltwater.

Then how he came to the Laestrygonians,
Who destroyed his ships and all their crews,
Leaving him with only one black-tarred hull.
Then all of Circe's tricks and wiles,   330
And how he sailed to the dank house of Hades
To consult the spirit of Theban Tiresias
And saw his old comrades there
And his aged mother who nursed him as a child.
Then how he heard the Sirens' eternal song,   335
And came to the Clashing Rocks,
And dread Charybdis and Scylla,
Whom no man had ever escaped before.
Then how his crew killed the cattle of the Sun,
And how Zeus, the high lord of thunder,   340
Slivered his ship with lightning, and all his men
Went down, and he alone survived.
And he told her how he came to Ogygia,
The island of the nymph Calypso,
Who kept him there in her scalloped caves,   345
Yearning for him to be her husband,
And how she took care of him, and promised
To make him immortal and ageless all his days
But did not persuade the heart in his breast.
Then how he crawled out of the sea in Phaeacia,   350
And how the Phaeacians honored him like a god
And sent him on a ship to his own native land
With gifts of bronze and clothing and gold.

He told the story all the way through,
And then sleep, which slackens our bodies,   355
Fell upon him and released him from care.

The Grey-eyed One knew what to do next.
When she felt that Odysseus was satisfied
With sleep and with lying next to his wife,
She roused the slumbering, golden Dawn,   360
Who climbed from Ocean with light for the world.
Odysseus got up from his rose-shadowed bed
And turned to Penelope with these instructions:

"My wife, we've had our fill of trials now,
You here, weeping over all the troubles   365
My absence caused, and I, bound by Zeus
To suffer far from the home I yearned for.
Now that we have both come to the bed
We have long desired, you must take charge
Of all that is mine in the house, while I   370
See to replenishing the flocks and herds
The insolent suitors have depleted.
I'll get some back on raids, some as tribute,
Until the pens are full again. But now,
I want you to know I am going to our farm   375
To see my father, who has suffered terribly
On my account. You don't need me to tell you
That when the sun rises the news will spread
That I have killed the suitors in our hall. So,
Go upstairs with your women and sit quietly.   380
Don't look outside or speak to anyone."

Odysseus spoke and put on his beautiful armor.
He woke Telemachus, and the cowherd
And swineherd, and had them arm also.
They strapped on their bronze, opened the doors   385
And went out, Odysseus leading the way.
It was light by now, but Athena hid them
In darkness, and spirited them out of the city.

ODYSSEY 24

Hermes, meanwhile, was calling forth
The ghosts of the suitors. He held the wand
He uses to charm mortal eyes to sleep
And make sleepers awake; and with this beautiful,
Golden wand he marshaled the ghosts,   5
Who followed along squeaking and gibbering.

> *Bats deep inside an eerie cave*
> *Flit and gibber when one of them falls*
> *From the cluster clinging to the rock overhead.*

So too these ghosts, as Hermes led them   10
Down the cold, dank ways, past
The streams of Ocean, past the White Rock,
Past the Gates of the Sun and the Land of Dreams,
Until they came to the Meadow of Asphodel,
Where the spirits of the dead dwell, phantoms   15
Of men outworn.

                Here was the ghost of Achilles,
And those of Patroclus, of flawless Antilochus,
And of Ajax, the best of the Achaeans
After Achilles, Peleus' incomparable son.
These ghosts gathered around Achilles   20
And were joined by the ghost of Agamemnon,
Son of Atreus, grieving, he himself surrounded
By the ghosts of those who had died with him
And met their fate in the house of Aegisthus.
The son of Peleus was the first to greet him: 25

"Son of Atreus, we believed that you of all heroes
Were dear to thundering Zeus your whole life through,
For you were the lord of the great army at Troy,
Where we Greeks endured a bitter campaign.

But you too had an early rendezvous with death,   30
Which no man can escape once he is born.
How much better to have died at Troy
With all the honor you commanded there!
The entire Greek army would have raised you a tomb,
And you would have won glory for your son as well.   35
As it was, you were doomed to a most pitiable death."

And the ghost of Agamemnon answered:

"Godlike Achilles, you did have the good fortune
To die in Troy, far from Argos. Around you fell
Some of the best Greeks and Trojans of their time,   40
Fighting for your body, as you lay there
In the howling dust of war, one of the great,
Your horsemanship forgotten. We fought all day
And would never have stopped, had not Zeus
Halted us with a great storm. Then we bore your body   45
Back to the ships and laid it on a bier, and cleansed
Your beautiful flesh with warm water and ointments,
And the men shed many hot tears and cut their hair.
Then your mother heard, and she came from the sea
With her saltwater women, and an eerie cry   50
Rose over the deep. The troops panicked,
And they would have run for the ships, had not
A man who was wise in the old ways stopped them,
Nestor, whose counsel had prevailed before.
Full of concern, he called out to the troops: 55

'Argives and Achaeans, halt! This is no time to flee.
It is his mother, with her immortal nymphs,
Come from the sea to mourn her dead son.'

"When he said that the troops settled down.
Then the daughters of the Old Man of the Sea   60
Stood all around you and wailed piteously,
And they dressed you in immortal clothing.
And the Muses, all nine, chanted the dirge,
Singing responsively in beautiful voices.

You couldn't have seen a dry eye in the army,   65
So poignant was the song of the Muses.
For seventeen days we mourned you like that,
Men and gods together. On the eighteenth day
We gave you to the fire, slaughtering sheep
And horned cattle around you. You were burned   70
In the clothing of the gods, with rich unguents
And sweet honey, and many Greek heroes
Paraded in arms around your burning pyre,
Both infantry and charioteers,
And the sound of their marching rose to heaven.   75
When the fire had consumed you,
We gathered your white bones at dawn, Achilles,
And laid them in unmixed wine and unguents.
Your mother had given us a golden urn,
A gift of Dionysus, she said, made by Hephaestus.   80
In this urn lie your white bones, Achilles,
Mingled with those of the dead Patroclus.
Just apart lie the bones of Antilochus
Whom you honored most after Patroclus died.
Over them all we spearmen of the great army   85
Heaped an immense and perfect barrow
On a headland beside the broad Hellespont
So that it might be seen from far out at sea
By men now and men to come.
                                    Your mother, Thetis,
Had collected beautiful prizes from the gods   90
And now set them down in the middle of the field
To honor the best of the Achaean athletes.
You have been to many heroes' funeral games
Where young men contend for prizes,
But you would have marveled at the sight   95
Of the beautiful prizes silver-footed Thetis
Set out for you. You were very dear to the gods.
Not even in death have you lost your name,
Achilles, nor your honor among men.
But what did I get for winding up the war?   100
Zeus worked out for me a ghastly death
At the hands of Aegisthus and my murderous wife."

As these two heroes talked with each other,
Quicksilver Hermes was leading down
The ghosts of the suitors killed by Odysseus.   *105*
When Hermes and these ghosts drew near,
The two heroes were amazed and went up to see
Who they were. The ghost of Agamemnon
Recognized one of them, Amphimedon,
Who had been his host in Ithaca, and called out: *110*

"Amphimedon! Why have you come down
Beneath the dark earth, you and your company,
All men of rank, all the same age? It's as if
Someone had hand-picked the city's best men.
Did Poseidon sink your ships and drown you   *115*
In the wind-whipped waves? Was it that, or
Did an enemy destroy you on land
As you cut off their cattle and flocks of sheep—
Or as they fought for their city and women?
Tell me. Remember who is asking—   *120*
An old friend of your house. I came there
With godlike Menelaus to urge Odysseus
To sail with the fleet to Ilion. A full month
That journey to Ithaca took us—hard work
Persuading Odysseus, destroyer of cities."   *125*

The ghost of Amphimedon responded:

"Son of Atreus, most glorious Agamemnon,
I remember all that, just as you tell it,
And I will tell you exactly what happened to us,
And how it ended in our bitter death.   *130*
We were courting the wife of Odysseus,
Long gone by then. She loathed the thought
Of remarrying, but she wouldn't give us a yes or no.
Her mind was bent on death and darkness for us.
Here is one of the tricks she dreamed up: *135*
She set up a loom in the hall and started weaving—
A huge, fine-threaded piece—and then came out and said:

'Young men—my suitors, since Odysseus is dead—
Eager as you are to marry me, you must wait
Until I finish this robe—it would be a shame   140
To waste my spinning—a shroud for the hero
Laertes, when death's doom lays him low.
I fear the Achaean women would reproach me
If he should lie shroudless for all his wealth.'

"We went along with this appeal to our honor.   145
Every day she would weave at the great loom,
And every night she would unweave by torchlight.
She fooled us for three years with her craft.
But in the fourth year, as the seasons rolled by,
And the moons waned, and the days dragged on,   150
One of her women who knew all about it
Told us, and we caught her unweaving
The gloried shroud. Then we forced her to finish it.
When it was done she washed it and showed it to us,
And it shone like the sun or the moon.
                                        It was then   155
That some evil spirit brought Odysseus
From who knows where to the border of his land,
Where the swineherd lived. Odysseus' son
Put in from Pylos in his black ship and joined him.
These two, after they had plotted an ugly death   160
For the suitors, came up to the town, first Telemachus
And then later Odysseus, led by the swineherd,
Who brought his master wearing tattered clothes,
Looking for all the world like a miserable old beggar,
Leaning on a staff, his rags hanging off him.   165
None of us could know who he was, not even
The older men, when he showed up like that.
We threw things at him and gave him a hard time.
He just took it, pelted and taunted in his own house,
Until, prompted by Zeus, he and Telemachus   170
Removed all the weapons from the hall
And locked them away in a storeroom.
Then he showed all his cunning. He told his wife
To set before the suitors his bow and grey iron—

Implements for a contest, and for our ill-fated death. *175*
None of us were able to string that bow.
We couldn't even come close. When it came
Around to Odysseus, we cried out and objected,
'Don't give the bow to that beggar,
No matter what he says!' Telemachus alone *180*
Urged him on and encouraged him to take it.
And he did. The great Odysseus
Took the bow, strung it easily, and shot an arrow
Straight through the iron. Then he stood on the threshold,
Poured the arrows out, and glaring around him *185*
He shot Lord Antinous. And then he shot others,
With perfect aim, and we fell thick and fast.
You could see that some god was helping them,
The way they raged through the hall, cutting us down
Right and left; and you could hear *190*
The hideous groans of men as their heads
Were bashed in. The floor smoked with blood.
  That's how we died, Agamemnon. Our bodies
Still lie uncared for in Odysseus' halls.
Word has not yet reached our friends and family, *195*
Who could wash the black blood from our wounds
And lay us out with wailing, as is due the dead."

And the ghost of Agamemnon responded:

"Well done, Odysseus, Laertes' wily son!
You won a wife of great character *200*
In Icarius' daughter. What a mind she has,
A woman beyond reproach! How well Penelope
Kept in her heart her husband, Odysseus.
And so her virtue's fame will never perish,
And the gods will make among men on earth *205*
A song of praise for steadfast Penelope.
But Tyndareus' daughter was evil to the core,
Killing her own husband, and her song will be
A song of scorn, bringing ill-repute
To all women, even the virtuous." *210*

That was the drift of their talk as they stood
In the Dark Lord's halls deep under the earth.

Odysseus and the others went from the town
And made good time getting down to Laertes'
Well-kept fields. The old man had worked hard   215
Reclaiming the land from the wilderness.
His farmhouse was there with a row of huts around it
Where the field hands ate and rested and slept.
These were his slaves, and they did as he wished.
There was an old Sicilian woman, too,   220
Who took good care of the old man out in the country.

Odysseus had a word with the herdsmen and his son:

"Go into the farmhouse and make yourselves busy.
Sacrifice the best pig and roast it for dinner.
I am going to test my father. Will he recognize me?   225
Will he know who I am after all these years?"

He disarmed and gave his weapons to the herdsmen.
They hurried off indoors, leaving Odysseus
To search through the rows of fruit trees and vines.
He did not find Dolius, or any of his sons   230
Anywhere in the orchard. Old Dolius had taken them
To gather fieldstones for a garden wall.
But he found his father, alone, on a well-banked plot,
Spading a plant. He had on an old, dirty shirt,
Mended and patched, and leather leggings   235
Pieced together as protection from scratches.
He wore gloves because of the bushes, and on his head
He had a goatskin cap, crowning his sorrow.
Odysseus, who had borne much, saw him like this,
Worn with age and a grieving heart,   240
And wept as he watched from a pear tree's shade.
He thought it over. Should he just throw his arms
Around his father, kiss him and tell him all he had done,
And how he'd returned to his homeland again—
Or should he question him and feel him out first?   245

Better that way, he thought, to feel him out first
With a few pointed remarks. With this in mind,
Godlike Odysseus walked up to his father,
Who kept his head down and went on digging.
His illustrious son stood close by him and said: 250

"Well, old-timer, you certainly know how to garden.
There's not a plant, a fig tree, a vine or an olive,
Not a pear tree or leek in this whole garden untended.
But if I may say so without getting you angry,
You don't take such good care of yourself. Old age   255
Is hard, yes. But unwashed, scruffy and dressed in rags?
It can't be that your lord is too lax to care for you,
And anyway there's nothing in your build or looks
To suggest you're a slave. You look more like a king,
The sort of man who after he has bathed and eaten   260
Sleeps on a soft bed, as is only right for elders.
Come on now and give me a straight answer.
Whose slave are you? Whose orchard is this?
And tell me this, too, so that I can be sure:
Is this really Ithaca I've come to, as I was told   265
By that man I ran into on my way over here?
He wasn't very polite, couldn't be bothered
To tell me what I wanted, or even to hear me out.
I've been trying to find out about an old friend
I entertained at my house once, whether he's still alive   270
Or is dead by now and gone down to Hades.
So I'll ask you, if you'll give me your attention.
I was host to a man once back in my own country,
A man who means more to me than anyone else
Who has ever visited my home from abroad.   275
He claimed his family was from Ithaca, and he said
His father was Laertes, son of Arcesius.
I took him into my home, and entertained him
In a style befitting the wealth in my house,
And gave him suitable gifts to seal our friendship: 280
Seven ingots of fine gold, a silver mixing bowl
Embossed with flowers, twelve cloaks, as many
Carpets, mantles and tunics, and his choice of four

Beautiful women superbly trained in handicrafts."

A tear wet his father's cheek as he answered: *285*

"You've come to the land you're looking for, stranger,
But it's in the hands of haughty and violent men.
You've given all those generous gifts in vain.
If you were to find him alive here in Ithaca
He would send you off with the beautiful gifts   *290*
And fine hospitality you deserve as his friend.
But tell me this now, and tell me the truth:
How many years has it been since you hosted
Your ill-fated guest, my son—if I ever had a son?
Born for sorrow he was, and now far from home,   *295*
Far from his loved ones, his bones are picked clean
By fish undersea; or on some wild shore
His body is feeding the scavenging birds,
Unburied, unmourned by his mother and me,
Who brought him into this world. Nor has his wife,   *300*
Penelope, patient and wise, who brought him so much,
Lamented her husband on a funeral bier
Or closed his eyelids, as is due the dead.
And tell me this, too, so that I will know.
Who are you?   *305*
What city are you from? Who are your parents?
And where have you moored the sailing ship
That brought you and your crew of heroes here?
Or did you come as a passenger on another's ship
That put you ashore and went on its way?"   *310*

And Odysseus, his great mind teeming:

"I'll tell you everything point by point.
I come from Alybas and have my home there.
I'm the son of Apheidas and Polypemon's grandson.
My name is Eperitus. Some storm spirit drove me   *315*
Off course from Sicily and, as luck had it, here.
My ship stands off wild country far from the town.
As for Odysseus, it's been five years now

Since he left my land, ill-fated maybe,
But the birds were good when he sailed out—   *320*
On the right. This cheered me as I sent him off,
And he was cheered, too, our hearts full of hope
We would meet again and exchange splendid gifts."

A black mist of pain shrouded Laertes.
He scooped up fistfuls of shimmering dust   *325*
And groaned as he poured it upon his grey head.
This wrung Odysseus' heart, and bitter longing
Stung his nostrils as he watched his father.
With a bound he embraced him, kissed him and said:

"I'm the one that you miss, Father, right here,   *330*
Back in my homeland after twenty years.
But don't cry now. Hold back your tears.
I'm telling you, we really have to hurry.
I've killed the suitors in our house and avenged
All of the wrongs that have grieved your heart."   *335*

But Laertes' voice rang out in answer:

"If you are really Odysseus and my son come back,
Give me a sign, a clear sign I can trust."

And Odysseus, the master strategist:

"First, here's the scar I got on Parnassus   *340*
From that boar's bright tusk. Mother and you
Had sent me to my grandfather Autolycus
To collect some presents he had promised me
When he had visited us here. And let me count off
All of the trees in the orchard rows   *345*
You gave me one day when I was still a boy.
You gave me thirteen pear trees, ten apple trees,
Forty fig trees, and fifty vine rows
That ripened one by one as the season went on
With heavy clusters of all sorts of grapes."   *350*

He spoke, and the old man's knees went slack
As he recognized the signs Odysseus showed him.
He threw his arms around his beloved son
And gasped for breath. And godly Odysseus,
Who had borne much, embraced him.   355
When he had caught his breath and his spirit returned,
Laertes' voice rang out to the sky:

"Father Zeus, there are still gods on high Olympus,
If the suitors have really paid the price!
But now I have a terrible fear   360
That all of Ithaca will be upon us soon,
And word will have gone out to Cephallenia, too."

And Odysseus, his mind teeming:

"We don't have to worry about that right now.
Let's go to the cottage near the orchard.   365
I sent Telemachus there, and the cowherd
And swineherd, to prepare a meal for us."

And they went together to the house
With its comfortable rooms and found
Telemachus and the two herdsmen there   370
Carving huge roasts and mixing wine.
While they were busy with these tasks,
The old Sicilian woman bathed great Laertes
In his own house and rubbed him down
With olive oil and threw about his shoulders   375
A handsome cloak. And Athena came
And made the shepherd of the people
Taller than before and added muscle to his frame.
When he came from the bath, his son marveled
At his deathless, godlike appearance,   380
And his words rose to his father on wings:

"Father, surely one of the gods eternal
Has made you larger, and more handsome, too."

And Laertes, feeling the magic, answered him:

"I wish by Zeus and Athena and Apollo   *385*
That I could have stood at your side yesterday
In our house, armor on my shoulders,
As the man I was when I took Nericus,
The mainland town, commanding the Cephallenians!
I would have beaten the daylights out of them   *390*
There in our halls, and made your heart proud."

While they were talking, the others
Had finished preparing the meal.
They all sat down on benches and chairs
And were just serving themselves food   *395*
When old Dolius came in with his sons,
Weary from their work in the fields.
Their mother, the old Sicilian woman,
Had gone out to call them. It was she
Who made their meals and took care   *400*
Of Dolius, now that old age had set in.
When they saw Odysseus, and realized
Who he was, they stood there dumbfounded.
Odysseus spoke to them gently and said:

"Old man, sit down to dinner, and all of you,   *405*
You can stop being amazed. Hungry as we are,
We've been waiting a long time for you."

He spoke, and Dolius ran up to him
With arms outstretched, and clasped
Odysseus' hand and kissed him on the wrist.   *410*
Trembling with excitement, the old man said:

"My dear Odysseus, you have come back home.
We missed you so much but never hoped
To see you again. The gods themselves
Have brought you back. Welcome, welcome,   *415*
And may the gods grant you happiness.
But tell me this—I have to know—

Does Penelope know that you have returned,
Or should we send her a messenger?"

And Odysseus, his mind teeming: 420

"She knows, old man. You don't have to worry."

He spoke, and Dolius sat down in a polished chair.
His sons then gathered around glorious Odysseus
And greeted him and clasped his hands
And then sat down in order next to their father.   425

 While they were busy with their meal,
Rumor, that swift messenger, flew
All through the city, telling everyone
About the grim fate the suitors had met.
Before long a crowd had gathered   430
Outside Odysseus' palace, and the sound
Of their lamentation hung in the air.
They carried their dead out of the hall
And buried them. Those from other cities
They put aboard ships to be brought home by sea.   435
Then they all went to the meeting place,
Sad at heart. When they were assembled,
Eupeithes rose and spoke among them,
Upon his heart an unbearable grief
For his son Antinous, the first man   440
Whom Odysseus killed. Weeping for him
He addressed the assembly and said:

"My friends, it is truly monstrous—
What this man has done to our city.
First, he sailed off with many of our finest men   445
And lost the ships and every man aboard.
Now he has come back and killed many others,
By far the best of the Cephallenians.
We must act now, before he runs off to Pylos
Or takes refuge with the Epean lords of Elis.   450
We will be disgraced forever if we don't avenge

Our sons' and brothers' deaths, and if we don't,
I see no point in living. I'd rather be dead.
Let's move now, before they cross the sea!"

He wept as he spoke, and they all pitied him.   455
Then up came Medon and the godlike bard
From Odysseus' halls. They had just woken up
From a long sleep and stood now in the midst
Of the wondering crowd. Medon had this to say:

"Hear me, men of Ithaca. It was not without the will   460
Of the deathless gods that Odysseus managed this.
I myself saw one of the immortals
Close to Odysseus. He looked just like Mentor
But was a god, now appearing in front of Odysseus,
Urging him on, then raging through the hall   465
Terrifying the suitors, who fell thick and fast."

He spoke, and they all turned pale with fear.
Then the old hero Halitherses, son of Mastor,
Rose to speak. He alone looked ahead and behind,
And spoke with the best of intentions to them: 470

"Now hear what I have to say, men of Ithaca.
You have only yourselves to blame, my friends,
For what has happened. You would not obey me
Nor Mentor, shepherd of the people, when we told you
To make your sons stop their foolishness.   475
It was what your sons did that was truly monstrous,
Wasting the wealth and dishonoring the wife
Of a great man, who they said would never return.
Now listen to me and keep your peace. Some of you
Are asking for trouble—and you just might find it."   480

Less than half of them took his advice
And stayed in their seats. Most of them
Jumped up with a whoop and went with Eupeithes.
They rushed to get weapons, and when the mob
Had armed themselves in glowing bronze,   485

They put the city behind them, following Eupeithes,
Who in his folly thought he would avenge
His son's death, but met his own fate instead.
Eupeithes would never return home again.

Athena, meanwhile, was having a word with Zeus: *490*

"Father of us all, Son of Cronus most high,
Tell me what is hidden in that mind of yours.
Will you let this grim struggle go on?
Or will you establish peace on Ithaca?"

And Zeus in his thunderhead responded: *495*

"Why question me, Daughter? Wasn't this
Your plan, to have Odysseus pay them back
With a vengeance? Do as you will,
But I will tell you what would be fitting.
Now that Odysseus has paid the suitors back,   *500*
Let all parties swear a solemn oath,
That he will be king on Ithaca all of his days.
We, for our part, will have them forget
The killing of their sons and brothers.
Let them live in friendship as before,   *505*
And let peace and prosperity abound."

This was all Athena needed to hear,
And she streaked down from Olympus' peaks.

The meal was over. Seeing that his company
Had satisfied their hunger, Odysseus said: *510*

"Someone should go out to see if they're coming."

One of Dolius' sons went to the doorway,
Looked out, and saw the mob closing in.
His words flew fast to Odysseus:

"They're almost here. We'd better arm quickly."   *515*

They jumped up and put on their gear,
Odysseus and his three men and Dolius' six sons.
Laertes and Dolius armed themselves, too,
Warriors in a pinch despite their white hair.
When they had strapped on their bronze   520
They opened the doors and headed out
Behind Odysseus.

              Athena joined them,
Looking for all the world like Mentor,
And Odysseus was glad to see her. He turned
To his son Telemachus and said: 525

"Telemachus, now you will see firsthand
What it means to distinguish yourself in war.
Don't shame your ancestors. We have been
Strong and brave in every generation."

And Telemachus coolly answered him: 530

"The way I feel now, I don't think you'll see me
Shaming my ancestors, as you put it, Father."

Laertes was delighted with this and exclaimed:

"What a day, dear gods! My son and grandson
Going head to head to see who is best."   535

The Grey-eyed One stood next to him and said:

"Son of Arcesius, my dearest comrade,
Say a prayer to Zeus and his grey-eyed daughter,
And then cast your long-shadowed spear."

Pallas Athena breathed great strength into him,   540
And with a prayer to Zeus' grey-eyed daughter,
Laertes cast his long-shadowed spear
And hit Eupeithes square in the helmet.
Bronze bored through bronze, and Eupeithes

Thudded to the ground, his armor clattering.   *545*
Odysseus and his glorious son
Charged the front lines, thrusting hard
With their swords and spears. They would have killed
Every last man—not one would have gone home—
Had not Athena, daughter of the Storm Cloud,   *550*
Given voice to a cry that stopped them all cold:

"ITHACANS!
                 Lay down your arms now,
And go your ways with no more bloodshed."

Thus Athena, and they turned pale with fear.
The weapons dropped from their trembling hands   *555*
And fell to the ground as the goddess' voice
Sent shock waves through them. They turned
Back toward the city and ran for their lives.
With a roar, the great, long-suffering Odysseus
Gathered himself and swept after them   *560*

   Like a soaring raptor.

                    At that moment
Zeus, Son of Cronus, hurled down
A flaming thunderbolt that landed at the feet
Of his owl-eyed daughter, who said:

"Son of Laertes in the line of Zeus,   *565*
Cunning Odysseus—restrain yourself.
End this quarrel and cease from fighting
Lest broad-browed Zeus frown upon you."

Thus Athena. The man obeyed and was glad,
And the goddess made both sides swear binding oaths—   *570*
Pallas Athena, daughter of the Storm Cloud,
Who looked like Mentor and spoke with his voice.

Glossary of Names: *Iliad*

Gods and Goddesses

Aphrodite (Af-ro-deye´-tee): Goddess of love and beauty. Daughter of Zeus and Dione in the *Iliad*. Aphrodite is pro-Trojan, due in part to her affinity for Paris Alexander, who in other versions awarded her the prize of the Golden Apple for being the most beautiful of the goddesses.

Apollo (A-pol´-oh): Patron god of many areas, including music and the arts. Son of Zeus and Leto; brother of Artemis. Also known as Phoebus Apollo, Lord of the Silver Bow, and the Far-Shooter (for his role in bringing death by natural causes to men). Apollo is pro-Trojan in the *Iliad*.

Ares (Ai´-reez): God of war. Son of Zeus and Hera. Ares is pro-Trojan in the *Iliad*, although at times he appears as an impartial representative of bloodshed and the cruelties of war.

Artemis (Ar´-te-mis): Goddess of the hunt and the moon. Daughter of Zeus and Leto; sister of Apollo. Like her brother, Artemis brings natural death to mortals, although she is the slaughterer of female mortals in particular. She is pro-Trojan in the *Iliad*.

Athena (A-thee´-na): Goddess of wisdom, crafts, and battle. Daughter of Zeus, usually said to have sprung from his head. Also called Pallas Athena. Athena is powerfully pro-Achaean in the *Iliad* and has particular favorite heroes on that side.

Charis (Ka´-ris): One of the Graces, goddesses of beauty and grace. Wife of Hephaestus in the *Iliad*.

Cronion (Kro´-nee-on): Son of Cronus. See Zeus.

Dione (Deye-oh´-nee): A goddess of the early generation, either a Titan or an Oceanid. Mother of Aphrodite in the *Iliad*.

Hades (Hay-deez): God of the Underworld, sometimes synonymous with death. Son of Cronus and Rhea; brother of Zeus, Poseidon, and Hera; husband of Persephone. Hades shows no partiality to the Achaeans or the Trojans.

Hebe (Hee´-bee): Goddess of youth and beauty. Daughter of Zeus and Hera. She serves as a palace helper to the gods on Olympus.

Hephaestus (He-feyes´-tus): God of fire and patron of metalworkers. Son of Zeus and Hera; husband of Charis in the *Iliad*. Hephaestus is pro-Achaean, although his major roles are to make peace between his parents and to create magically endowed objects, in particular Achilles' armor.

Hera (Hee´-ra): Queen of the Olympian gods. Daughter of Cronus and Rhea; wife of Zeus; mother of Ares, Hephaestus, and Hebe. Hera is powerfully pro-Achaean in the *Iliad*, to the extent that she is at war with her husband.

Hermes (Hur´-meez): God who serves as messenger for the Olympians. Son of Zeus and Maia. Hermes is technically pro-Achaean, but has a larger role as a messenger and guide, including guiding Priam, the Trojan king, to the Achaean camp.

Iris (Eye´-ris): Goddess of the rainbow and a messenger for the Olympians. Daughter of the Titan Thaumas and the Oceanid Electra.

Leto (Lee´-toh): A Titan goddess. Daughter of Coeus and Phoebe; mother of the twins Apollo and Artemis, sired by Zeus. Leto is pro-Trojan, given that her beloved children are strong allies of the Trojans.

Poseidon (Po-seye´-don): God of the sea. Son of Cronus and Rhea; brother of Zeus, Hades, and Hera. In the *Iliad*, Poseidon is generally pro-Achaean, although at times he favors certain Trojans.

Themis (The´-mis): Titan goddess of law and order. Daughter of Uranus and Gaia.

Thetis (The´-tis): A sea goddess, one of the Nereids. Daughter of Nereus and Doris; wife of Peleus; mother of Achilles. Thetis' main concern in the *Iliad* is watching out for her mighty son and securing his desires.

Xanthus (Xan´-thus): God of the river near Troy, called by men Scamander. In the battle of the gods, Xanthus fittingly takes his place on the Trojan side.

Zeus (Zyoos): The supreme god of Olympus, known as the father of gods and men. Son of Cronus and Rhea; husband of Hera; father of Athena, Aphrodite, Ares, Apollo, Artemis, Hephaestus, and others. Zeus' position in the *Iliad* is generally impartial except when he is influenced by special requests.

The Greeks (Achaeans, Argives, and Danaans)

Achilles (A-kil´-eez): Son of Peleus, King of Phthia, and Thetis, a sea goddess. Leader of the Myrmidons, the contingent from Phthia, and their fifty ships. Central character whose actions determine the course of the epic.

Agamemnon (Ag-a-mem´-non): Son of Atreus and Aerope; brother of Menelaus; husband of Clytemnestra. Commander in chief of the Greek forces and leader of the contingent from Argos and Mycenae and their hundred ships. His quarrel with Achilles sets the plot in motion.

Ajax (Ay´-jax) (1): Son of Telamon and Periboea; half-brother of Teucer. Leader of the contingent from Salamis and their twelve ships. Also called Great Ajax and Telamonian Ajax. Since he is known as the greatest in battle next to Achilles, his ships guard the flank opposite that guarded by Achilles. To be distinguished from the lesser Ajax (2).

Ajax (2): Son of Oïleus and Eriopis. Leader of the contingent from Locris and their forty ships. He is called Little Ajax, Oïlean Ajax, or Locrian Ajax to distinguish him from Great Ajax (1).

Antilochus (An-ti´-lo-kus): Son of Nestor and Eurydice or Anaxibia. Brother of Thrasymedes and co-leader with him and their father of the contingent from Pylos and its ninety ships. Antilochus contributes significantly in combat throughout the epic.

Automedon (Aw-to´-me-don): Son of Diores. Charioteer of Achilles' immortal horses.

Calchas (Kal´-kas): Son of Thestor. The foremost Greek seer, consulted by the Greeks at key moments of the expedition to Troy.

Diomedes (Deye-o-mee´-deez): Son of Tydeus and Deïpyle. Leader with Sthenelus of the contingent from Argos and Tiryns and their eighty ships. Known as one of the greatest Greek fighters and sometimes paired with Odysseus in exploits.

Epeius (E-pee´-us): Son of Panopeus. A Phocian fighter who participates in the funeral games as a boxing champion and is known elsewhere as the builder of the Trojan Horse, the war machine that eventually conquers Troy.

Eumelus (Yoo-mee´-lus): Son of Admetus and Alcestis. Leader of the Thessalian contingent from Pherae and their eleven ships. Known for his famous horses, he participates in the funeral games as a charioteer.

Euryalus (Yoo-reye´-a-lus): Son of Mecisteus. One of the leaders of the contingent from Argos under Diomedes. He participates in the funeral games as a boxer.

Eurybates (Yoo-ri´-ba-teez): A principal herald or official messenger of Agamemnon and the Greek forces; his name means "wide walker."

Eurypylus (Yoo-ri´-pi-lus): Son of Euaemon and Opis. Leader of one of the Thessalian contingents, with forty ships.

Helen (He´-len): Daughter of Zeus and Leda. Originally the wife of Menelaus of Sparta; in the *Iliad*, wife of Paris of Troy. According to ancient mythology, she was the most beautiful woman in the world. In spite of her married status, she was offered as a bride to Paris Alexander by the goddess Aphrodite, on the condition that he would award the Golden Apple of Discord to her. Helen then became known as the cause of the Trojan war, although other reasons for the war are mentioned in Homer and other versions of Helen's story exist in other sources.

Idomeneus (Eye-do´-men-yoos): Son of Deucalion. Leader of the contingent from the island of Crete and its eighty ships. One of the most prominent Greek fighters, although older than most.

Leitus (Lee´-i-tus): Son of Alectryon and Cleobule. Co-leader with Peneleos of the Boeotian contingent and its fifty ships.

Leonteus (Le-on´-tyoos): Son of Coronus. Co-leader with Polypoetes of the Lapith contingent and its forty ships. The two are instrumental in repelling the Trojans' attack on the ships.

Machaon (Ma-kay´-on): Son of Asclepius. Co-leader with his brother Podalirius of the Thessalian contingent from Tricca and Oechalia and its thirty ships. A Greek warrior best known, like his brother, for medical skills inherited from his famous father.

Meges (Me'-jeez): Son of Phyleus and Ctimene. Leader of the contingent from Dulichium and its forty ships.

Menelaus (Me-ne-lay'-us): Son of Atreus and Aerope; brother of Agamemnon, the commander in chief; husband of Helen, who was taken from his home by Paris. Leader of the Lacedaemonian contingent from the Peloponnese and its sixty ships. A prominent Greek warrior.

Menestheus (Me-nes'-thyoos): Son of Peteos. Leader of the Athenian contingent and its fifty ships.

Meriones (Me-reye'-o-neez): Son of Molus. Second in command under Idomeneus of the contingent from Crete and its eighty ships. A leading Greek warrior and a major participant in the funeral games.

Nestor (Nes'-tor): Son of Neleus and Chloris. Leader with his two sons, Antilochus and Thrasymedes, of the contingent from Pylos and its ninety ships. Although known principally as a wise counsellor to the Greeks and as the oldest among their warriors, Nestor still participates in battle to some degree.

Odysseus (O-dis'-yoos): Son of Laertes and Anticleia. Leader of the contingent from the island of Ithaca and its twelve ships. Odysseus serves as a prominent fighter, orator, and general troubleshooter for the Greeks. He is the hero of Homer's *Odyssey*, which tells of his return home.

Patroclus (Pa-tro'-klus): Son of Menoetius. Greek warrior with the Myrmidon contingent and best friend of Achilles, its leader. Patroclus is a key figure in the *Iliad* because of his decision to fight in Achilles' place.

Peneleos (Pee-ne'-lee-ohs): Son of Hippalcimus and Asterope. Co-leader with Leitus of the Boeotian contingent and its fifty ships.

Phoenix (Fee'-nix): Son of Amyntor. Greek warrior with the Myrmidons and friend and mentor of Achilles, whose father Peleus made Phoenix king of the Dolopians.

Podalirius (Po-da-leye'-ri-us): Son of Asclepius and Epione. Co-leader with his brother Machaon of the Thessalian contingent from Tricca and Oechalia and its thirty ships. A Greek warrior best known, along with his brother, for medical skills inherited from his famous father.

Polypoetes (Po-li-pee´-teez): Son of Peirithous and Hippodameia. Co-leader with Leonteus of the Lapith contingent and its forty ships. The two are instrumental in repelling the Trojans' attack on the ships.

Sthenelus (Sthen´-e-lus): Son of Capaneus and Evadne. A close friend of Diomedes and second in command under him of the contingent from Argos and its eighty ships.

Talthybius (Tal-thi´-bi-us): The principal herald, or official messenger, for Agamemnon and the Greek forces.

Teucer (Tyoo´-sur): Son of Telamon and Hesione. The illegitimate half-brother of Telamonian (or Great) Ajax, he accompanies the contingent from Salamis and is a notable Greek warrior, particularly with the bow.

Thersites (Thur-seye´-teez): Son of Agrius. A Greek warrior known for raucous and rebellious speeches in assemblies.

Thrasymedes (Thra-si-mee´-deez): Son of Nestor and Eurydice or Anaxibia. Brother of Antilochus and co-leader with him and their father of the contingent from Pylos. He was known as chief among the sentinels.

Tlepolemus (Tle-po´-le-mus): Son of the great hero Heracles and Astyocheia. Leader of the contingent from Rhodes and its nine ships.

The Trojans (Dardanians) and Allies

Aeneas (Ee-nee´-as): Son of Anchises and the goddess Aphrodite. A Trojan fighter of repute who would survive to establish the ruling line of Rome.

Andromache (An-dro´-ma-kee): Daughter of Eëtion; wife of Hector; mother of Scamandrius, who was also called Astyanax ("city lord") for his father's glory. She lost her birth family to Achilles earlier in the war and fears losing her husband and child as well.

Antenor (An-tee´-nor): Wise Trojan counsellor. Husband of the priestess of Athena, Theano, and father of many sons killed by the Achaeans.

Astyanax (A-steye´-a-nax): Infant son of the Trojan hero Hector and his wife Andromache. His given name is Scamandrius, but he is called Astyanax ("city lord") to honor his father. The child is the most likely heir to the Trojan realm and the subject of much concern on the part of his parents.

Briseis (Breye-see´-is): Daughter of Briseus. A war prize awarded to Achilles after he sacked Lyrnessus, she was subsequently taken away by Agamemnon.

Cassandra (Ka-san´-dra): Daughter of King Priam and Hecuba; sister of Hector, Paris, Helenus, and Deïphobus. Known elsewhere for her prophetic abilities and as an oracle who is never believed.

Cebriones (Se-breye´-o-neez): Illegitimate son of King Priam. Warrior and charioteer of his half-brother Hector.

Chryseis (Kreye-see´-is): Daughter of Chryses. War prize awarded to Agamemnon as his share of the looting and subsequently ransomed by her father.

Chryses (Kreye´-seez): Priest of Apollo who comes to the Achaean camp to ransom his daughter Chryseis, war prize of Agamemnon.

Deïphobus (Dee-i´-fo-bus): Son of King Priam and Hecuba; brother of Hector, Paris, Helenus, and Cassandra. Trojan warrior who consults with Hector on strategy.

Dolon (Doh´-lon): Son of Eumedes. A Trojan sent to spy on the Achaean forces, he runs into the enemy with disastrous consequences.

Euphorbus (Yoo-for´-bus): Son of Panthous and Phrontis. Trojan warrior who wounds Patroclus.

Glaucus (Glaw´-kus): Son of Hippolochus. Co-leader with his cousin Sarpedon of the Lycians, Trojan allies. Glaucus is notable as well for his descent from Bellerophon, one of the great heroes of Greek mythology, who in other mythological versions performed glorious feats on the back of the winged horse Pegasus.

Hector (Hek´-tor): Oldest son of King Priam and Hecuba; brother of Paris, Helenus, Deïphobus, and Cassandra; husband of Andromache. Leader of the Trojans in battle and their foremost fighter; known as the defense of the city of Troy.

Hecuba (He´-kew-ba): Daughter of Dymas, King of Phrygia, and Eunoe. Official consort of King Priam of Troy and mother of many of his children, including Hector, Paris, Helenus, Deïphobus, Cassandra, and Laodice. Known as a prototype of the grieving mother who must face tragic losses in war.

Helenus (He´-le-nus): Son of King Priam and Hecuba; brother of Hector, Paris, Deïphobus, and Cassandra. A Trojan fighter and seer, he was awarded the gift of prophecy by Apollo. In other mythological versions, he is said to have become dissatisfied with the Trojans for various reasons and to have gone over to the Achaean side, helping them by means of his prophetic knowledge.

Idaeus (Eye-dee´-us): The principal herald, or official messenger, of King Priam and the Trojan forces.

Laodice (Lay-o´-di-see): Daughter of King Priam and Hecuba. Sometimes called the most beautiful of their daughters.

Pandarus (Pan´-da-rus): Son of King Lycaon of Lycia. Leader of the Troes and a bowman whose role in the *Iliad* is limited mainly to that of peace-breaker. In later mythology Pandarus' role is expanded considerably, although it generally involves the aspect of treachery.

Paris (Pa´-ris): Son of King Priam and Hecuba; brother of Hector, Helenus, Deïphobus, and Cassandra. Also called Alexander. A leading Trojan fighter, Paris is better known as the cause of the Trojan war through his seduction of Helen, wife of Menelaus of Sparta.

Polydamas (Po-li´-da-mas): Son of Panthous and Phrontis. A Trojan fighter who sometimes advises Hector on strategy.

Priam (Preye´-am): Son of Laomedon; husband of Hecuba; father of Hector, Paris, Helenus, Deïphobus, Cassandra, Laodice, and many others. The wealthy and aged ruler of Troy.

Rhesus (Ree´-sus): Son of Eïoneus. A Thracian king and ally of the Trojans who arrives late in the war with his famous snow-white horses to do battle with the Achaeans.

Sarpedon (Sar-pee´-don): Son of Zeus and Laodamia. Co-leader with his cousin Glaucus of the Lycians, allies of the Trojans. A notable warrior on the Trojan side and famous as progeny of Zeus.

Theano (Thee-ay´-no): Daughter of Cisseus, a king of Thrace; wife of Antenor and mother of his many sons. Priestess of Athena at Troy.

Glossary of Names: *Odyssey*

Achaeans (A-kee´-unz): General term used by Homer to refer to Greeks.

Acheron (A´-ker-on): River in the Underworld, land of the dead.

Achilles (A-kil´-eez): Son of Peleus and Thetis. He is the heroic leader of the Myrmidons in the Trojan War and is slain by Paris. Odysseus consults him in the Underworld.

Aeaea (Ee-ee´-a): Island on which Circe lives.

Aegisthus (Ee-jis´-thus): Son of Thyestes and Pelopia. He seduces Clytemnestra, wife of Agamemnon, while Agamemnon is away fighting the Trojan War and helps her slay Agamemnon when he returns. Orestes avenges this action years later by murdering both Clytemnestra and Aegisthus.

Aegyptus (Ee-jip´-tus): The Nile River.

Aeolus (Ee´-oh-lus): King of the island Aeolia and keeper of the winds.

Aeson (Ee´-son): Son of Cretheus and Tyro; father of Jason, leader of the Argonauts.

Aethon (Ee´-thon): One of Odysseus' aliases used in his conversation with Penelope.

Agamemnon (Ag-a-mem´-non): Son of Atreus and Aerope; brother of Menelaus; husband of Clytemnestra. He commands the Greek forces in the Trojan War. He is killed by his wife and her lover when he returns home; his son, Orestes, avenges this murder.

Agelaus (A-je-lay´-us): One of Penelope's suitors; son of Damastor; killed by Odysseus.

Ajax (1) (Ay´-jax): Son of Telamon and Perioboea; also called Great Ajax or Telamonian Ajax. He contends with Odysseus for the prize of Achilles' arms, given in honor of service to the Greek cause in the Trojan War. When

Ajax loses, he temporarily takes leaves of his wits and commits suicide when he regains his senses.

Ajax (2) (Ay´-jax): Son of Oïleus and Eriopes; also called Little Ajax or Oïlean Ajax. He survives the Trojan War, but his boasting angers Poseidon, who kills Ajax on his return home.

Alcinous (Al-si´-no-us): Grandson of Poseidon; king of the Phaeacians; husband of Arete and father of Nausicaa. He graciously entertains Odysseus and gives him riches and safe transport to Ithaca.

Alcmene (Alk-mee´-nee): Wife of Amphitryon; mother of Heracles (by Zeus).

Amphimedon (Am-fi´-me-don): One of Penelope's suitors. He is killed by Telemachus. In the Underworld he tells Agamemnon about the slaughter of the suitors.

Amphinomus (Am-fi´-no-mus): Son of Nisus. A leader of Penelope's suitors, he convinces other suitors not to slay Telemachus on his return from Pylos unless the gods give a sign of favor. Although warned by Odysseus, Amphinomus is slain with the other suitors.

Amphion (Am-feye´-on): Son of Zeus and Antiope; husband of Niobe.

Amphithea (Am-fi´-the-a): Wife of Autolycus; grandmother of Odysseus.

Amphitryon (Am-fi´-tri-on): King of Tiryns; husband of Alcmene; mortal father of Heracles.

Anticleia (An-ti-klay´-a): Daughter of Autolycus; wife of Laertes and mother of Odysseus. She is able to speak to Odysseus when he visits her in the Underworld.

Anticlus (An´-ti-klus): One of the Greek warriors who hides in the wooden horse at Troy. Odysseus restrains him from responding when Helen imitates the voices of Greek wives.

Antinous (An-ti´-no-us): Son of Eupeithes; an Ithacan noble and the primary leader of Penelope's suitors. He is the first suitor slain by Odysseus.

Antiphates (An-ti´-fa-teez): King of the Laestrygonians.

Antiphus (An´-ti-fus): Name given to two of Odysseus' companions, one of whom is the son of Aegyptius, the last of Odysseus' companions eaten by the Cyclops.

Aphrodite (Af-ro-deye´-tee): Goddess of love and beauty. Daughter of Zeus and Dione; wife of Hephaestus. During a sexual liaison, Aphrodite and Ares are caught in a trap set by Hephaestus and exposed to the laughter of the gods.

Apollo (A-pol´-oh): Patron god of music and the arts. Son of Zeus and Leto; brother of Artemis. Also called Phoebus Apollo, he is associated with the lyre and archery. It is on the day of his festival that the suitors are murdered.

Arcesius (Ar-ke´-si-us): Father of Laertes and grandfather of Odysseus.

Ares (Ai´-reez): God of War. Son of Zeus and Hera; lover of Aphrodite.

Arete (A-ree´-tee): Wife of Alcinous; mother of Nausicaa. Queen of the Phaeacians, to whom Odysseus, shipwrecked on the island, kneels as a suppliant first, rather than to Alcinous.

Argives (Ar´-geyvz): The Greeks who fight at Troy under the leadership of Agamemnon.

Argo (Ar´-goh): The ship of the Argonauts.

Argos (Ar´-gos): City or district in the northeastern Peloponnese, Greek region of the Achaeans.

Argus (Ar´-gos): Odysseus' dog, the only creature to recognize Odysseus on his return to Ithaca. Argus dies almost immediately thereafter.

Ariadne (A-ri-ad´-nee): Daughter of Minos, king of Crete, and Pasiphae. She helps Theseus overcome the Minotaur, is killed by Artemis, and is seen by Odysseus in the Underworld.

Artemis (Ar´-te-mis): Goddess of the hunt and the moon. Daughter of Zeus and Leto; sister of Apollo. Like her brother, Artemis brings natural death to mortals, but she is the slaughterer of female mortals in particular.

Athena (A-thee´-na): Goddess of wisdom, crafts, and battle. Daughter of Zeus; usually said to have sprung from his head. She is also called Pallas

Athena and the Grey-eyed One. She frequently appears to Odysseus and helps him return home.

Atlas (At´-las): Titan who holds up the pillars of the sky; father of Calypso.

Atreus (Ay´-tryoos): Son of Pelops and Hippodameia; brother of Thyestes; father of Agamemnon and Menelaus.

Autolycus (Aw-to´-li-kus): Father of Anticleia; maternal grandfather of Odysseus. He gives Odysseus his name.

Boreas (Bo´-re-as): The North Wind. Husband of Oreithyia and father of Calais and Zetes.

Cadmus (Kad´-mus): Founder and king of Cadmea (Thebes). Married to Harmonia; father of Polydorus, Autonoë, Semele, Ino, and Agave.

Calypso (Ka-lip´-soh): Goddess, daughter of Atlas. Her name is a play on a Greek word meaning "to conceal." She detains Odysseus for seven years on her island, Ogygia, offering him immortality if he remains.

Cassandra (Ka-san´-dra): Trojan princess and prophetess, daughter of Priam and Hecuba. Taken as a war prize by Agamemnon, she is murdered with him by Clytemnestra and Aegisthus on his return home.

Castor (Kas´-tor): Son of Tyndareus and Leda; brother of Polydeuces, Clytemnestra, and Helen.

Cephallenians (Se-fa-lee´-ni-unz): Inhabitants of a much larger island near Ithaca under Odysseus' command.

Charybdis (Ka-rib´-dis): Whirlpool situated opposite Scylla.

Cicones (Si-koh´-neez): Allies of Troy, the first people Odysseus encounters (and raids) on his return home. Maron, the priest, gives Odysseus some excellent wine in return for sparing his and his family's lives.

Circe (Sir´-see): Goddess and sorceress; daughter of Helios and Perse. When Odysseus lands on her island, Aeaea, she turns many of his men into swine, but Odysseus (with Hermes' help) resists her magic and convinces her to undo her spell. He and his men remain on her island for one year.

Clytemnestra (Kleye-tem-nes´-tra): Daughter of Tyndareus and Leda; married first to Tantalus and then to Agamemnon, to whom she bore Iphigeneia, Electra, Chrysothemis, and Orestes. She killed her husband and his concubine Cassandra with the aid of her lover, Aegisthus. Years later Orestes avenged his father's death by murdering his mother.

Cnossus (Knos´-os): Principal city on the island of Crete.

Cocytus (Ko-kee´-tos): River forming one of the boundaries of Hades.

Crete: Island in the Aegean Sea south of the Peloponnese, ruled by Idomeneus.

Ctessipus (Kte-si´-pus): Wealthy suitor of Penelope. He throws an ox's hoof at Odysseus' head when Odysseus is disguised as a beggar. He is killed by Philoetius.

Ctimene (Kti-mee´-nee): Daughter of Laertes and Anticleia; sister of Odysseus.

Cyclopes (Seye´-klops): One-eyed, man-eating giants. Their occupation of Hyperia forces the Phaeacians to relocate. The term in the singular (Cyclops) also refers to Polyphemus.

Cytherean (Si-the-ree´-an): Epithet of Aphrodite, perhaps from the name of the island Cythera, where some claim the goddess was born.

Danaans (Da-nay´-unz): One of three general names Homer uses when referring to Greeks. The other two are Achaeans and Argives.

Deiphobus (Dee-i´-fo-bus)): Prince of Troy, son of Priam and Hecuba. He marries Helen after Paris' death and is killed at Troy by Menelaus.

Demeter (Dee-mee´-tur): Goddess of crops and the harvest. Daughter of Cronus and Rhea; mother of Persephone.

Demodocus (Dee-mo´-do-kus): Blind singer of tales at Phaeacia.

Demoptolemus (Dee-mop-to´-le-mus): One of Penelope's suitors.

Diocles (Deye´-o-kleez): Inhabitant of Pherae who receives Telemachus on his trip to Sparta and on his return.

Diomedes (Deye-o-mee´-deez): Son of Tydeus and Deipyle; king of Argos. He accompanies Odysseus at night around the city and is one of the few Greeks to return home quickly after the destruction of Troy.

Dodona (Doh-doh´-na): City in northwestern Greece; home to a famous oracle of Zeus.

Dolios (Do´-li-us): Old servant of Odysseus who remains faithful during Odysseus' absence. He later defends Odysseus against the relatives of the slain suitors.

Dorians (Doh´-ri-unz): Greek-speaking inhabitants of Crete.

Echephron (E-ke´-fron): Son of Nestor.

Echetus (E´-ke-tus): King of Eperius who acquires a reputation for cruelty.

Egypt: Country in Africa or its king.

Eidothea (Eye-do´-the-a): Daughter of Proteus who advises Menelaus on his journey home with Helen.

Elatus (E´-la-tus): One of Penelope's suitors; slain by Eumaeus.

Elpenor (El-pee´-nor): Member of Odysseus' crew who dies when he falls asleep on a roof on Circe's island and falls off. When Odysseus visits the Underworld, Elpenor's shade asks Odysseus for a proper funeral.

Epeius (E-pee´-us): Son of Panopeus. With Athena's help, he builds the Trojan Horse.

Epicaste (E-pi-kas´-tee): Also known as Jocasta. Daughter of Menoeceus; wife of Laius and mother of Oedipus.

Erebus (E´-re-bus): Another name for Hades; sometimes refers to an especially dark place within the Underworld.

Eriphyle (E-ri-feye´-lee): Daughter of Talaus and Lysimache; wife and betrayer of Amphiaraus. Her shade appears to Odysseus in the Underworld.

Eumaeus (Yoo-mee´-us): Odysseus' loyal swineherd who generously hosts Odysseus, disguised as a beggar upon his return to Ithaca. Eumaeus later assists Odysseus in the slaughter of the suitors.

Eupeithes (Yoo-pay´-theez): Father of Antinous. He rallies the relatives of the slain suitors against Odysseus and is killed by Laertes.

Euryades (Yoo-reye´-a-deez): One of Penelope's suitors. He is killed by Telemachus.

Eurybates (Yoo-ri´-ba-teez): Round-shouldered, swarthy, and curly haired herald whom Odysseus values for his quick mind.

Eurycleia (Yoo-ri-klay´-a): Daughter of Ops; nurse to Odysseus and later to Telemachus. She recognizes Odysseus' scar on his thigh but at his request does not reveal his identity.

Eurydamas (Yoo-ri´-da-mas): One of Penelope's suitors killed by Odysseus.

Eurylochus (Yoo-ri´-lo-kus): Leading member of Odysseus' crew. He tells Odysseus that Circe transformed several crew members, and he incites the crew to slaughter Helios' cattle.

Eurymachus (Yoo-ri´-ma-kus): One of Penelope's suitors.

Eurynome (Yoo-ri´-no-mee): Penelope's housekeeper.

Eurynomus (Yoo-ri´-no-mus): Son of Antiphus; suitor to Penelope.

Hades (Hay´-deez): God of the Underworld. Son of Cronus and Rhea. His name probably means "Unseen One." Also refers to the dwelling place of the dead, named for its ruler.

Halitherses (Ha-li-thur´-seez): Son of Mastor; Ithacan soothsayer. He predicts Odysseus' return to Ithaca.

Helen (He´-len): Daughter of Leda and Zeus or Tyndareus; wife of Menelaus. She is the most beautiful woman in the world and is given to Paris by Aphrodite. Menelaus' efforts to regain Helen are the basis of the Trojan War.

Helios (Hee´-li-os): The Sun God.

Hephaestus (He-feyes´-tus): God of fire and patron of metalworkers and crafts. Son of Zeus and Hera. He marries Aphrodite, who is not always faithful. He forges Achilles' armor.

Hera (Hee´-ra): Queen of the Olympian gods. Daughter of Cronus and Rhea; Zeus' sister and wife. Goddess of childbirth and marriage.

Hermes (Hur´-meez): Divine messenger of the gods and guide to mortal travelers. Son of Zeus and Maia.

Hermione (Hur-meye´-o-nee): Daughter of Menelaus and Helen.

Hypereia (Hi-pe-reye´-a): First homeland of the Phaeacians whence they are driven by the Cyclopes.

Icarius (I-ka´-ri-us): Father of Penelope; brother of Menelaus.

Ilion (Il´-i-on): Troy.

Ino (Eye´-noh): Daughter of Cadmus and Harmonia. She disguises and rears her nephew Dionysus to protect him from Hera's wrath. She becomes a nereid and is renamed Leucothea, meaning "White Goddess."

Iphitus (I´-fi-tus): Son of Eurytus, king of Oechalia. He gives Odysseus his bow.

Irus (Eye´-rus): Ithacan beggar who frequents the gatherings of Penelope's suitors at the palace. He loses a boxing match to the disguised Odysseus.

Ithaca (Ith´-a-ka): Rocky island home of Odysseus.

Jason (Jay´-son): Son of Aeson and leader of the Argonauts.

Lacedaemon (La-ke-deye´-mon): Sparta. City and kingdom of Menelaus.

Laertes (Lay-er´-teez): Son of Arcesius; husband of Anticleia and father of Odysseus and Ctimene.

Laestrygonians (Leye-stri-goh´-ni-unz): Giant cannibals who eat part of Odysseus' crew and destroy all the ships but Odysseus'.

Lampetië (Lam-pe´-ti-ee): Daughter of Helios and Neaera. When Odysseus' men slaughter Helios' cattle, the nymph tells her father.

Leda (Lee´-da): Wife of Tyndareus; mother of Castor, Polydeuces, Clytemnestra, and Helen.

Leocritus (Lee-o´-kri-tus): Suitor killed by Telemachus.

Leodes (Lee-oh´-deez): Suitor with prophetic gifts, killed by Odysseus.

Leto (Lee´-toh): Titan goddess. Daughter of Coeus and Phoebe; mother of Artemis and Apollo.

Malea (Ma-lay´-a): Cape on the southeast tip of the Peloponnese known for its difficulty in navigation.

Marathon (Ma´-ra-thon): Attic city northeast of Athens.

Maron (May´-ron): Priest of Apollo at Ismarus who gives Odysseus the wine that is used to intoxicate the Cyclops.

Medon (Mee´-don): Ithacan herald who remains faithful to his lord, Odysseus, and is spared when the suitors are killed.

Megapenthes (Me-ga-pen´-theez): Son of Menelaus by a slave woman. His name means "great sorrow," presumably because Menelaus was unable to have children with Helen after the birth of Hermione. He marries the daughter of Alector on the day that Telemachus arrives in Sparta.

Megara (Me´-ga-ra): Daughter of Creon and the wife of Heracles.

Melanthius (Me-lan´-thi-us): Odysseus' goatherd; son of Dolius. He aligns himself with the suitors while Odysseus is away and insults his master, who is disguised as a beggar. He is killed for his disloyalty.

Melantho (Me-lan´-thoh): Daughter of Dolius; sister of Melanthius; handmaid of Penelope. She becomes the mistress of Eurymachus during Odysseus' absence and a deceitful antagonist. Telemachus hangs her for her betrayal.

Memnon (Mem´-non): Son of Dawn and Tithonus; nephew of Priam. He kills Nestor's son Antilochus and in turn is killed by Achilles. Zeus grants him immortality when he dies.

Menelaus (Me-ne-lay´-us): Son of Atreus and Aerope; brother of Agamemnon; ruler of Lacedaemon; husband of Helen.

Mentes (Men´-teez): Taphian captain, son of Anchialus, in whose form Athena first appears to Telemachus.

Mentor (Men´-tor): Close friend of Odysseus who is to look after the household during Odysseus' absence. Athena often appears in his form.

Minos (Meye´-nos): Son of Zeus and Europa; king of Crete; husband of Pasiphae; father of Ariadne, Phaedra, and Deucalion; brother of Rhadamanthus. After his death he becomes a judge of the dead in Hades.

Muses (Mu´-zez): Goddesses of the arts who inspire poets and musicians. Daughters of Zeus and Mnemosyne.

Mycenae (Meye-see´-nee): Ancient city in Argos ruled by Agamemnon.

Mycene (Meye-see´-neh): Legendary daughter of Inachus. The namesake of Mycenae.

Myrmidons (Mur´-mi-donz): A people inhabiting southern Thessaly. Achilles' crack troops in the *Iliad*.

Nausicaa (Naw-si´-kay-a): Phaeacian princess; daughter of Alcinous and Arete.

Nausithous (Naw-si´-tho-us): Son of Poseidon and Periboea; father of Alcinous. He leads the Phaeacians to Schería where they find a peaceful existence.

Neleus (Neel´-yoos): Son of Poseidon and Tyro; brother of Pelias; father of Nestor.

Neoptolemus (Nee-op-to´-le-mus): Son of Achilles and Deidameia.

Nericus (Nee´-ri-cus): A coastal town in western Greece once conquered by Laertes.

Neriton (Nee´-ri-ton): A thickly forested mountain on Ithaca.

Nestor (Nes´-tor): Son of Neleus and Chloris; king of Pylos. He fights in the Trojan War, although already an old man, and is known for his valuable counsel. Father of Peisistratus, Thrasymedes, and Antilochus.

Noemon (No-ee´-mon): Wealthy Ithacan who, inspired by Athena, lends Telemachus a ship to sail to Pylos. His name means "thoughtful."

Ocean: The river encircling the earth. Son of Uranus and Earth; husband of Tethys.

Odysseus (O-dis´-yoos): Son of Laertes and Anticlea; husband of Penelope; father of Telemachus. *Odysseus* may mean either "giver of woe" or "woeful one."

Oedipus (Ee´-di-pus): Son of Laius and Epicaste who unknowingly kills his father and marries his mother.

Ogygia (Oh-gi´-ja): Mythical island where the nymph Calypso resides.

Olympus (O-lim´-pus): Mount Olympus, the tallest mountain in Greece, believed to be the abode of the gods.

Ops (Ops): Father of Eurycleia, nurse to Odysseus and Telemachus.

Orestes (O-res´-teez): Son of Agamemnon and Clytemnestra. He avenges his father's murder by killing his mother and her lover, Aegisthus.

Orion (O-reye´-on): Mythical hunter famed for his size and handsome looks. The goddess Dawn falls in love with him and bears him away to her island, Ortygia. The other gods become envious of the love affair and urge Artemis to slay the hunter.

Pallas (Pal´-as): Epithet of the goddess Athena that may mean "maiden" or "weapon-brandishing."

Pandareus (Pan-dar´-yoos): A king of Miletas in Crete; father of Aedon. He steals a golden dog from the temple of Zeus in Crete, and consequently both he and his wife are killed.

Paphos (Pa´-fos): A city on the southern coast of Cyprus and an important center for the cult of Aphrodite.

Patroclus (Pa-tro´-klus): Son of Menoetius. Greek warrior of the Myrmidon contingent at Troy and dear friend of Achilles. He rallies his Achaean comrades by donning Achilles' armor but is then killed by Hector.

Peirithous (Peye-ri´-tho-us): Son of Ixion and king of the Lapiths. The centaur Eurytion becomes drunk and attempts to abduct his fiancée Hippodamia during their wedding. This causes the war between the Lapiths and the Centaurs.

Peisander (Peye-sand´-er): One of Penelope's suitors.

Peisistratus (Peye-sis´-tra-tus): Youngest son of Nestor who accompanies Telemachus to Sparta.

Peleus (Pee´-li-as): Husband of the sea-goddess Thetis and father of the hero Achilles.

Penelope (Pe-ne´-lo-pee): Daughter of Icarius and Periboea; wife of Odysseus; mother of Telemachus.

Perse (Pur´-see): Daughter of Oceanus and mother of Circe by Helios.

Persephone (Pur-se´-fo-nee): Daughter of Demeter and Zeus; wife of Hades; queen of the Underworld.

Perseus (Purs´-yoos): A son of Nestor (not to be confused with the son of Zeus and Danae, the hero who beheads Medusa).

Phaeacians (Fee-ay´-shunz): The people who inhabit Phaeacia (sometimes called Schería). As descendants of Poseidon they are loved by the gods and have remarkable seafaring abilities. According to legend, they have ships that move without the aid of rudder or sail.

Phaedra (Fay´-dra): Daughter of Minos and Pasiphae. Wife of Theseus but falls in love with his son Hippolytus and hangs herself. Odysseus is visited by her ghost in the Underworld.

Pharos (Fa´-ros): An island off the coast of Egypt where Proteus and his seals reside.

Phemius (Fee´-mi-us): Son of Terpius; a bard in Ithaca. Although he is forced to entertain the suitors, he remains faithful to the house of Laertes. Odysseus spares him because of his fidelity.

Pherae (Feh´-ree): Town between Pylos and Sparta where Telemachus and Peisistratus stay on their way to Sparta.

Philoctetes (Fi-lok-tee´-teez): Son of Poias and great archer hero. On his way to Troy a serpent bites him. The smell of the festering wound is so foul that the Greeks abandon him on the island of Lemnos. However, it was predetermined that Troy would not fall without his help.

Philoetius (Fi-lee´-tee-us): Cowherd who remains faithful to Odysseus.

Phoebus (Fee´-bus): An epithet of Apollo meaning "bright," identifying him with the sun.

Phoenicia (Fee-ni´-sha): A country on the Mediterranean coast in Syria. The Phoenicians were known for being skilled seafarers and traders.

Phorcys (For´-kis): Sea-god; father of Thoösa; grandfather of Polyphemus.

Pleiades (Plee´-a-deez): A constellation of seven stars used by ancient seamen for nocturnal navigation. The Pleiades were originally the seven daughters of Atlas and Pleione.

Polybus (Pol´-i-bus): Father of Eurymachus; Theban man visited by Menelaus and Helen; Phaeacian craftsman; one of Penelope's suitors killed by Eumaeus.

Polydamna (Po-li-dam´-na): Egyptian wife of Thon who supplies Helen with herbal somnifers.

Polydeuces (Po-li-dyoo´-seez): Son of Leda and Tyndareus; brother of Helen; twin brother of Castor. He is known for his skill as a boxer.

Polyphemus (Po-li-fee´-mus): One of the Cyclopes, son of Poseidon and Thoösa. This one-eyed giant consumes some of Odysseus' men after he traps them in his cave. To escape from the cave, Odysseus and his men drive a heated pole into Polyphemus' only eye. As punishment for his son's blinding, Poseidon torments Odysseus until he reaches Ithaca.

Poseidon (Po-seye´-don): God of the sea. Son of Cronus and Rhea; brother of Zeus, Hades, and Hera; father of the Cyclops Polyphemus.

Priam (Preye´-am): King of Troy; son of Laomedon and Strymo; husband of Hecuba; father of Hector and Paris. He is killed by Neoptolemus as Troy falls to the Greeks.

Proteus (Proh´-tyoos): A shape-shifting sea-god; son of Oceanus and Tethys; father of Eidothea. Also known as the "Old Man of the Sea." He is generally associated with the island of Pharos.

Pylos (Peye-los): City on the southwest coast of the Peloponnese ruled by Nestor.

Pyriphlegethon (Peye-ri-fle´-ge-thon): One of the three rivers near the entrance to Hades.

Rhadamanthus (Ra-da-man´-thus): A son of Europa and Zeus and brother of Minos. Because he is a fair king, he is granted eternal life in the Elysian fields.

Rhexenor (Rex-ee´-nor): Son of Nausithous; brother of Alcinous; father of Arete.

Schería (Ske-ri´-a): The island inhabited by the Phaeacians.

Scylla (Sil´-a): The cave-dwelling monster possessing female attributes from the waist up but six dog heads and a dozen canine feet from the waist down. *Scylla* is Greek for "she-pup." She inhabits the cliff across the strait from Charybdis.

Scyros (Skeye´-ros): Island in the Aegean where Achilles is hidden to prevent him from going to the Trojan War.

Sirens (Seye´-rens): Singing creatures with female heads and breasts, and large birdlike bodies. They lure sailors to their island with an irresistible song.

Sisyphus (Si´-si-fus): Son of Aeolus, and a king of Corinth. He was condemned to spend eternity in Hades perpetually pushing a huge stone up a hill.

Sparta (Spar´-ta): City in the southwest Peleponnese that was ruled by Menelaus.

Styx (Stix): One of the rivers that flows near Hades. When gods swear by this river their oaths are irretractable.

Tantalus (Tan´-ta-lus): Father of Pelops and Niobe; mythical king of Phrygia. He was forced to suffer in Hades with everlasting hunger and thirst for trying to serve the gods the mortal flesh of his son Pelops.

Taphians (Ta´-fi-unz): The inhabitants of Taphos, a seafaring people ruled by Mentes. Taphos is a city on the west coast of Greece.

Telamon (Tel´-a-mon): Father of the hero Ajax.

Telemachus (Te-lem´-a-kus): Son of Odysseus and Penelope. His name means "battle from afar."

Telemos (Te´-le-mus): A seer among the Cyclopes who had warned Polyphemus that he would lose his eye to a mortal named Odysseus.

Telepylus (Te-le´-pi-lus): The fortress of the Laestrygonians.

Tenedos (Te´-ne-dos): A small island off the coast of Asia Minor.

Themis (The´-mis): Titan goddess of law and order. Daughter of Uranus and Gaia.

Theseus (Thees´-yoos): Athenian hero; son of Aegeus. He slays the Minotaur with the help of Minos' daughter Ariadne, who had fallen in love with Theseus.

Thetis (Thee´-tis): A sea-goddess, one of the Nereids. Daughter of Nereus and Doris; wife of Peleus; mother of Achilles.

Thoösa (Tho-oh´-sa): A nymph; mother of Polyphemus by Poseidon.

Thrinacia (Thri-nay´-sha): Island where Helios' cattle pastured.

Thyestes (Theye-es´-teez): Father of Aegisthus and brother of Atreus.

Tiresias (Teye-ree´-si-as): The blind seer from Thebes whose shade counsels Odysseus in the Underworld.

Tithonus (Ti-thoh´-nus): Son of Laomedon and husband of Dawn.

Tityus (Ti´-ti-yus): A giant and son of Gaia. He attempted to rape Leto. He was killed and was eternally punished by two vultures that tore at his liver.

Tritogeneia (Tri-to-ge-nee´-a): Epithet of Athena meaning "third born."

Trojans (Troh´-junz): The inhabitants of Troy.

Troy (Troy): City in northwestern Asia Minor; ruled by Priam; conquered by the Greeks in the Trojan War. Site at which the *Iliad* takes place.

Tyndareus (Tin-da´-ri-us): Husband of Leda; father of Castor, Polydeuces, and Clytemnestra; foster father of Helen.

Zeus (Zyoos): The supreme god of Olympus, known as the father of gods and men. Son of Cronus and Rhea; husband and brother of Hera; father of Athena, Aphrodite, Ares, Apollo, Artemis, Hephaestus, and others.

Suggestions for Further Reading

A. General Interest

Arnold, Matthew. "On Translating Homer." In *On the Classical Tradition*, ed. R. H. Super. Michigan University Press. Ann Arbor and London, 1960.

Beye, Charles R. *The Iliad, the Odyssey, and the Epic Tradition*. New York and London, 1966.

Carter, Jane B., and Sarah P. Morris, eds. *The Ages of Homer: A Tribute to Emily Townsend Vermeule*. University of Texas Press. Austin, 1995.

Clarke, Howard. *Homer's Readers: A Historical Introduction to the Iliad and the Odyssey*. University of Delaware Press. Newark, 1981.

Griffin, Jasper. *Homer on Life and Death*. Clarendon Press. Oxford, 1980.

Kirk, G. S. *The Songs of Homer*. Cambridge University Press. Cambridge, England, 1962.

Lamberton, R., and J. J. Keaney, eds. *Homer's Ancient Readers: The Hermeneutics of Greek Epic's Earliest Exegetes*. Princeton University Press. Princeton, N.J., 1992.

Lord, Albert. *The Singer of Tales*. Harvard University Press. Cambridge, Mass., 1960.

——— . *The Singer Resumes the Tale*. M. L. Lord, ed. Cornell University Press. Ithaca, N.Y., 1995.

Moulton, Carroll. *Similes in the Homeric Poems*. Vandenhoeck und Ruprecht. Göttingen, Germany, 1977.

Myrsiades, Kostas, ed. *Approaches to Teaching Homer's Iliad and Odyssey*. Modern Language Association of America. New York, 1987.

Nagler, Michael. *Spontaneity and Tradition: A Study in the Oral Art of Homer*. University of California Press. Berkeley, Los Angeles, and London, 1974.

Parry, Milman. *The Making of Homeric Verse: The Collected Papers of Milman Parry*. Adam Parry, ed. Clarendon Press. Oxford, 1971.

Powell, Barry, and Ian Morris, eds. *A New Companion to Homer*. Brill. Leiden, 1997.

Reece, Steve. *The Stranger's Welcome: Oral Theory and the Aesthetics of the Homeric Hospitality Scene*. University of Michigan Press. Ann Arbor, 1993.

Rutherford, R. B. *Homer.* Greece and Rome. New surveys in the classics, no. 26. Oxford University Press. Oxford, 1966.

Scully, Stephen. *Homer and the Sacred City.* Cornell University Press. Ithaca, N.Y. and London, 1991.

Steiner, George, and Robert Fagles, eds. *Homer: A Collection of Critical Essays.* Maynard Mack, ed. Twentieth Century Views. Englewood Cliffs, N.J., 1962.

Vivante, Paolo. *Homer.* John Herington, ed. Hermes Books. Yale University Press. New Haven, Conn., and London, 1985.

———. *Homeric Rhythm: A Philosophical Study.* Greenwood Press. Westport, Conn., 1997.

Wace, Alan J. B., and Frank Stubbings. *A Companion to Homer.* Macmillan. London, 1962.

Whitman, Cedric H. *Homer and the Heroic Tradition.* Harvard University Press. Cambridge, Mass., and London, 1958.

B. On the *Iliad*

Homeri Opera. Ed. D. B. Monro and T. W. Allen. 2nd ed., Vols. I and II. Oxford Classical Texts. London, 1920.

The Iliad: A Commentary. General Ed., G. S. Kirk. Vol. I: Books 1–4, Kirk. Cambridge, England, 1985. Vol. II: Books 5–8, Kirk, 1990. Vol. III: Books 9–12, J. B. Hainsworth; Vol. IV: Books 13–16, Richard Janko; Vol. V: Books 17–20, Mark W. Edwards; Vol. VI: Books 21–24, Nicholas Richardson.

Bespaloff, Rachel. *On the Iliad.* Mary McCarthy, trans. New York, 1947.

Bowra, Sir Maurice. *Tradition and Design in the Iliad.* Clarendon Press. Oxford, 1930.

Edwards, Mark W. *Homer: Poet of the Iliad.* Johns Hopkins University Press. Baltimore, Md., and London, 1987.

Martin, Richard. *The Language of Heroes: Speech and Performance in the Iliad.* Cornell University Press. Ithaca, N.Y., 1989.

Mueller, Martin. *The Iliad.* Allen & Unwin. London, 1984.

Nagy, Gregory. *The Best of the Achaeans: Concepts of the Hero in Archaic Greek Poetry.* Johns Hopkins University Press. Baltimore, Md., and London, 1979.

Owen, E. T. *The Story of the Iliad.* Reprint Bolchazy-Carducci. Wauconda, Ill., 1989.

Page, Sir Denys. *History and the Homeric Iliad*. Sather Classical Lectures, vol. 31. University of California Press. Berkeley, Los Angeles, and London, 1959.

Redfield, J. M. *Nature and Culture in the Iliad: The Tragedy of Hector*. University of Chicago Press. Chicago, Ill., and London, 1975. Expanded edition: Duke University Press. Durham, N.C., and London, 1994.

Schein, Seth L. *The Mortal Hero: An Introduction to Homer's Iliad*. University of California Press. Berkeley, Los Angeles, and London, 1984.

Segal, Charles. *The Theme of the Mutilation of the Corpse in the Iliad*. *Mnemosyne*, supp. vol. 17. Leiden, The Netherlands, 1971.

Shay, Jonathan. *Achilles in Vietnam: Combat Trauma and the Undoing of Character*. Athenaeum. New York, 1994.

Shive, David M. *Naming Achilles*. Oxford University Press. New York, 1987.

Silk, M. S. *Homer: The Iliad*. Cambridge University Press. Cambridge, England, 1987.

Slatkin, Laura M. *The Power of Thetis: Allusion and Interpretation in the Iliad*. University of California Press. Berkeley, Los Angeles, and London, 1991.

Taplin, Oliver. *Homeric Soundings: The Shaping of the Iliad*. Oxford University Press. New York and London, 1995.

Wade-Gery, H. T. *The Poet of the Iliad*. Cambridge, England, 1952.

Weil, Simone. *The Iliad or The Poem of Force*. Mary McCarthy, trans. Politics Pamphlet No. 1. New York, n.d. Reprint. Wallingford, Penn., n.d.

Wright, John. *Essays on the Iliad: Selected Modern Criticism*. Indiana University Press. Bloomington, 1978.

C. On the *Odyssey*

Homeri Opera. Ed. T. W. Allen. 2nd ed., Vols. III and IV. Oxford Classical Texts. London and New York, 1917.

The Odyssey. Ed. with Introduction, Commentary, and Indexes by W. B. Stanford. 2nd ed., 2 vols. London and New York, 1967.

Homer, *The Odyssey*. Ed. with English translation by A. T. Murray, revised by George E. Dimock. 2 vols. The Loeb Classical Library. Cambridge, Mass., and London, 1995.

A Commentary on Homer's Odyssey. Vol. I: Books I–VIII, A. Heubeck, S. West, J. B. Hainsworth. Vol. II: Books IX–XVI, A. Heubeck, A. Hoekstra. Vol. III: Books XVII–XXIV, J. Russo, M. Fernández-Galiano, A. Heubeck. New York and Oxford, 1988–92.

Ahl, Frederick, and Hanna M. Roisman. *The Odyssey Re-Formed*. Cornell University Press. Ithaca, N.Y., and London, 1996.

Auerbach, Erich. *Mimesis: The Representation of Reality in Western Literature*. Willard Trask, trans. Chapter 1, "Odysseus' Scar." Princeton University Press. Princeton, N.J., 1953.

Austin, Norman. *Archery at the Dark of the Moon: Poetic Problems in Homer's Odyssey*. University of California Press. Berkeley, Los Angeles, and London, 1975.

Bloom, Harold, ed. *Homer's Odyssey*. Chelsea House. New York, 1996.

Buitron, Diana, and Beth Cohen, eds. *The Odyssey and Ancient Art: An Epic in Word and Image*. The Edith C. Blum Art Institute, Bard College, Annandale-on-Hudson, New York, 1992.

Clarke, Howard. *The Art of the Odyssey*. Prentice-Hall. Englewood Cliffs, N.J., 1967.

Clay, Jenny Strauss. *The Wrath of Athena: Gods and Men in the Odyssey*. Princeton, N.J., 1983.

Cohen, Beth, ed. *The Distaff Side: Representing the Female in Homer's Odyssey*. Oxford University Press. New York and London, 1995.

Cook, Erwin F., *The Odyssey in Athens: Myths of Cultural Origins*. Cornell University Press. Ithaca, N.Y., 1995.

Doherty, Lillian Eileen. *Siren Songs: Gender, Audiences, and Narrators in the Odyssey*. University of Michigan Press. Ann Arbor, 1995.

Felson, Nancy. *Regarding Penelope: From Character to Poetics*, revised paperback edition. University of Oklahoma Press. Norman, 1997.

Finley, M. I. *The World of Odysseus*. Viking Press. New York, 1978.

Frame, Douglas. *The Myth of Return in Early Greek Epic*. Yale University Press. New Haven, Conn., 1978.

Katz, Marilyn A. *Penelope's Renown: Meaning and Indeterminacy in the Odyssey*. Princeton University Press. Princeton, N.J., 1991.

Murnaghan, Sheila. *Disguise and Recognition in the Odyssey*. Princeton University Press. Princeton, N.J., 1987.

Page, Denys. *Folktales in Homer's Odyssey*. Harvard University Press. Cambridge, Mass., 1973.

———. *The Homeric Odyssey*. Clarendon Press. Oxford, 1955.

Peradotto, John. *Man in the Middle Voice: Name and Narration in the Odyssey*. Martin Classical Lectures, New Series, Vol. 1. Princeton University Press. Princeton, N.J., 1990.

Pucci, Pietro. *Odysseus Polutropos: Intertextual Readings in the Odyssey and the Iliad*. 2nd ed. Cornell University Press. Ithaca, N.Y., 1995.

Rubens, Beaty, and Oliver Taplin. *An Odyssey Round Odysseus: The Man and His Story Traced Through Time and Place*. London, 1989.

Schein, Seth, ed. *Reading the Odyssey: Selected Interpretive Essays*. Princeton University Press. Princeton, N.J., 1996.

Segal, Charles. *Singers, Heroes, and Gods in the Odyssey*. Cornell University Press. Ithaca, N.Y., 1994.

Stanford, W. B. *The Ulysses Theme: A Study in the Adaptability of the Homeric Hero*. Clarendon Press. Oxford, 1983.

Thalmann, William G. *The Odyssey: Poem of Return*. Twayne. New York, 1992.

———. *The Swineherd and the Bow: Representations of Class in the Odyssey*. Cornell University Press. Ithaca, N.Y., 1998.

Tracy, Stephen W. *The Story of the Odyssey*. Princeton University Press. Princeton, N.J., 1990.